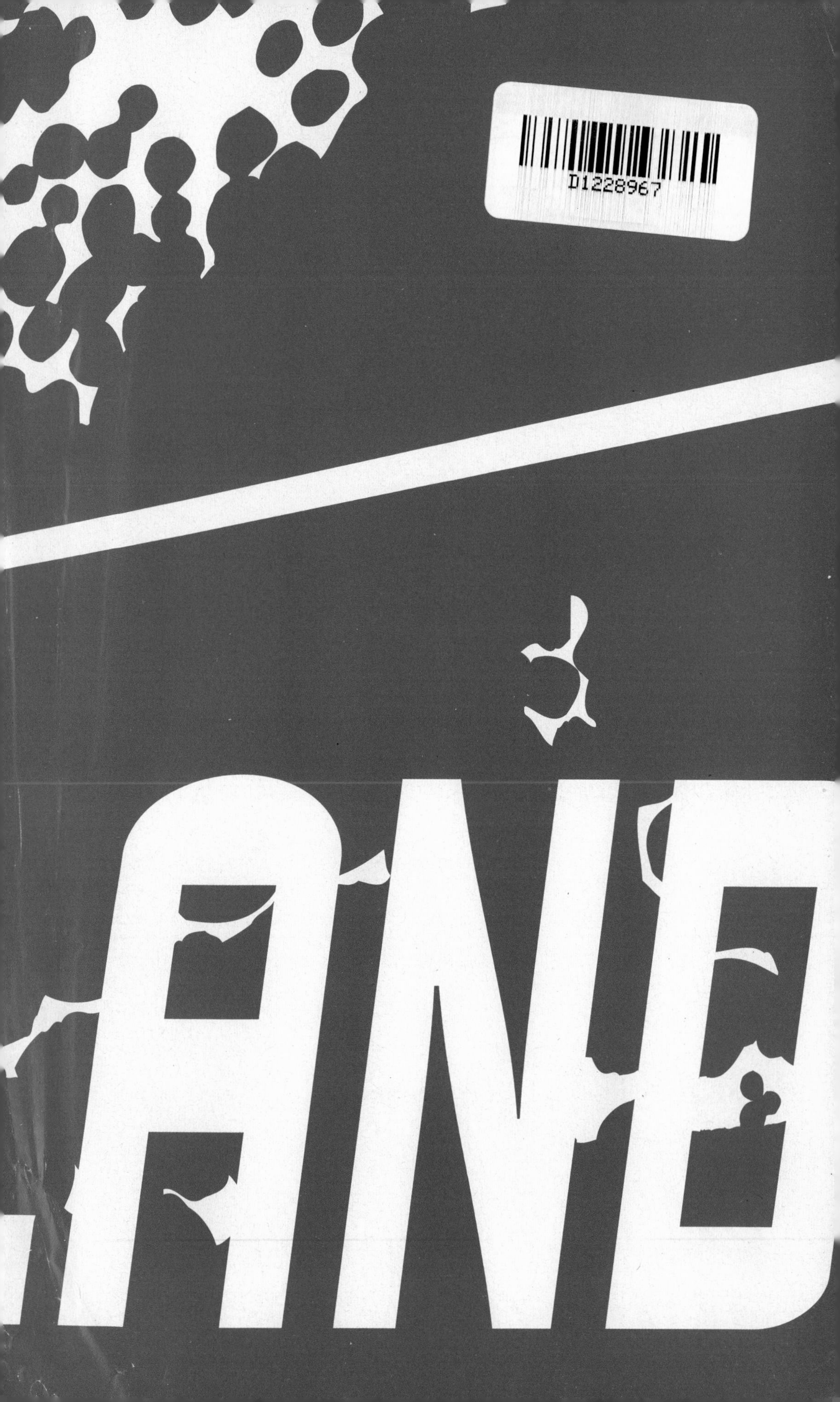
AND

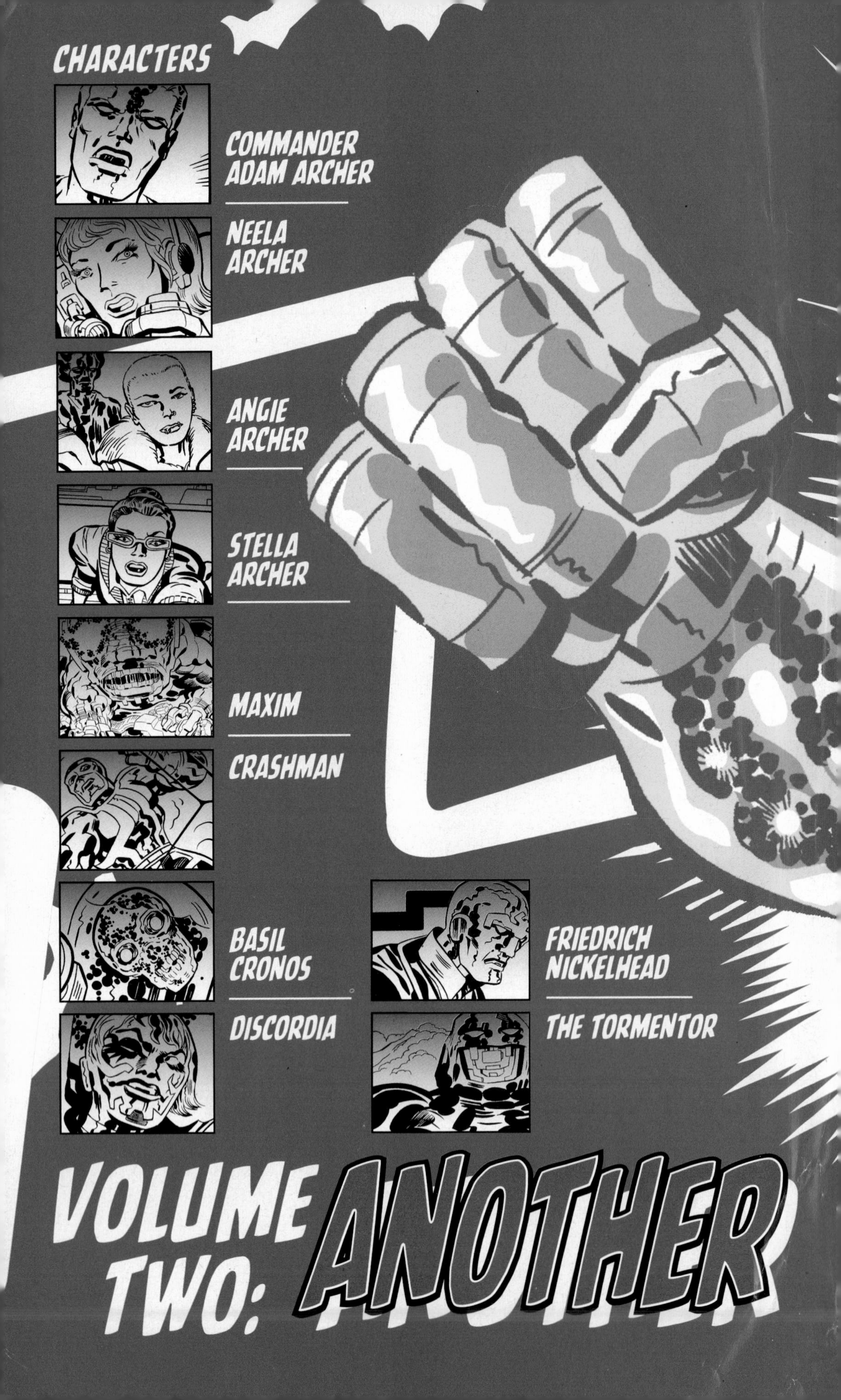

CHARACTERS
COMMANDER ADAM ARCHER
NEELA ARCHER
ANGIE ARCHER
STELLA ARCHER
MAXIM
CRASHMAN
BASIL CRONOS
FRIEDRICH NICKELHEAD
DISCORDIA
THE TORMENTOR
VOLUME TWO: ANOTHER

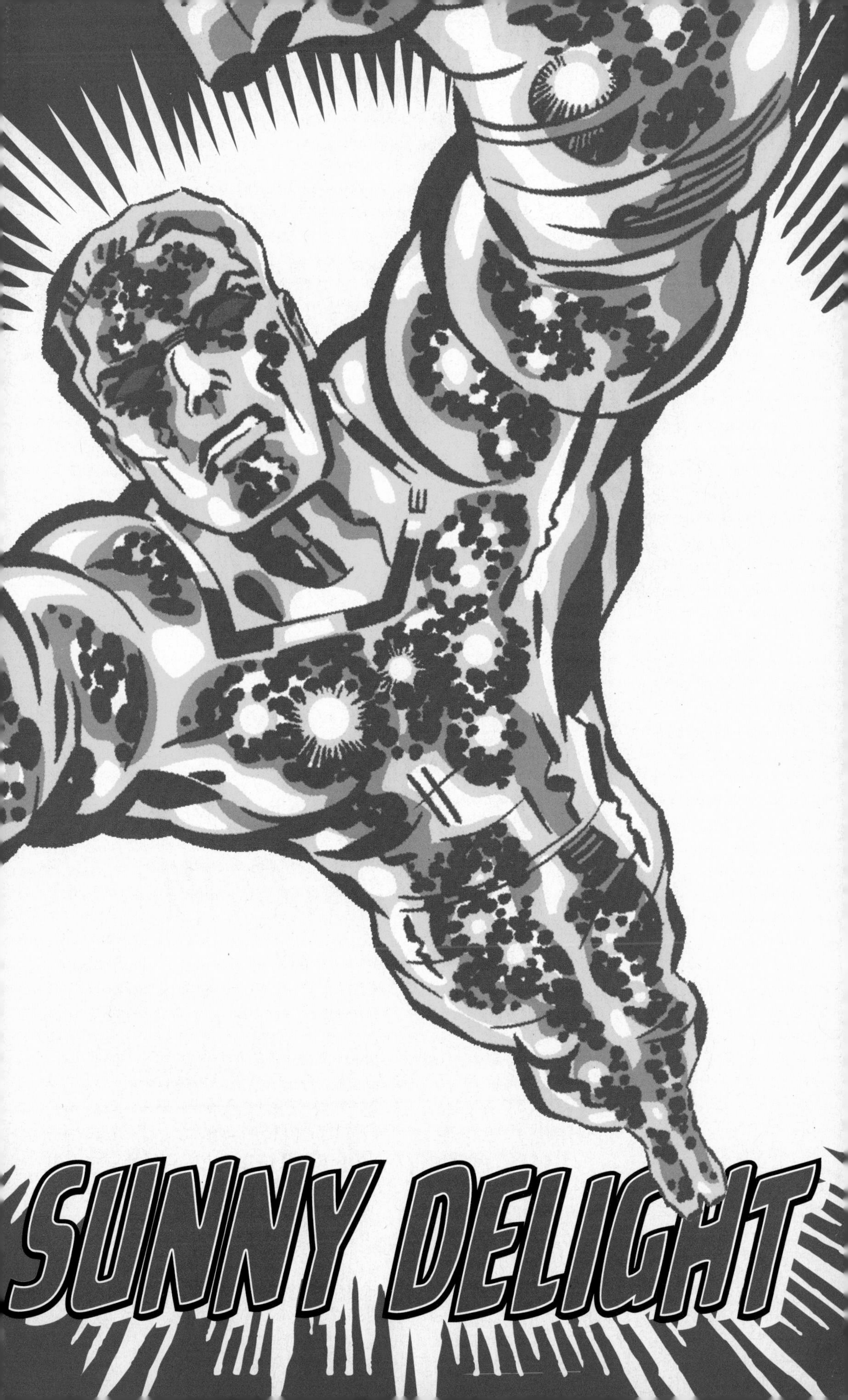
SUNNY DELIGHT

BY

CO-CREATORS:
JOE CASEY · TOM SCIOLI

DESIGN:
RICHARD STARKINGS

CIW

COLORS:
NICK FILARDI

LETTERS:
COMICRAFT'S ALBERT DESCHESNE & JIMMY BETANCOURT

WWW.IMAGECOMICS.COM

PUBLISHER: ERIK LARSEN · PRESIDENT: TODD MCFARLANE
CEO: MARC SILVESTRI · VICE-PRESIDENT: JIM VALENTINO

EXECUTIVE DIRECTOR: ERIC STEPHENSON
PR & MARKETING COORDINATOR: JIM DEMONAKOS
ACCOUNTS MANAGER: MIA MACHATTON
ADMINISTRATIVE ASSISTANT: TRACI HUI
TRAFFIC MANAGER: JOE KEATINGE
PRODUCTION MANAGER: ALLEN HUI
PRODUCTION ARTIST: JONATHAN CHAN
PRODUCTION ARTIST: DREW GILL

THE STORY SO FAR...

Commander ADAM ARCHER is a former Nasa astronaut who possesses incredible cosmic powers -- the unexpected result of a failed mission to Mars. He lives in Manhattan with his sisters, NEELA, STELLA and ANGIE, in a hi-tech facility built by the U.S. government known as the INFINITY TOWER.

While investigating a mysterious meteor crash at the Great Wall of China, Commander Archer is the first to encounter a visiting alien lifeform that he soon suspects has come in peace. That peace is shattered when the super-villain junkie, BASIL CRONUS, arrives on the scene to confiscate the alien for his own hallucinogenic experiments. Adam soon launches an all-out assault on Basil's deep sea sub lab, freeing the captive alien, appropriately named MAXIM, in the process. Although he loses his head in the melee, Basil escapes Adam's retribution via blind teleportation. Unfortunately, Basil -- head and body still separated -- falls into the possession of rival super-villain, FRIEDRICH NICKELHEAD.

Meanwhile, Adam discovers that sister NEELA -- also a former Nasa astronaut experiencing rising resentment toward her brother -- has embarked on a solo rescue mission to free America's most cherished hero (and Adam's rival for the general public's respect and affection), CRASHMAN, who was kidnapped by the self-styled "Queen of Pain", DISCORDIA. Before Adam can get to her, Neela soon joins Crashman in captivity. Thankfully, Adam rescues them both Discordia is placed into custody. However, after being found guilty by a jury of her peers (yeah, right!) in a Federal court, Discordia shocks the world when her head inexplicably explodes on live television, killing her instantly. Simultaneously, Neela has willfully allied herself with an independent, privately owned space flight program...

(Of course, all this and more can be found in the first collection in this series, GØDLAND VOL. 1: HELLO, COSMIC! Available where all good graphic novels are sold. Buy it and enjoy all its cosmic goodness!)

BOOK SEVEN:

ACID RAIN DROPS

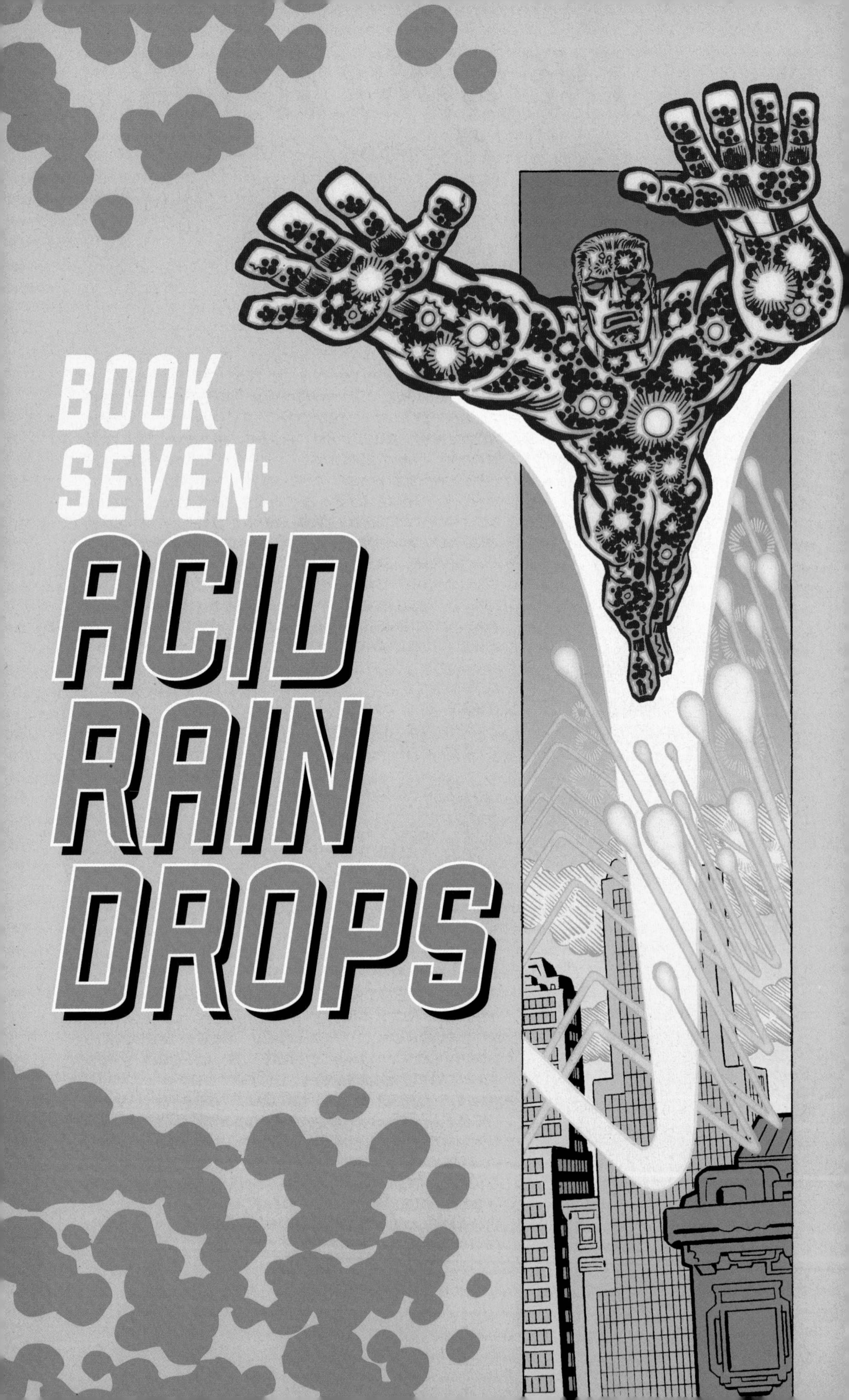

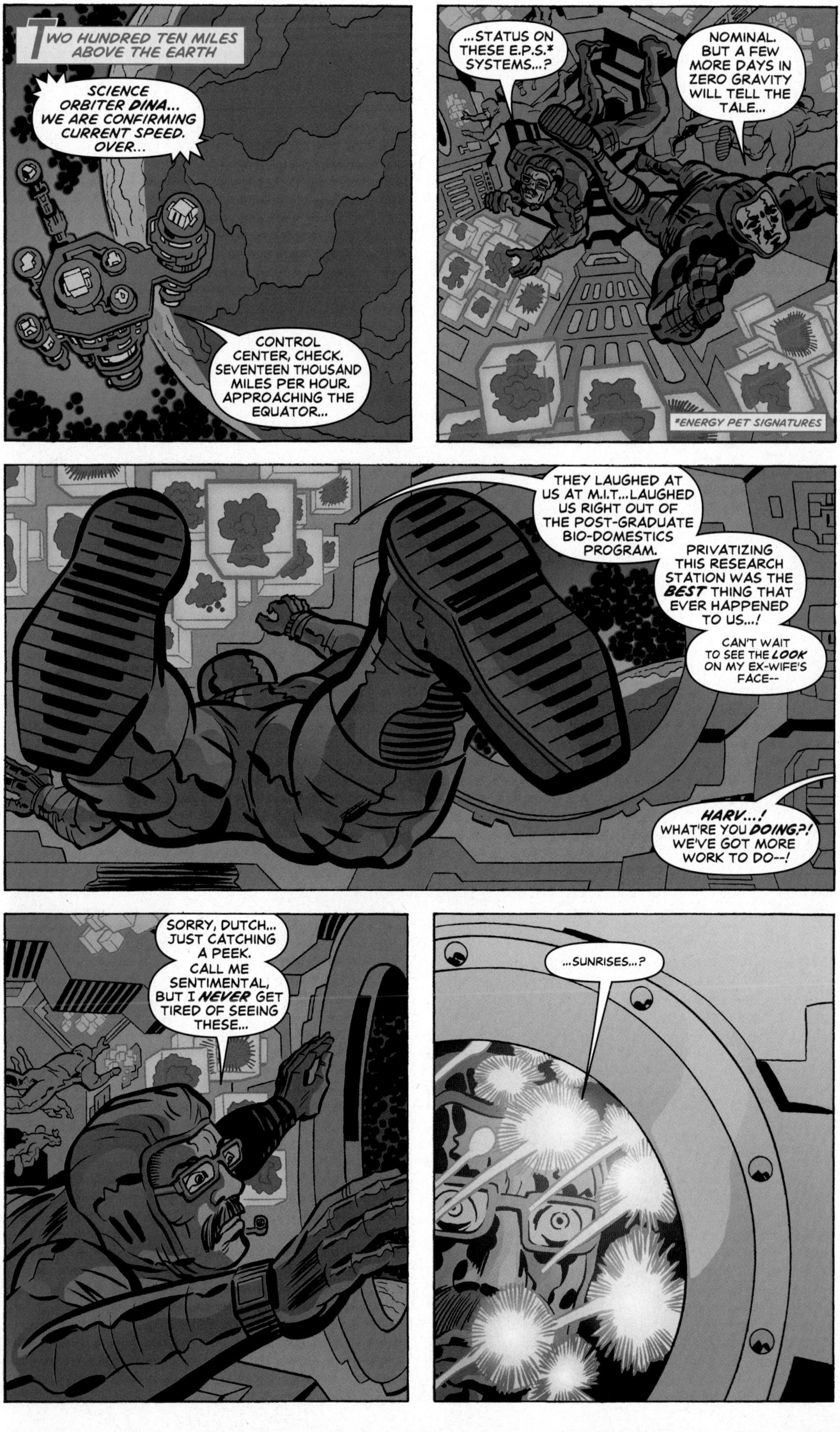
TWO HUNDRED TEN MILES ABOVE THE EARTH
SCIENCE ORBITER DINA... WE ARE CONFIRMING CURRENT SPEED. OVER...
CONTROL CENTER, CHECK. SEVENTEEN THOUSAND MILES PER HOUR. APPROACHING THE EQUATOR...
...STATUS ON THESE E.P.S.* SYSTEMS...?
NOMINAL. BUT A FEW MORE DAYS IN ZERO GRAVITY WILL TELL THE TALE...
*ENERGY PET SIGNATURES
THEY LAUGHED AT US AT M.I.T...LAUGHED US RIGHT OUT OF THE POST-GRADUATE BIO-DOMESTICS PROGRAM.
PRIVATIZING THIS RESEARCH STATION WAS THE BEST THING THAT EVER HAPPENED TO US...!
CAN'T WAIT TO SEE THE LOOK ON MY EX-WIFE'S FACE--
HARV...! WHAT'RE YOU DOING?! WE'VE GOT MORE WORK TO DO--!
SORRY, DUTCH... JUST CATCHING A PEEK. CALL ME SENTIMENTAL, BUT I NEVER GET TIRED OF SEEING THESE...
...SUNRISES...?

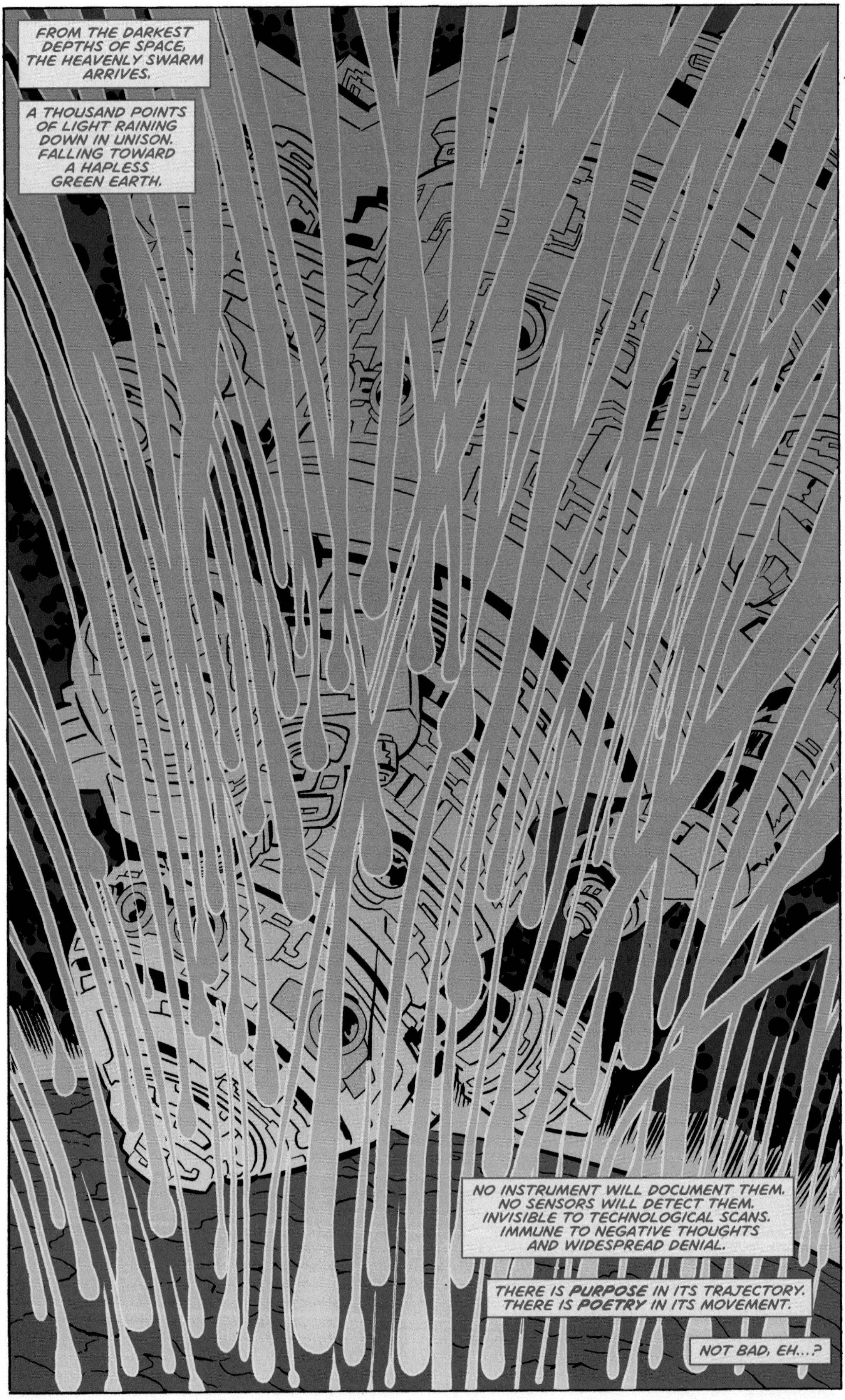
FROM THE DARKEST DEPTHS OF SPACE, THE HEAVENLY SWARM ARRIVES.
A THOUSAND POINTS OF LIGHT RAINING DOWN IN UNISON. FALLING TOWARD A HAPLESS GREEN EARTH.
NO INSTRUMENT WILL DOCUMENT THEM. NO SENSORS WILL DETECT THEM. INVISIBLE TO TECHNOLOGICAL SCANS. IMMUNE TO NEGATIVE THOUGHTS AND WIDESPREAD DENIAL.
THERE IS PURPOSE IN ITS TRAJECTORY. THERE IS POETRY IN ITS MOVEMENT.
NOT BAD, EH...?

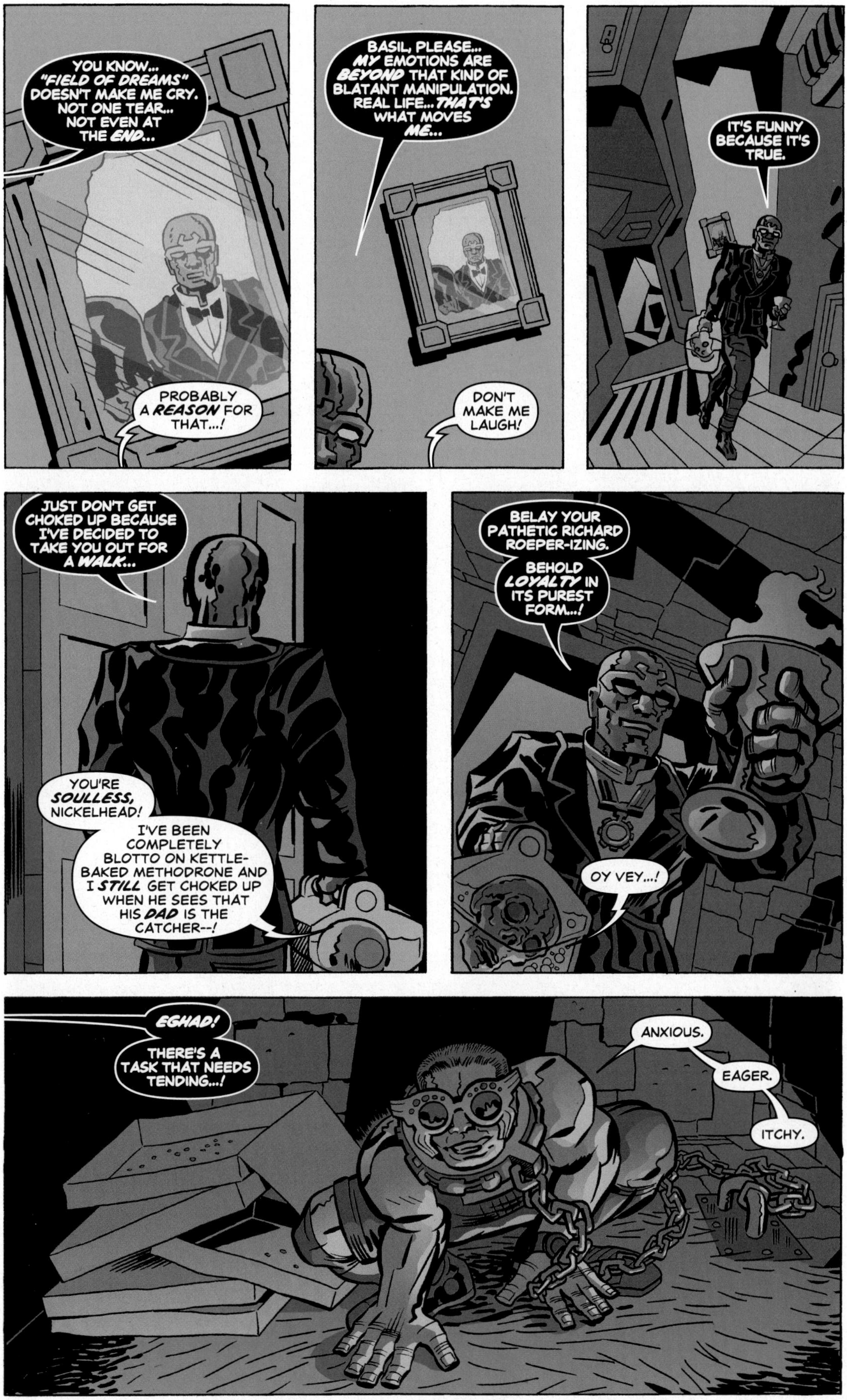
YOU KNOW... "FIELD OF DREAMS" DOESN'T MAKE ME CRY. NOT ONE TEAR... NOT EVEN AT THE END...
PROBABLY A REASON FOR THAT...!
BASIL, PLEASE... MY EMOTIONS ARE BEYOND THAT KIND OF BLATANT MANIPULATION. REAL LIFE... THAT'S WHAT MOVES ME...
DON'T MAKE ME LAUGH!
IT'S FUNNY BECAUSE IT'S TRUE.
JUST DON'T GET CHOKED UP BECAUSE I'VE DECIDED TO TAKE YOU OUT FOR A WALK...
YOU'RE SOULLESS, NICKELHEAD!
I'VE BEEN COMPLETELY BLOTTO ON KETTLE-BAKED METHODRONE AND I STILL GET CHOKED UP WHEN HE SEES THAT HIS DAD IS THE CATCHER--!
BELAY YOUR PATHETIC RICHARD ROEPER-IZING.
BEHOLD LOYALTY IN ITS PUREST FORM...!
OY VEY...!
EGHAD!
THERE'S A TASK THAT NEEDS TENDING...!
ANXIOUS.
EAGER.
ITCHY.

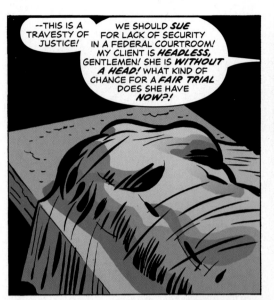

--THIS IS A TRAVESTY OF JUSTICE!

WE SHOULD *SUE* FOR LACK OF SECURITY IN A FEDERAL COURTROOM! MY CLIENT IS *HEADLESS*, GENTLEMEN! SHE IS *WITHOUT A HEAD!* WHAT KIND OF CHANCE FOR A *FAIR TRIAL* DOES SHE HAVE *NOW?!*

UMMM... YOU ALREADY GOT A *GUILTY* VERDICT.

A WELL-TIMED RETORT, FRIEND.

COMMANDER ARCHER... CRASHMAN...EVERYONE JUST CALM DOWN. THIS IS OBVIOUSLY A... *UNIQUE* SITUATION...

"UNIQUE!" AN *UNDERSTATEMENT*, TO SAY THE LEAST. HEADS DON'T JUST SPONTANEOUSLY *EXPLODE!*

I SMELL A *CONSPIRACY...!*

THAT... MAY JUST BE *DECOMPOSITION* YOU'RE... SMELLING...

JUSTICE *WILL* BE SERVED IN THIS MATTER, TANKROUS! SO SWEARS *CRASHMAN!*

OH, WHATEVER...!

MR. TANKROUS...PERHAPS IT WOULD BE BEST IF YOU LEFT THE ROOM. THE *CORONERS*--

OH, YOU'D *LOVE* IT IF I LEFT, *WOULDN'T* YOU, MR. HIGH-AND-MIGHTY PROSECUTOR! ANOTHER NOTCH IN *YOUR* BELT, EH...?!

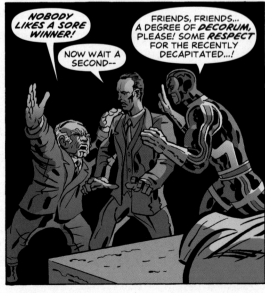

NOBODY LIKES A SORE WINNER!

NOW WAIT A SECOND--

FRIENDS, FRIENDS... A DEGREE OF *DECORUM*, PLEASE! SOME *RESPECT* FOR THE RECENTLY DECAPITATED...!

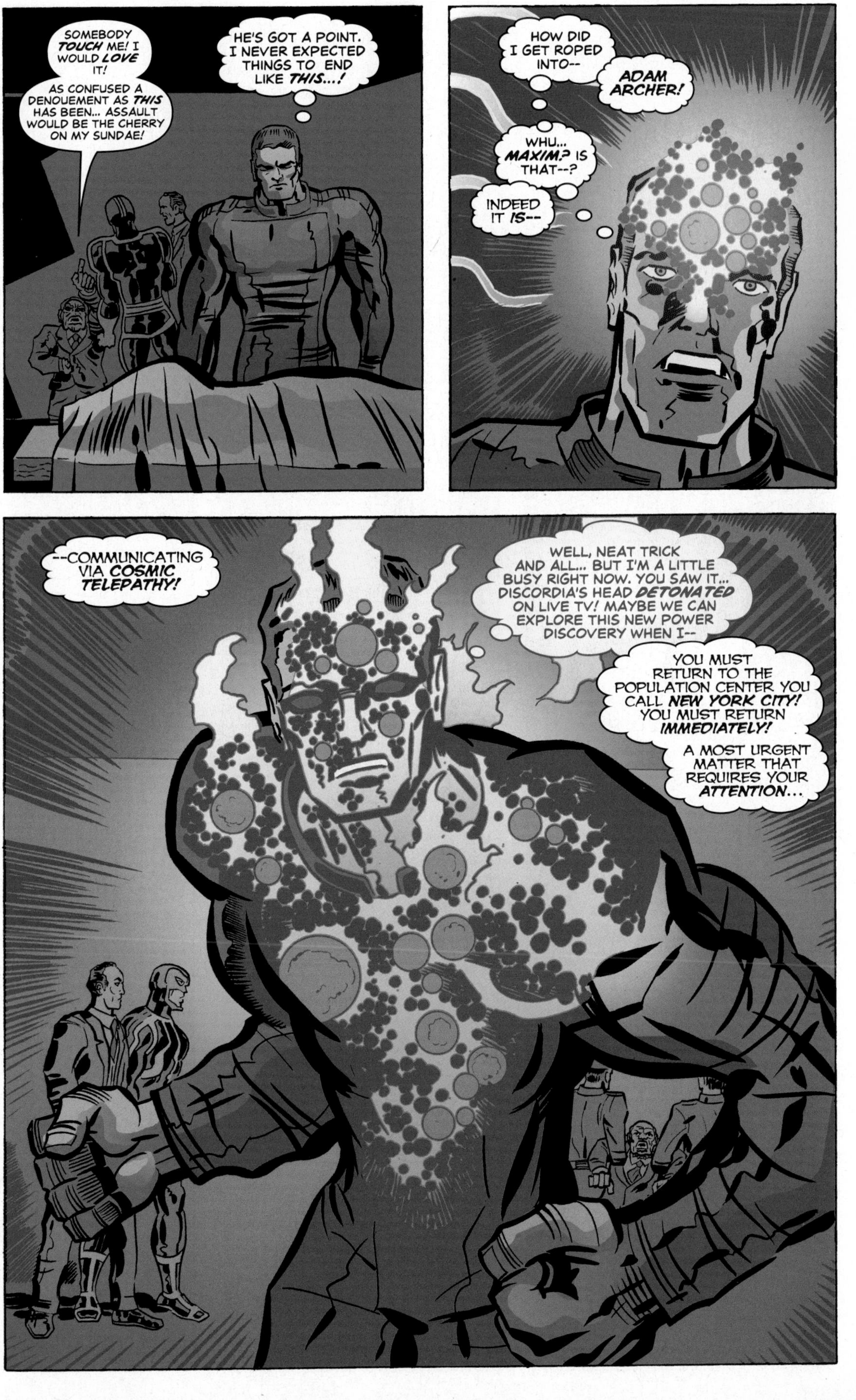
SOMEBODY TOUCH ME! I WOULD LOVE IT!
AS CONFUSED A DENOUEMENT AS THIS HAS BEEN... ASSAULT WOULD BE THE CHERRY ON MY SUNDAE!
HE'S GOT A POINT. I NEVER EXPECTED THINGS TO END LIKE THIS...!
HOW DID I GET ROPED INTO--
ADAM ARCHER!
WHU... MAXIM? IS THAT--?
INDEED IT IS--
--COMMUNICATING VIA COSMIC TELEPATHY!
WELL, NEAT TRICK AND ALL... BUT I'M A LITTLE BUSY RIGHT NOW. YOU SAW IT... DISCORDIA'S HEAD DETONATED ON LIVE TV! MAYBE WE CAN EXPLORE THIS NEW POWER DISCOVERY WHEN I--
YOU MUST RETURN TO THE POPULATION CENTER YOU CALL NEW YORK CITY! YOU MUST RETURN IMMEDIATELY!
A MOST URGENT MATTER THAT REQUIRES YOUR ATTENTION...

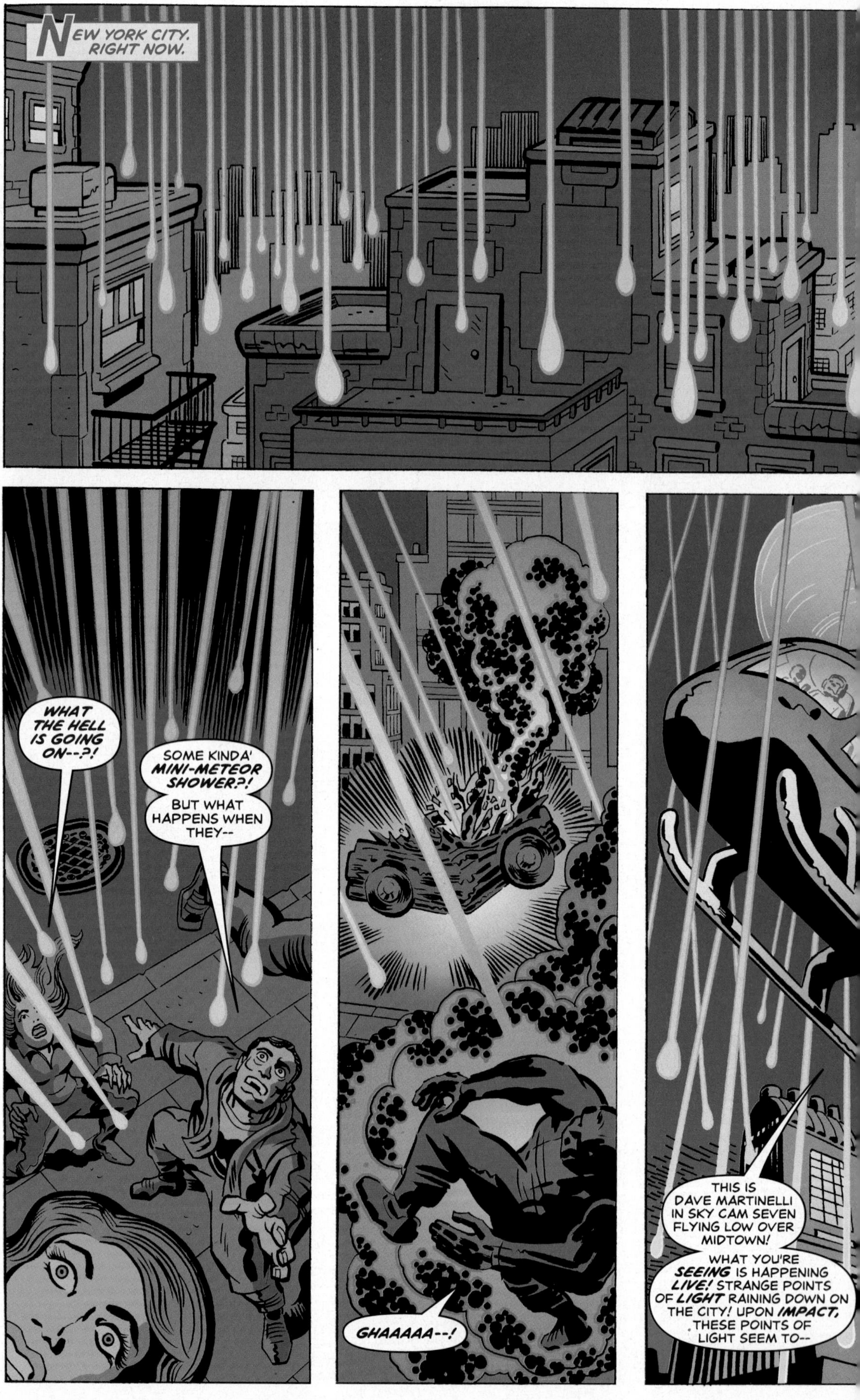
NEW YORK CITY. RIGHT NOW.
WHAT THE HELL IS GOING ON--?!
SOME KINDA' MINI-METEOR SHOWER?!
BUT WHAT HAPPENS WHEN THEY--
GHAAAAA--!
THIS IS DAVE MARTINELLI IN SKY CAM SEVEN FLYING LOW OVER MIDTOWN!
WHAT YOU'RE SEEING IS HAPPENING LIVE! STRANGE POINTS OF LIGHT RAINING DOWN ON THE CITY! UPON IMPACT, THESE POINTS OF LIGHT SEEM TO--

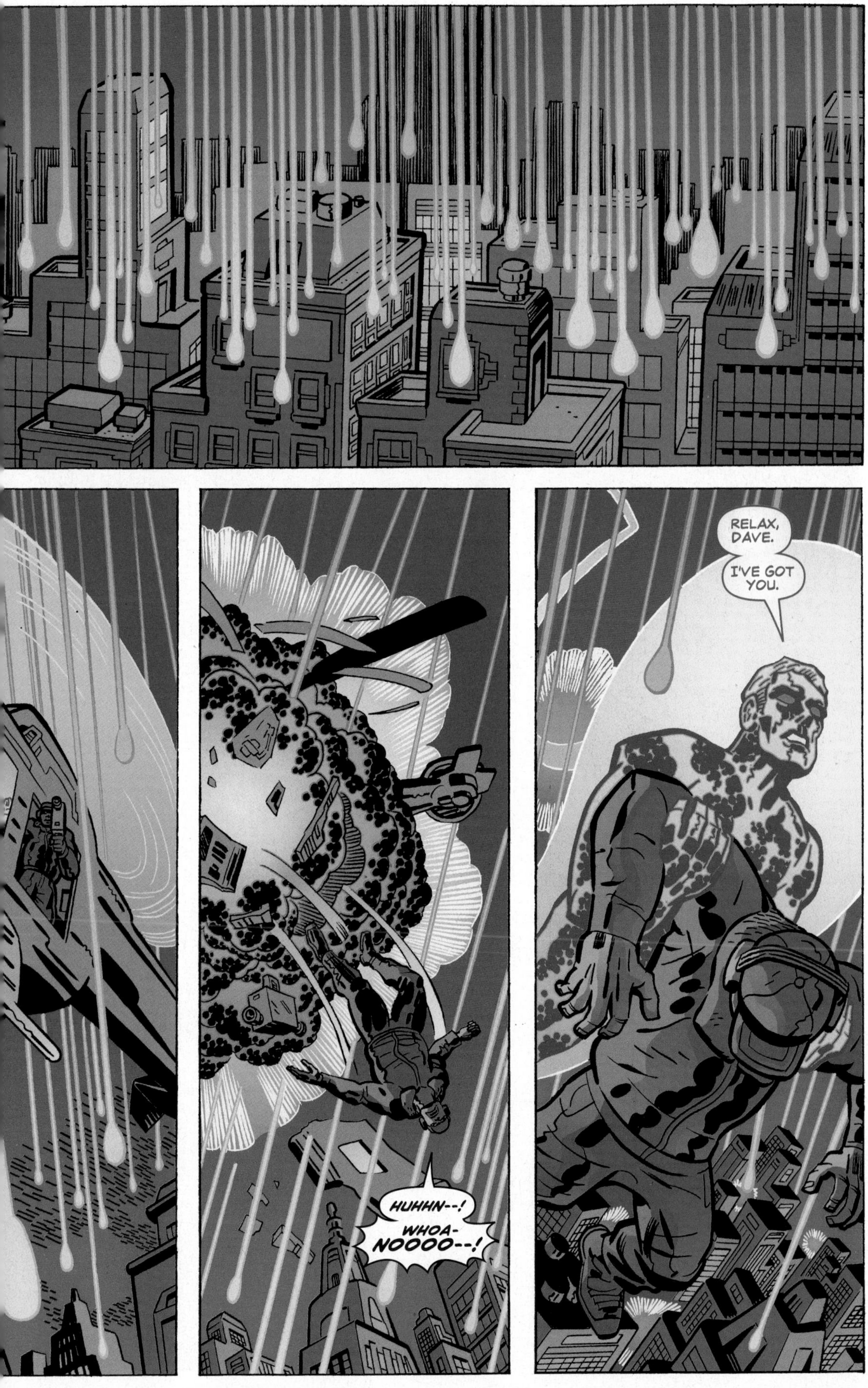
RELAX, DAVE.
I'VE GOT YOU.
HUHHN--!
WHOA-NOOOO--!

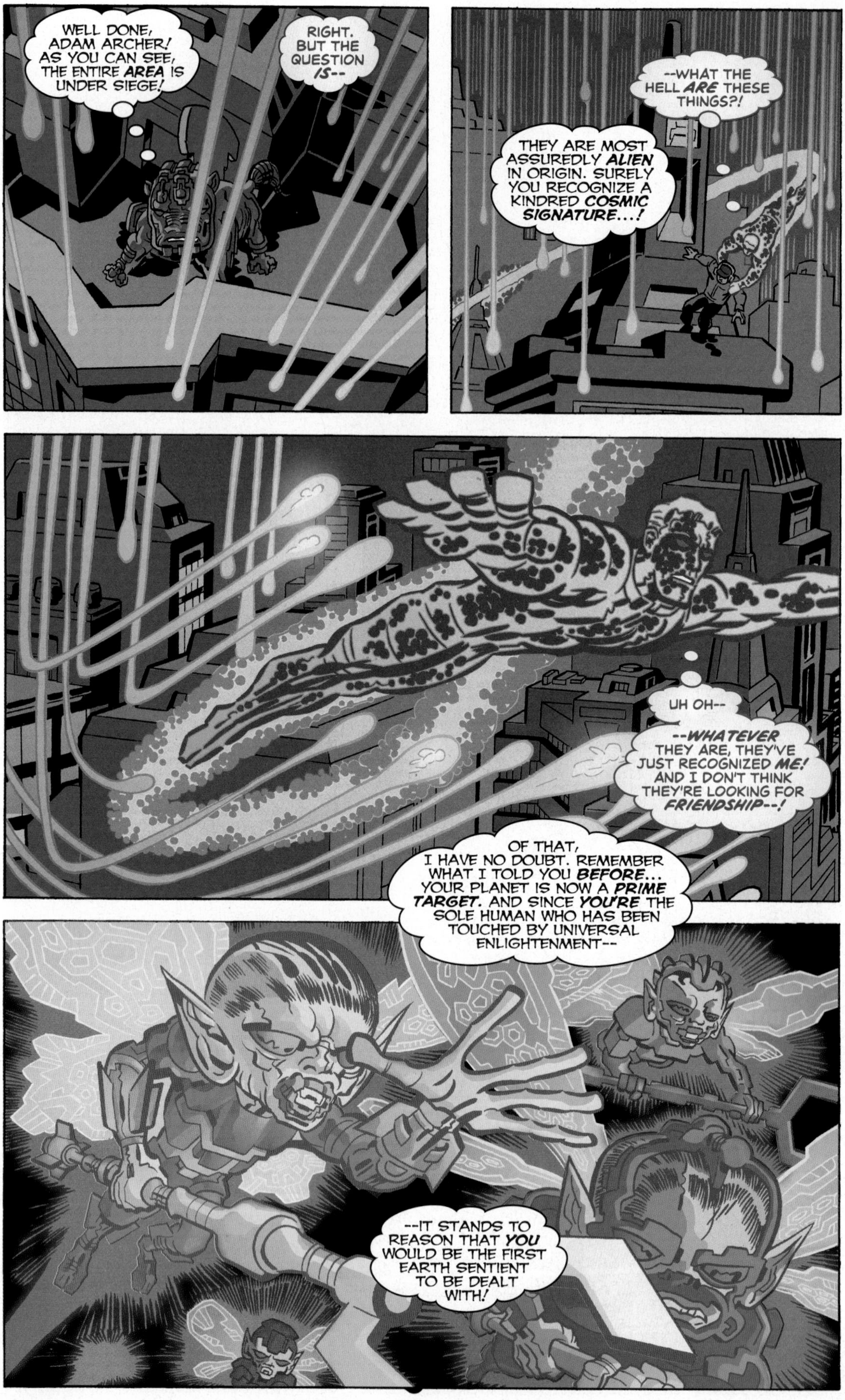

WELL DONE, ADAM ARCHER! AS YOU CAN SEE, THE ENTIRE AREA IS UNDER SIEGE!
RIGHT. BUT THE QUESTION IS--
--WHAT THE HELL ARE THESE THINGS?!
THEY ARE MOST ASSUREDLY ALIEN IN ORIGIN. SURELY YOU RECOGNIZE A KINDRED COSMIC SIGNATURE...!
UH OH--
--WHATEVER THEY ARE, THEY'VE JUST RECOGNIZED ME! AND I DON'T THINK THEY'RE LOOKING FOR FRIENDSHIP--!
OF THAT, I HAVE NO DOUBT. REMEMBER WHAT I TOLD YOU BEFORE... YOUR PLANET IS NOW A PRIME TARGET. AND SINCE YOU'RE THE SOLE HUMAN WHO HAS BEEN TOUCHED BY UNIVERSAL ENLIGHTENMENT--
--IT STANDS TO REASON THAT YOU WOULD BE THE FIRST EARTH SENTIENT TO BE DEALT WITH!

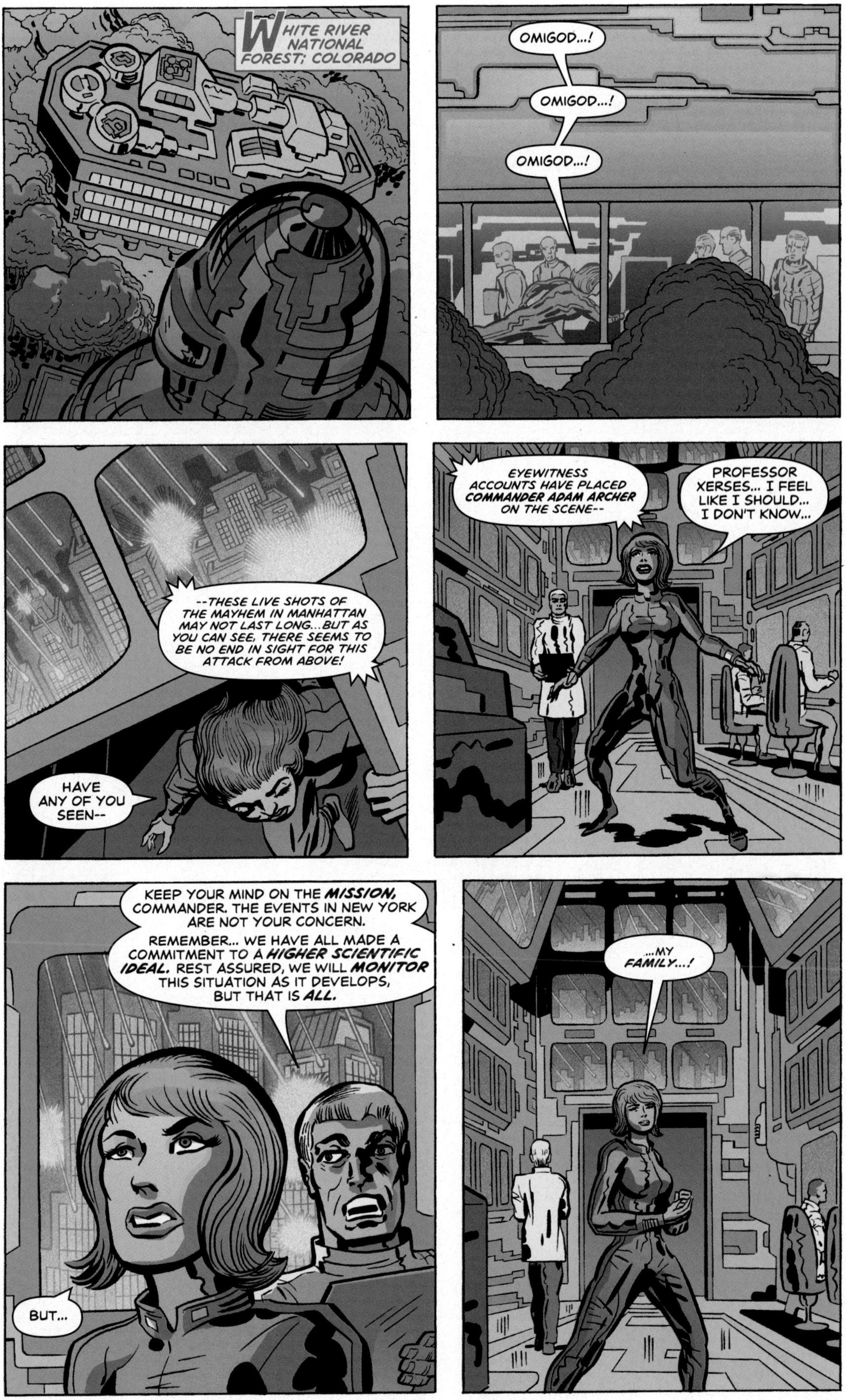
WHITE RIVER NATIONAL FOREST; COLORADO
OMIGOD...!
OMIGOD...!
OMIGOD...!
--THESE LIVE SHOTS OF THE MAYHEM IN MANHATTAN MAY NOT LAST LONG...BUT AS YOU CAN SEE, THERE SEEMS TO BE NO END IN SIGHT FOR THIS ATTACK FROM ABOVE!
HAVE ANY OF YOU SEEN--
EYEWITNESS ACCOUNTS HAVE PLACED COMMANDER ADAM ARCHER ON THE SCENE--
PROFESSOR XERSES... I FEEL LIKE I SHOULD... I DON'T KNOW...
KEEP YOUR MIND ON THE MISSION, COMMANDER. THE EVENTS IN NEW YORK ARE NOT YOUR CONCERN.
REMEMBER... WE HAVE ALL MADE A COMMITMENT TO A HIGHER SCIENTIFIC IDEAL. REST ASSURED, WE WILL MONITOR THIS SITUATION AS IT DEVELOPS, BUT THAT IS ALL.
BUT...
...MY FAMILY...!

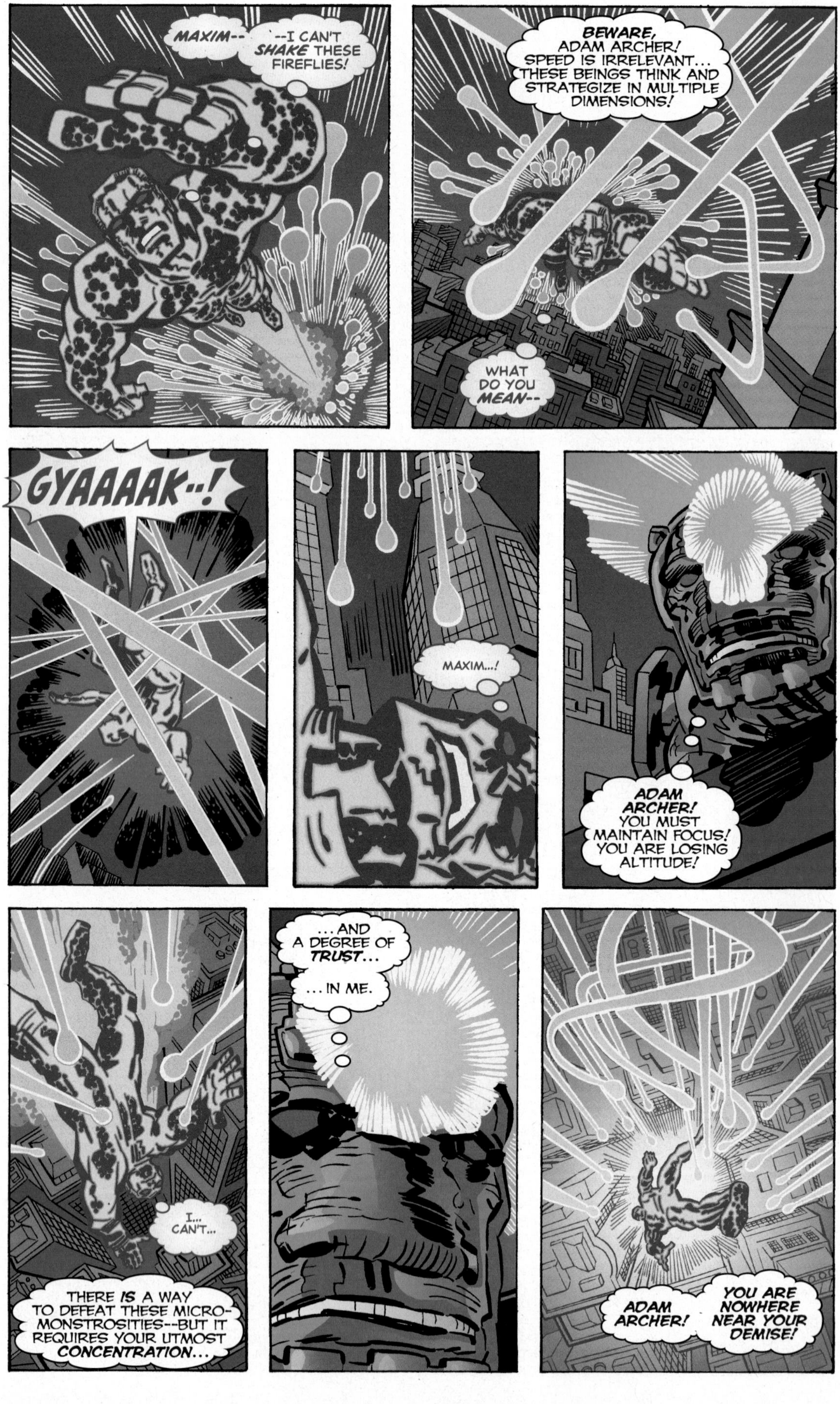
MAXIM--
--I CAN'T SHAKE THESE FIREFLIES!
BEWARE, ADAM ARCHER! SPEED IS IRRELEVANT... THESE BEINGS THINK AND STRATEGIZE IN MULTIPLE DIMENSIONS!
WHAT DO YOU MEAN--
GYAAAAK--!
MAXIM...!
ADAM ARCHER! YOU MUST MAINTAIN FOCUS! YOU ARE LOSING ALTITUDE!
I... CAN'T...
THERE IS A WAY TO DEFEAT THESE MICRO-MONSTROSITIES--BUT IT REQUIRES YOUR UTMOST CONCENTRATION...
...AND A DEGREE OF TRUST...
...IN ME.
ADAM ARCHER!
YOU ARE NOWHERE NEAR YOUR DEMISE!

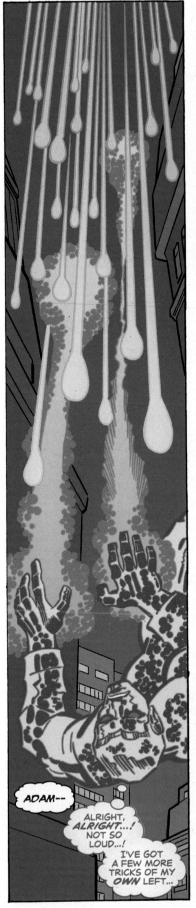

ADAM--

ALRIGHT, *ALRIGHT*...! NOT SO LOUD...!

I'VE GOT A FEW MORE TRICKS OF MY *OWN* LEFT...

NOT THAT ANY OF THEM ARE *WORKING*...!

ADAM... THIS IS *STELLA* ON THE QUANTUM PARTICLE WAVE COMMUNICATOR! COME IN...!

WE'RE MONITORING THE ACTION--YOU'RE GETTING *KILLED* OUT THERE--!

I CAN'T *RAISE* HIM--!

THERE IS NO *NEED*, STELLA ARCHER. AT THE MOMENT, OUR MINDS ARE AS *ONE*...

UHHH... *MAXIM*...?

YOU SAID THERE WAS A WAY TO *DEAL* WITH THESE THINGS...

...*NOW* WOULD BE A GOOD TIME TO FILL ME IN!

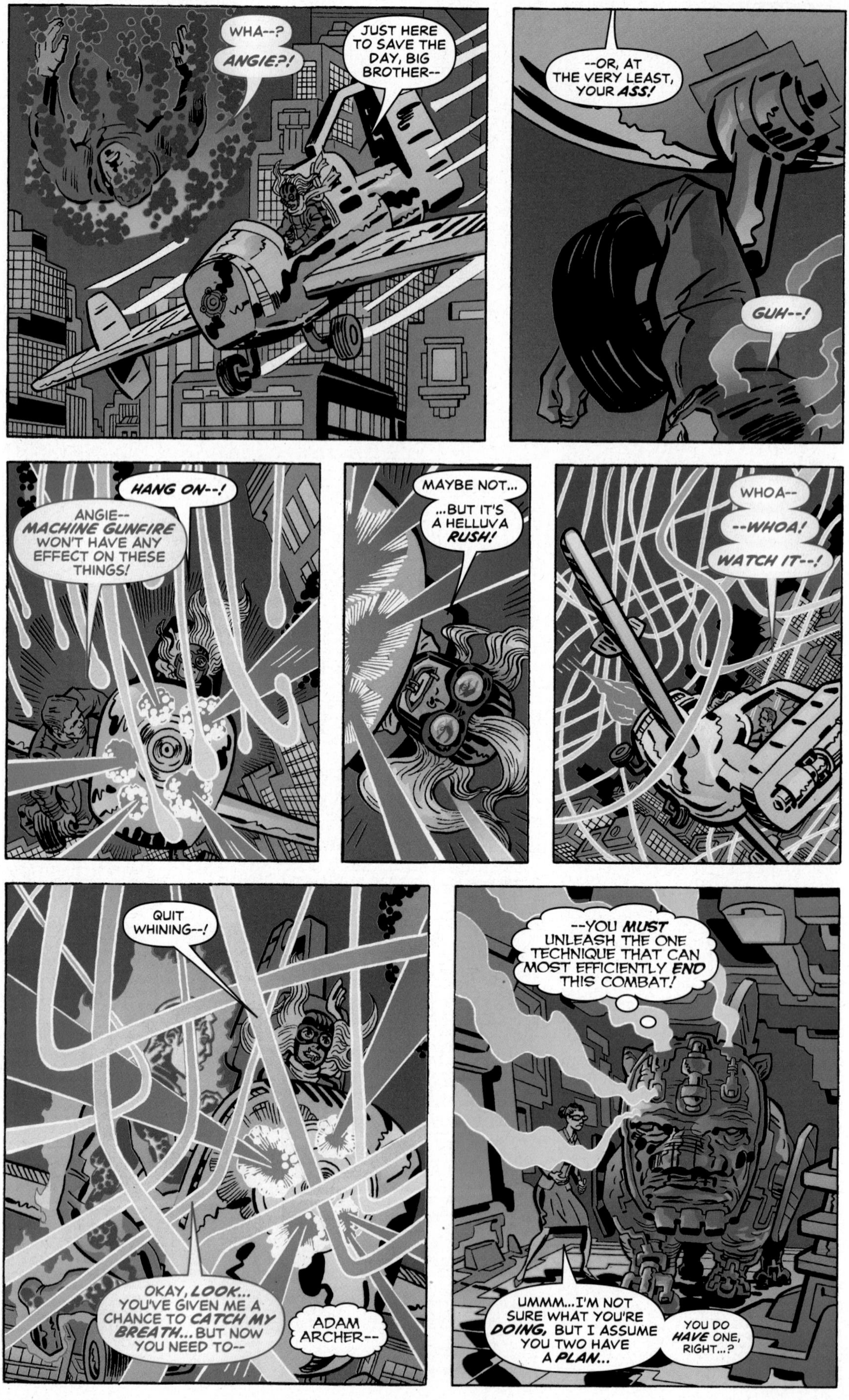
WHA--? ANGIE?!
JUST HERE TO SAVE THE DAY, BIG BROTHER--
--OR, AT THE VERY LEAST, YOUR ASS!
GUH--!
HANG ON--!
ANGIE-- MACHINE GUNFIRE WON'T HAVE ANY EFFECT ON THESE THINGS!
MAYBE NOT...
...BUT IT'S A HELLUVA RUSH!
WHOA--
--WHOA!
WATCH IT--!
QUIT WHINING--!
OKAY, LOOK... YOU'VE GIVEN ME A CHANCE TO CATCH MY BREATH... BUT NOW YOU NEED TO--
ADAM ARCHER--
--YOU MUST UNLEASH THE ONE TECHNIQUE THAT CAN MOST EFFICIENTLY END THIS COMBAT!
UMMM...I'M NOT SURE WHAT YOU'RE DOING, BUT I ASSUME YOU TWO HAVE A PLAN...
YOU DO HAVE ONE, RIGHT...?

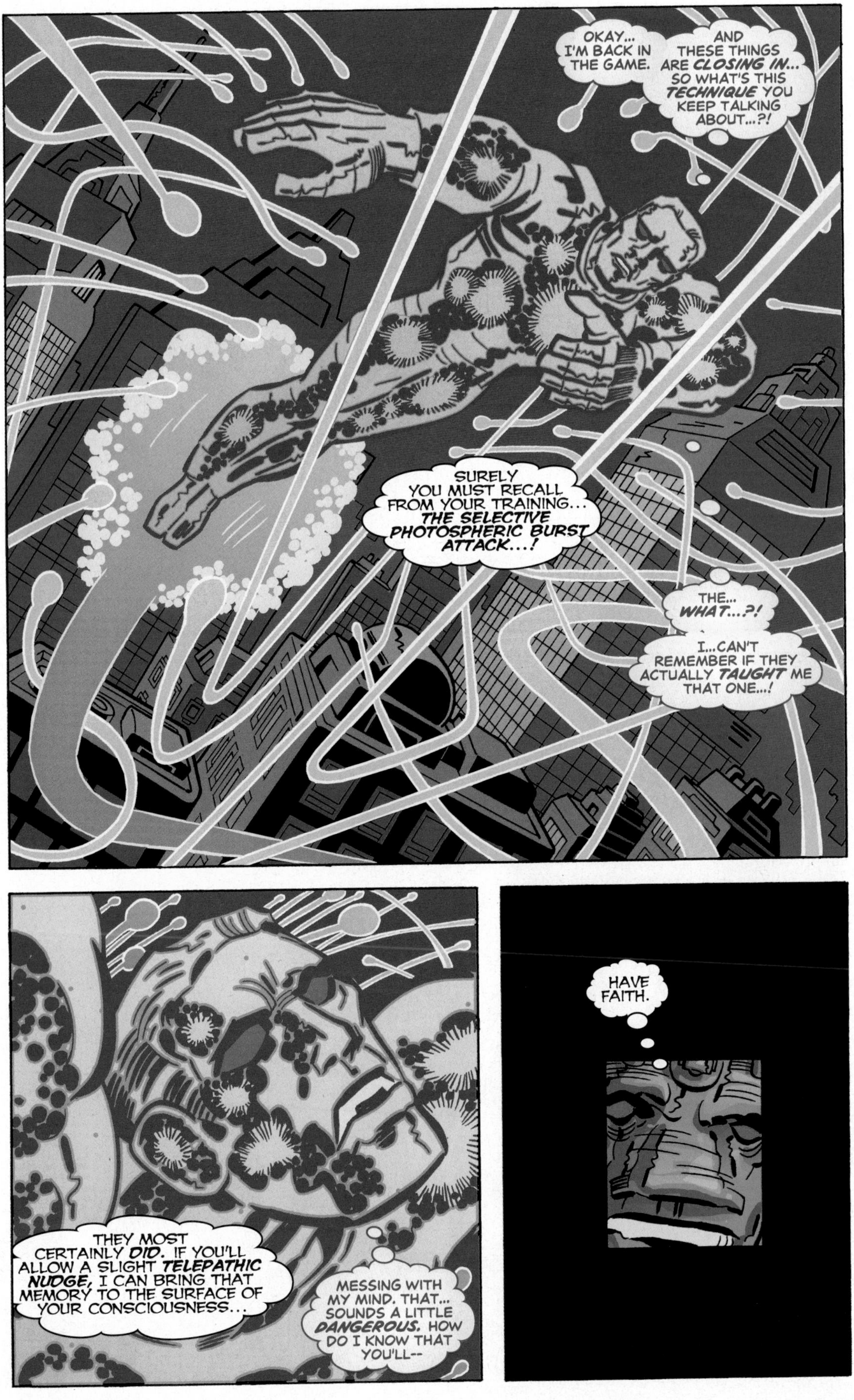
OKAY... I'M BACK IN THE GAME.
AND THESE THINGS ARE CLOSING IN... SO WHAT'S THIS TECHNIQUE YOU KEEP TALKING ABOUT...?!
SURELY YOU MUST RECALL FROM YOUR TRAINING... THE SELECTIVE PHOTOSPHERIC BURST ATTACK...!
THE... WHAT...?!
I...CAN'T REMEMBER IF THEY ACTUALLY TAUGHT ME THAT ONE...!
THEY MOST CERTAINLY DID. IF YOU'LL ALLOW A SLIGHT TELEPATHIC NUDGE, I CAN BRING THAT MEMORY TO THE SURFACE OF YOUR CONSCIOUSNESS...
MESSING WITH MY MIND. THAT... SOUNDS A LITTLE DANGEROUS. HOW DO I KNOW THAT YOU'LL--
HAVE FAITH.

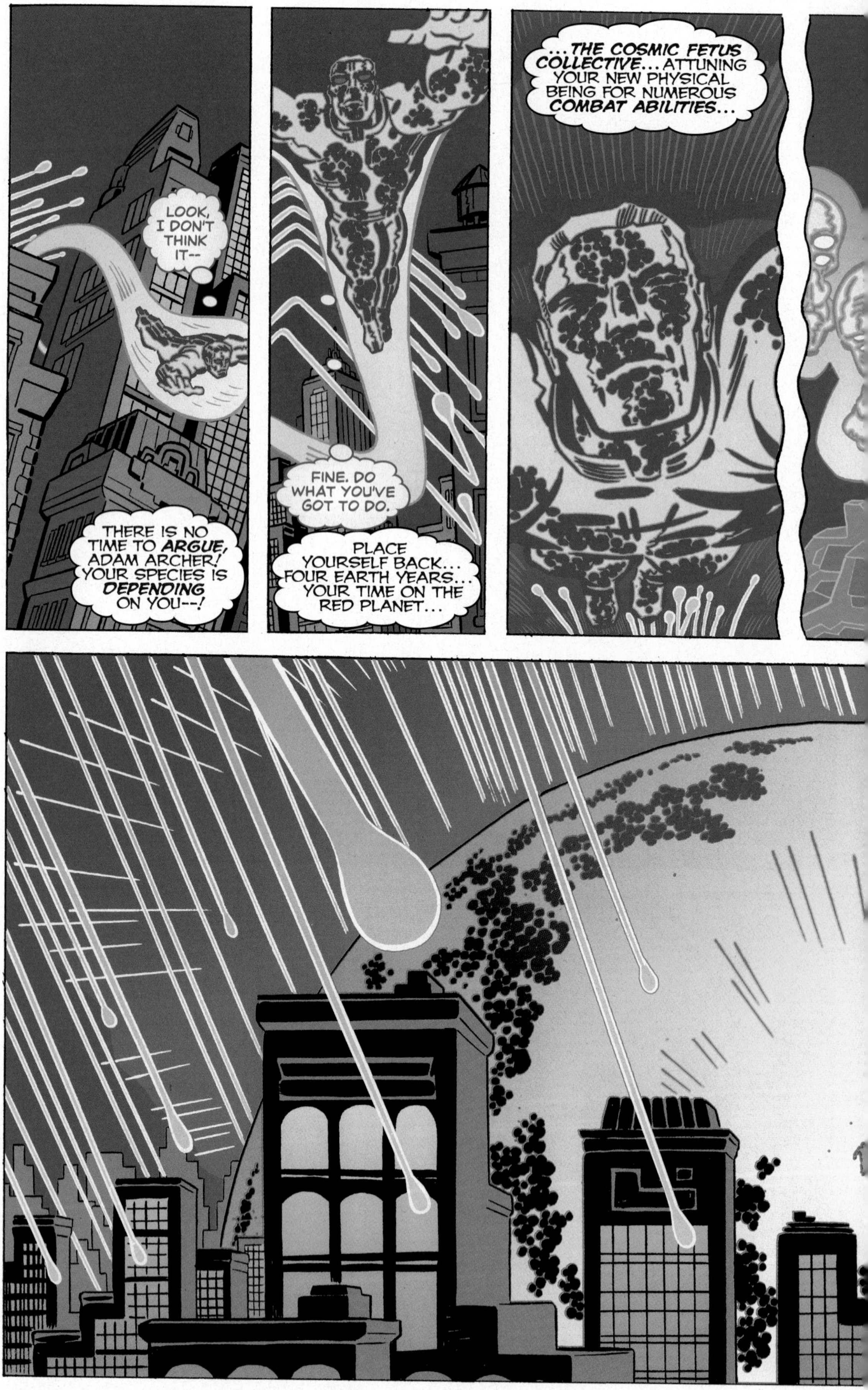
LOOK, I DON'T THINK IT--
THERE IS NO TIME TO ARGUE, ADAM ARCHER! YOUR SPECIES IS DEPENDING ON YOU--!
FINE. DO WHAT YOU'VE GOT TO DO.
PLACE YOURSELF BACK... FOUR EARTH YEARS... YOUR TIME ON THE RED PLANET...
...THE COSMIC FETUS COLLECTIVE... ATTUNING YOUR NEW PHYSICAL BEING FOR NUMEROUS COMBAT ABILITIES...

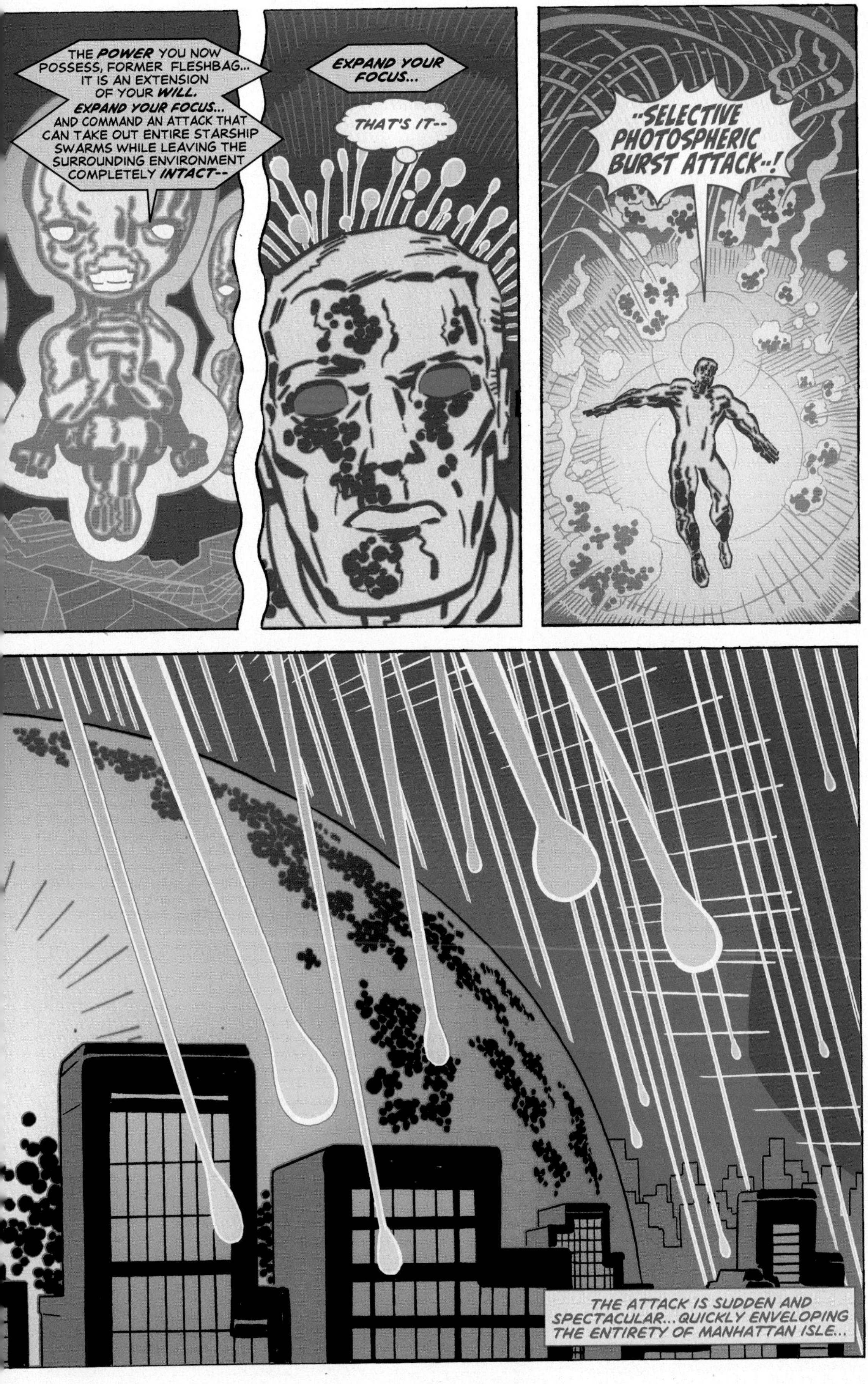
THE POWER YOU NOW POSSESS, FORMER FLESHBAG... IT IS AN EXTENSION OF YOUR WILL.
EXPAND YOUR FOCUS... AND COMMAND AN ATTACK THAT CAN TAKE OUT ENTIRE STARSHIP SWARMS WHILE LEAVING THE SURROUNDING ENVIRONMENT COMPLETELY INTACT--
EXPAND YOUR FOCUS...
THAT'S IT--
--SELECTIVE PHOTOSPHERIC BURST ATTACK--!
THE ATTACK IS SUDDEN AND SPECTACULAR... QUICKLY ENVELOPING THE ENTIRETY OF MANHATTAN ISLE...

...ITS UNSUSPECTING *DENIZENS* SCATTER AND SCREAM AS THE COSMIC WIND WHIPS THROUGH THEIR FRAMES...

...NO ONE ABLE TO PROCESS THAT THEY REMAIN RELATIVELY *UNHARMED*--

--THE HEAVENLY SWARM, HOWEVER, IS NOT SO LUCKY.

I'VE... NEVER FELT *ANYTHING*... LIKE *THIS*...

REMEMBER YOUR TRAINING, ADAM ARCHER.

NOW, EASE IT BACK. TAKE IT ALL BACK IN--

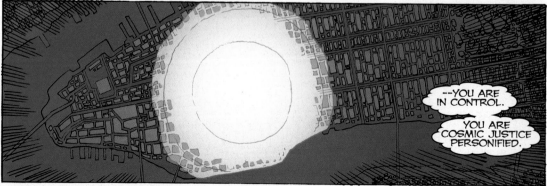

--YOU ARE IN CONTROL.

YOU ARE COSMIC JUSTICE PERSONIFIED.

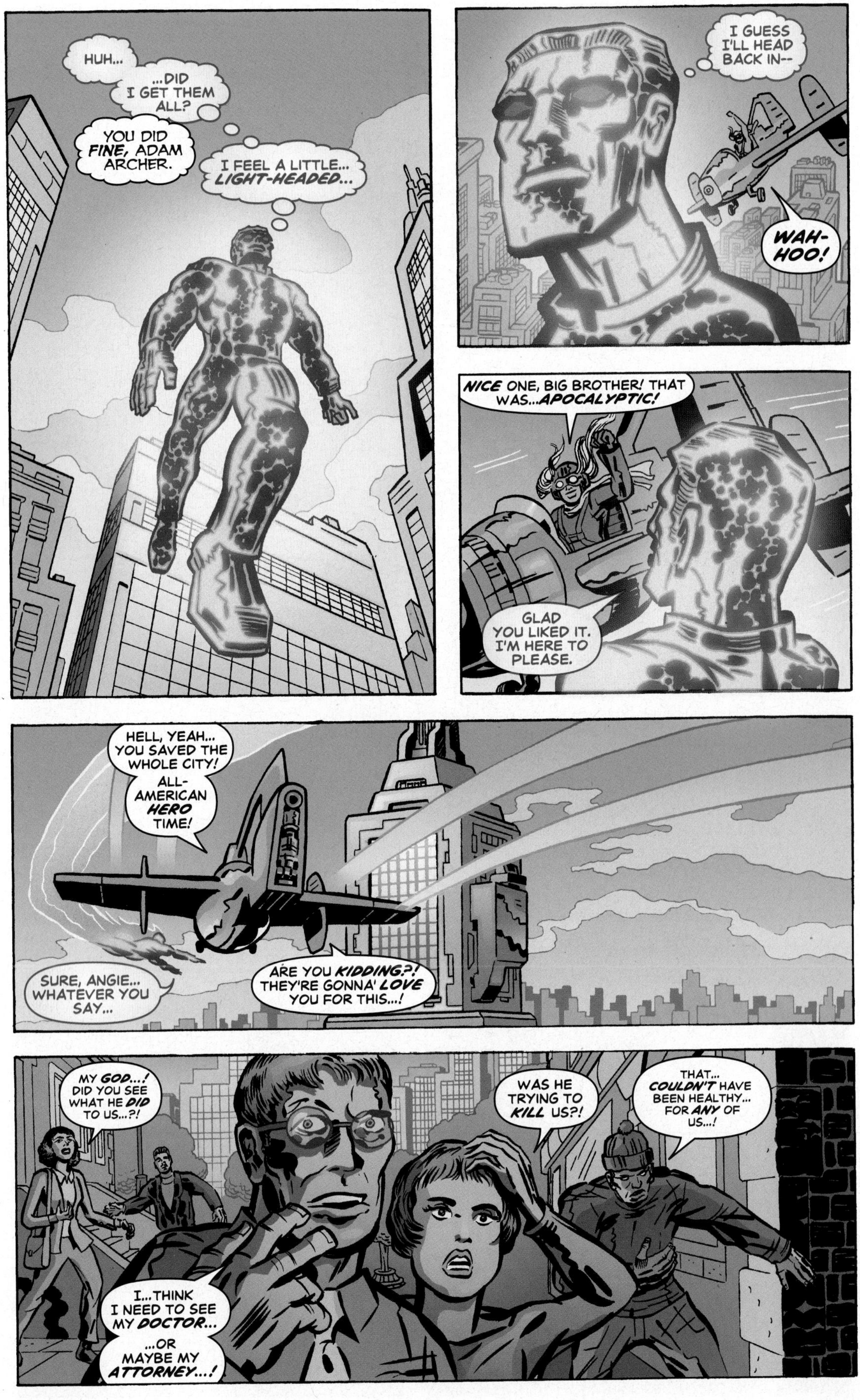
HUH...
...DID I GET THEM ALL?
YOU DID FINE, ADAM ARCHER.
I FEEL A LITTLE... LIGHT-HEADED...
I GUESS I'LL HEAD BACK IN--
WAH-HOO!
NICE ONE, BIG BROTHER! THAT WAS...APOCALYPTIC!
GLAD YOU LIKED IT. I'M HERE TO PLEASE.
HELL, YEAH... YOU SAVED THE WHOLE CITY!
ALL-AMERICAN HERO TIME!
SURE, ANGIE... WHATEVER YOU SAY...
ARE YOU KIDDING?! THEY'RE GONNA' LOVE YOU FOR THIS...!
MY GOD...! DID YOU SEE WHAT HE DID TO US...?!
WAS HE TRYING TO KILL US?!
THAT... COULDN'T HAVE BEEN HEALTHY... FOR ANY OF US...!
I...THINK I NEED TO SEE MY DOCTOR...
...OR MAYBE MY ATTORNEY...!

WASHINGTON, D.C. FEDERAL MORGUE. SECURITY SUB-LEVEL D.

SUB-LEVEL C.

STEALTHY. EFFICIENCY. TADPOLE.

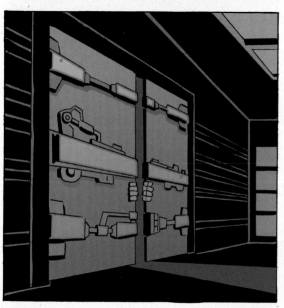

COMPANY.

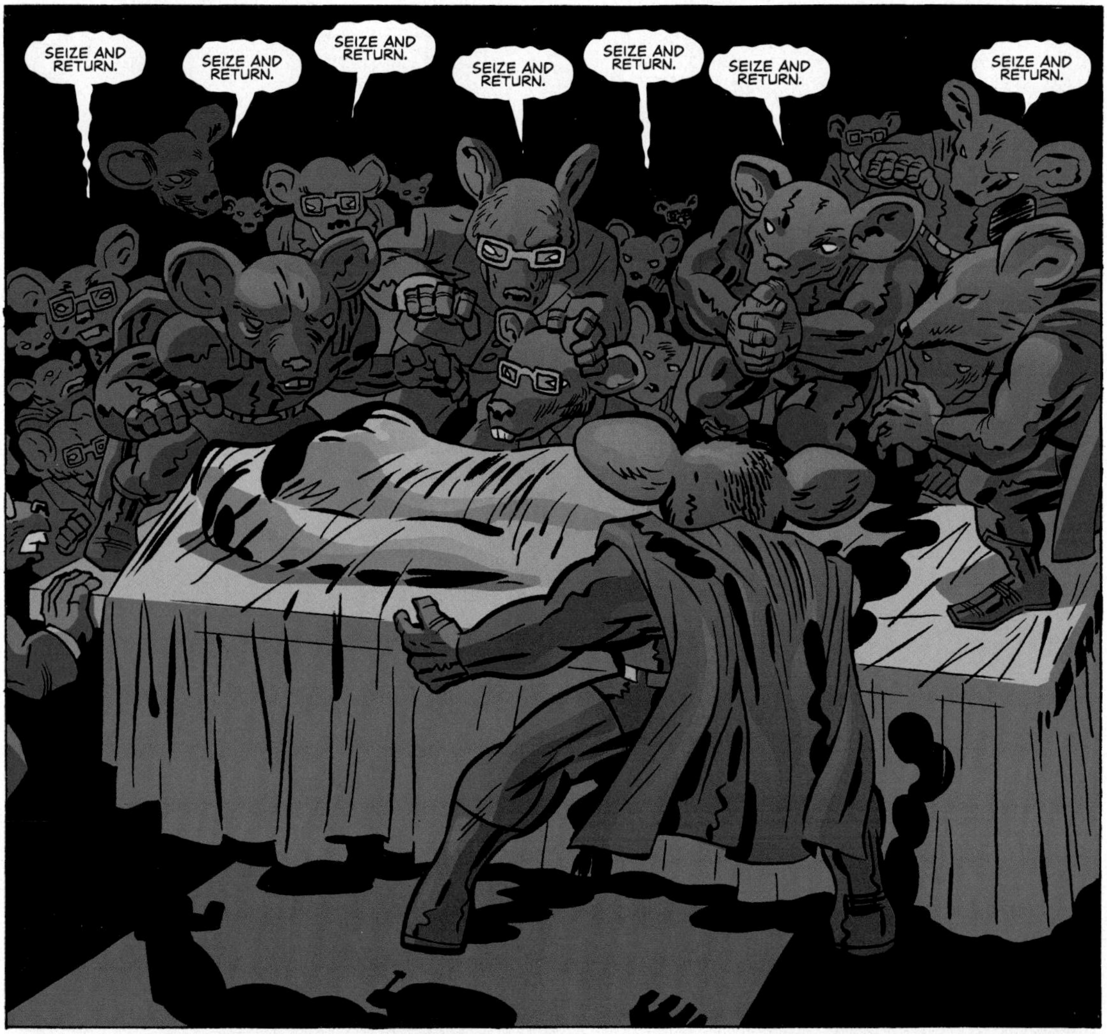
SEIZE AND RETURN.
SEIZE AND RETURN.
SEIZE AND RETURN.
SEIZE AND RETURN.
SEIZE AND RETURN.
SEIZE AND RETURN.
SEIZE AND RETURN.

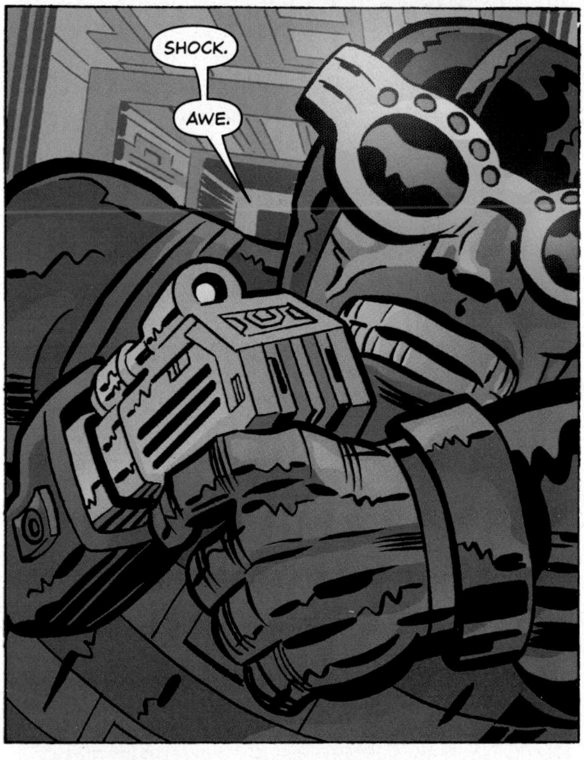
SHOCK.
AWE.

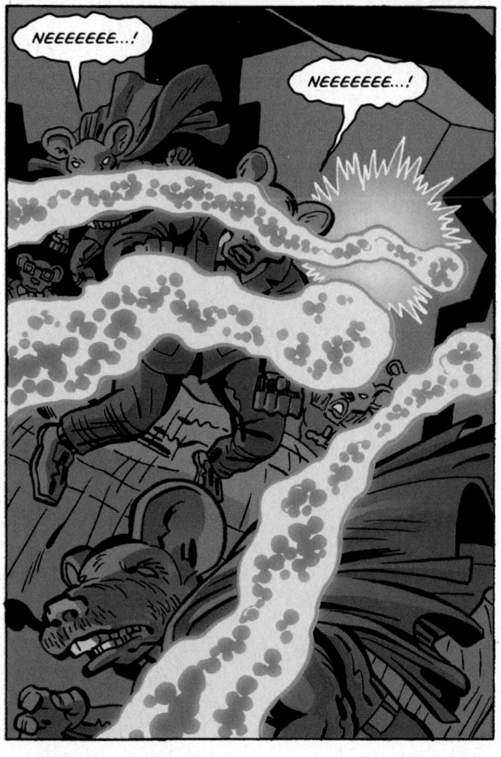
NEEEEEEE...!
NEEEEEEE...!

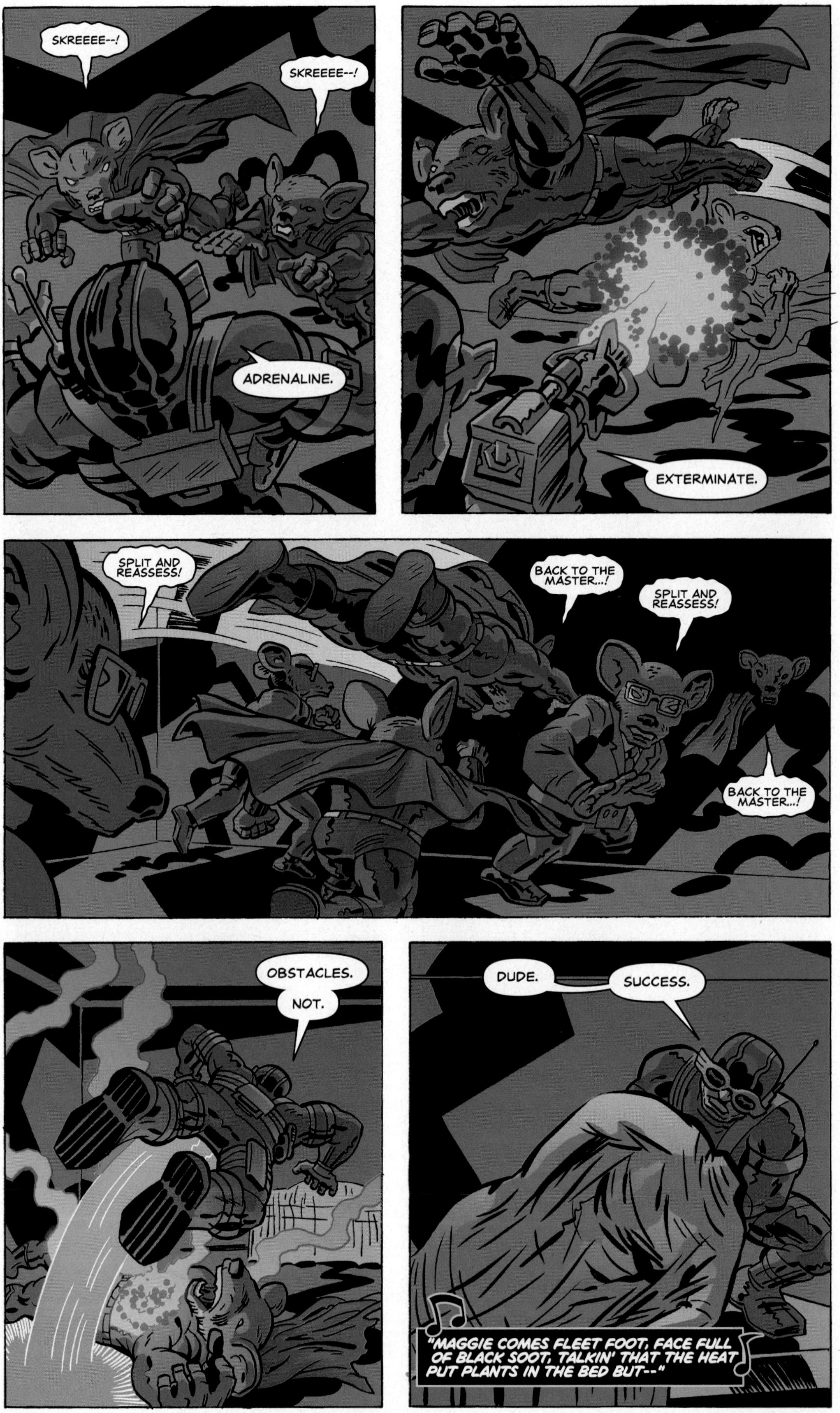
SKREEEE--!
SKREEEE--!
ADRENALINE.
EXTERMINATE.
SPLIT AND REASSESS!
BACK TO THE MASTER...!
SPLIT AND REASSESS!
BACK TO THE MASTER...!
OBSTACLES.
NOT.
DUDE.
SUCCESS.
"MAGGIE COMES FLEET FOOT, FACE FULL OF BLACK SOOT, TALKIN' THAT THE HEAT PUT PLANTS IN THE BED BUT--"

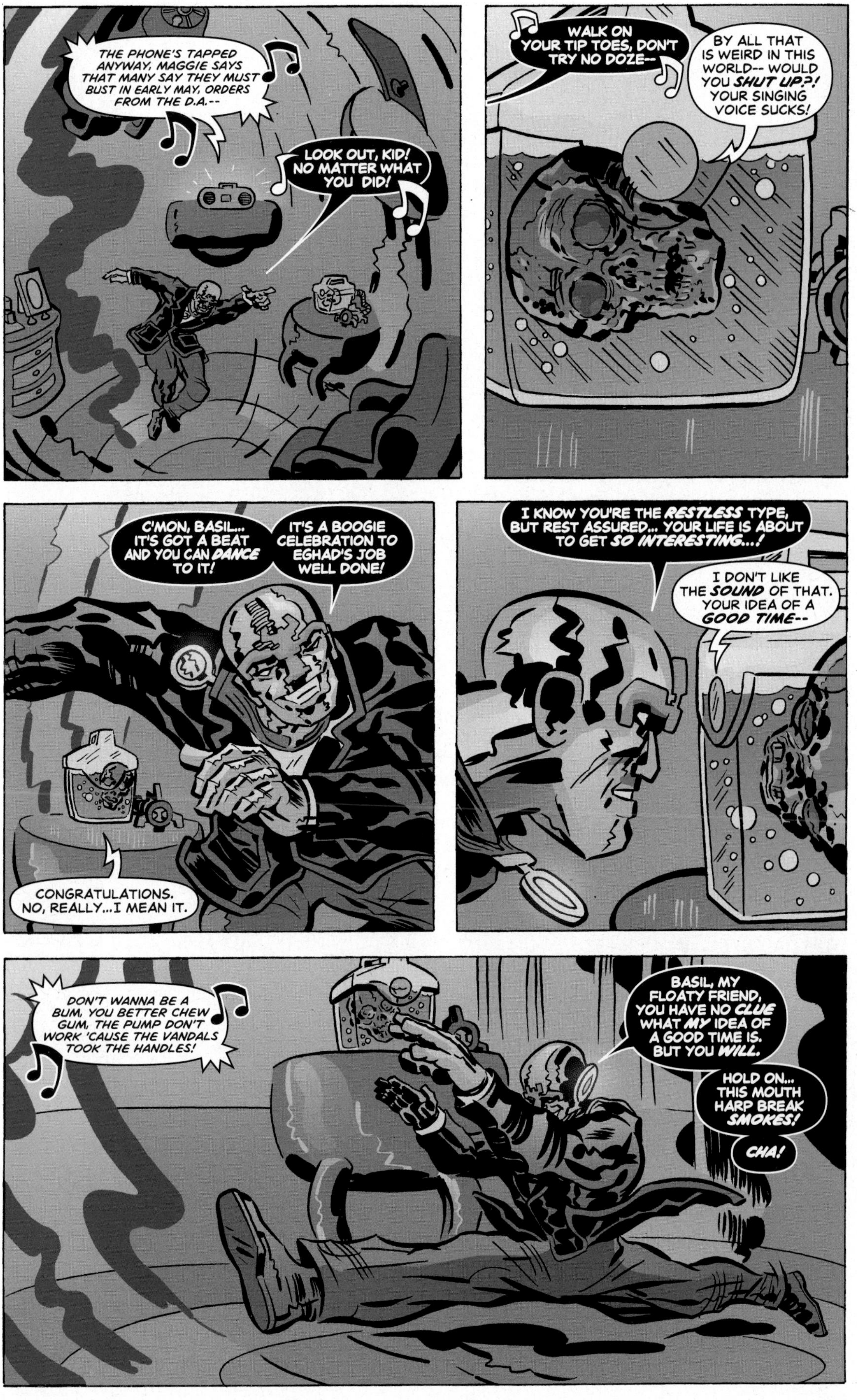
THE PHONE'S TAPPED ANYWAY, MAGGIE SAYS THAT MANY SAY THEY MUST BUST IN EARLY MAY, ORDERS FROM THE D.A.--
LOOK OUT, KID! NO MATTER WHAT YOU DID!
WALK ON YOUR TIP TOES, DON'T TRY NO DOZE--
BY ALL THAT IS WEIRD IN THIS WORLD-- WOULD YOU SHUT UP?! YOUR SINGING VOICE SUCKS!
C'MON, BASIL... IT'S GOT A BEAT AND YOU CAN DANCE TO IT!
IT'S A BOOGIE CELEBRATION TO EGHAD'S JOB WELL DONE!
CONGRATULATIONS. NO, REALLY...I MEAN IT.
I KNOW YOU'RE THE RESTLESS TYPE, BUT REST ASSURED... YOUR LIFE IS ABOUT TO GET SO INTERESTING...!
I DON'T LIKE THE SOUND OF THAT. YOUR IDEA OF A GOOD TIME--
DON'T WANNA BE A BUM, YOU BETTER CHEW GUM, THE PUMP DON'T WORK 'CAUSE THE VANDALS TOOK THE HANDLES!
BASIL, MY FLOATY FRIEND, YOU HAVE NO CLUE WHAT MY IDEA OF A GOOD TIME IS. BUT YOU WILL.
HOLD ON... THIS MOUTH HARP BREAK SMOKES!
CHA!

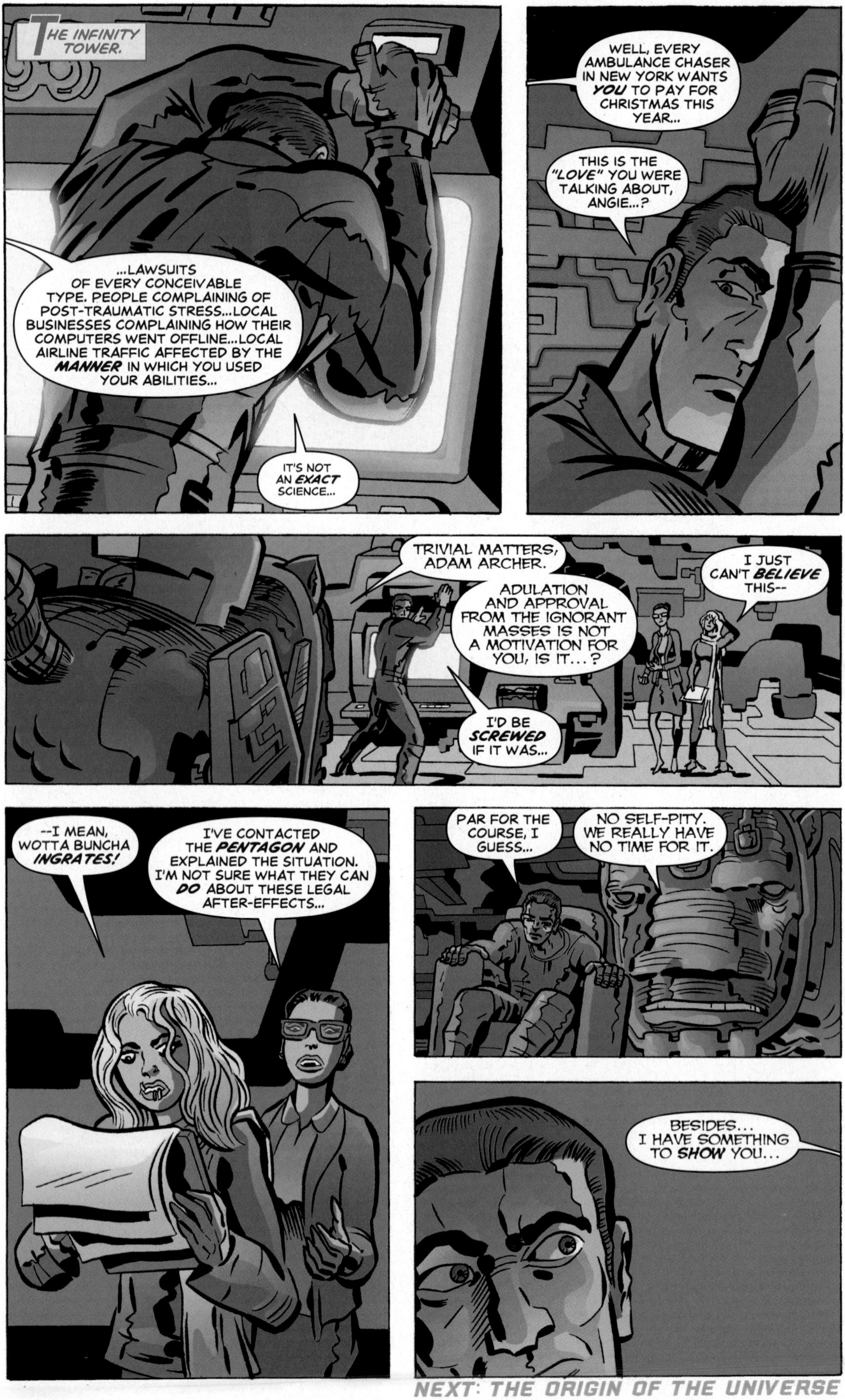
THE INFINITY TOWER.
...LAWSUITS OF EVERY CONCEIVABLE TYPE. PEOPLE COMPLAINING OF POST-TRAUMATIC STRESS...LOCAL BUSINESSES COMPLAINING HOW THEIR COMPUTERS WENT OFFLINE...LOCAL AIRLINE TRAFFIC AFFECTED BY THE MANNER IN WHICH YOU USED YOUR ABILITIES...
IT'S NOT AN EXACT SCIENCE...
WELL, EVERY AMBULANCE CHASER IN NEW YORK WANTS YOU TO PAY FOR CHRISTMAS THIS YEAR...
THIS IS THE "LOVE" YOU WERE TALKING ABOUT, ANGIE...?
TRIVIAL MATTERS, ADAM ARCHER.
ADULATION AND APPROVAL FROM THE IGNORANT MASSES IS NOT A MOTIVATION FOR YOU, IS IT...?
I'D BE SCREWED IF IT WAS...
I JUST CAN'T BELIEVE THIS--
--I MEAN, WOTTA BUNCHA INGRATES!
I'VE CONTACTED THE PENTAGON AND EXPLAINED THE SITUATION. I'M NOT SURE WHAT THEY CAN DO ABOUT THESE LEGAL AFTER-EFFECTS...
PAR FOR THE COURSE, I GUESS...
NO SELF-PITY. WE REALLY HAVE NO TIME FOR IT.
BESIDES... I HAVE SOMETHING TO SHOW YOU...

NEXT: THE ORIGIN OF THE UNIVERSE

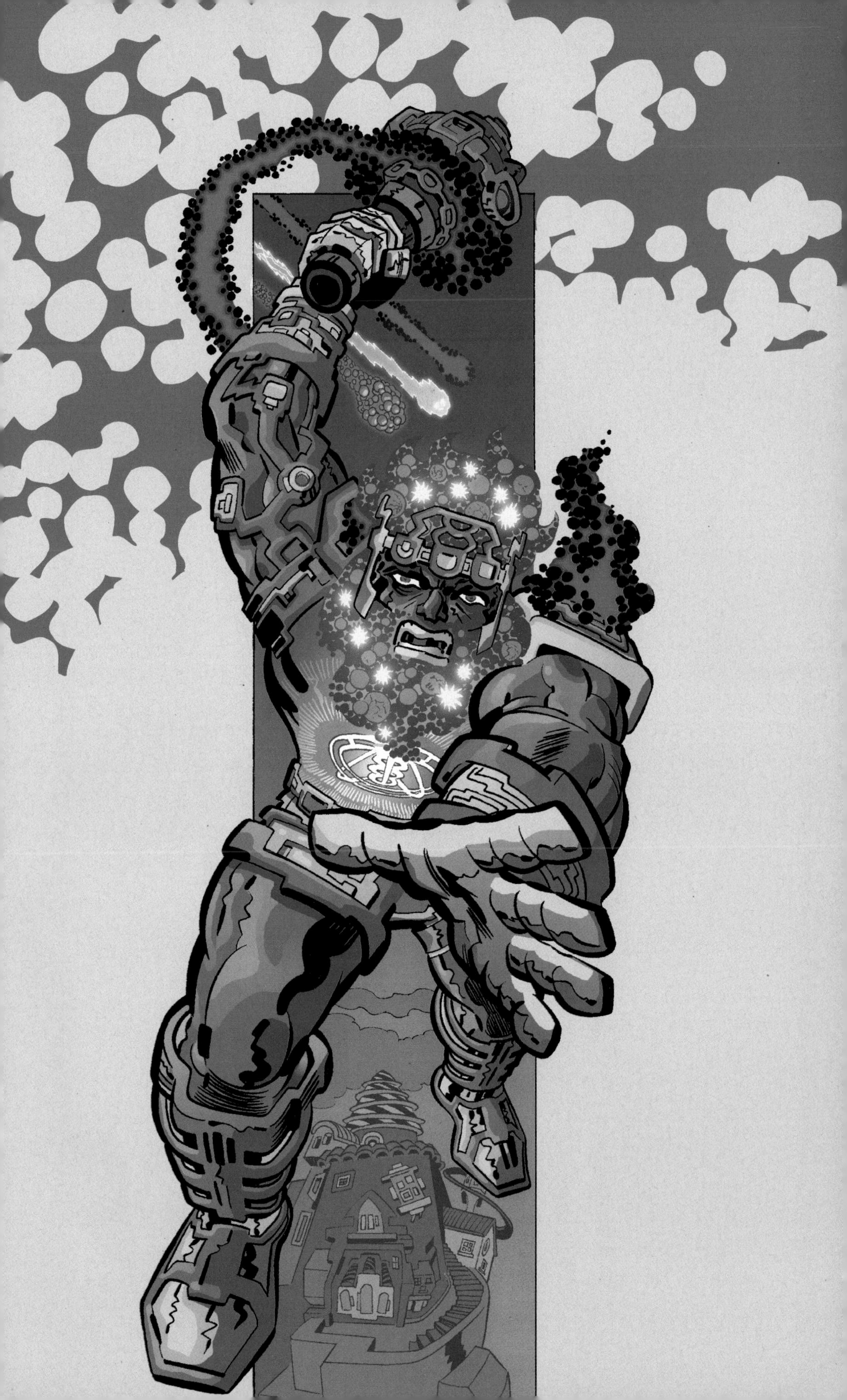

BOOK EIGHT:
ORIGIN OF THE UNIVERSE

THE INFINITE COSMOS

"WORD UP, FELLOW FRANTICS! REMEMBER THE MIND-BLOWING *VASTNESS*... RECALL THE GALACTOSTROPHIC *MULTITUDES* THAT LAY FAR BEYOND THE FIELDS WE KNOW!

"COLD AND FOREBODING, NO DOUBT...

"...BUT NOT *EMPTY!*

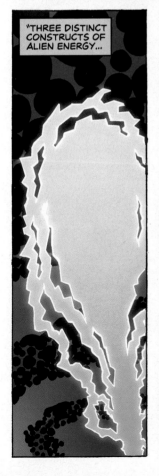

"THREE DISTINCT CONSTRUCTS OF ALIEN ENERGY...

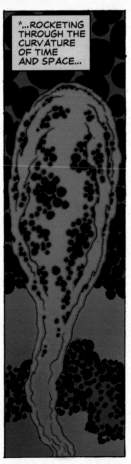

"...ROCKETING THROUGH THE CURVATURE OF TIME AND SPACE...

"...THEY HAVE *DIRECTION*... THEY HAVE *PURPOSE!*

"AND THEIR *TARGET*--

"-- WHERE *ELSE?* THE NEW EPICENTER OF UNIVERSAL HAPPENSTANCE... THE THIRD PLANET FROM SOL...

"...*EARTH!*"

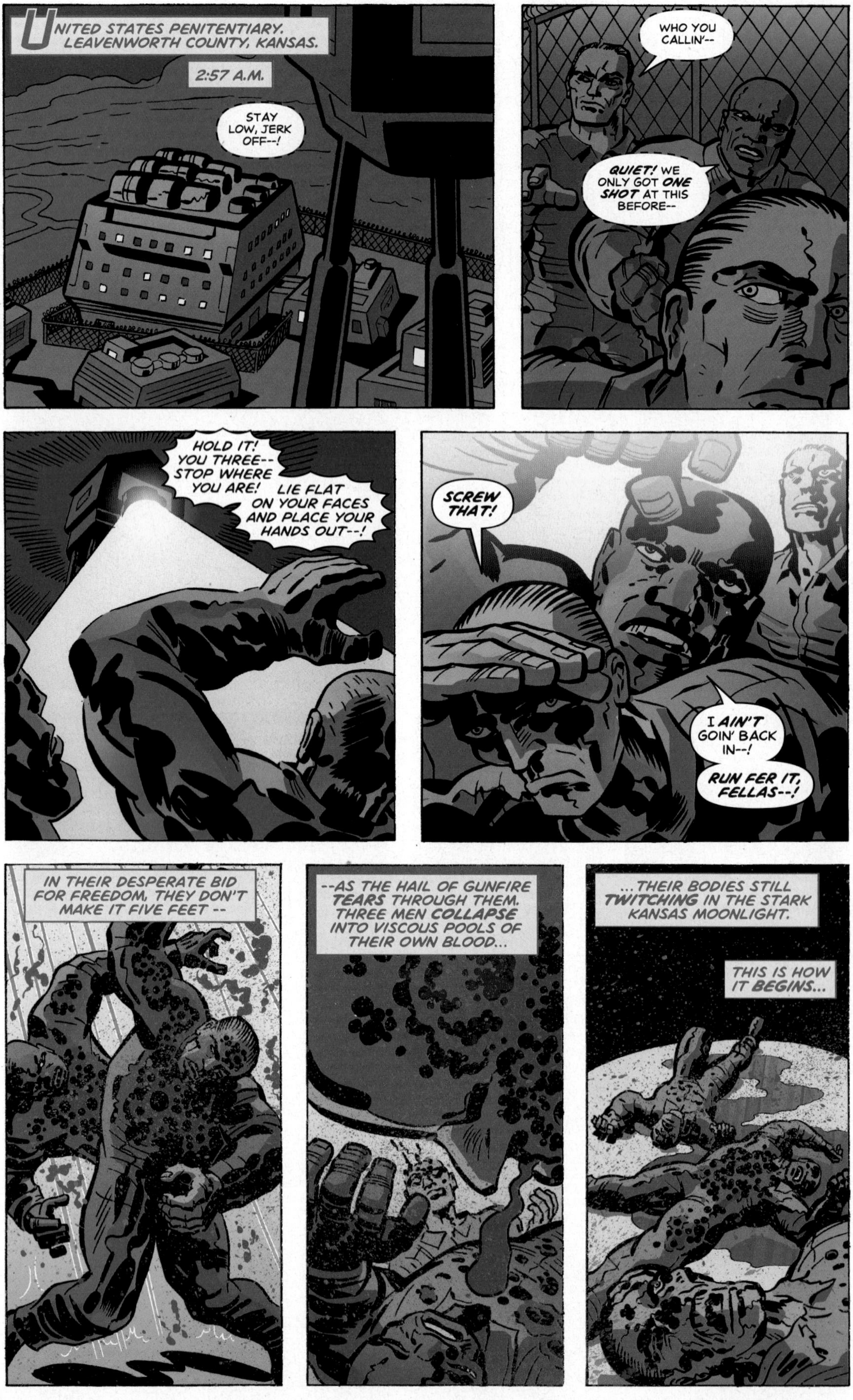

UNITED STATES PENITENTIARY. LEAVENWORTH COUNTY, KANSAS.
2:57 A.M.
STAY LOW, JERK OFF--!
WHO YOU CALLIN'--
QUIET! WE ONLY GOT ONE SHOT AT THIS BEFORE--
HOLD IT! YOU THREE-- STOP WHERE YOU ARE!
LIE FLAT ON YOUR FACES AND PLACE YOUR HANDS OUT--!
SCREW THAT!
I AIN'T GOIN' BACK IN--!
RUN FER IT, FELLAS--!
IN THEIR DESPERATE BID FOR FREEDOM, THEY DON'T MAKE IT FIVE FEET --
--AS THE HAIL OF GUNFIRE TEARS THROUGH THEM. THREE MEN COLLAPSE INTO VISCOUS POOLS OF THEIR OWN BLOOD...
...THEIR BODIES STILL TWITCHING IN THE STARK KANSAS MOONLIGHT.
THIS IS HOW IT BEGINS...

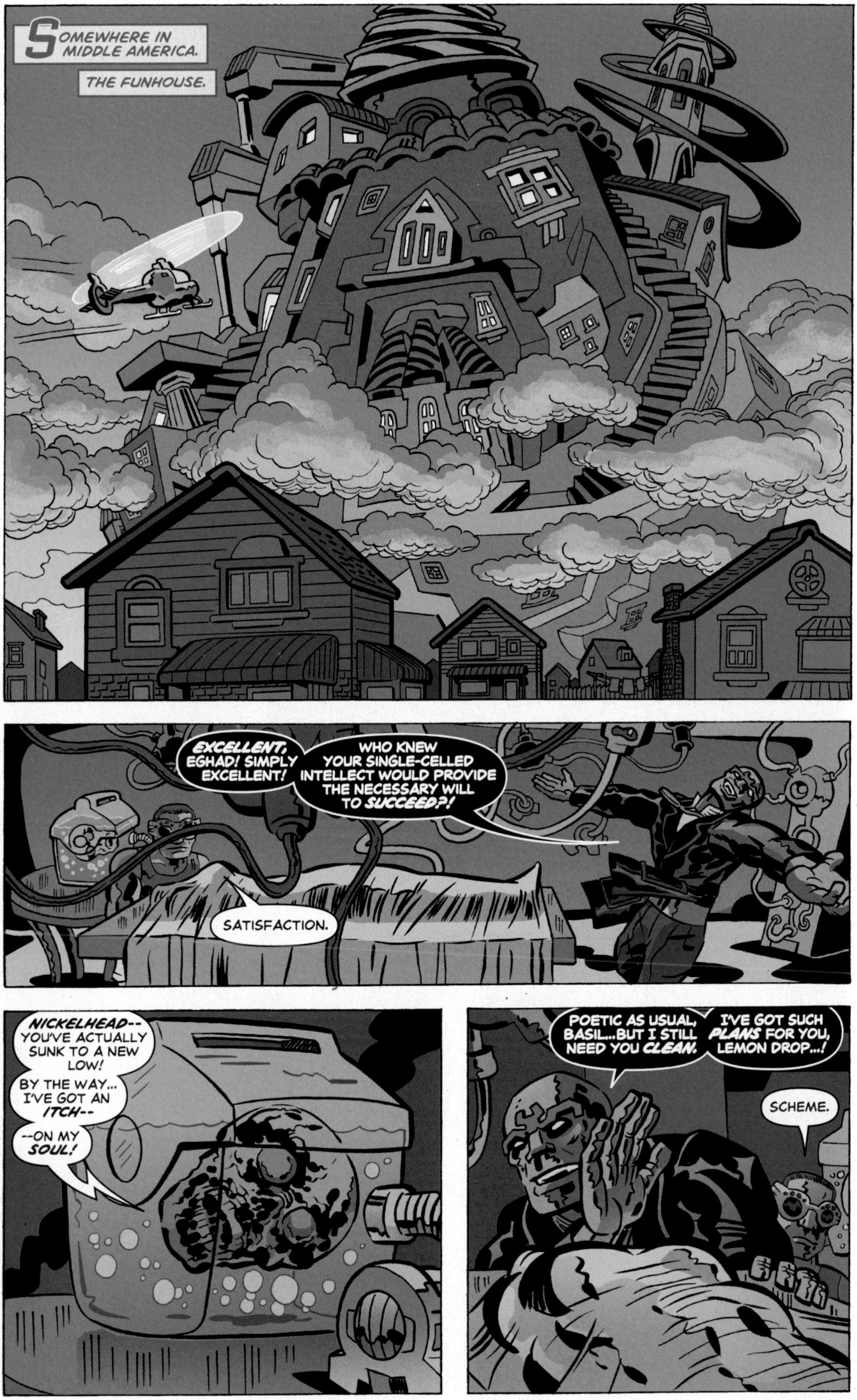
SOMEWHERE IN MIDDLE AMERICA.
THE FUNHOUSE.
EXCELLENT, EGHAD! SIMPLY EXCELLENT!
WHO KNEW YOUR SINGLE-CELLED INTELLECT WOULD PROVIDE THE NECESSARY WILL TO SUCCEED?!
SATISFACTION.
NICKELHEAD-- YOU'VE ACTUALLY SUNK TO A NEW LOW!
BY THE WAY... I'VE GOT AN ITCH--
--ON MY SOUL!
POETIC AS USUAL, BASIL...BUT I STILL NEED YOU CLEAN.
I'VE GOT SUCH PLANS FOR YOU, LEMON DROP...!
SCHEME.

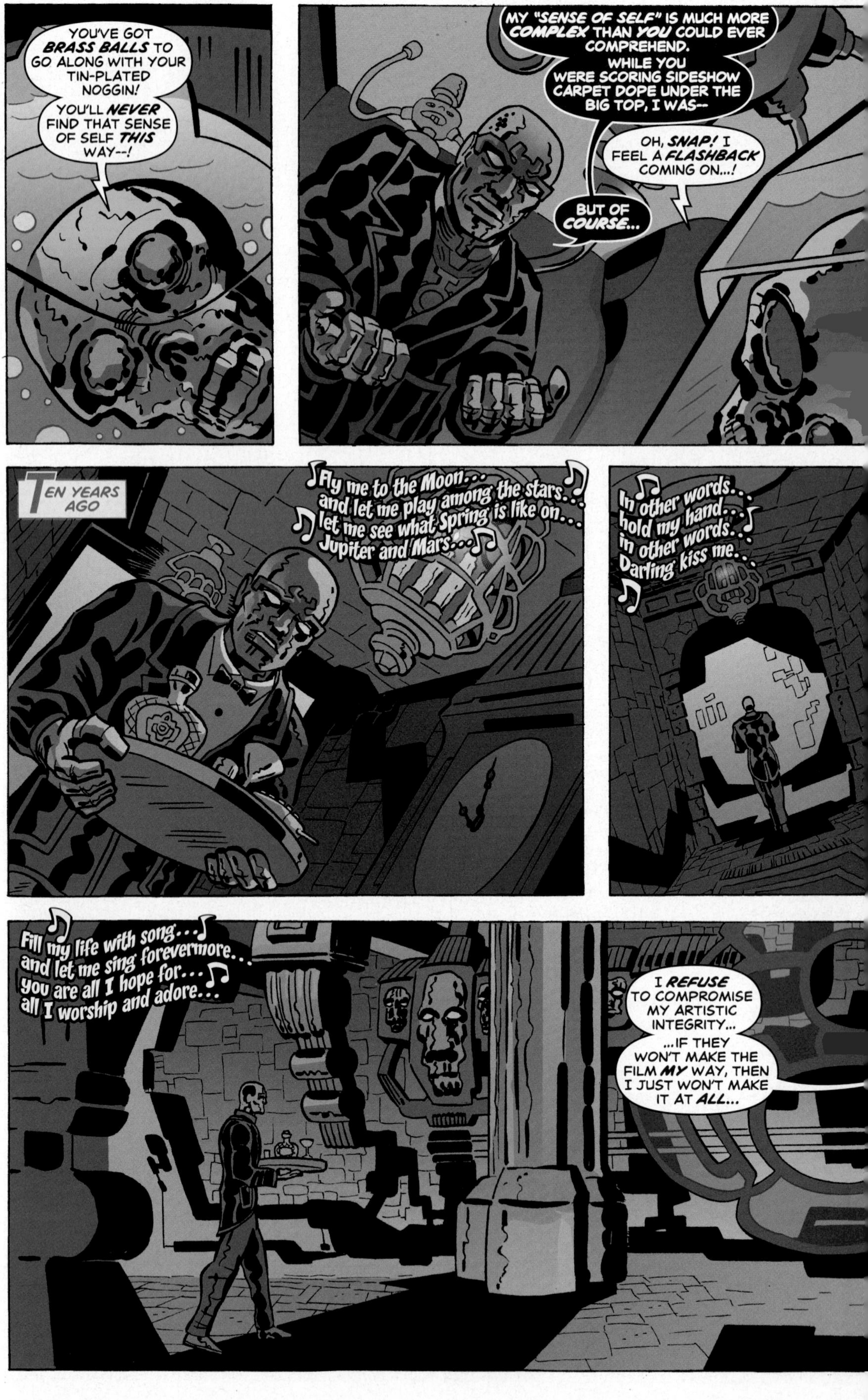

YOU'VE GOT BRASS BALLS TO GO ALONG WITH YOUR TIN-PLATED NOGGIN!
YOU'LL NEVER FIND THAT SENSE OF SELF THIS WAY--!
MY "SENSE OF SELF" IS MUCH MORE COMPLEX THAN YOU COULD EVER COMPREHEND.
WHILE YOU WERE SCORING SIDESHOW CARPET DOPE UNDER THE BIG TOP, I WAS--
OH, SNAP! I FEEL A FLASHBACK COMING ON...!
BUT OF COURSE...
TEN YEARS AGO
Fly me to the Moon... and let me play among the stars... let me see what Spring is like on... Jupiter and Mars...
In other words... hold my hand... in other words... Darling kiss me...
Fill my life with song... and let me sing forevermore... you are all I hope for... all I worship and adore...
I REFUSE TO COMPROMISE MY ARTISTIC INTEGRITY...
...IF THEY WON'T MAKE THE FILM MY WAY, THEN I JUST WON'T MAKE IT AT ALL...

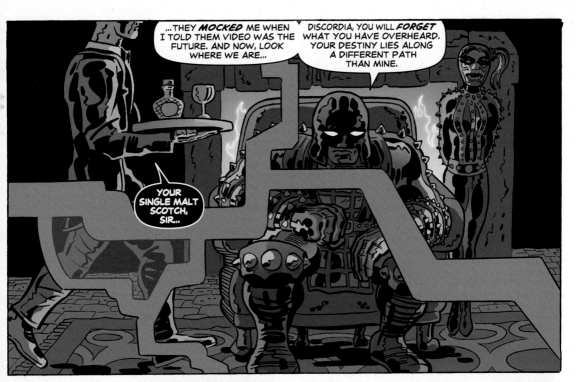

...THEY *MOCKED* ME WHEN I TOLD THEM VIDEO WAS THE FUTURE. AND NOW, LOOK WHERE WE ARE...

DISCORDIA, YOU WILL *FORGET* WHAT YOU HAVE OVERHEARD. YOUR DESTINY LIES ALONG A DIFFERENT PATH THAN MINE.

YOUR SINGLE MALT SCOTCH, SIR...

I FEAR I AM ONCE AGAIN FORCED TO ADMINISTER THE *CRUELEST* OF ALL TORTURES...

...LEGAL ACTION.

ONCE MORE UNTO THE BREACH OF PAIN FOR--

FRIEDRICH... IS THIS GLENFIDDICH OR GLENLIVET?

AHHH... GLENFIDDICH, SIR...

DISHWATER--!

I REFUSE TO ALLOW MY LIPS TO TOUCH GLENFIDDICH WHEN I AM STRUGGLING WITH THE EXTREMITIES OF MY CIRCUMSTANCES.

WAIT IN YOUR QUARTERS UNTIL I CALL YOU TO MAKE BREAKFAST!

BISCUITS AND GRAVY!

"BISCUITS AND GRAVY...HOW *ANY* HUMAN COULD EAT SO MUCH WHITE FLOUR...!

"SITTING IN THOSE STABLES EVERY NIGHT, I PLOTTED *REVOLUTION*... LIKE CAESAR IN CONQUEST. AND *REVENGE*..."

...AND NOW, I SHALL *HAVE* IT!

PUT ME DOWN! YOU'RE MAKING *WAVES* IN HERE--!

I THINK YOU'RE JUST PISSED BECAUSE HE EVENTUALLY *FIRED* YOU!

A FAILED *MANSERVANT*--!

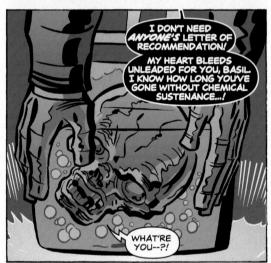

I DON'T NEED *ANYONE'S* LETTER OF RECOMMENDATION!

MY HEART BLEEDS UNLEADED FOR YOU, BASIL. I KNOW HOW LONG YOU'VE GONE WITHOUT CHEMICAL SUSTENANCE...!

WHAT'RE YOU--?!

ALL THIS TIME, I HAVE BEEN WAITING FOR THE PIECES OF THIS PUZZLE TO COALESCE. AND SO THEY HAVE. WITH MY NEW ACQUISITION--AND YOUR HELP--I WILL *STRIKE* AT THE TORMENTOR WHERE IT HURTS HIM THE *MOST*:

BRAINS.

BEAUTY.

BASTARD.

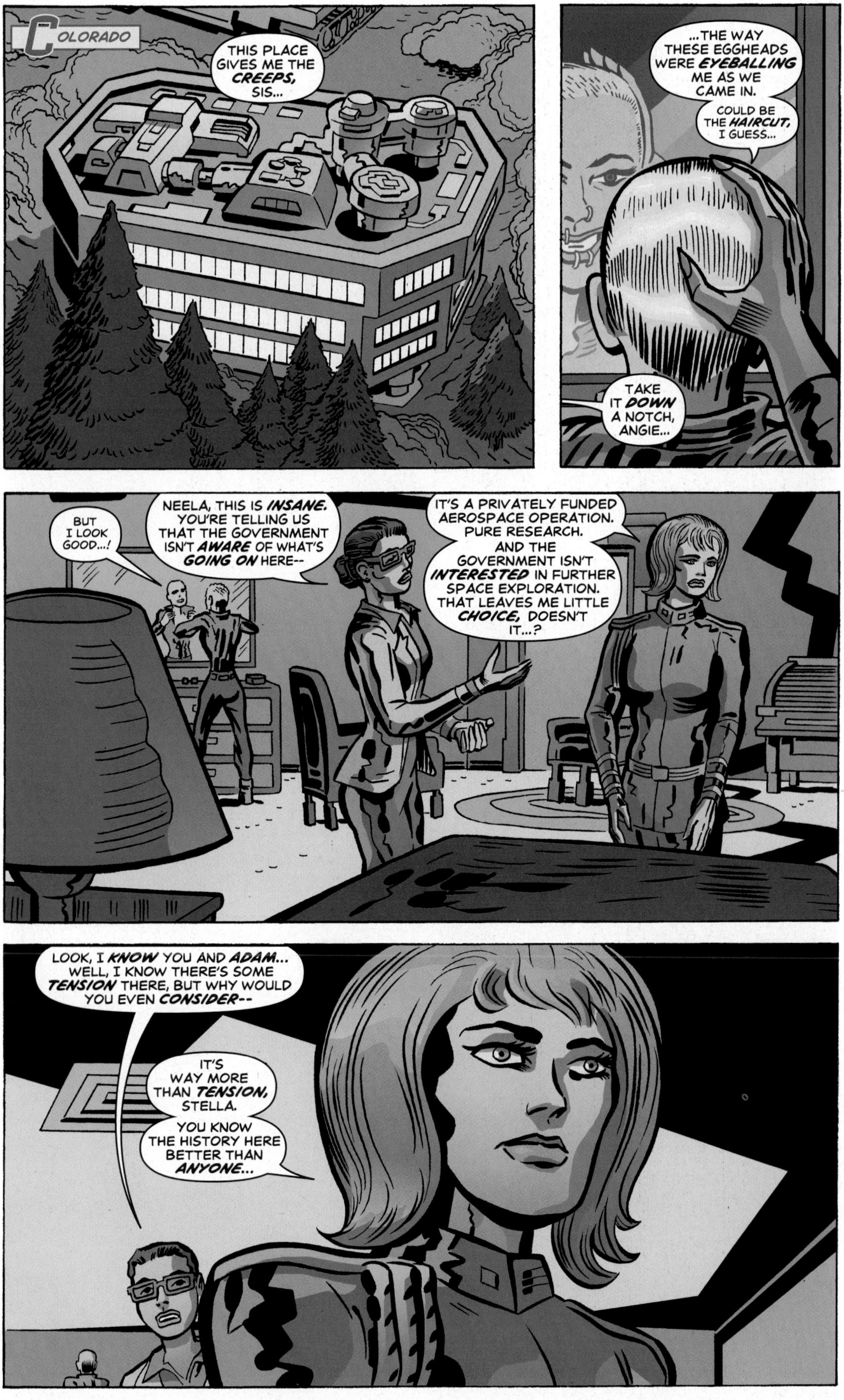
COLORADO
THIS PLACE GIVES ME THE CREEPS, SIS...
...THE WAY THESE EGGHEADS WERE EYEBALLING ME AS WE CAME IN.
COULD BE THE HAIRCUT, I GUESS...
TAKE IT DOWN A NOTCH, ANGIE...
BUT I LOOK GOOD...!
NEELA, THIS IS INSANE. YOU'RE TELLING US THAT THE GOVERNMENT ISN'T AWARE OF WHAT'S GOING ON HERE--
IT'S A PRIVATELY FUNDED AEROSPACE OPERATION. PURE RESEARCH.
AND THE GOVERNMENT ISN'T INTERESTED IN FURTHER SPACE EXPLORATION. THAT LEAVES ME LITTLE CHOICE, DOESN'T IT...?
LOOK, I KNOW YOU AND ADAM... WELL, I KNOW THERE'S SOME TENSION THERE, BUT WHY WOULD YOU EVEN CONSIDER--
IT'S WAY MORE THAN TENSION, STELLA.
YOU KNOW THE HISTORY HERE BETTER THAN ANYONE...

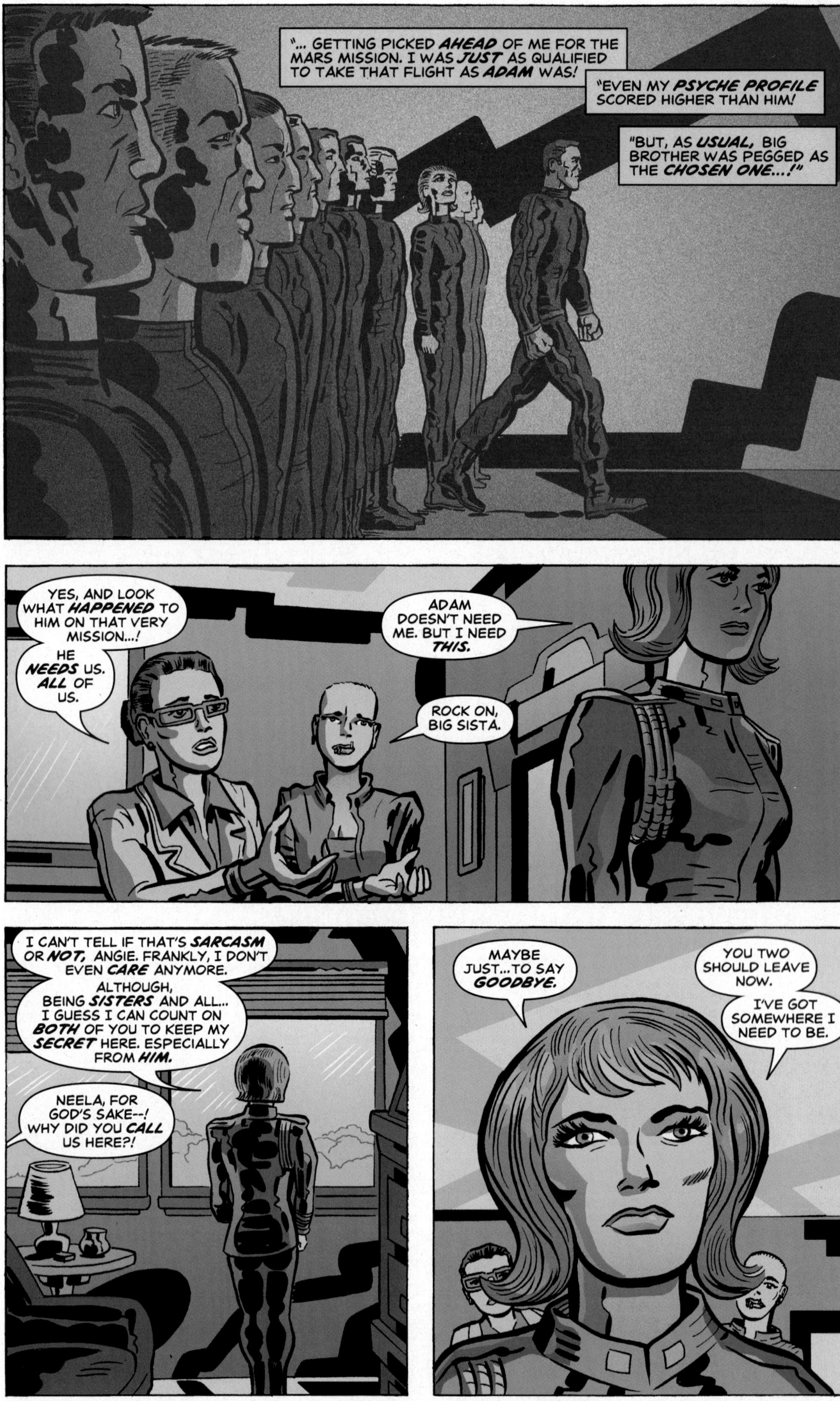
"... GETTING PICKED AHEAD OF ME FOR THE MARS MISSION. I WAS JUST AS QUALIFIED TO TAKE THAT FLIGHT AS ADAM WAS!
"EVEN MY PSYCHE PROFILE SCORED HIGHER THAN HIM!
"BUT, AS USUAL, BIG BROTHER WAS PEGGED AS THE CHOSEN ONE...!"
YES, AND LOOK WHAT HAPPENED TO HIM ON THAT VERY MISSION...!
HE NEEDS US. ALL OF US.
ADAM DOESN'T NEED ME. BUT I NEED THIS.
ROCK ON, BIG SISTA.
I CAN'T TELL IF THAT'S SARCASM OR NOT, ANGIE. FRANKLY, I DON'T EVEN CARE ANYMORE.
ALTHOUGH, BEING SISTERS AND ALL... I GUESS I CAN COUNT ON BOTH OF YOU TO KEEP MY SECRET HERE. ESPECIALLY FROM HIM.
NEELA, FOR GOD'S SAKE--! WHY DID YOU CALL US HERE?!
MAYBE JUST...TO SAY GOODBYE.
YOU TWO SHOULD LEAVE NOW.
I'VE GOT SOMEWHERE I NEED TO BE.

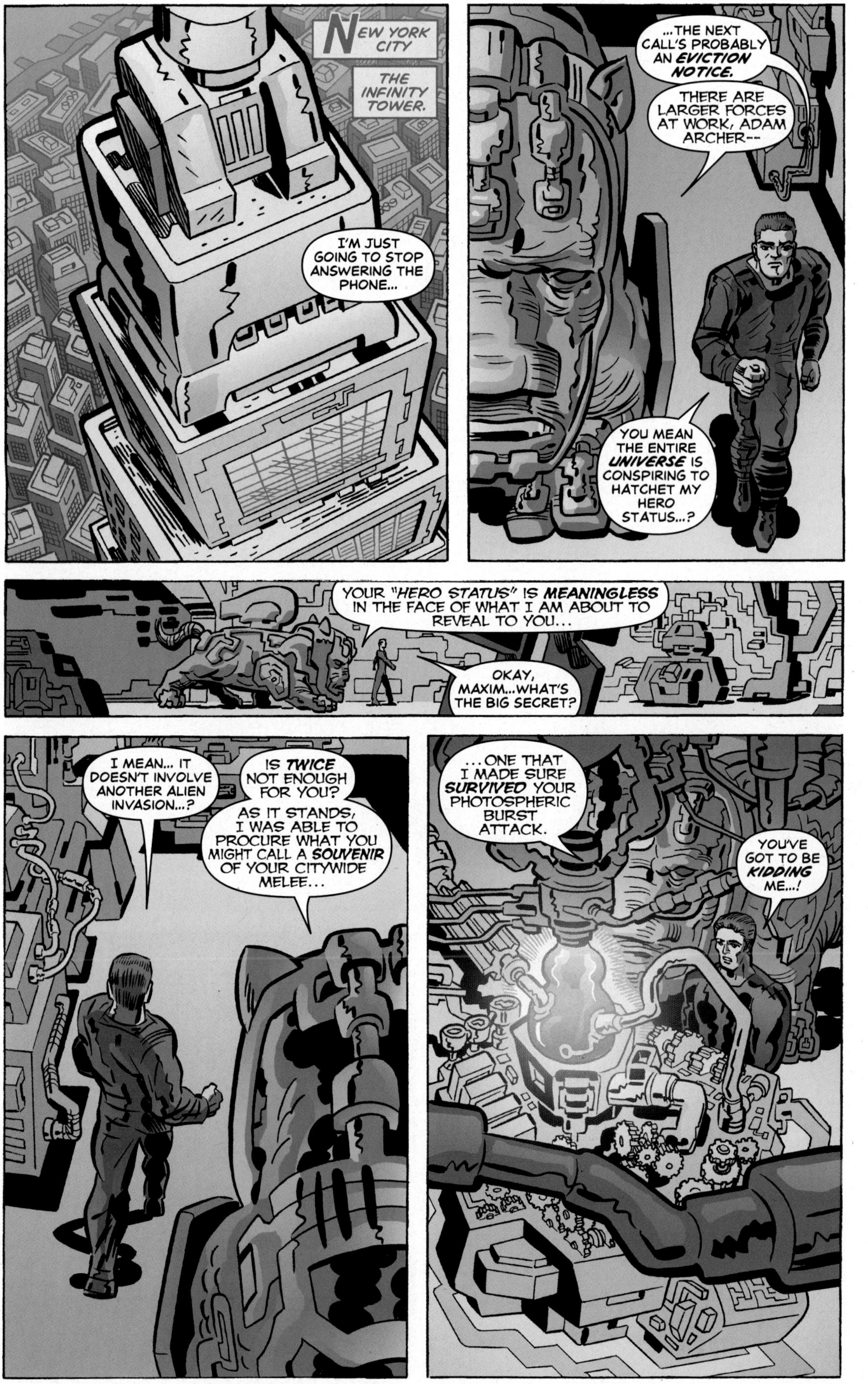
NEW YORK CITY
THE INFINITY TOWER.
I'M JUST GOING TO STOP ANSWERING THE PHONE...
...THE NEXT CALL'S PROBABLY AN EVICTION NOTICE.
THERE ARE LARGER FORCES AT WORK, ADAM ARCHER--
YOU MEAN THE ENTIRE UNIVERSE IS CONSPIRING TO HATCHET MY HERO STATUS...?
YOUR "HERO STATUS" IS MEANINGLESS IN THE FACE OF WHAT I AM ABOUT TO REVEAL TO YOU...
OKAY, MAXIM...WHAT'S THE BIG SECRET?
I MEAN... IT DOESN'T INVOLVE ANOTHER ALIEN INVASION...?
IS TWICE NOT ENOUGH FOR YOU?
AS IT STANDS, I WAS ABLE TO PROCURE WHAT YOU MIGHT CALL A SOUVENIR OF YOUR CITYWIDE MELEE...
...ONE THAT I MADE SURE SURVIVED YOUR PHOTOSPHERIC BURST ATTACK.
YOU'VE GOT TO BE KIDDING ME...!

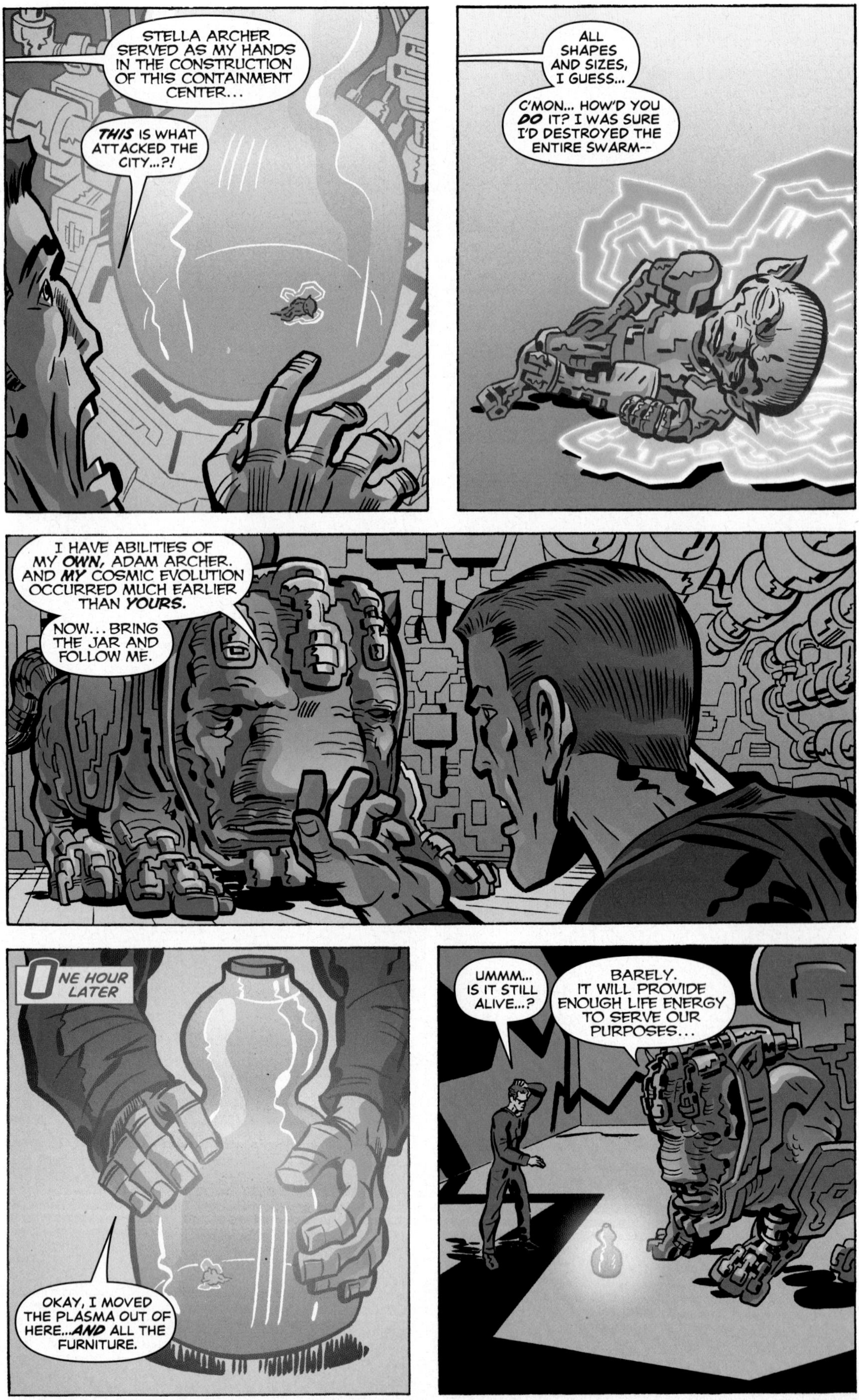
STELLA ARCHER SERVED AS MY HANDS IN THE CONSTRUCTION OF THIS CONTAINMENT CENTER...
THIS IS WHAT ATTACKED THE CITY...?!
ALL SHAPES AND SIZES, I GUESS...
C'MON... HOW'D YOU *DO* IT? I WAS SURE I'D DESTROYED THE ENTIRE SWARM--
I HAVE ABILITIES OF MY *OWN,* ADAM ARCHER. AND *MY* COSMIC EVOLUTION OCCURRED MUCH EARLIER THAN *YOURS.*
NOW... BRING THE JAR AND FOLLOW ME.
ONE HOUR LATER
OKAY, I MOVED THE PLASMA OUT OF HERE...*AND* ALL THE FURNITURE.
UMMM... IS IT STILL ALIVE...?
BARELY. IT WILL PROVIDE ENOUGH LIFE ENERGY TO SERVE OUR PURPOSES...

...NOW, YOU SIT *THERE.* A SPECIFIC CONFIGURATION IS NECESSARY--

YOU'RE... WELL, YOU'RE *SCARING* ME A LITTLE, MAXIM...

NONSENSE. THE THREE-SIDED GEOMEX IS STANDARD FOR VISIONARY SÉANCE.

THIS FRAGILE, WEAKENED THING-- SENT IN AS PART OF THE SWARM TO *KILL* YOU--*COMPLETES* THE TRIANGLE.

FIRST... RELAX YOUR *SPIRIT,* ADAM ARCHER. QUIET YOUR INNER VOICE.

WE ARE ALL STAR STUFF CONSTRUCTS...

...ALL OF US *PIECES* OF A GREATER WHOLE. WE'VE SIMPLY *FORGOTTEN* THE TRUTHS THAT RESIDE *WITHIN* US.

WITHIN THIS SIMPLE *RITUAL,* WE SHALL EXPERIENCE SHARED REMEMBRANCE. AHHH, YES. THERE IT IS. IT *BEGINS...*

EACH OF US... MERELY A *CONDUIT...*

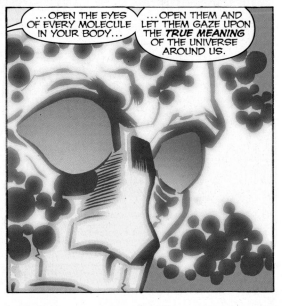

...OPEN THE EYES OF EVERY MOLECULE IN YOUR BODY...

...OPEN THEM AND LET THEM GAZE UPON THE *TRUE MEANING* OF THE UNIVERSE AROUND US.

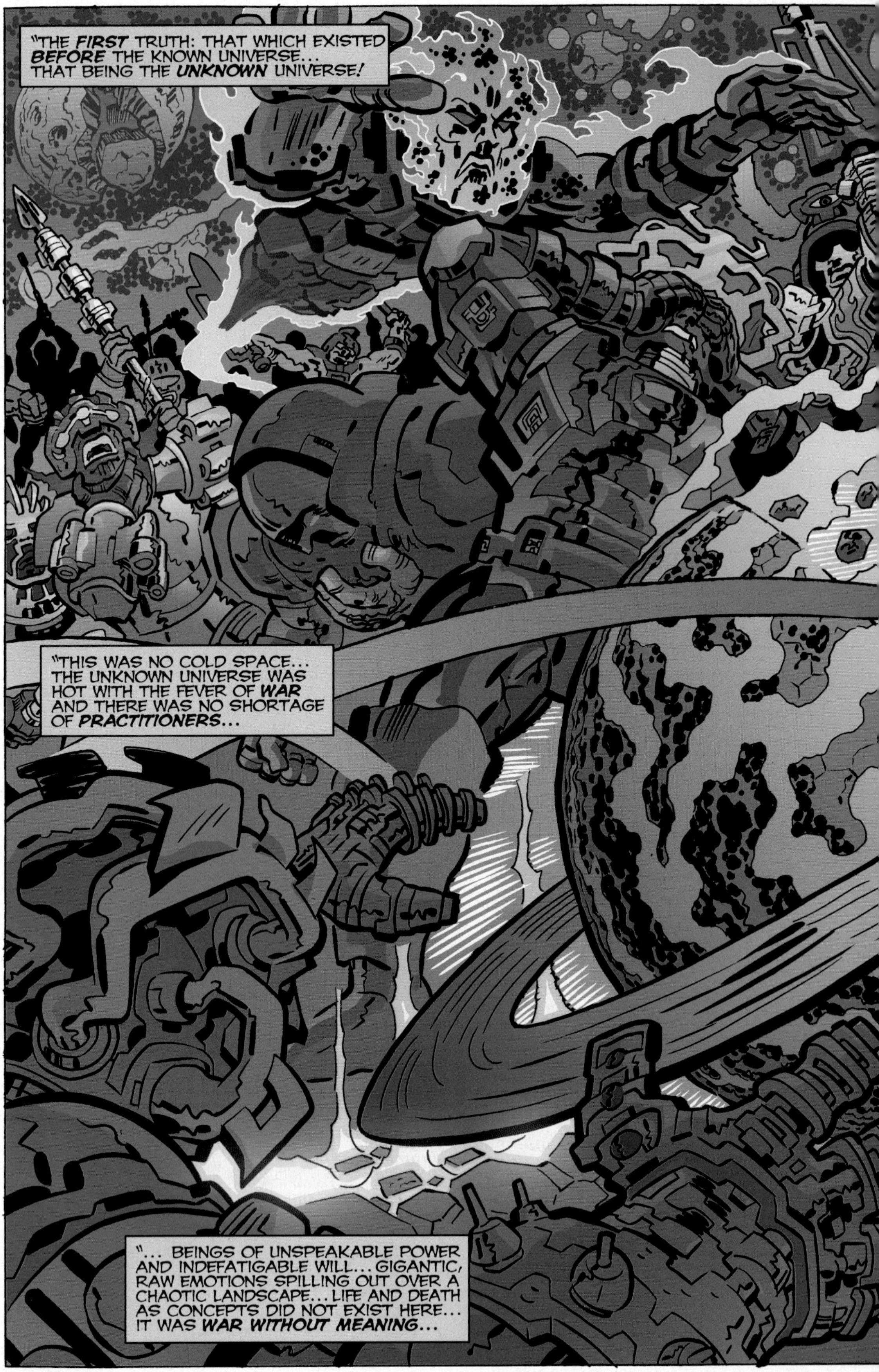
"THE FIRST TRUTH: THAT WHICH EXISTED BEFORE THE KNOWN UNIVERSE... THAT BEING THE UNKNOWN UNIVERSE!
"THIS WAS NO COLD SPACE... THE UNKNOWN UNIVERSE WAS HOT WITH THE FEVER OF WAR AND THERE WAS NO SHORTAGE OF PRACTITIONERS...
"... BEINGS OF UNSPEAKABLE POWER AND INDEFATIGABLE WILL... GIGANTIC, RAW EMOTIONS SPILLING OUT OVER A CHAOTIC LANDSCAPE... LIFE AND DEATH AS CONCEPTS DID NOT EXIST HERE... IT WAS WAR WITHOUT MEANING...

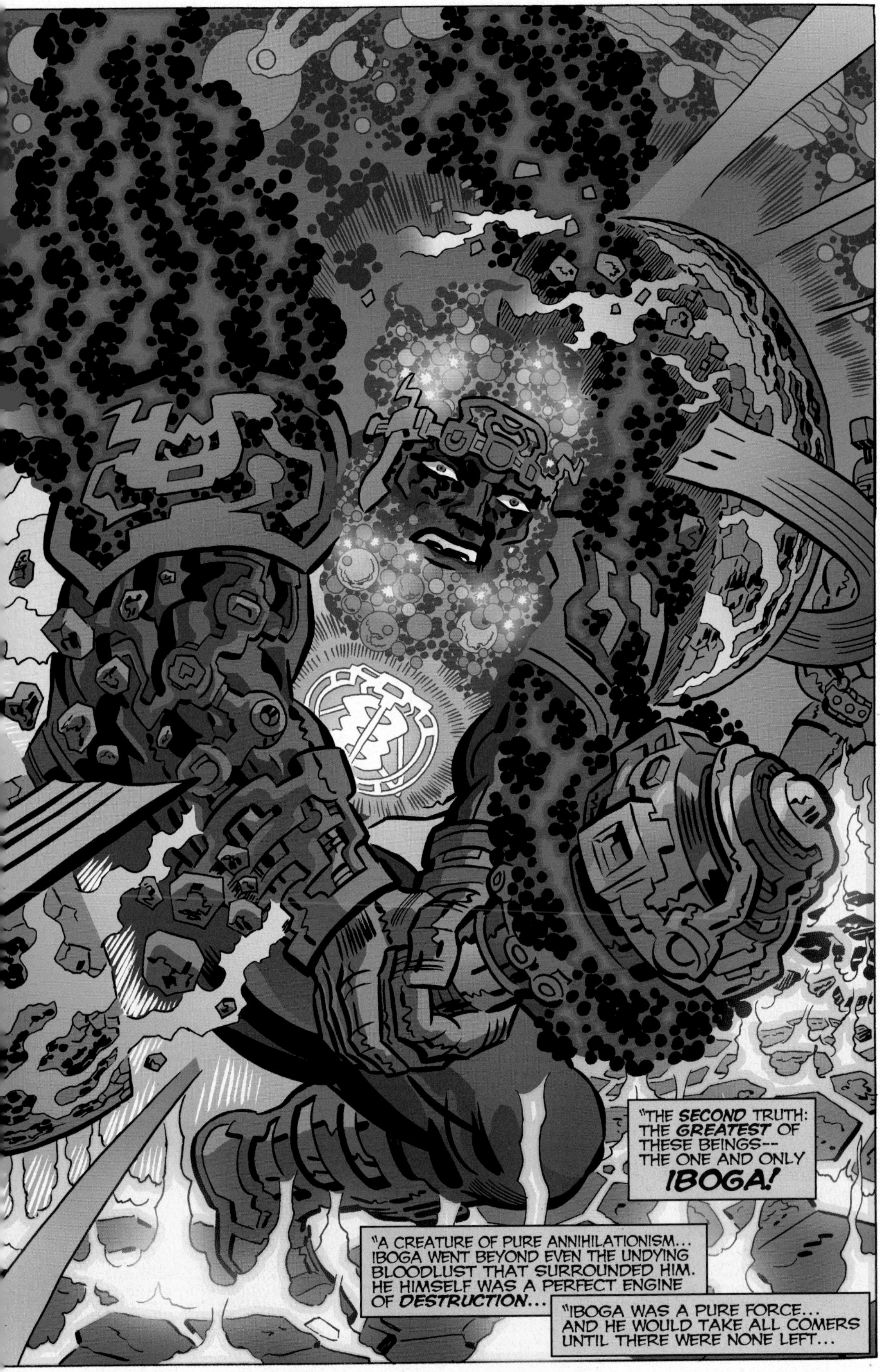
"THE SECOND TRUTH: THE GREATEST OF THESE BEINGS-- THE ONE AND ONLY IBOGA!
"A CREATURE OF PURE ANNIHILATIONISM... IBOGA WENT BEYOND EVEN THE UNDYING BLOODLUST THAT SURROUNDED HIM. HE HIMSELF WAS A PERFECT ENGINE OF DESTRUCTION...
"IBOGA WAS A PURE FORCE... AND HE WOULD TAKE ALL COMERS UNTIL THERE WERE NONE LEFT...

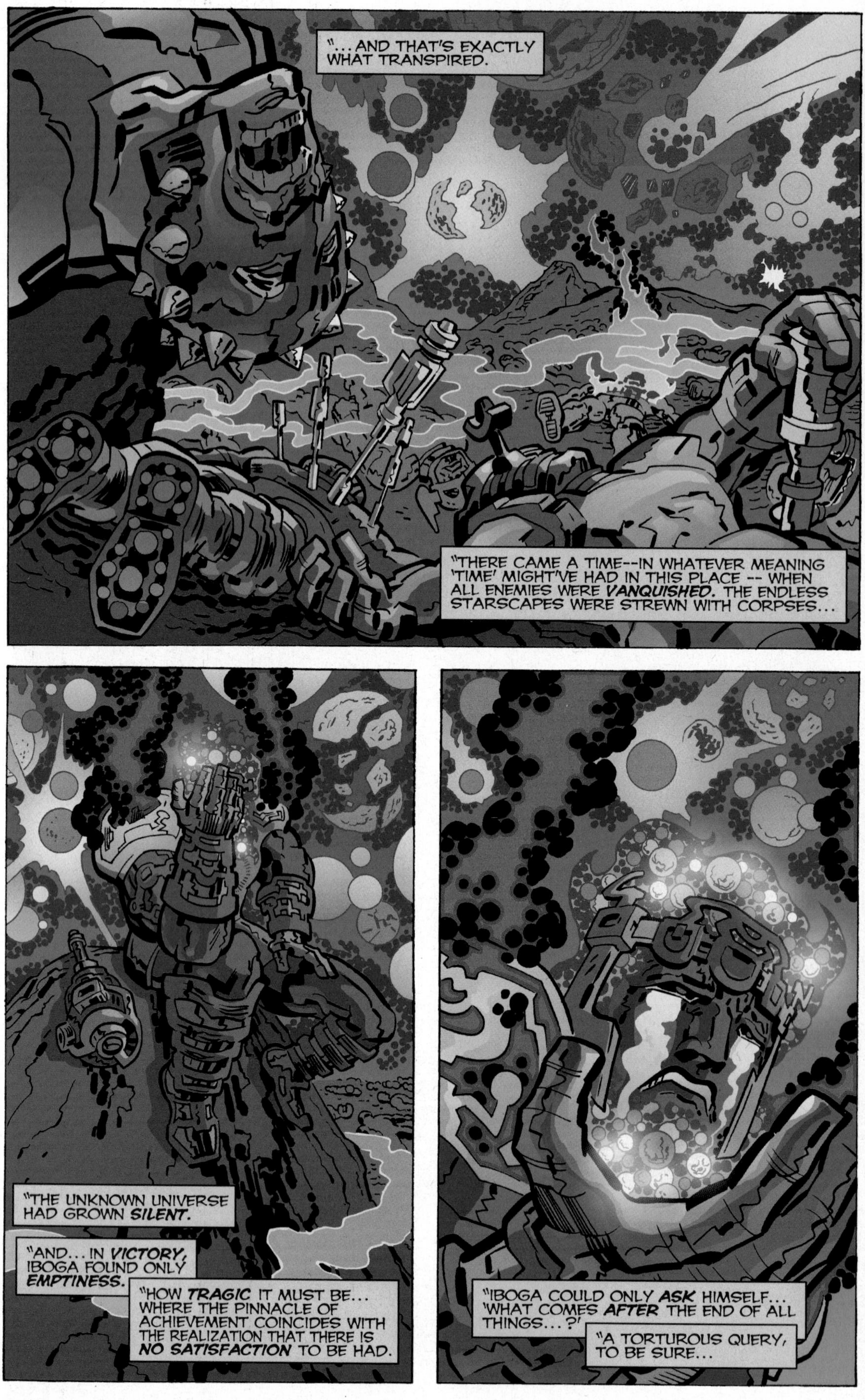
"...AND THAT'S EXACTLY WHAT TRANSPIRED.
"THERE CAME A TIME--IN WHATEVER MEANING 'TIME' MIGHT'VE HAD IN THIS PLACE -- WHEN ALL ENEMIES WERE VANQUISHED. THE ENDLESS STARSCAPES WERE STREWN WITH CORPSES...
"THE UNKNOWN UNIVERSE HAD GROWN SILENT.
"AND... IN VICTORY, IBOGA FOUND ONLY EMPTINESS.
"HOW TRAGIC IT MUST BE... WHERE THE PINNACLE OF ACHIEVEMENT COINCIDES WITH THE REALIZATION THAT THERE IS NO SATISFACTION TO BE HAD.
"IBOGA COULD ONLY ASK HIMSELF... 'WHAT COMES AFTER THE END OF ALL THINGS...?'
"A TORTUROUS QUERY, TO BE SURE...

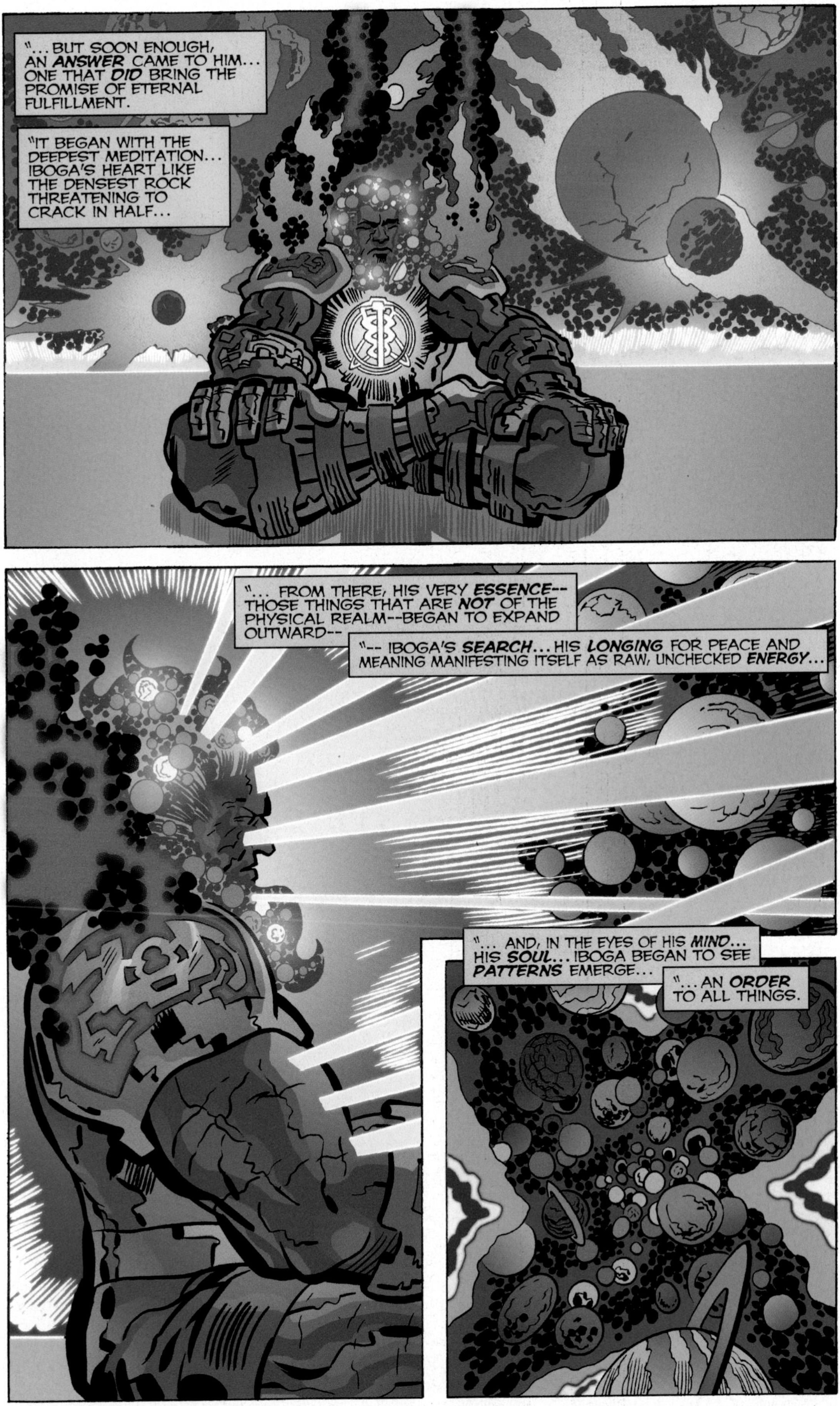
"... BUT SOON ENOUGH, AN ANSWER CAME TO HIM... ONE THAT DID BRING THE PROMISE OF ETERNAL FULFILLMENT.
"IT BEGAN WITH THE DEEPEST MEDITATION... IBOGA'S HEART LIKE THE DENSEST ROCK THREATENING TO CRACK IN HALF...
"... FROM THERE, HIS VERY ESSENCE-- THOSE THINGS THAT ARE NOT OF THE PHYSICAL REALM--BEGAN TO EXPAND OUTWARD--
"-- IBOGA'S SEARCH... HIS LONGING FOR PEACE AND MEANING MANIFESTING ITSELF AS RAW, UNCHECKED ENERGY...
"... AND, IN THE EYES OF HIS MIND... HIS SOUL... IBOGA BEGAN TO SEE PATTERNS EMERGE...
"... AN ORDER TO ALL THINGS.

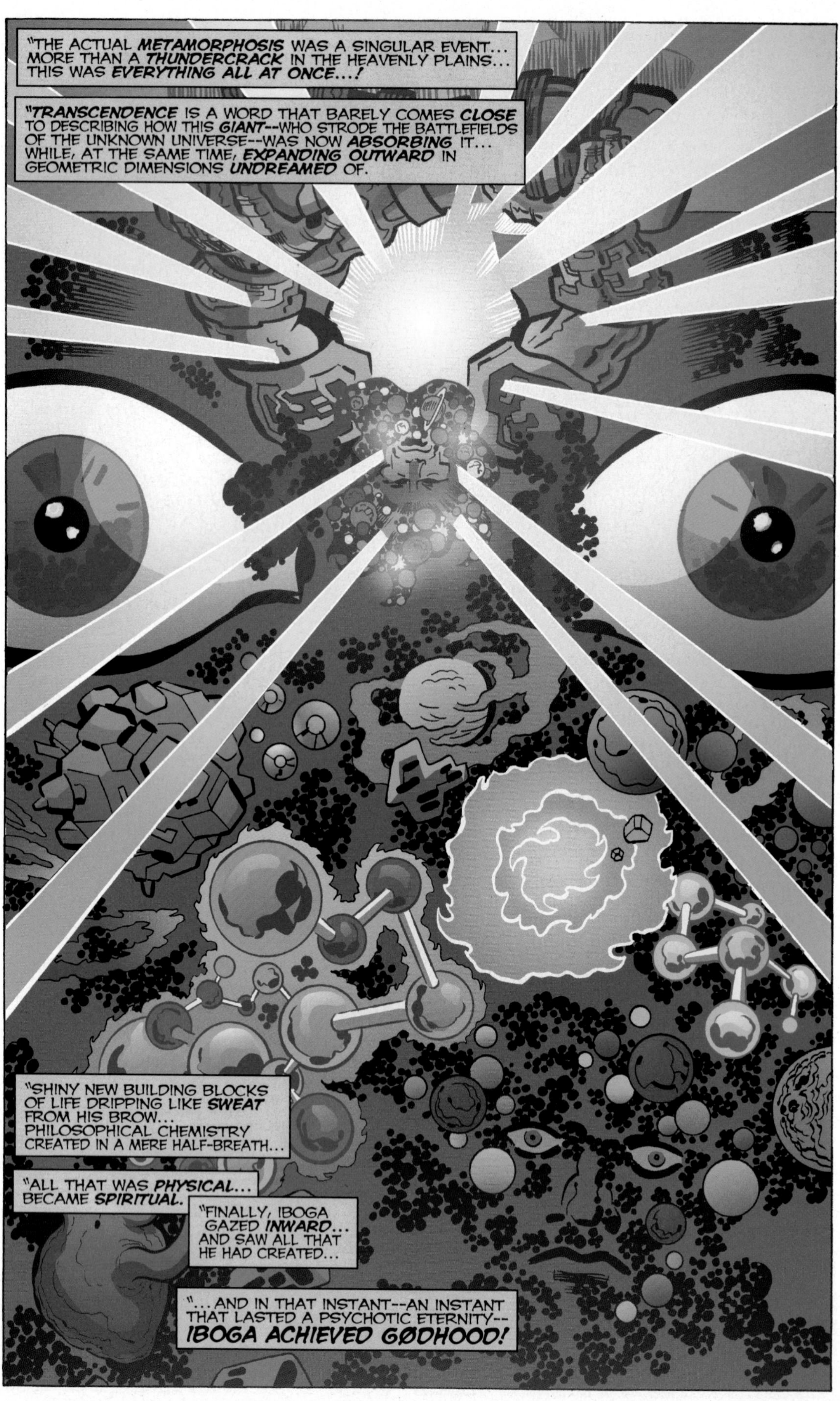
"THE ACTUAL METAMORPHOSIS WAS A SINGULAR EVENT... MORE THAN A THUNDERCRACK IN THE HEAVENLY PLAINS... THIS WAS EVERYTHING ALL AT ONCE...!
"TRANSCENDENCE IS A WORD THAT BARELY COMES CLOSE TO DESCRIBING HOW THIS GIANT--WHO STRODE THE BATTLEFIELDS OF THE UNKNOWN UNIVERSE--WAS NOW ABSORBING IT... WHILE, AT THE SAME TIME, EXPANDING OUTWARD IN GEOMETRIC DIMENSIONS UNDREAMED OF.
"SHINY NEW BUILDING BLOCKS OF LIFE DRIPPING LIKE SWEAT FROM HIS BROW... PHILOSOPHICAL CHEMISTRY CREATED IN A MERE HALF-BREATH...
"ALL THAT WAS PHYSICAL... BECAME SPIRITUAL.
"FINALLY, IBOGA GAZED INWARD... AND SAW ALL THAT HE HAD CREATED...
"...AND IN THAT INSTANT--AN INSTANT THAT LASTED A PSYCHOTIC ETERNITY--
IBOGA ACHIEVED GØDHOOD!

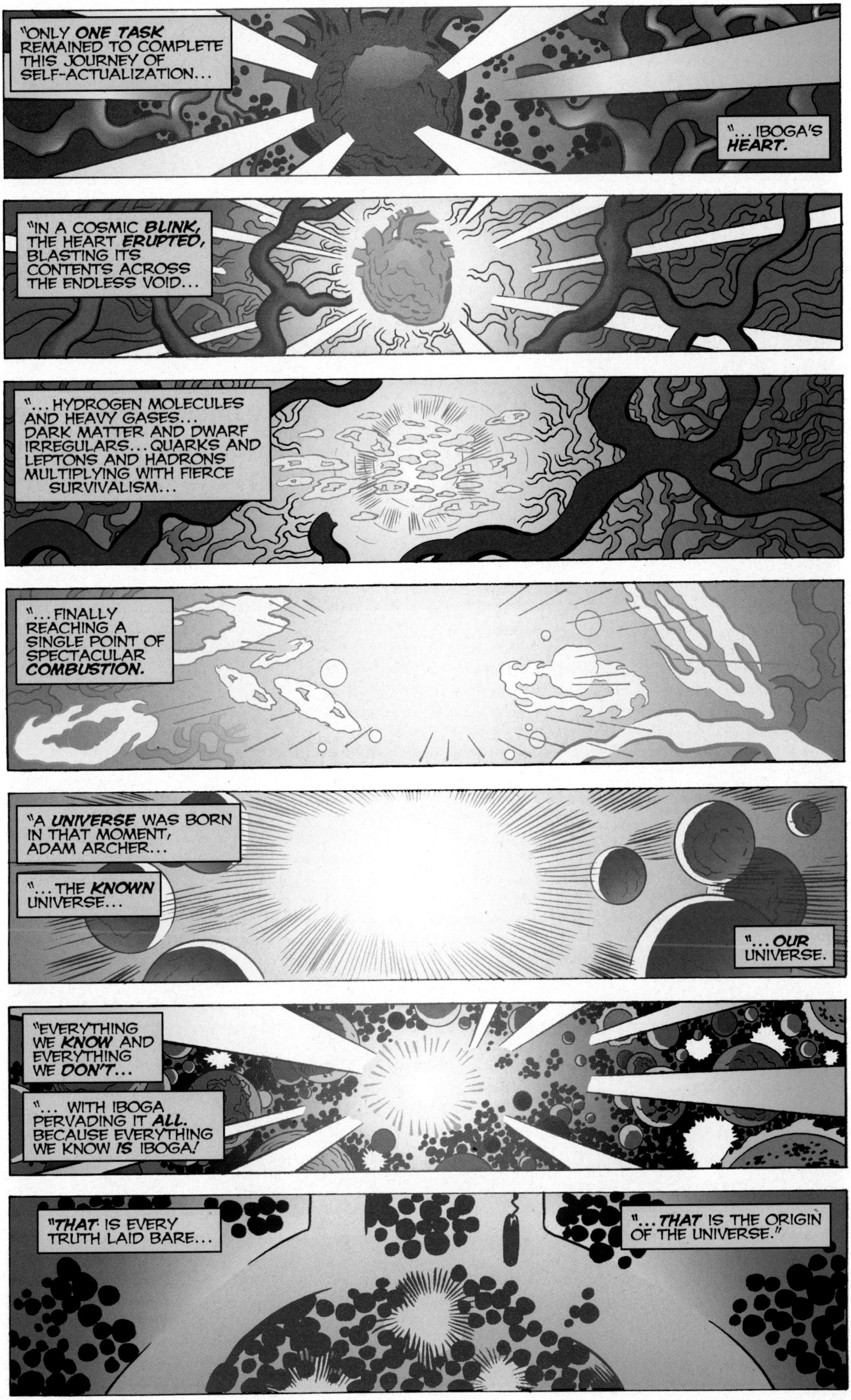
"ONLY ONE TASK REMAINED TO COMPLETE THIS JOURNEY OF SELF-ACTUALIZATION...
"...IBOGA'S HEART.
"IN A COSMIC BLINK, THE HEART ERUPTED, BLASTING ITS CONTENTS ACROSS THE ENDLESS VOID...
"...HYDROGEN MOLECULES AND HEAVY GASES... DARK MATTER AND DWARF IRREGULARS... QUARKS AND LEPTONS AND HADRONS MULTIPLYING WITH FIERCE SURVIVALISM...
"...FINALLY REACHING A SINGLE POINT OF SPECTACULAR COMBUSTION.
"A UNIVERSE WAS BORN IN THAT MOMENT, ADAM ARCHER...
"...THE KNOWN UNIVERSE...
"...OUR UNIVERSE.
"EVERYTHING WE KNOW AND EVERYTHING WE DON'T...
"... WITH IBOGA PERVADING IT ALL. BECAUSE EVERYTHING WE KNOW IS IBOGA!
"THAT IS EVERY TRUTH LAID BARE...
"...THAT IS THE ORIGIN OF THE UNIVERSE."

OH... JEEZUS...

FOR THOSE OF US *COSMICALLY ATTUNED,* IBOGA EVENTUALLY MAKES HIS EXISTENCE-- HIS *PRESENCE* IN OUR LIVES-- *KNOWN* TO US...

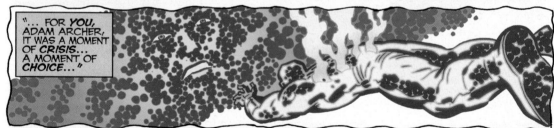

"... FOR *YOU,* ADAM ARCHER, IT WAS A MOMENT OF *CRISIS...* A MOMENT OF *CHOICE...*"

EVERYTHING... ALL AROUND US...

I-I... CAN'T...

LET IT *OUT,* ADAM ARCHER...

IN *TIME,* YOU WILL BE AT *PEACE* WITH WHAT YOU HAVE LEARNED TODAY...

T-TOO BIG...M-MUCH TOO...

≶SOB!≷

FOR *NOW,* THIS REACTION IS *NORMAL...*

THIS REACTION...

... IS *HUMAN.*

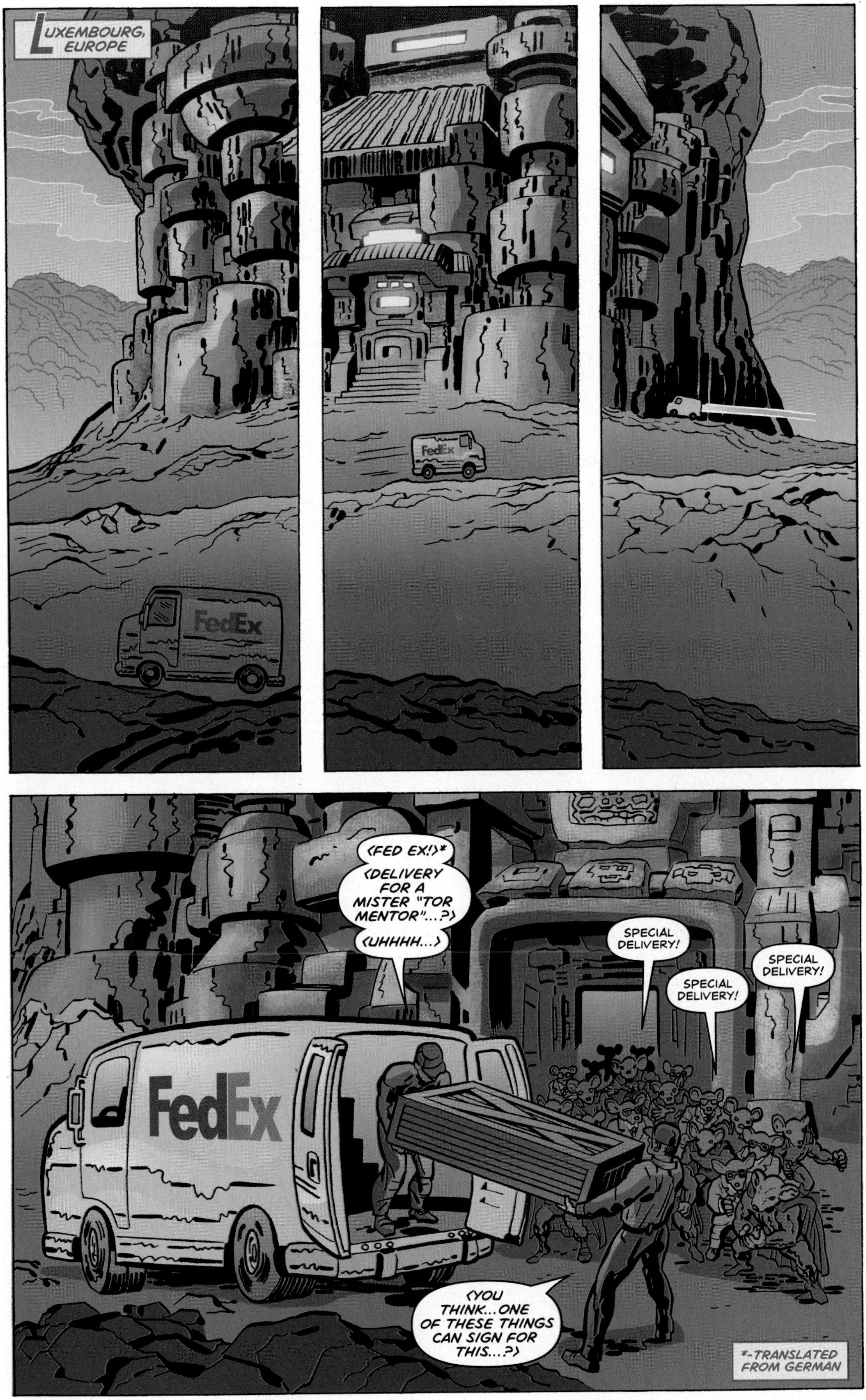
LUXEMBOURG, EUROPE
FedEx
FedEx
<FED EX!>*
<DELIVERY FOR A MISTER "TOR MENTOR"...?>
<UHHHH...>
SPECIAL DELIVERY!
SPECIAL DELIVERY!
SPECIAL DELIVERY!
FedEx
<YOU THINK...ONE OF THESE THINGS CAN SIGN FOR THIS...?>
*-TRANSLATED FROM GERMAN

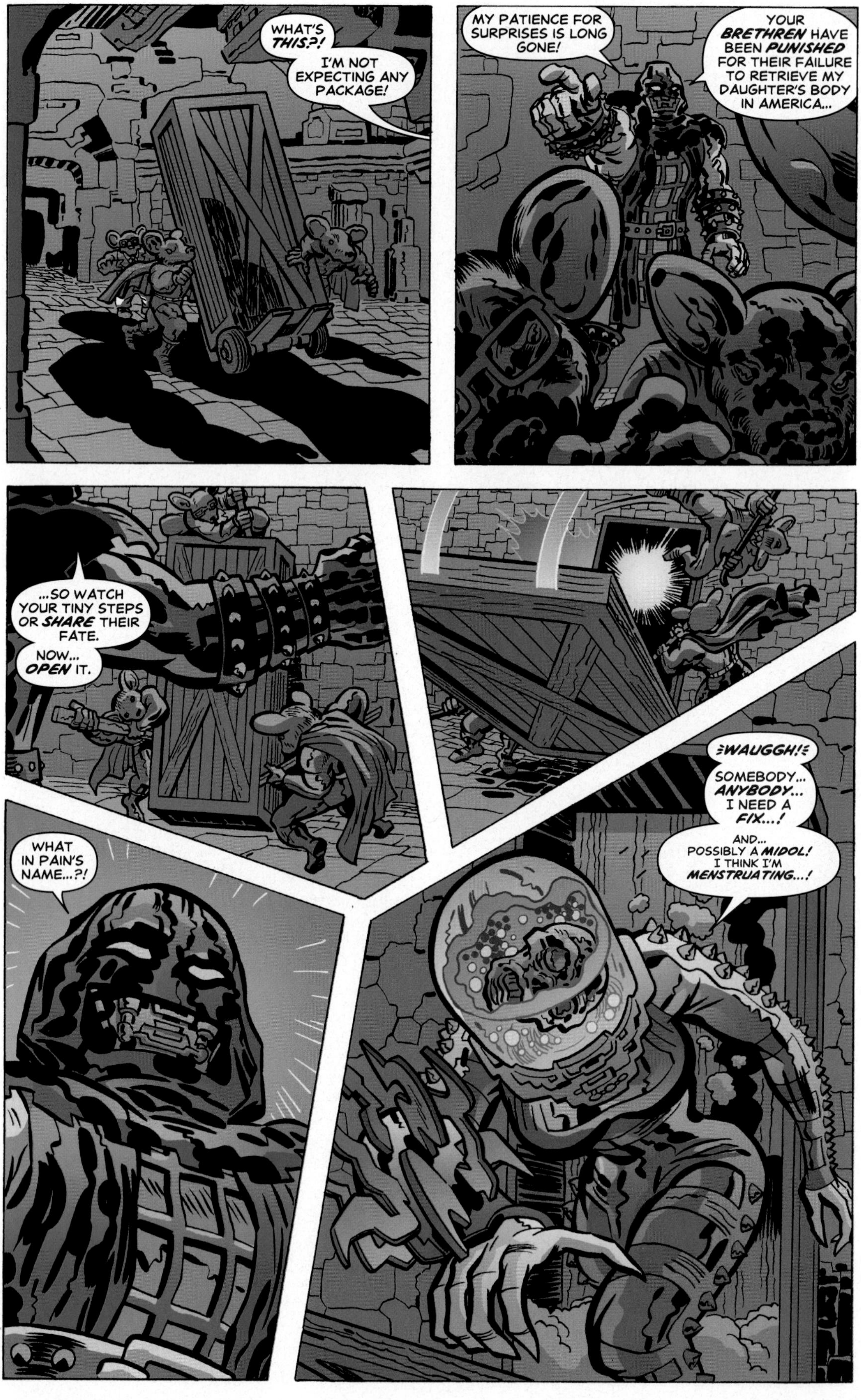

WHAT'S THIS?!
I'M NOT EXPECTING ANY PACKAGE!
MY PATIENCE FOR SURPRISES IS LONG GONE!
YOUR BRETHREN HAVE BEEN PUNISHED FOR THEIR FAILURE TO RETRIEVE MY DAUGHTER'S BODY IN AMERICA...
...SO WATCH YOUR TINY STEPS OR SHARE THEIR FATE.
NOW... OPEN IT.
WHAT IN PAIN'S NAME...?!
WAUGGH!
SOMEBODY... ANYBODY... I NEED A FIX...!
AND... POSSIBLY A MIDOL! I THINK I'M MENSTRUATING...!

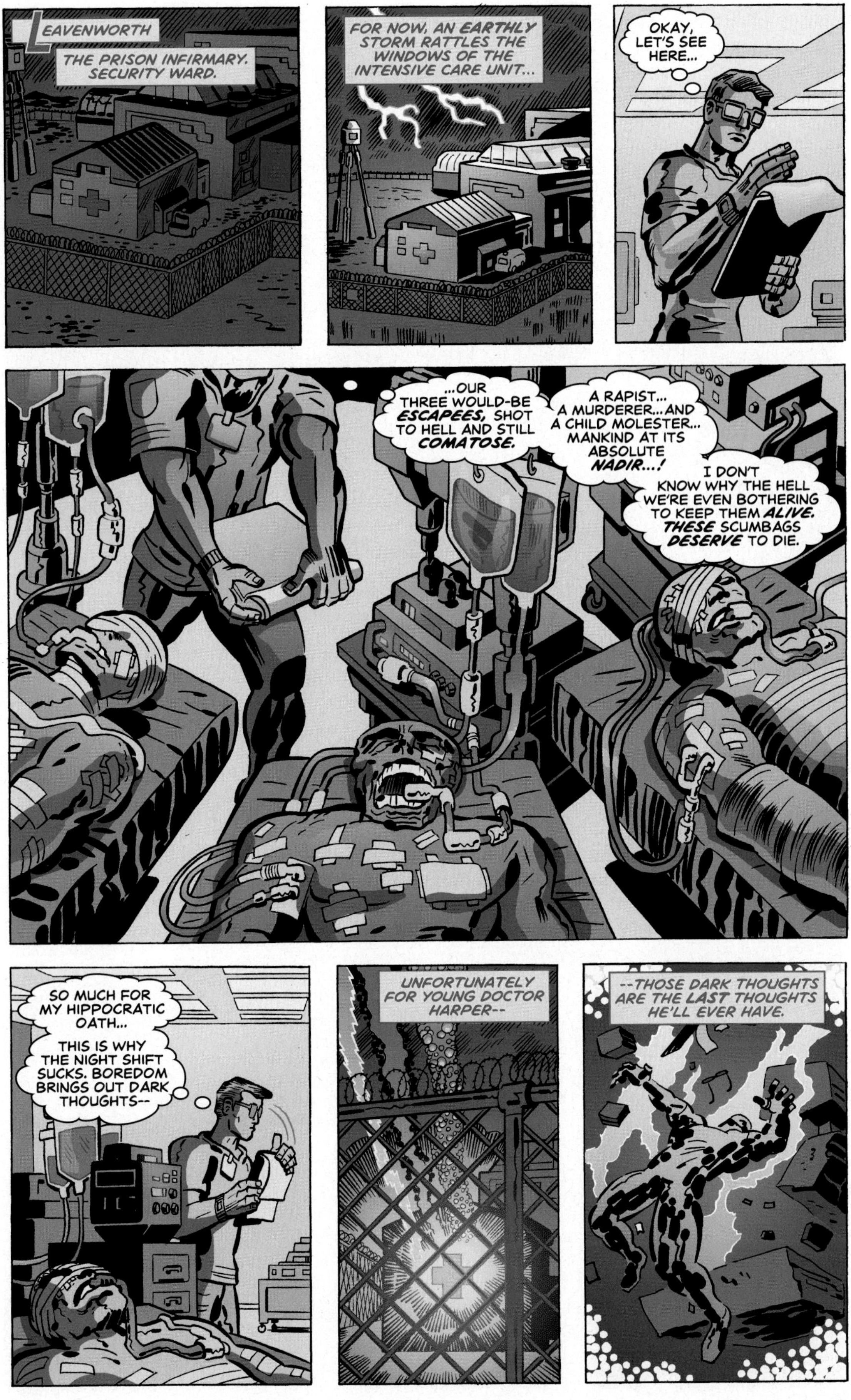
LEAVENWORTH
THE PRISON INFIRMARY. SECURITY WARD.
FOR NOW, AN EARTHLY STORM RATTLES THE WINDOWS OF THE INTENSIVE CARE UNIT...
OKAY, LET'S SEE HERE...
...OUR THREE WOULD-BE ESCAPEES, SHOT TO HELL AND STILL COMATOSE.
A RAPIST... A MURDERER...AND A CHILD MOLESTER... MANKIND AT ITS ABSOLUTE NADIR...!
I DON'T KNOW WHY THE HELL WE'RE EVEN BOTHERING TO KEEP THEM ALIVE. THESE SCUMBAGS DESERVE TO DIE.
SO MUCH FOR MY HIPPOCRATIC OATH...
THIS IS WHY THE NIGHT SHIFT SUCKS. BOREDOM BRINGS OUT DARK THOUGHTS--
UNFORTUNATELY FOR YOUNG DOCTOR HARPER--
--THOSE DARK THOUGHTS ARE THE LAST THOUGHTS HE'LL EVER HAVE.

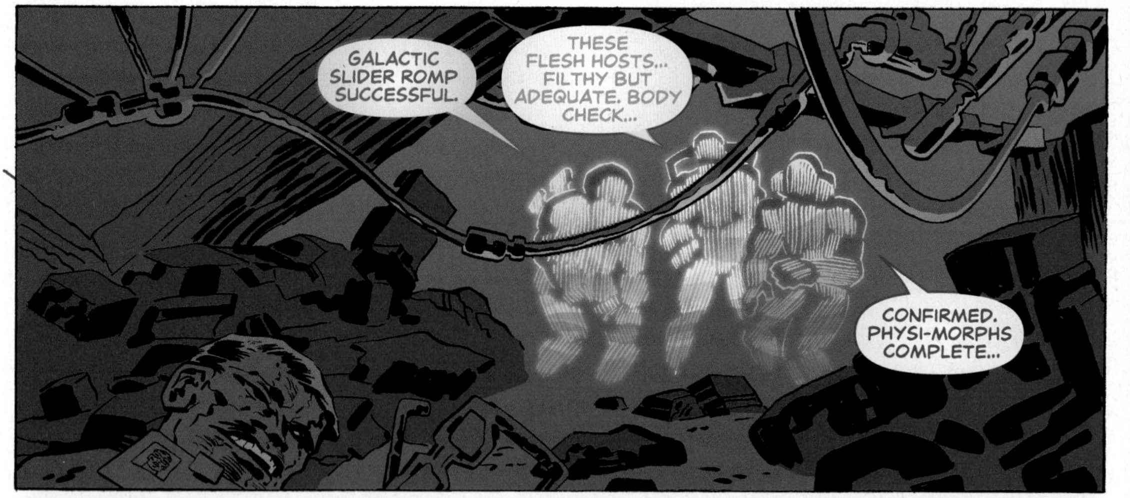
GALACTIC SLIDER ROMP SUCCESSFUL.
THESE FLESH HOSTS... FILTHY BUT ADEQUATE. BODY CHECK...
CONFIRMED. PHYSI-MORPHS COMPLETE...

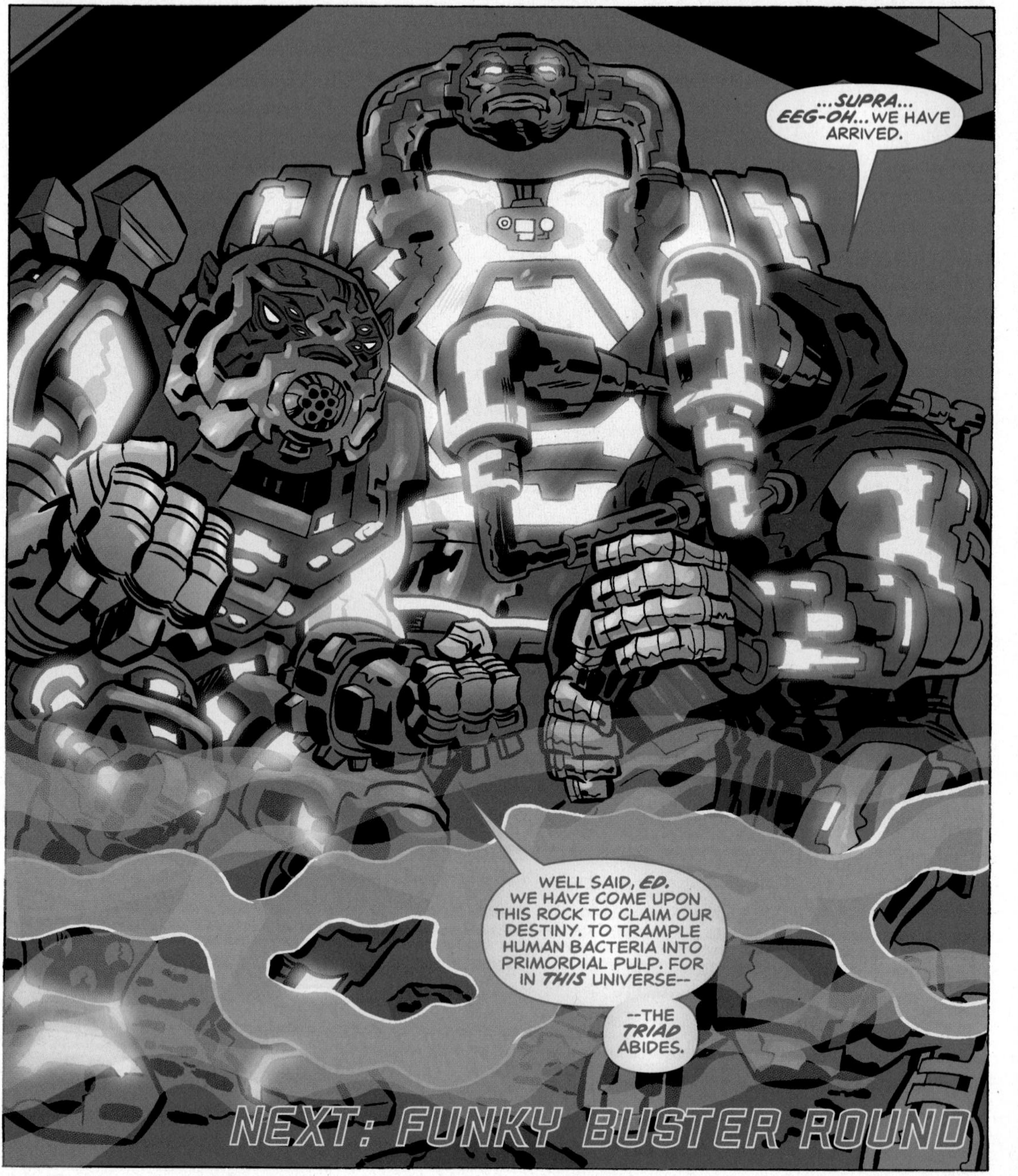
...SUPRA... EEG-OH... WE HAVE ARRIVED.
WELL SAID, ED. WE HAVE COME UPON THIS ROCK TO CLAIM OUR DESTINY. TO TRAMPLE HUMAN BACTERIA INTO PRIMORDIAL PULP. FOR IN THIS UNIVERSE--
--THE TRIAD ABIDES.
NEXT: FUNKY BUSTER ROUND

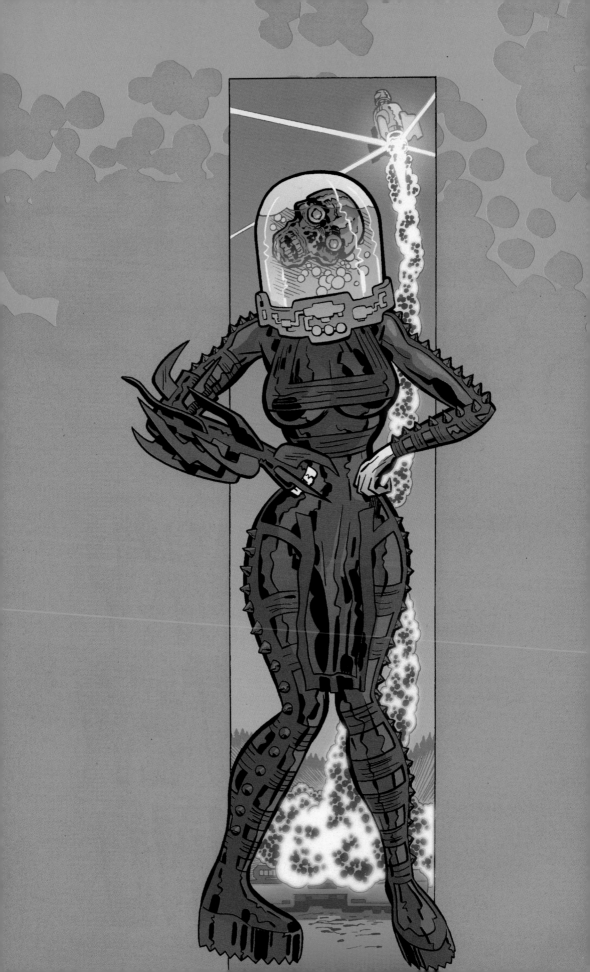

BOOK NINE:
FUNKY BUSTER ROUND

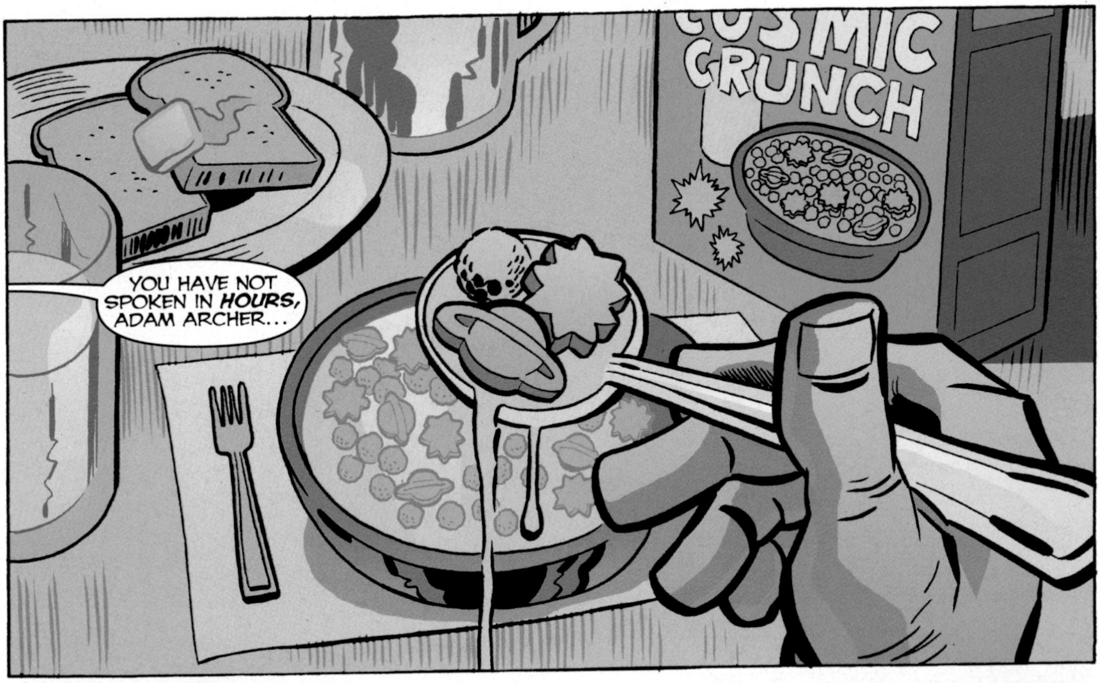
COSMIC CRUNCH
YOU HAVE NOT SPOKEN IN HOURS, ADAM ARCHER...

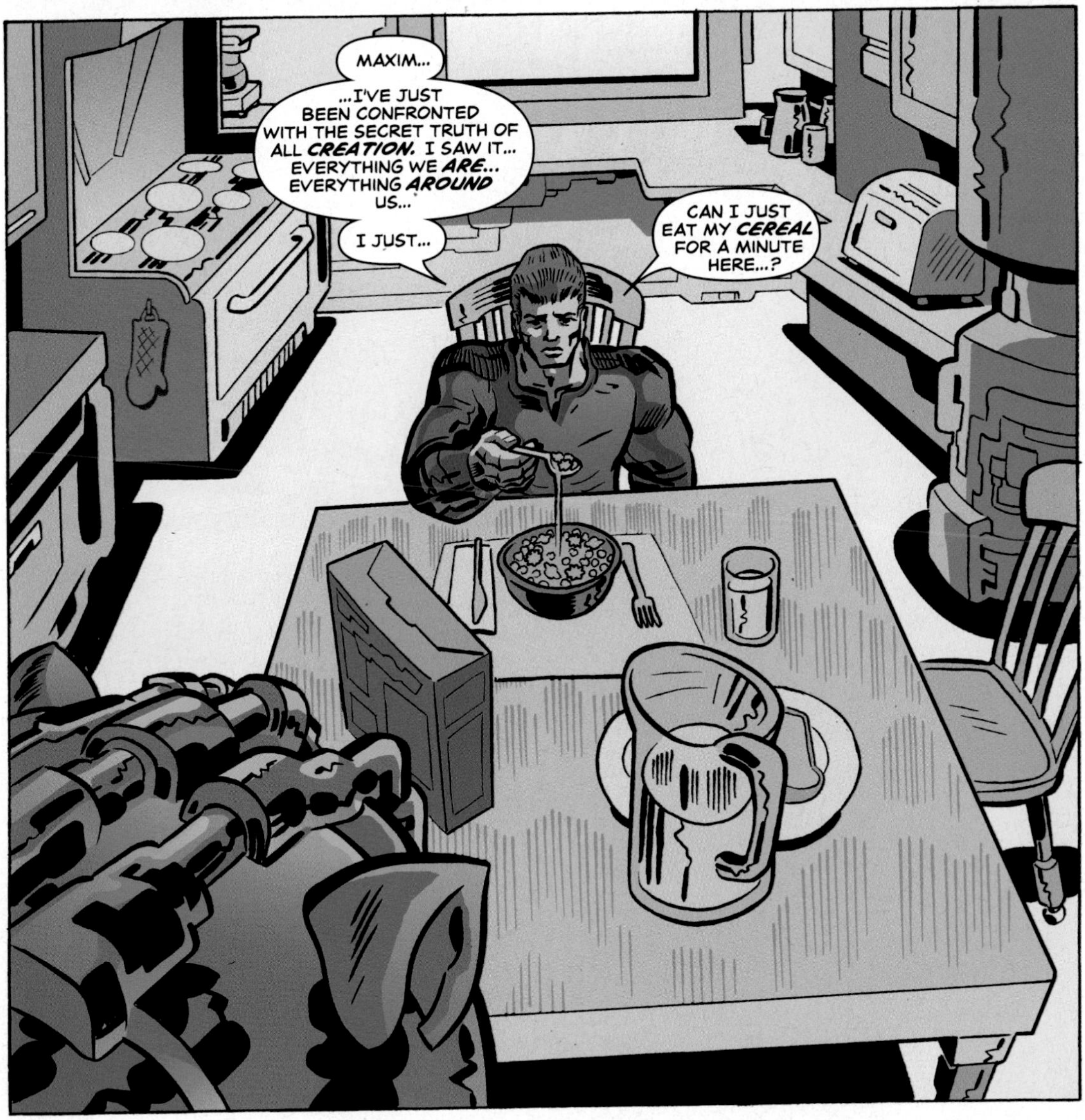
MAXIM...
...I'VE JUST BEEN CONFRONTED WITH THE SECRET TRUTH OF ALL CREATION. I SAW IT... EVERYTHING WE ARE... EVERYTHING AROUND US...
I JUST...
CAN I JUST EAT MY CEREAL FOR A MINUTE HERE...?

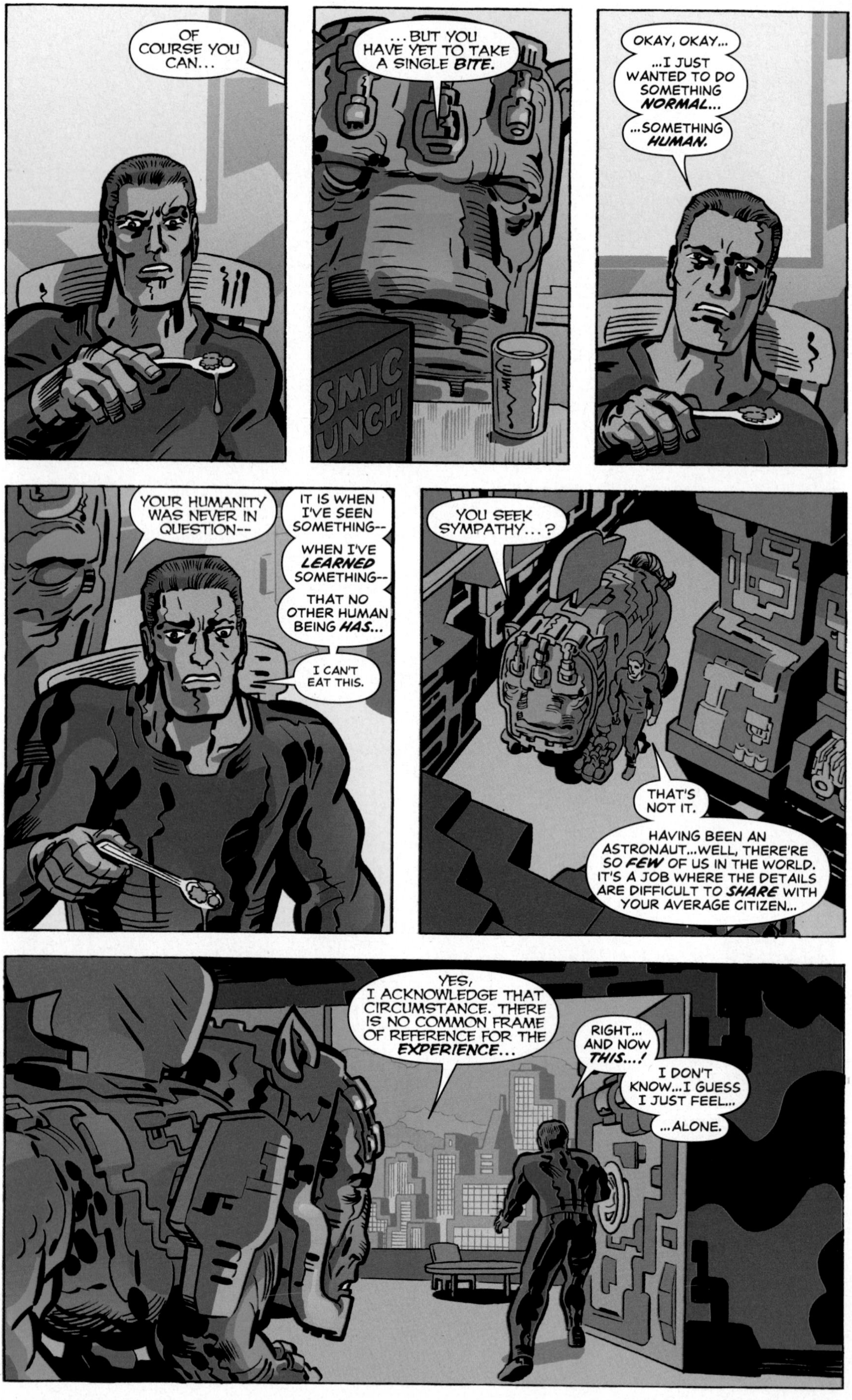
OF COURSE YOU CAN...
...BUT YOU HAVE YET TO TAKE A SINGLE BITE.
SMIC UNCH
OKAY, OKAY...
...I JUST WANTED TO DO SOMETHING NORMAL...
...SOMETHING HUMAN.
YOUR HUMANITY WAS NEVER IN QUESTION--
IT IS WHEN I'VE SEEN SOMETHING--
WHEN I'VE LEARNED SOMETHING--
THAT NO OTHER HUMAN BEING HAS...
I CAN'T EAT THIS.
YOU SEEK SYMPATHY...?
THAT'S NOT IT.
HAVING BEEN AN ASTRONAUT...WELL, THERE'RE SO FEW OF US IN THE WORLD. IT'S A JOB WHERE THE DETAILS ARE DIFFICULT TO SHARE WITH YOUR AVERAGE CITIZEN...
YES, I ACKNOWLEDGE THAT CIRCUMSTANCE. THERE IS NO COMMON FRAME OF REFERENCE FOR THE EXPERIENCE...
RIGHT... AND NOW THIS...!
I DON'T KNOW...I GUESS I JUST FEEL...
...ALONE.

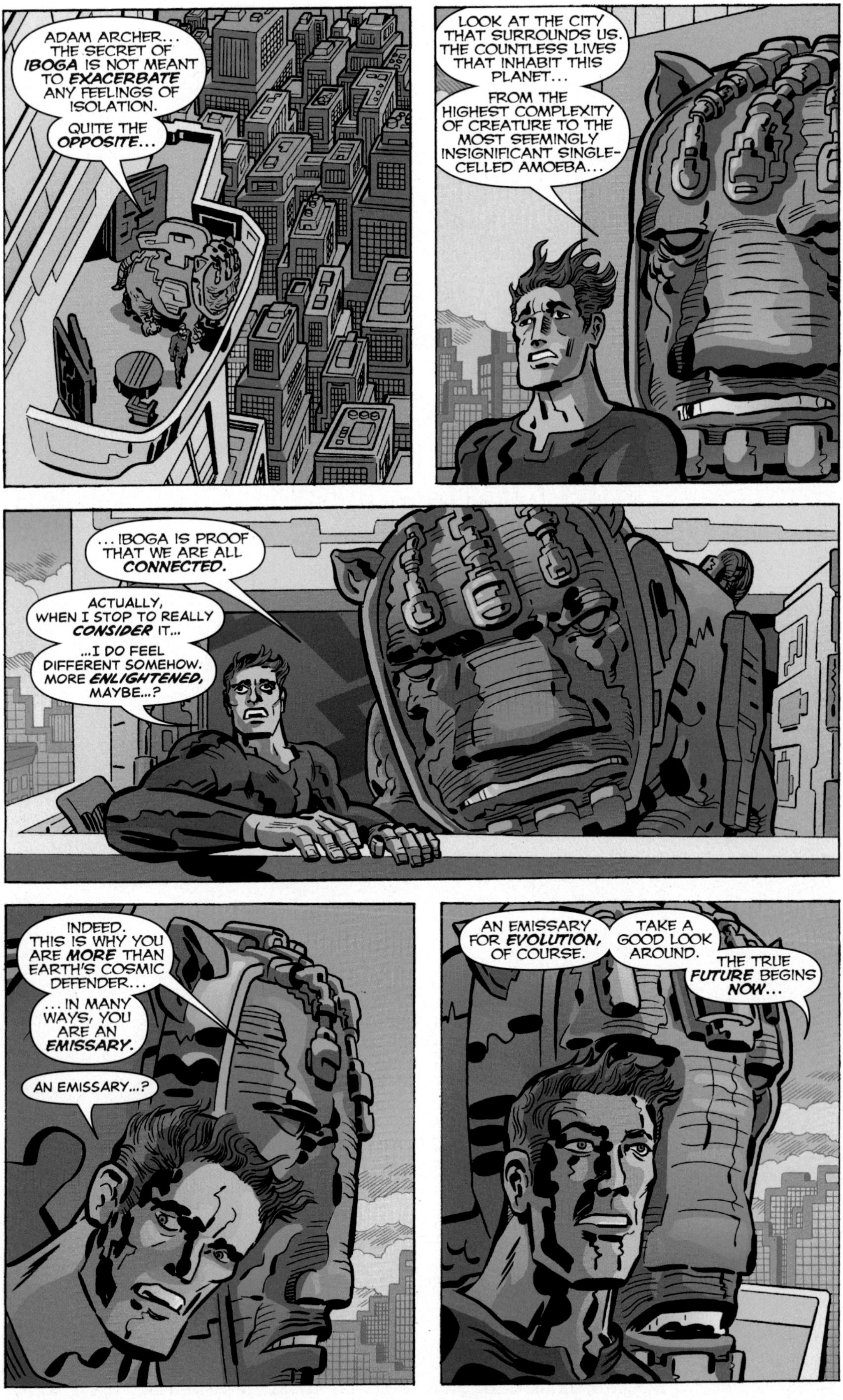
ADAM ARCHER... THE SECRET OF IBOGA IS NOT MEANT TO EXACERBATE ANY FEELINGS OF ISOLATION.
QUITE THE OPPOSITE...
LOOK AT THE CITY THAT SURROUNDS US. THE COUNTLESS LIVES THAT INHABIT THIS PLANET...
FROM THE HIGHEST COMPLEXITY OF CREATURE TO THE MOST SEEMINGLY INSIGNIFICANT SINGLE-CELLED AMOEBA...
...IBOGA IS PROOF THAT WE ARE ALL CONNECTED.
ACTUALLY, WHEN I STOP TO REALLY CONSIDER IT...
...I DO FEEL DIFFERENT SOMEHOW. MORE ENLIGHTENED, MAYBE...?
INDEED. THIS IS WHY YOU ARE MORE THAN EARTH'S COSMIC DEFENDER...
...IN MANY WAYS, YOU ARE AN EMISSARY.
AN EMISSARY...?
AN EMISSARY FOR EVOLUTION, OF COURSE.
TAKE A GOOD LOOK AROUND.
THE TRUE FUTURE BEGINS NOW...

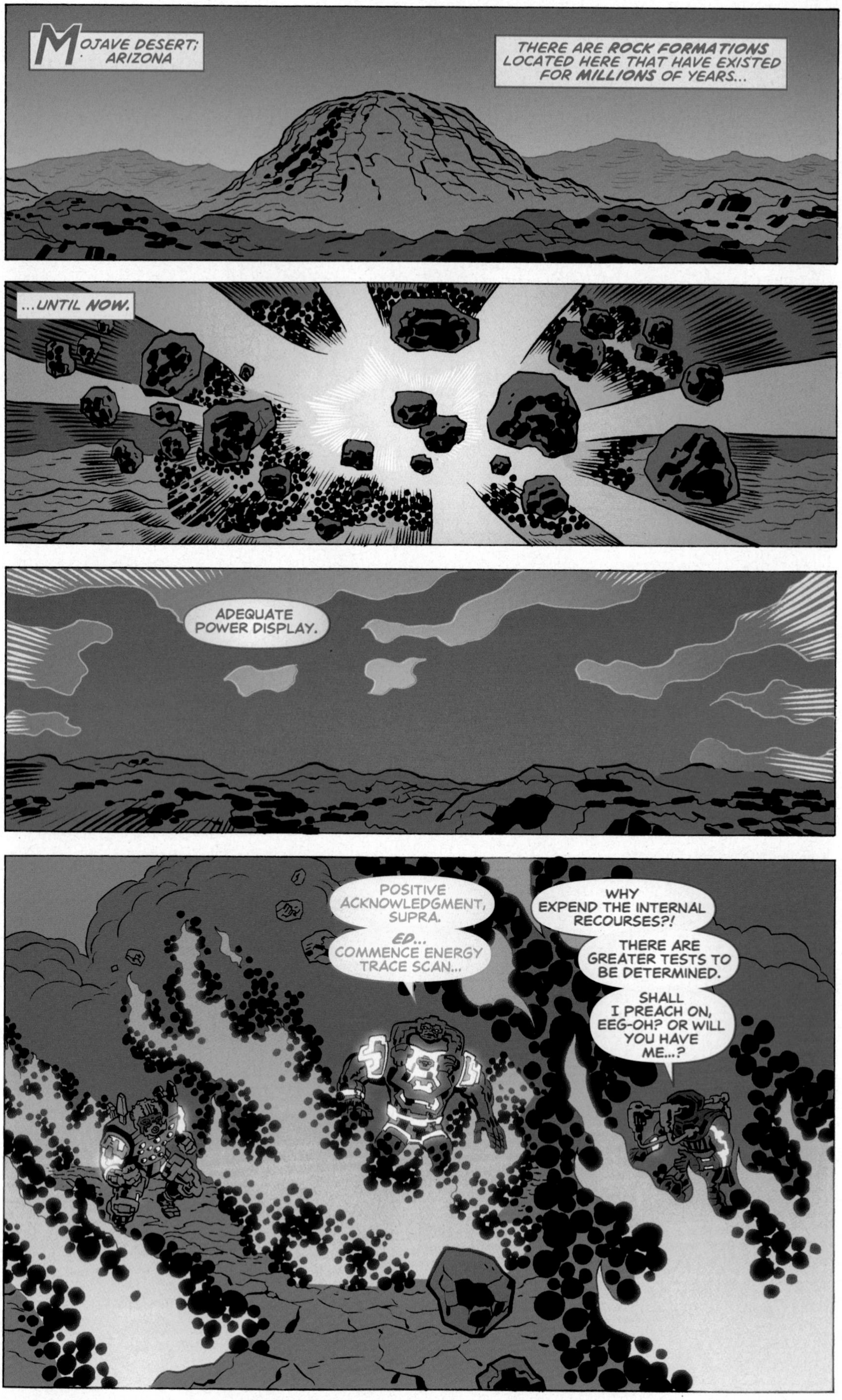
MOJAVE DESERT; ARIZONA
THERE ARE ROCK FORMATIONS LOCATED HERE THAT HAVE EXISTED FOR MILLIONS OF YEARS...
...UNTIL NOW.
ADEQUATE POWER DISPLAY.
POSITIVE ACKNOWLEDGMENT, SUPRA.
ED... COMMENCE ENERGY TRACE SCAN...
WHY EXPEND THE INTERNAL RECOURSES?!
THERE ARE GREATER TESTS TO BE DETERMINED.
SHALL I PREACH ON, EEG-OH? OR WILL YOU HAVE ME...?

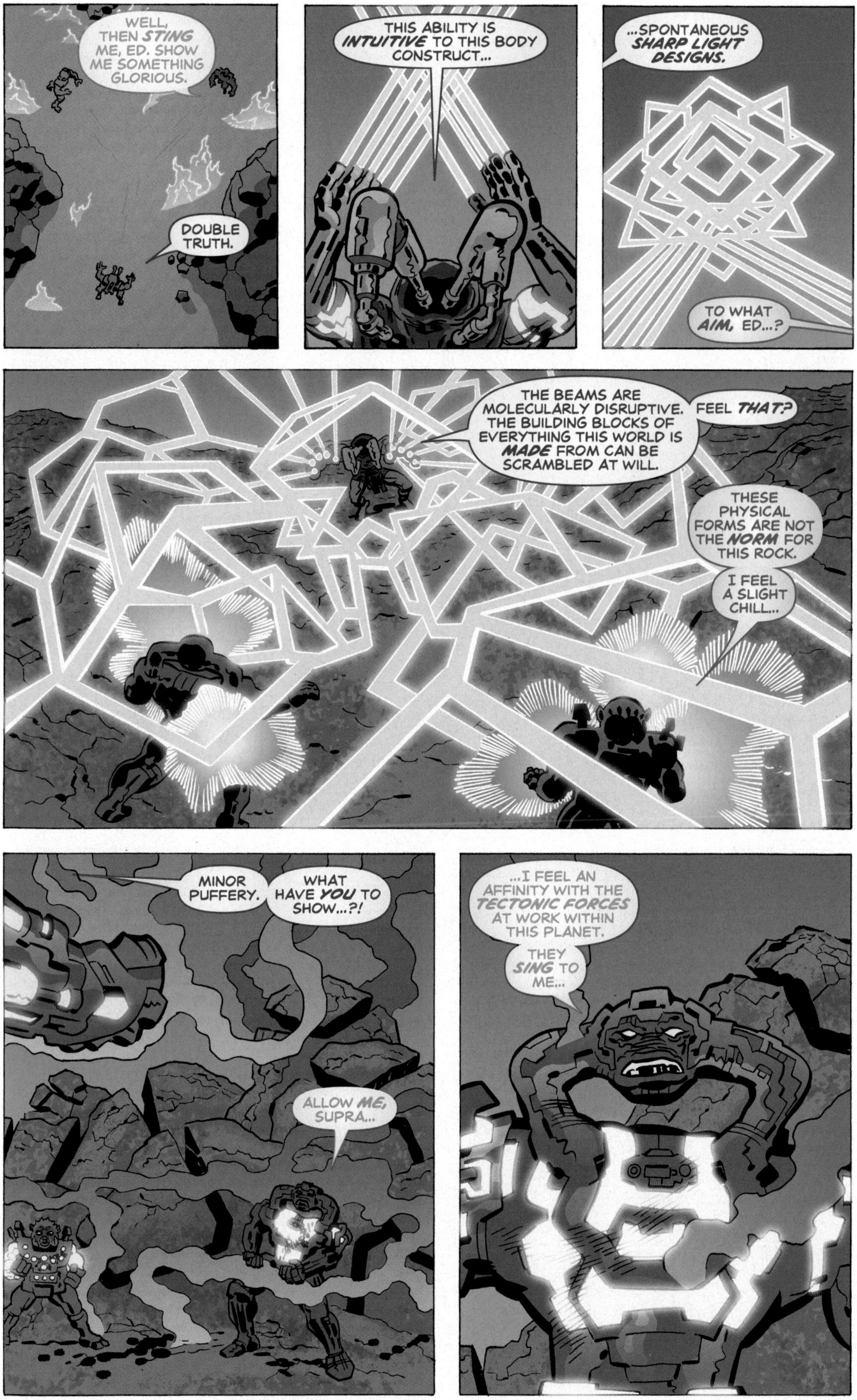
WELL, THEN STING ME, ED. SHOW ME SOMETHING GLORIOUS.
DOUBLE TRUTH.
THIS ABILITY IS INTUITIVE TO THIS BODY CONSTRUCT...
...SPONTANEOUS SHARP LIGHT DESIGNS.
TO WHAT AIM, ED...?
THE BEAMS ARE MOLECULARLY DISRUPTIVE. THE BUILDING BLOCKS OF EVERYTHING THIS WORLD IS MADE FROM CAN BE SCRAMBLED AT WILL.
FEEL THAT?
THESE PHYSICAL FORMS ARE NOT THE NORM FOR THIS ROCK.
I FEEL A SLIGHT CHILL...
MINOR PUFFERY.
WHAT HAVE YOU TO SHOW...?!
ALLOW ME, SUPRA...
...I FEEL AN AFFINITY WITH THE TECTONIC FORCES AT WORK WITHIN THIS PLANET.
THEY SING TO ME...

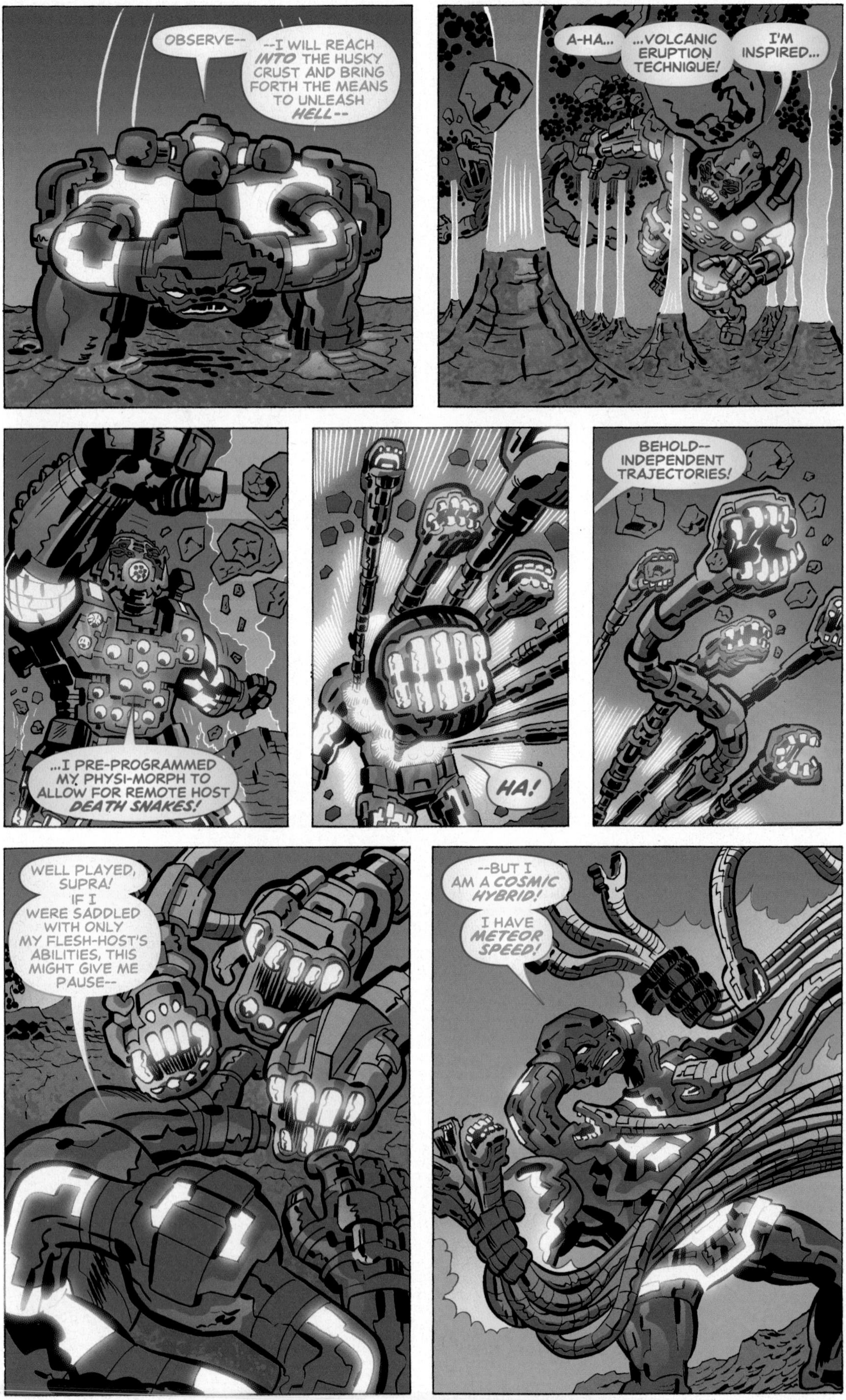
OBSERVE--
--I WILL REACH INTO THE HUSKY CRUST AND BRING FORTH THE MEANS TO UNLEASH HELL--
A-HA...
...VOLCANIC ERUPTION TECHNIQUE!
I'M INSPIRED...
...I PRE-PROGRAMMED MY PHYSI-MORPH TO ALLOW FOR REMOTE HOST DEATH SNAKES!
HA!
BEHOLD-- INDEPENDENT TRAJECTORIES!
WELL PLAYED, SUPRA! IF I WERE SADDLED WITH ONLY MY FLESH-HOST'S ABILITIES, THIS MIGHT GIVE ME PAUSE--
--BUT I AM A COSMIC HYBRID!
I HAVE METEOR SPEED!

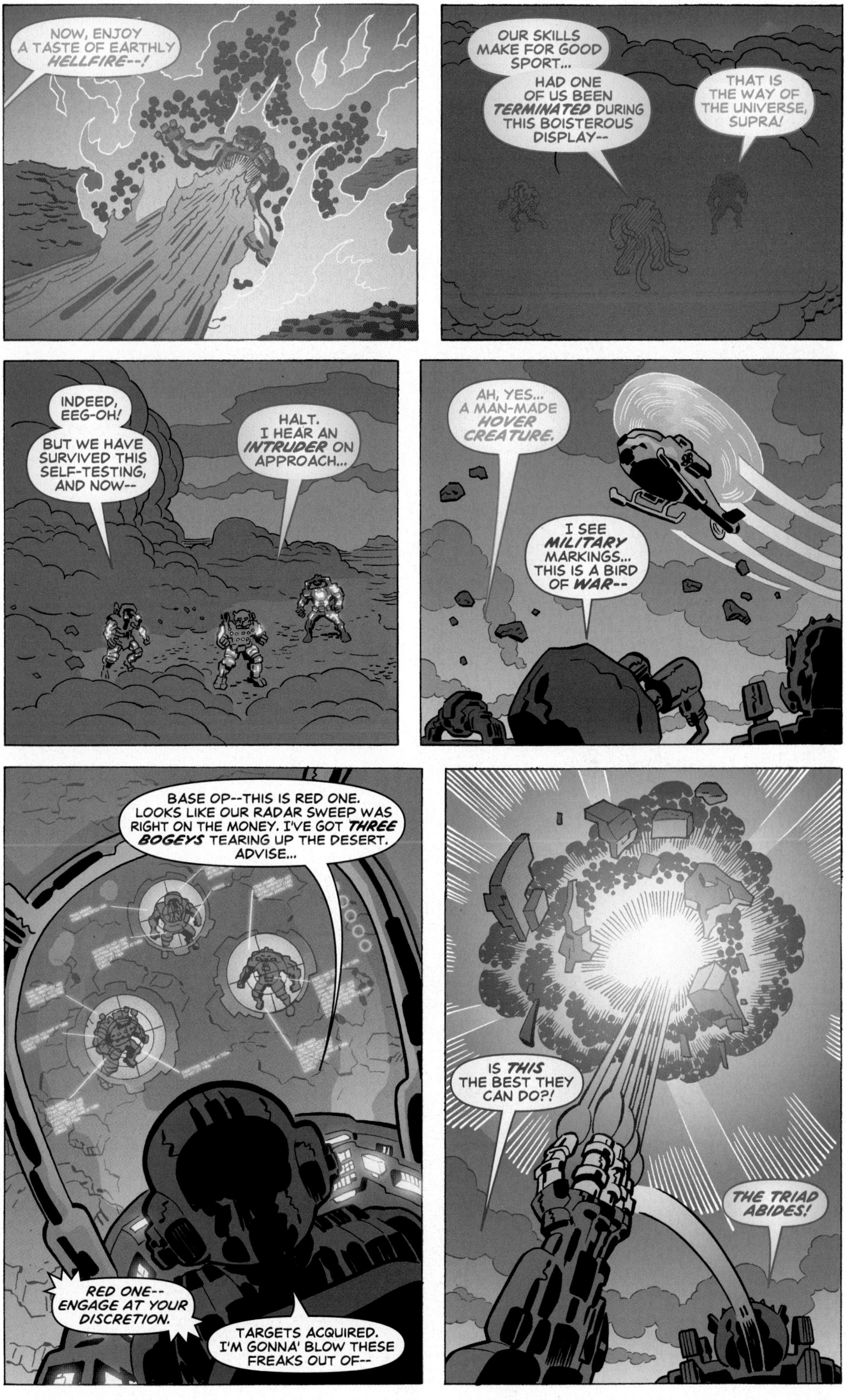
NOW, ENJOY A TASTE OF EARTHLY HELLFIRE--!
OUR SKILLS MAKE FOR GOOD SPORT...
HAD ONE OF US BEEN TERMINATED DURING THIS BOISTEROUS DISPLAY--
THAT IS THE WAY OF THE UNIVERSE, SUPRA!
INDEED, EEG-OH!
BUT WE HAVE SURVIVED THIS SELF-TESTING, AND NOW--
HALT. I HEAR AN INTRUDER ON APPROACH...
AH, YES... A MAN-MADE HOVER CREATURE.
I SEE MILITARY MARKINGS... THIS IS A BIRD OF WAR--
BASE OP--THIS IS RED ONE. LOOKS LIKE OUR RADAR SWEEP WAS RIGHT ON THE MONEY. I'VE GOT THREE BOGEYS TEARING UP THE DESERT. ADVISE...
RED ONE--ENGAGE AT YOUR DISCRETION.
TARGETS ACQUIRED. I'M GONNA' BLOW THESE FREAKS OUT OF--
IS THIS THE BEST THEY CAN DO?!
THE TRIAD ABIDES!

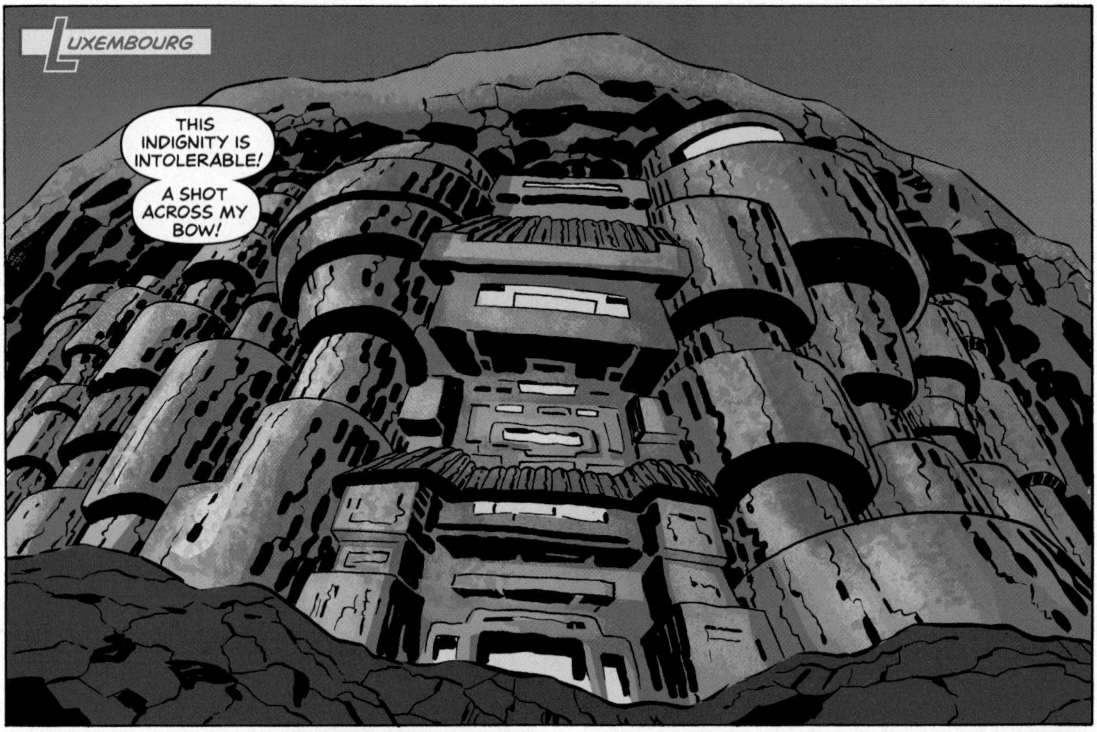
LUXEMBOURG
THIS INDIGNITY IS INTOLERABLE!
A SHOT ACROSS MY BOW!

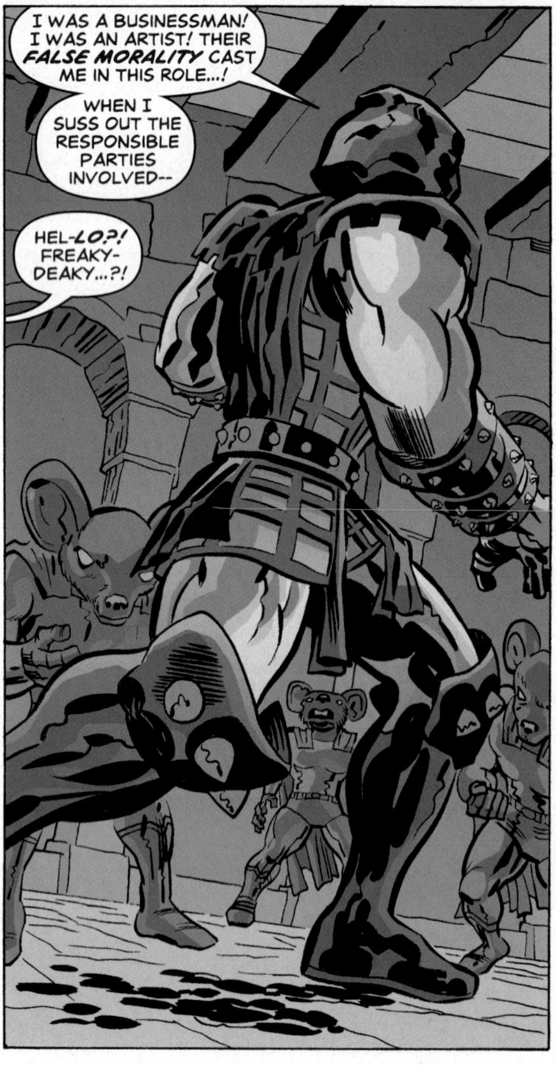
I WAS A BUSINESSMAN! I WAS AN ARTIST! THEIR FALSE MORALITY CAST ME IN THIS ROLE...!
WHEN I SUSS OUT THE RESPONSIBLE PARTIES INVOLVED--
HEL-LO?! FREAKY-DEAKY...?!

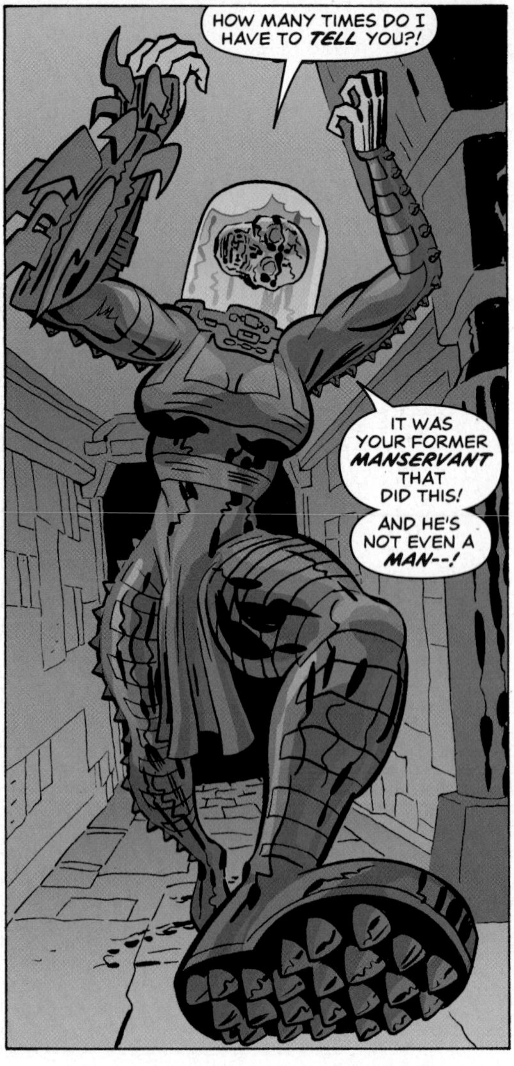
HOW MANY TIMES DO I HAVE TO TELL YOU?!
IT WAS YOUR FORMER MANSERVANT THAT DID THIS!
AND HE'S NOT EVEN A MAN--!

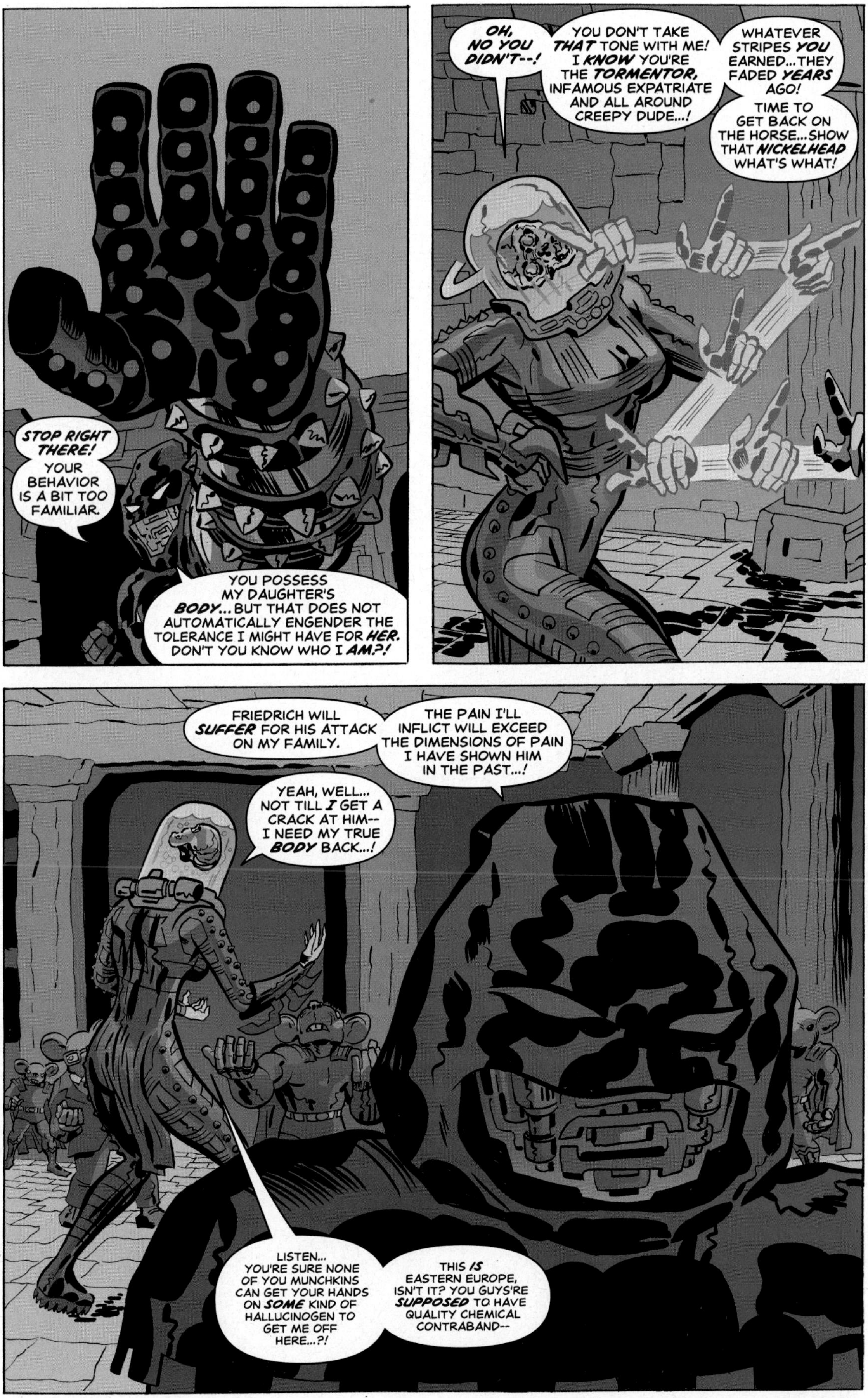
STOP RIGHT THERE! YOUR BEHAVIOR IS A BIT TOO FAMILIAR.
YOU POSSESS MY DAUGHTER'S BODY... BUT THAT DOES NOT AUTOMATICALLY ENGENDER THE TOLERANCE I MIGHT HAVE FOR HER. DON'T YOU KNOW WHO I AM?!
OH, NO YOU DIDN'T--!
YOU DON'T TAKE THAT TONE WITH ME! I KNOW YOU'RE THE TORMENTOR, INFAMOUS EXPATRIATE AND ALL AROUND CREEPY DUDE...!
WHATEVER STRIPES YOU EARNED...THEY FADED YEARS AGO!
TIME TO GET BACK ON THE HORSE...SHOW THAT NICKELHEAD WHAT'S WHAT!
FRIEDRICH WILL SUFFER FOR HIS ATTACK ON MY FAMILY.
THE PAIN I'LL INFLICT WILL EXCEED THE DIMENSIONS OF PAIN I HAVE SHOWN HIM IN THE PAST...!
YEAH, WELL... NOT TILL I GET A CRACK AT HIM-- I NEED MY TRUE BODY BACK...!
LISTEN... YOU'RE SURE NONE OF YOU MUNCHKINS CAN GET YOUR HANDS ON SOME KIND OF HALLUCINOGEN TO GET ME OFF HERE...?!
THIS IS EASTERN EUROPE, ISN'T IT? YOU GUYS'RE SUPPOSED TO HAVE QUALITY CHEMICAL CONTRABAND--

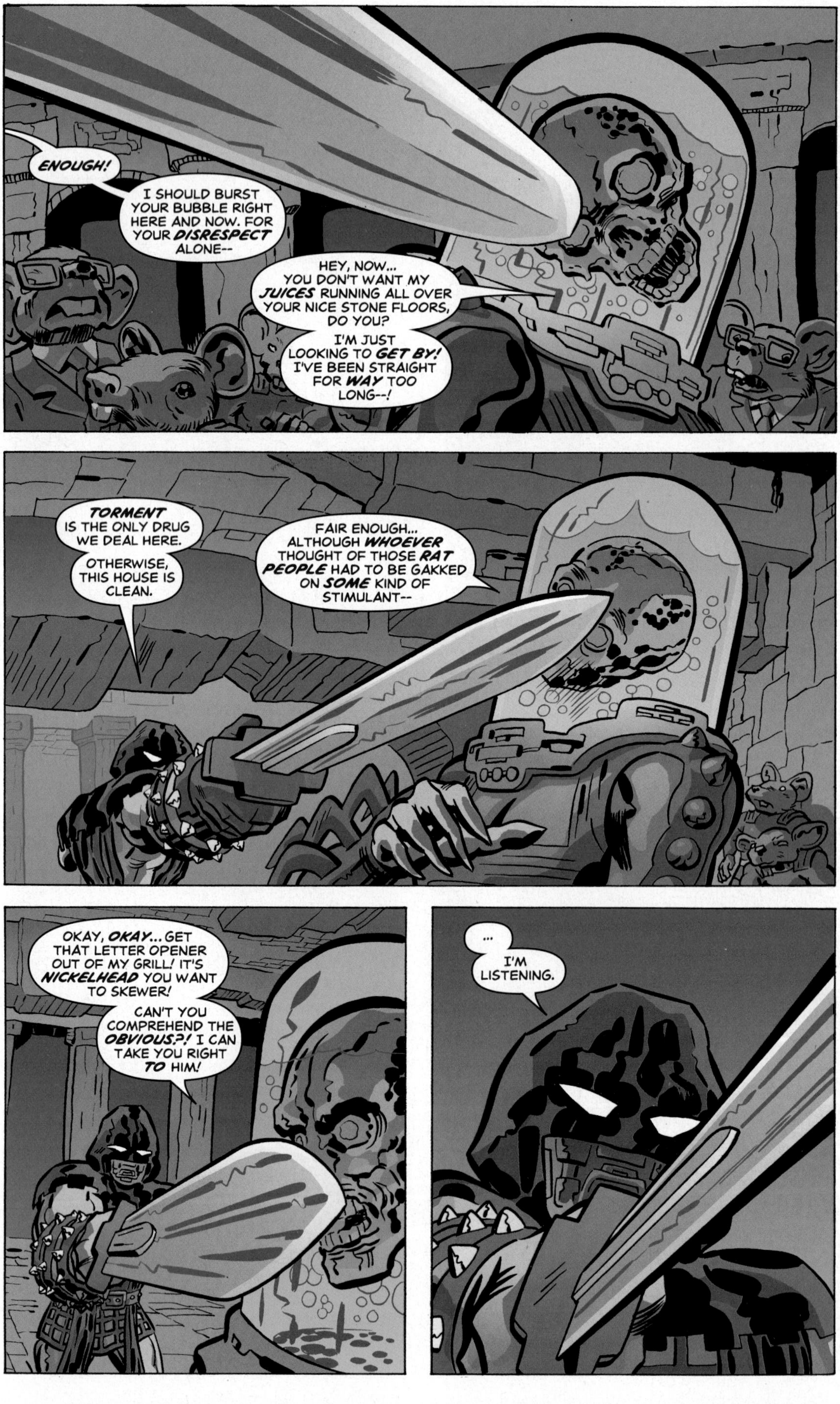
ENOUGH!
I SHOULD BURST YOUR BUBBLE RIGHT HERE AND NOW. FOR YOUR DISRESPECT ALONE--
HEY, NOW... YOU DON'T WANT MY JUICES RUNNING ALL OVER YOUR NICE STONE FLOORS, DO YOU?
I'M JUST LOOKING TO GET BY! I'VE BEEN STRAIGHT FOR WAY TOO LONG--!
TORMENT IS THE ONLY DRUG WE DEAL HERE.
OTHERWISE, THIS HOUSE IS CLEAN.
FAIR ENOUGH... ALTHOUGH WHOEVER THOUGHT OF THOSE RAT PEOPLE HAD TO BE GAKKED ON SOME KIND OF STIMULANT--
OKAY, OKAY... GET THAT LETTER OPENER OUT OF MY GRILL! IT'S NICKELHEAD YOU WANT TO SKEWER!
CAN'T YOU COMPREHEND THE OBVIOUS?! I CAN TAKE YOU RIGHT TO HIM!
...
I'M LISTENING.

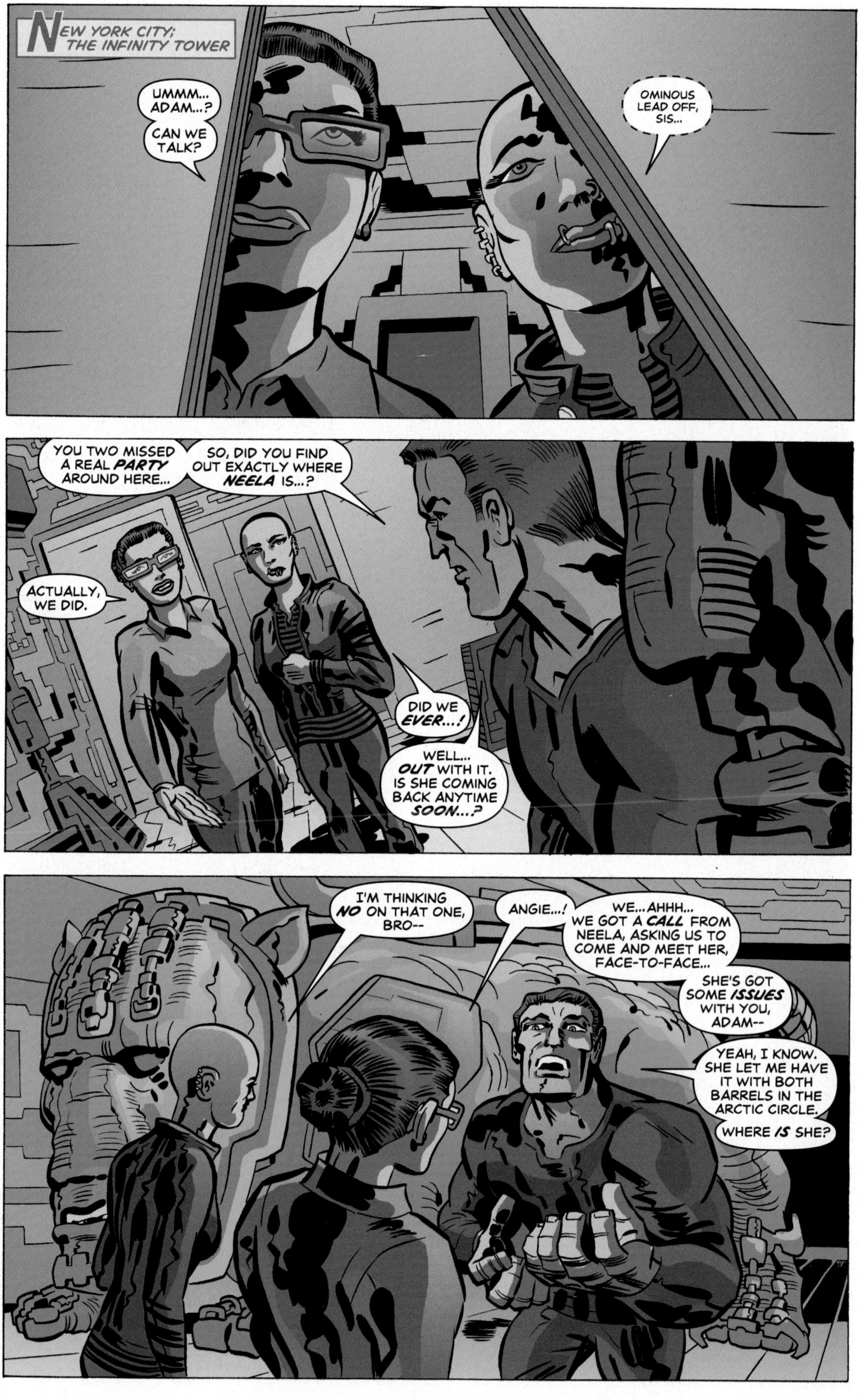
NEW YORK CITY:
THE INFINITY TOWER
UMMM... ADAM...?
CAN WE TALK?
OMINOUS LEAD OFF, SIS...
YOU TWO MISSED A REAL PARTY AROUND HERE...
SO, DID YOU FIND OUT EXACTLY WHERE NEELA IS...?
ACTUALLY, WE DID.
DID WE EVER...!
WELL... OUT WITH IT. IS SHE COMING BACK ANYTIME SOON...?
I'M THINKING NO ON THAT ONE, BRO--
ANGIE...!
WE...AHHH... WE GOT A CALL FROM NEELA, ASKING US TO COME AND MEET HER, FACE-TO-FACE...
SHE'S GOT SOME ISSUES WITH YOU, ADAM--
YEAH, I KNOW. SHE LET ME HAVE IT WITH BOTH BARRELS IN THE ARCTIC CIRCLE.
WHERE IS SHE?

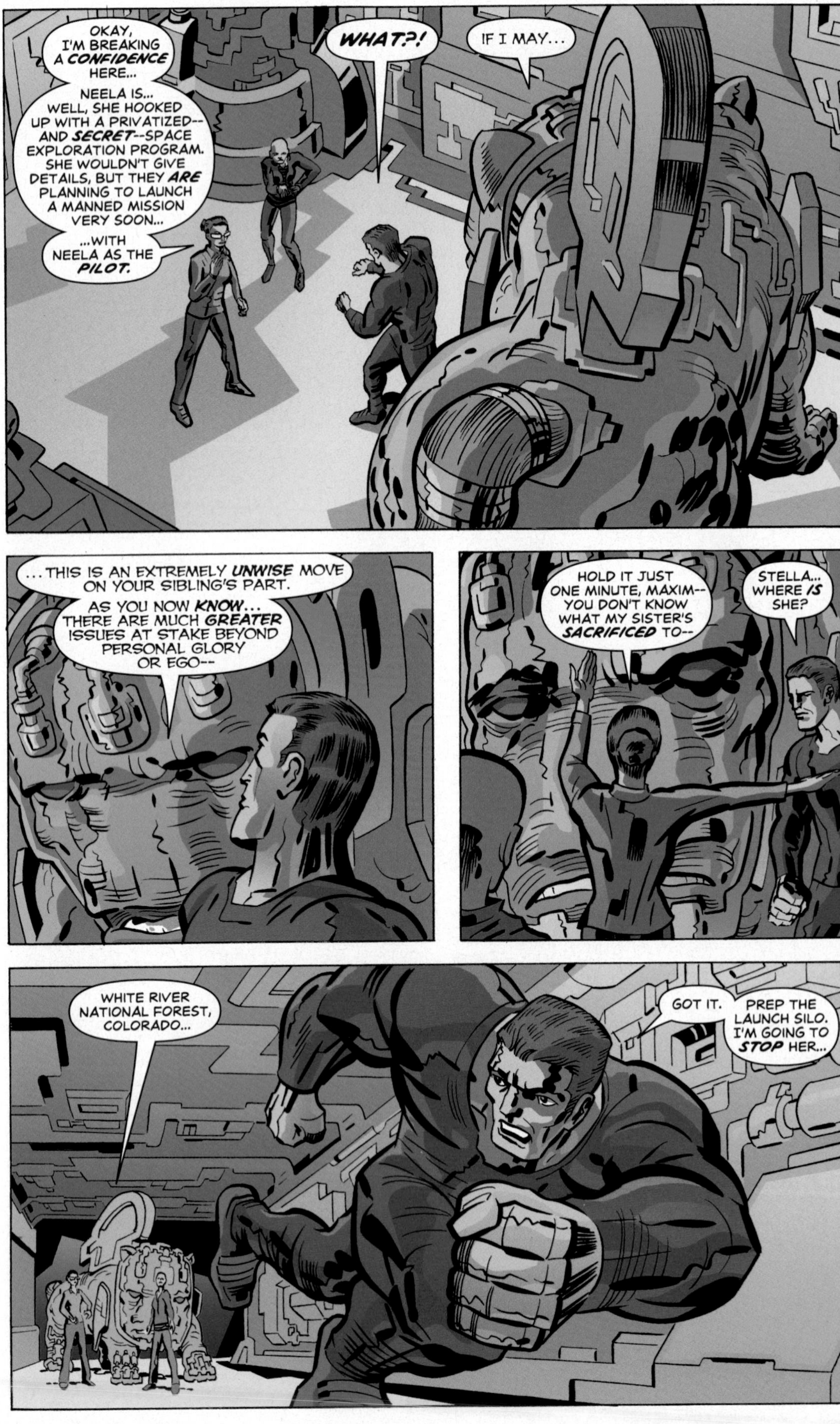
OKAY, I'M BREAKING A CONFIDENCE HERE...
NEELA IS... WELL, SHE HOOKED UP WITH A PRIVATIZED-- AND SECRET--SPACE EXPLORATION PROGRAM. SHE WOULDN'T GIVE DETAILS, BUT THEY ARE PLANNING TO LAUNCH A MANNED MISSION VERY SOON...
...WITH NEELA AS THE PILOT.
WHAT?!
IF I MAY...
...THIS IS AN EXTREMELY UNWISE MOVE ON YOUR SIBLING'S PART.
AS YOU NOW KNOW... THERE ARE MUCH GREATER ISSUES AT STAKE BEYOND PERSONAL GLORY OR EGO--
HOLD IT JUST ONE MINUTE, MAXIM-- YOU DON'T KNOW WHAT MY SISTER'S SACRIFICED TO--
STELLA... WHERE IS SHE?
WHITE RIVER NATIONAL FOREST, COLORADO...
GOT IT.
PREP THE LAUNCH SILO. I'M GOING TO STOP HER...

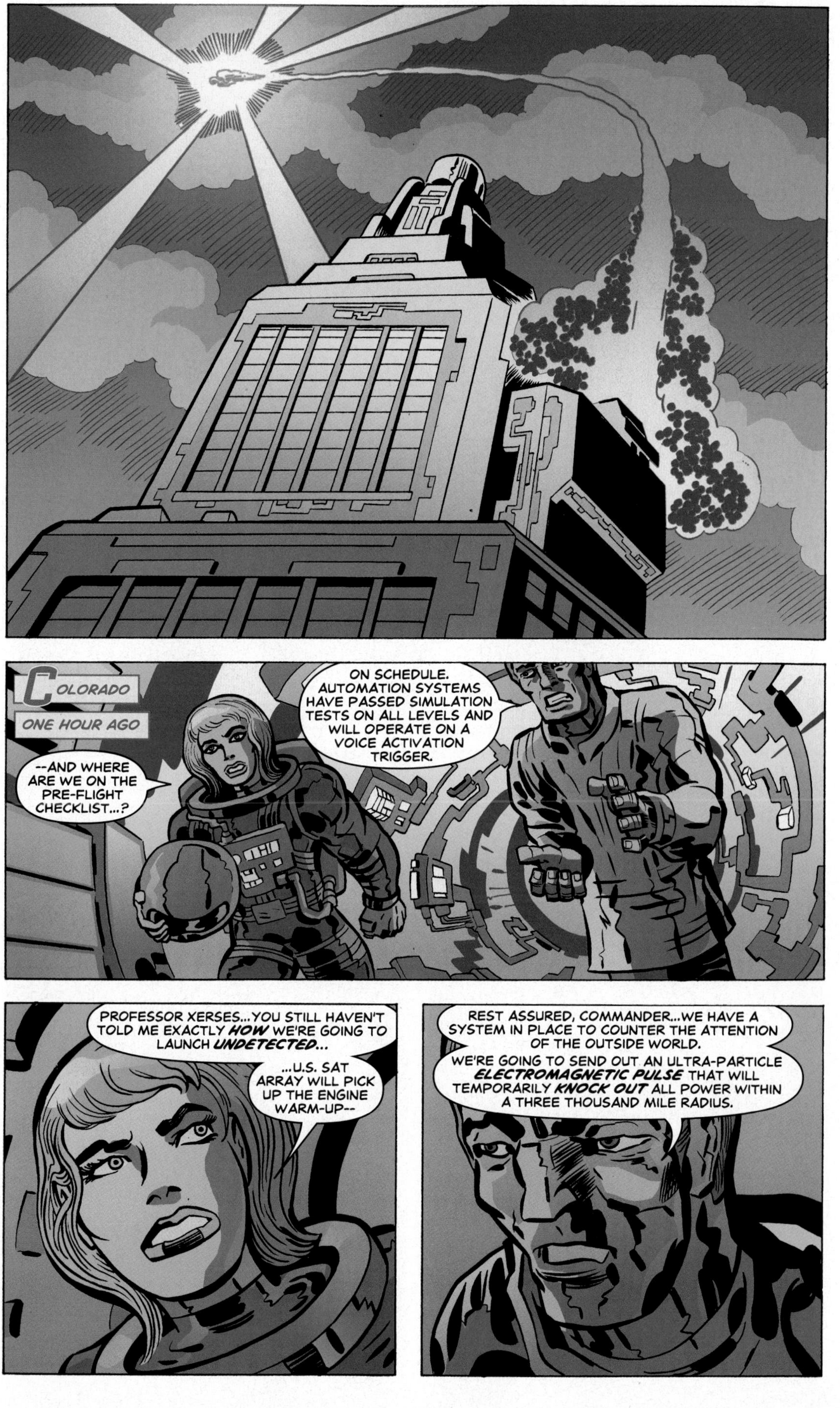
COLORADO
ONE HOUR AGO
--AND WHERE ARE WE ON THE PRE-FLIGHT CHECKLIST...?
ON SCHEDULE. AUTOMATION SYSTEMS HAVE PASSED SIMULATION TESTS ON ALL LEVELS AND WILL OPERATE ON A VOICE ACTIVATION TRIGGER.
PROFESSOR XERSES...YOU STILL HAVEN'T TOLD ME EXACTLY HOW WE'RE GOING TO LAUNCH UNDETECTED...
...U.S. SAT ARRAY WILL PICK UP THE ENGINE WARM-UP--
REST ASSURED, COMMANDER...WE HAVE A SYSTEM IN PLACE TO COUNTER THE ATTENTION OF THE OUTSIDE WORLD.
WE'RE GOING TO SEND OUT AN ULTRA-PARTICLE ELECTROMAGNETIC PULSE THAT WILL TEMPORARILY KNOCK OUT ALL POWER WITHIN A THREE THOUSAND MILE RADIUS.

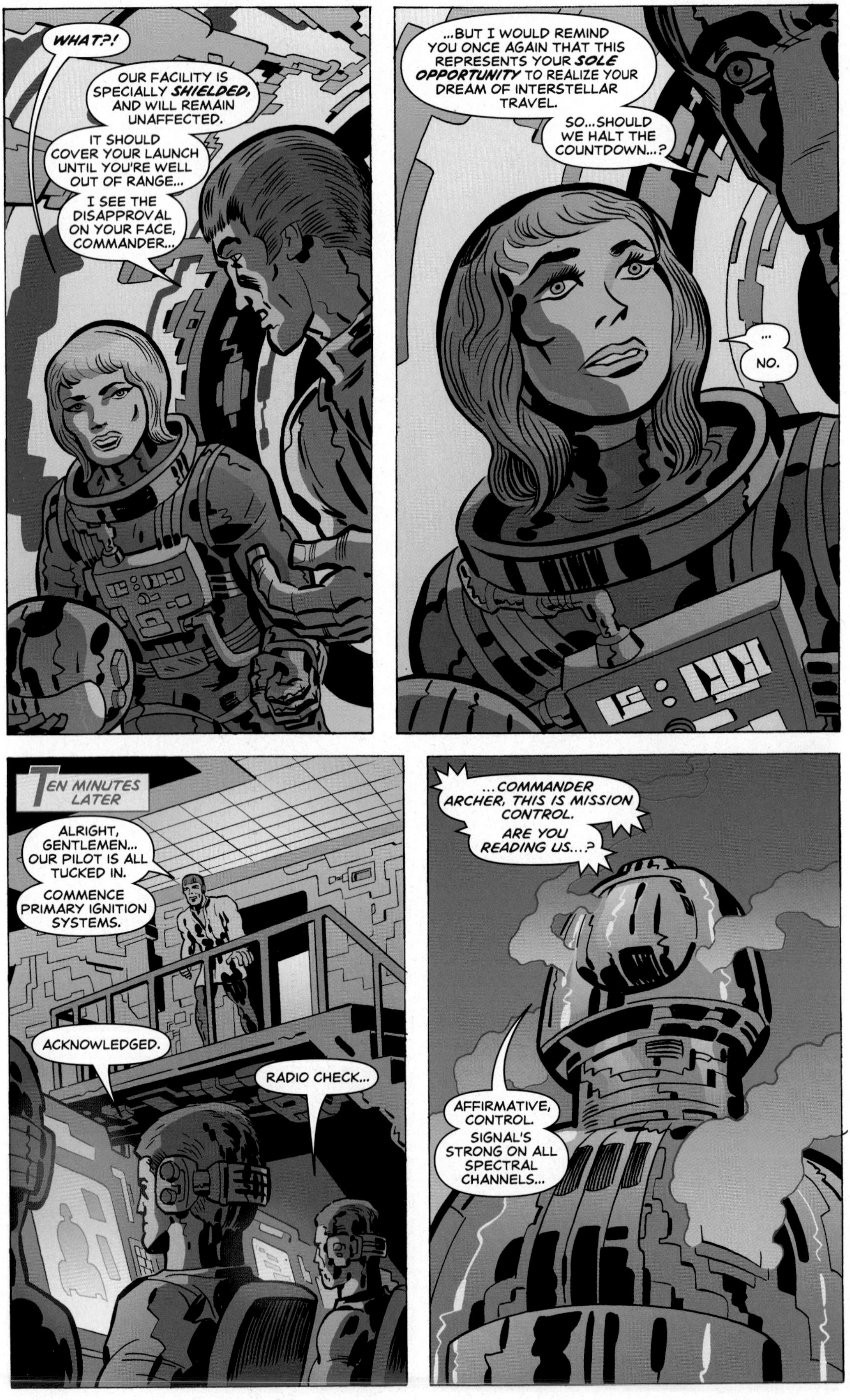
WHAT?!
OUR FACILITY IS SPECIALLY SHIELDED, AND WILL REMAIN UNAFFECTED.
IT SHOULD COVER YOUR LAUNCH UNTIL YOU'RE WELL OUT OF RANGE...
I SEE THE DISAPPROVAL ON YOUR FACE, COMMANDER...
...BUT I WOULD REMIND YOU ONCE AGAIN THAT THIS REPRESENTS YOUR SOLE OPPORTUNITY TO REALIZE YOUR DREAM OF INTERSTELLAR TRAVEL.
SO...SHOULD WE HALT THE COUNTDOWN...?
... NO.
TEN MINUTES LATER
ALRIGHT, GENTLEMEN... OUR PILOT IS ALL TUCKED IN.
COMMENCE PRIMARY IGNITION SYSTEMS.
ACKNOWLEDGED.
RADIO CHECK...
...COMMANDER ARCHER, THIS IS MISSION CONTROL.
ARE YOU READING US...?
AFFIRMATIVE, CONTROL.
SIGNAL'S STRONG ON ALL SPECTRAL CHANNELS...

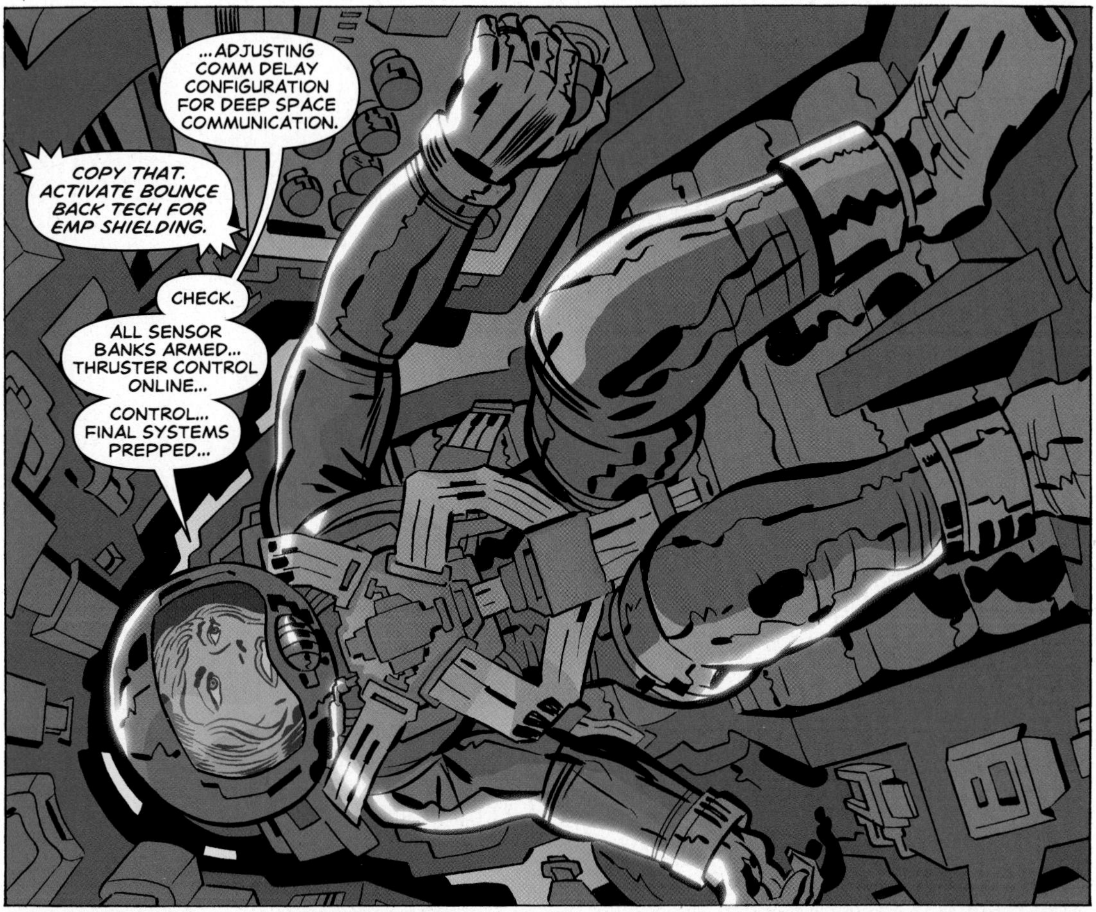
...ADJUSTING COMM DELAY CONFIGURATION FOR DEEP SPACE COMMUNICATION.
COPY THAT. ACTIVATE BOUNCE BACK TECH FOR EMP SHIELDING.
CHECK.
ALL SENSOR BANKS ARMED... THRUSTER CONTROL ONLINE...
CONTROL... FINAL SYSTEMS PREPPED...

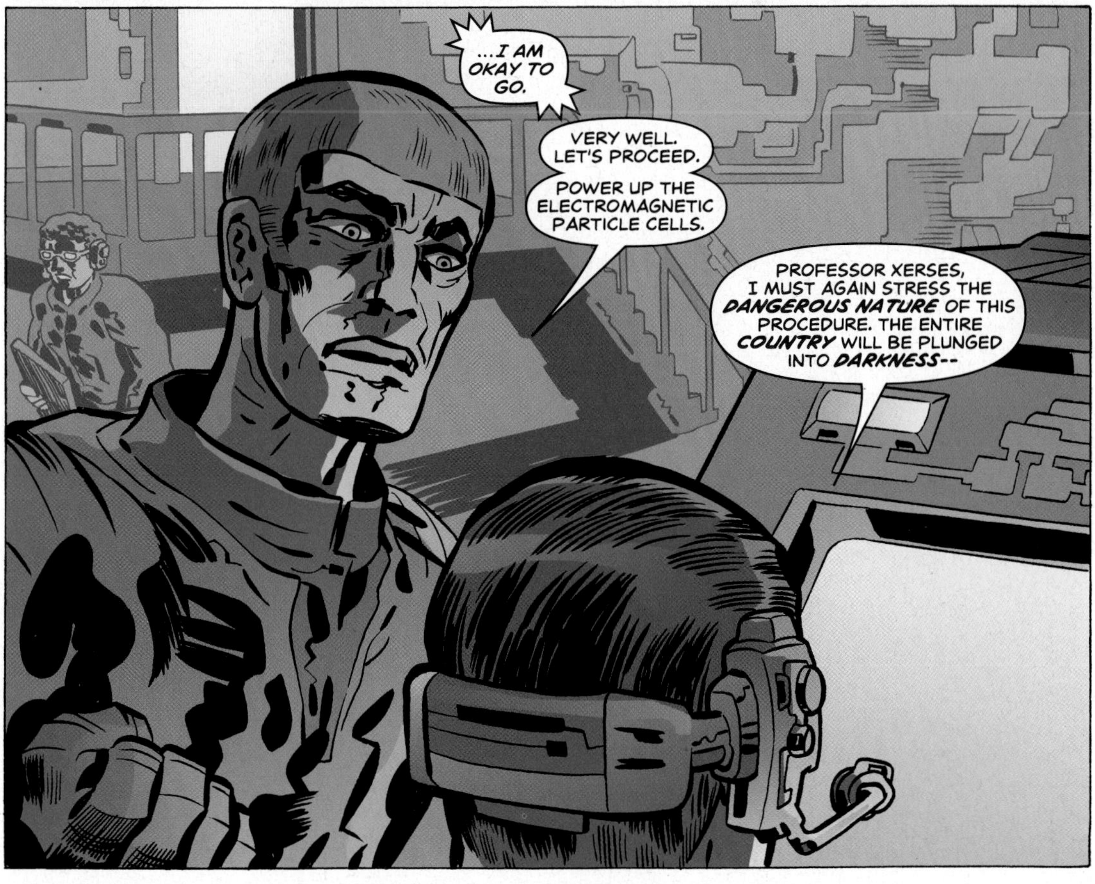
...I AM OKAY TO GO.
VERY WELL. LET'S PROCEED.
POWER UP THE ELECTROMAGNETIC PARTICLE CELLS.
PROFESSOR XERSES, I MUST AGAIN STRESS THE *DANGEROUS NATURE* OF THIS PROCEDURE. THE ENTIRE *COUNTRY* WILL BE PLUNGED INTO *DARKNESS*--

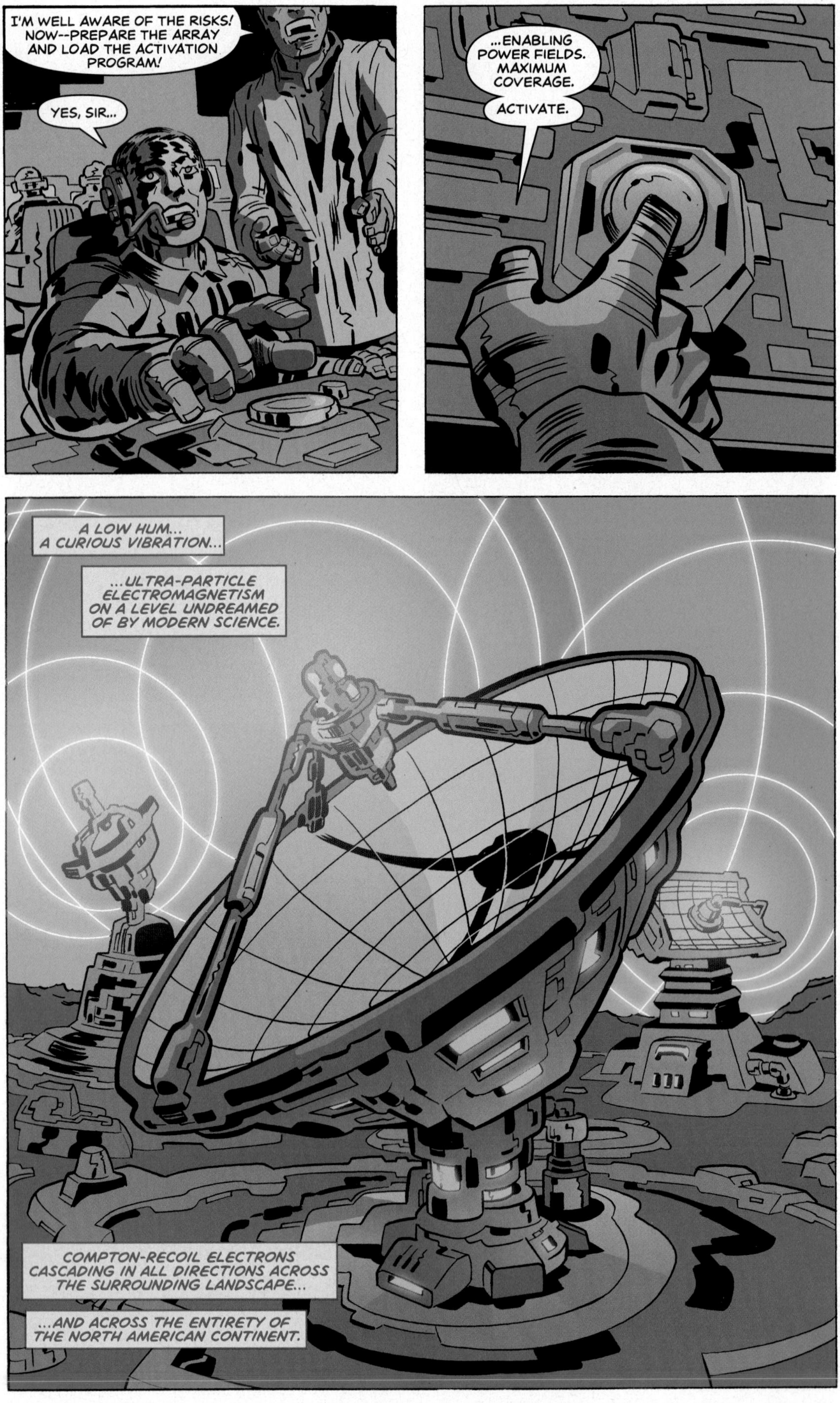
I'M WELL AWARE OF THE RISKS! NOW--PREPARE THE ARRAY AND LOAD THE ACTIVATION PROGRAM!
YES, SIR...
...ENABLING POWER FIELDS. MAXIMUM COVERAGE.
ACTIVATE.
A LOW HUM... A CURIOUS VIBRATION...
...ULTRA-PARTICLE ELECTROMAGNETISM ON A LEVEL UNDREAMED OF BY MODERN SCIENCE.
COMPTON-RECOIL ELECTRONS CASCADING IN ALL DIRECTIONS ACROSS THE SURROUNDING LANDSCAPE...
...AND ACROSS THE ENTIRETY OF THE NORTH AMERICAN CONTINENT.

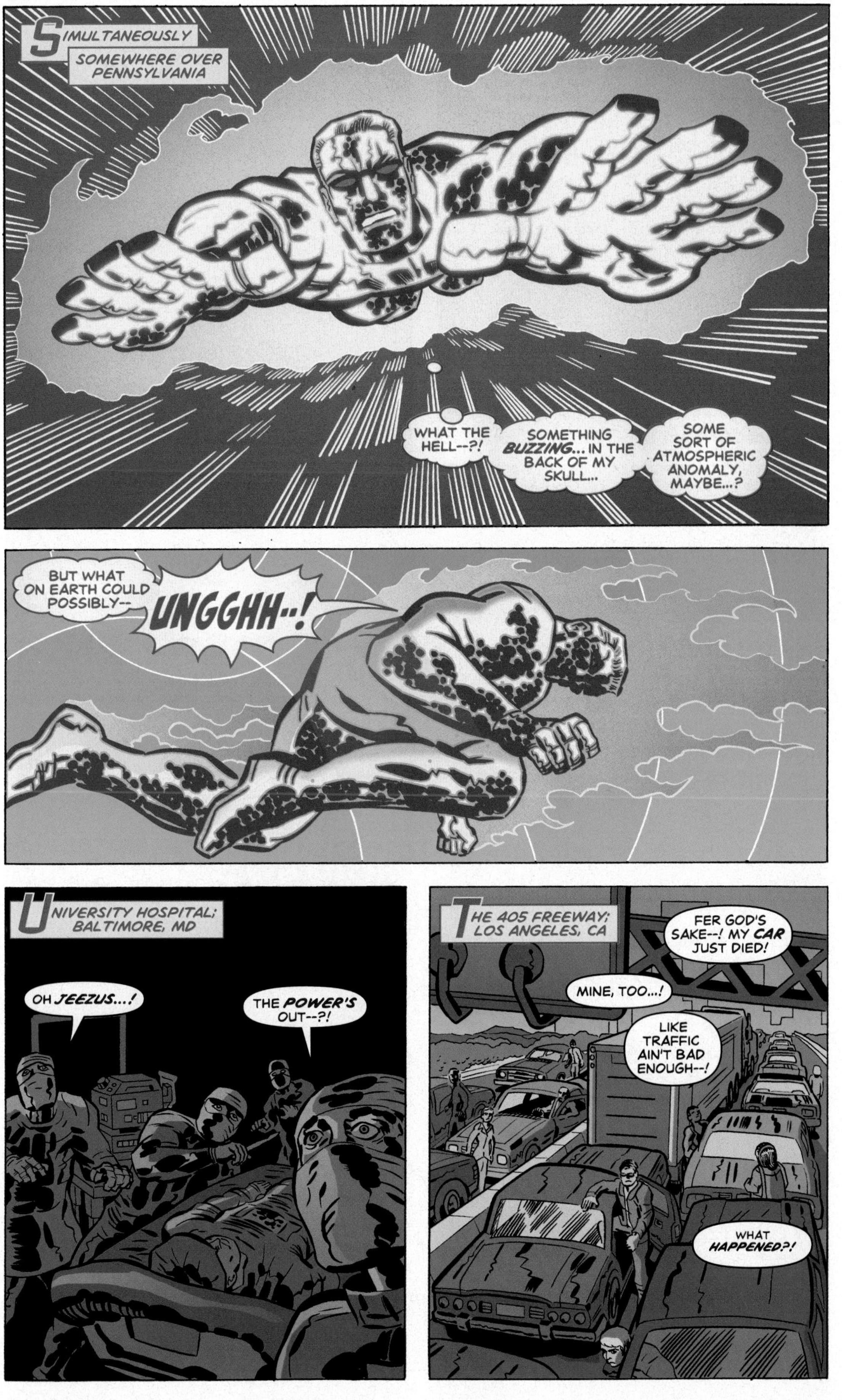
SIMULTANEOUSLY
SOMEWHERE OVER PENNSYLVANIA
WHAT THE HELL--?!
SOMETHING BUZZING... IN THE BACK OF MY SKULL...
SOME SORT OF ATMOSPHERIC ANOMALY, MAYBE...?
BUT WHAT ON EARTH COULD POSSIBLY--
UNGGHH--!
UNIVERSITY HOSPITAL; BALTIMORE, MD
OH JEEZUS...!
THE POWER'S OUT--?!
THE 405 FREEWAY; LOS ANGELES, CA
FER GOD'S SAKE--! MY CAR JUST DIED!
MINE, TOO...!
LIKE TRAFFIC AIN'T BAD ENOUGH--!
WHAT HAPPENED?!

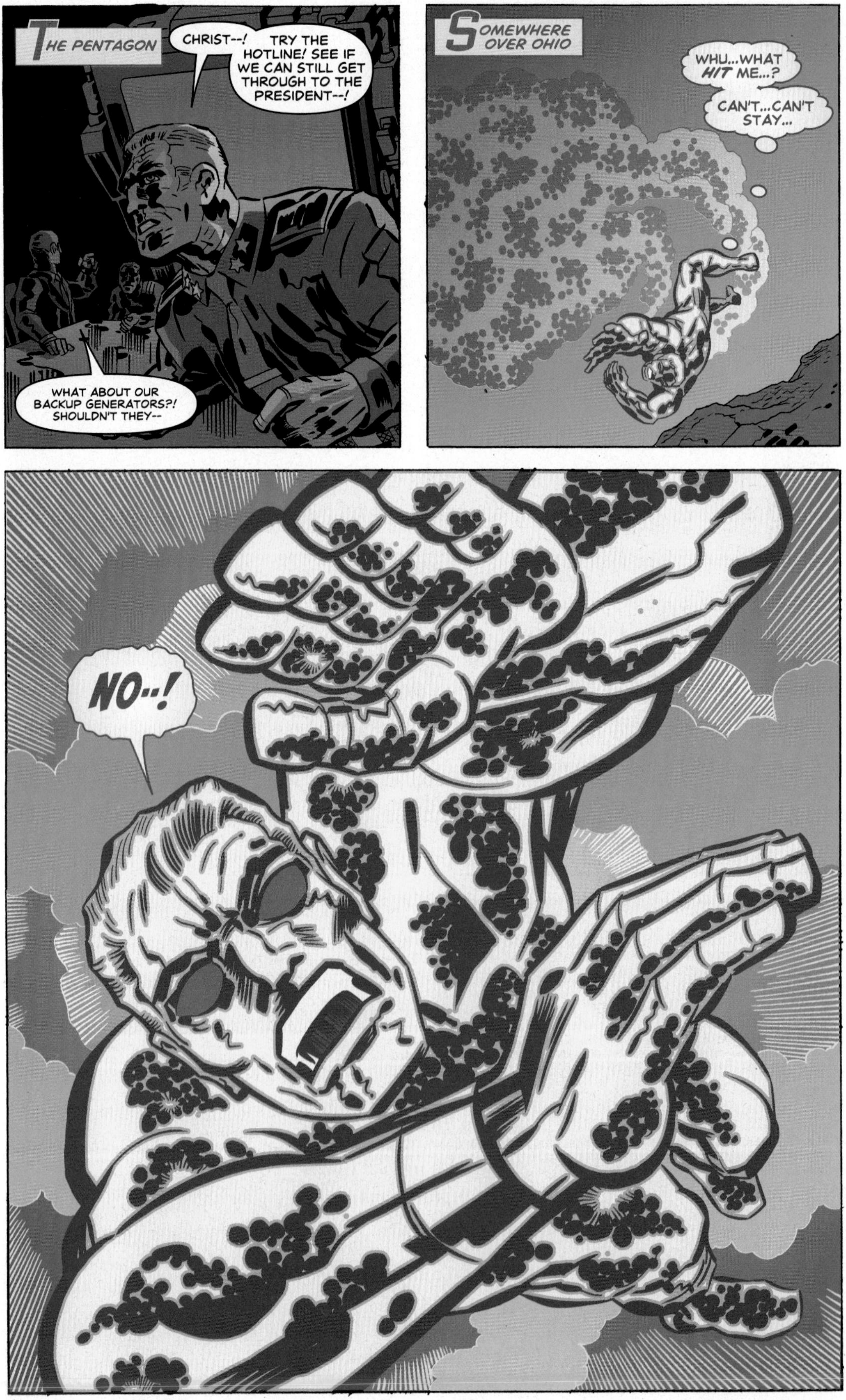
THE PENTAGON
CHRIST--!
TRY THE HOTLINE! SEE IF WE CAN STILL GET THROUGH TO THE PRESIDENT--!
WHAT ABOUT OUR BACKUP GENERATORS?! SHOULDN'T THEY--
SOMEWHERE OVER OHIO
WHU...WHAT HIT ME...?
CAN'T...CAN'T STAY...
NO--!

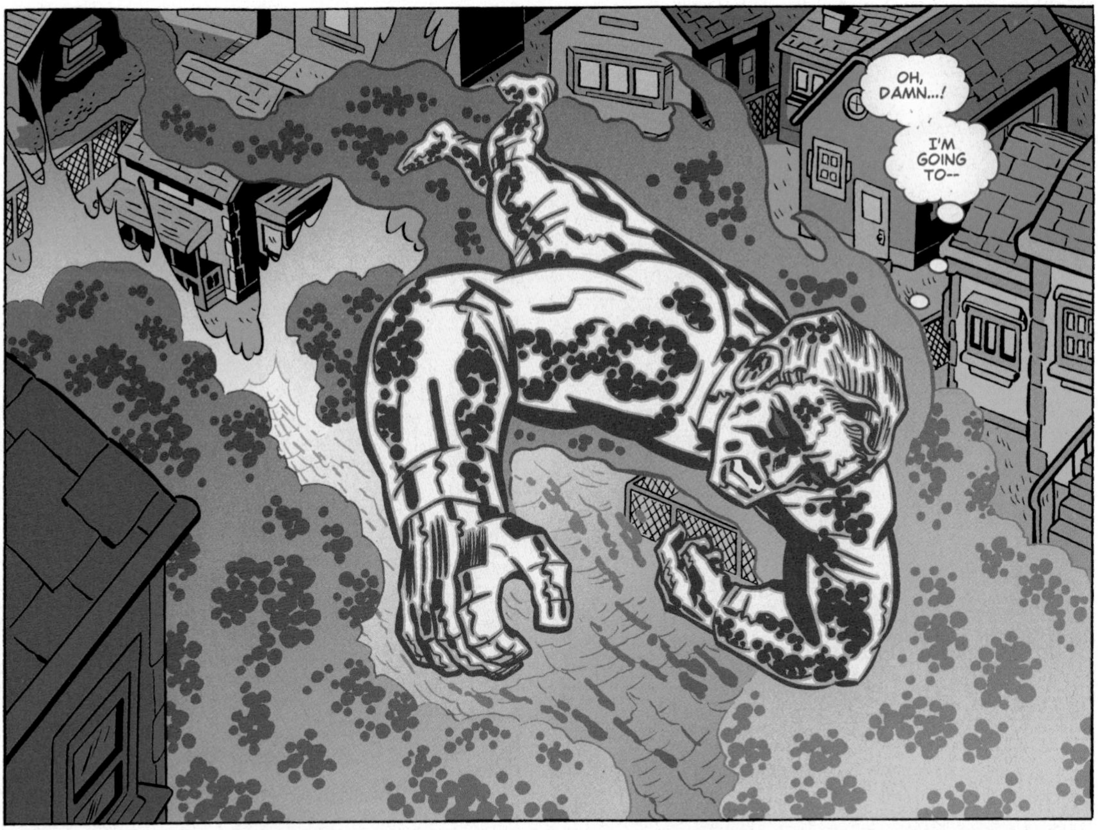
OH, DAMN...!
I'M GOING TO--

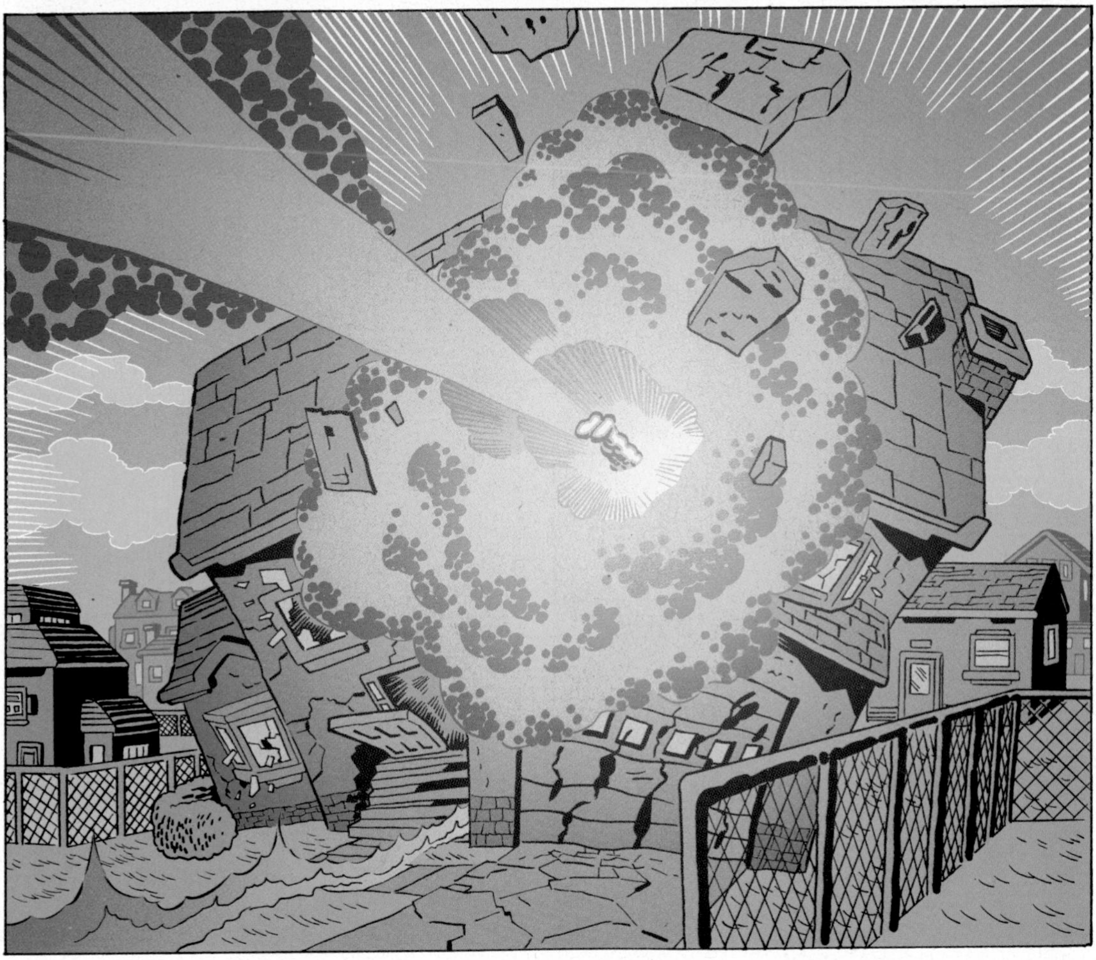

COLORADO
SIR, WE HAVE SAT-WIDE CONFIRMATION... NORTH AMERICA HAS GONE DARK.
ESTIMATES ARE ANOTHER TWO MINUTES...
EXCELLENT.
INITIATE LAUNCH!
COMMANDER... PREPARE FOR LIFTOFF...
T-MINUS FIVE... FOUR... THREE...
HERE GOES NOTHING...!
...TWO...ONE...
ALL THRUSTERS-- IGNITE FULL!
LIFTOFF!

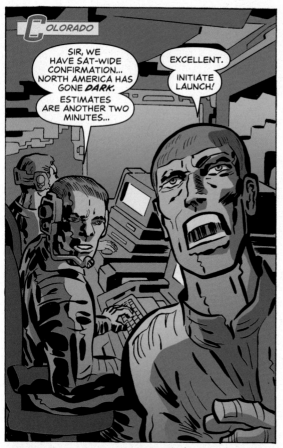

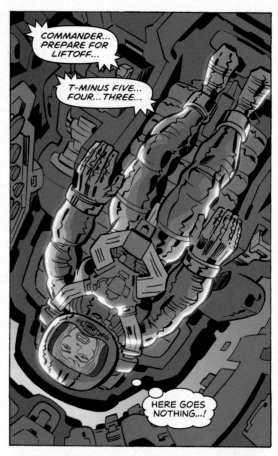

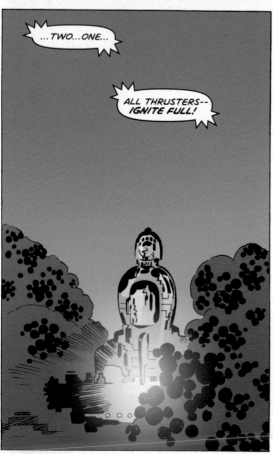

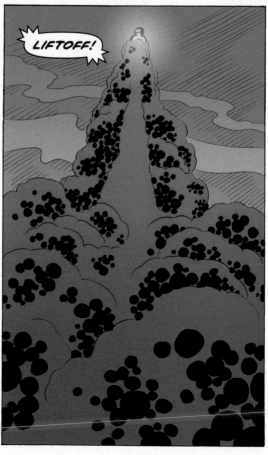

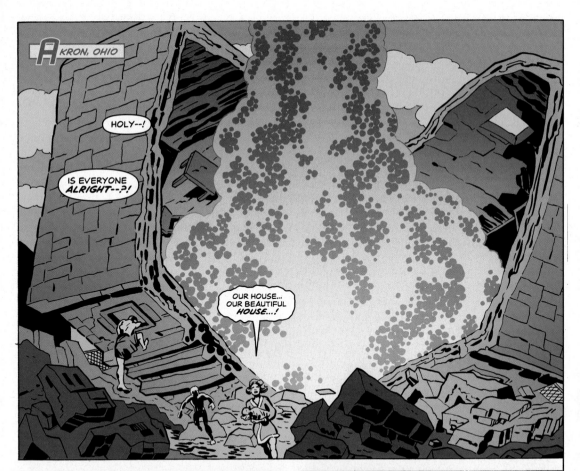

AKRON, OHIO

HOLY--!

IS EVERYONE ALRIGHT--?!

OUR HOUSE... OUR BEAUTIFUL HOUSE...!

I'M...

...S-SORRY... I...

...I COULDN'T...

HHNNN...

--⌖

WELL, WELL, WELL...

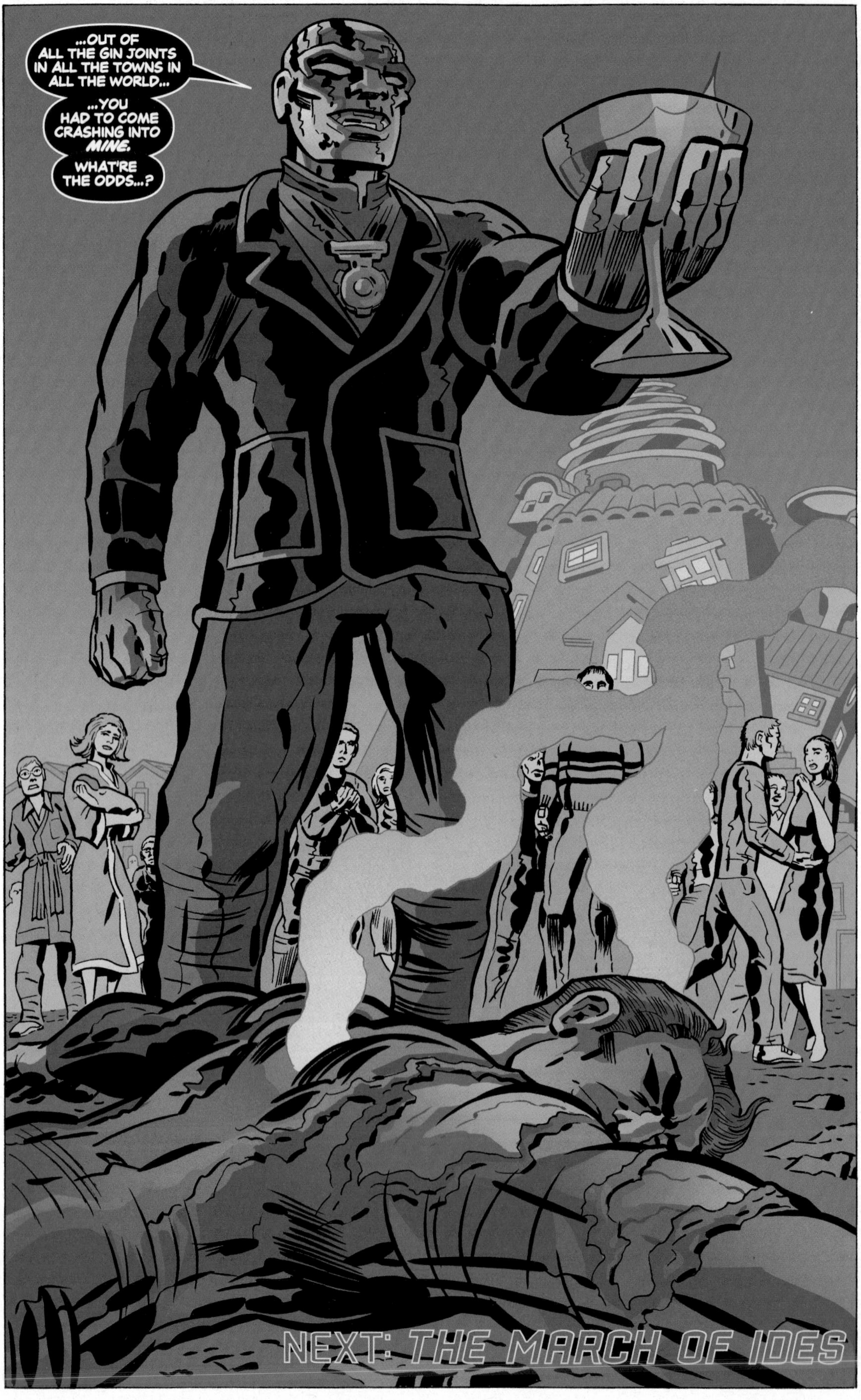
...OUT OF ALL THE GIN JOINTS IN ALL THE TOWNS IN ALL THE WORLD...
...YOU HAD TO COME CRASHING INTO *MINE.*
WHAT'RE THE ODDS...?
NEXT: *THE MARCH OF IDES*

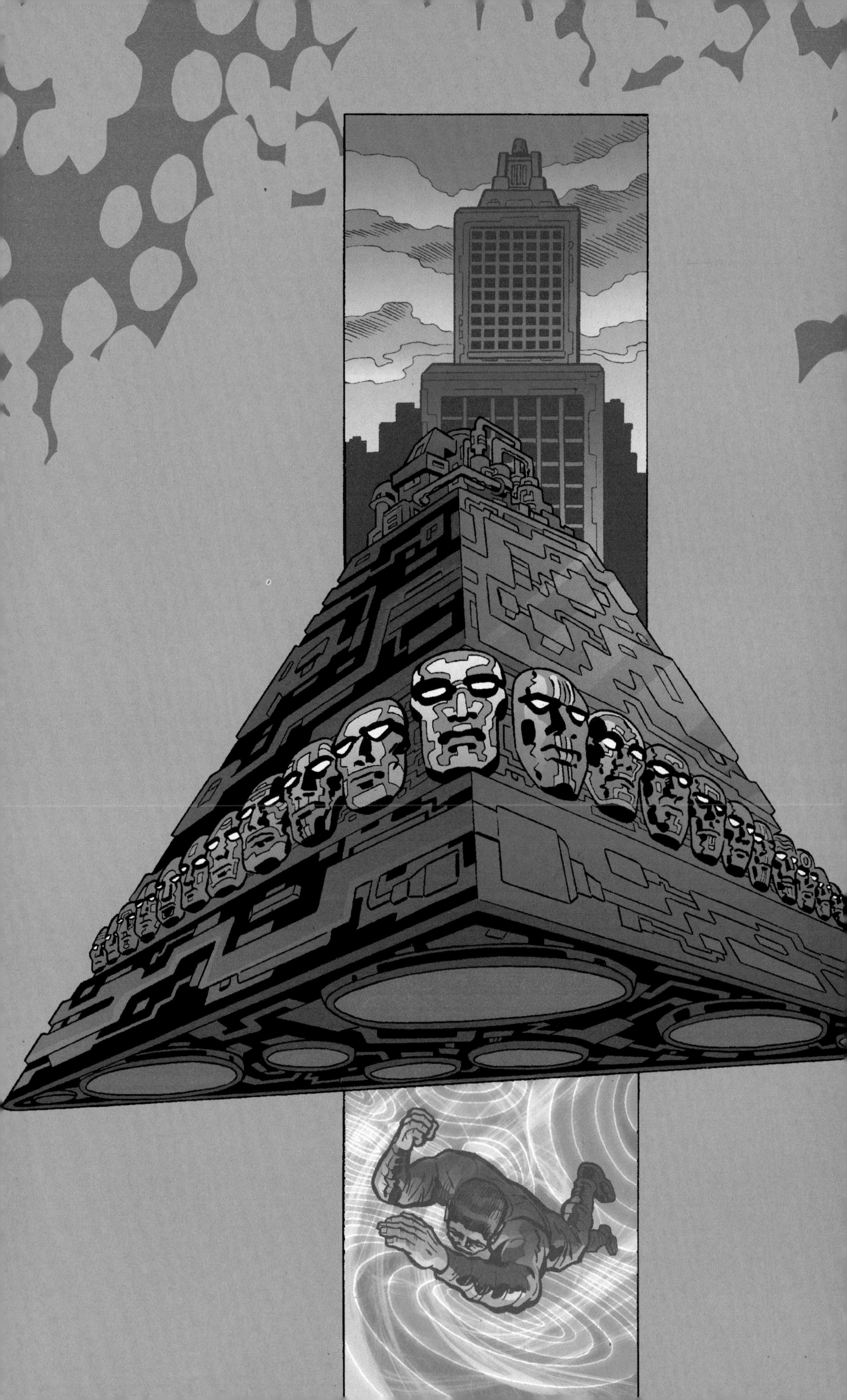

BOOK TEN:

THE MARCH OF IDES

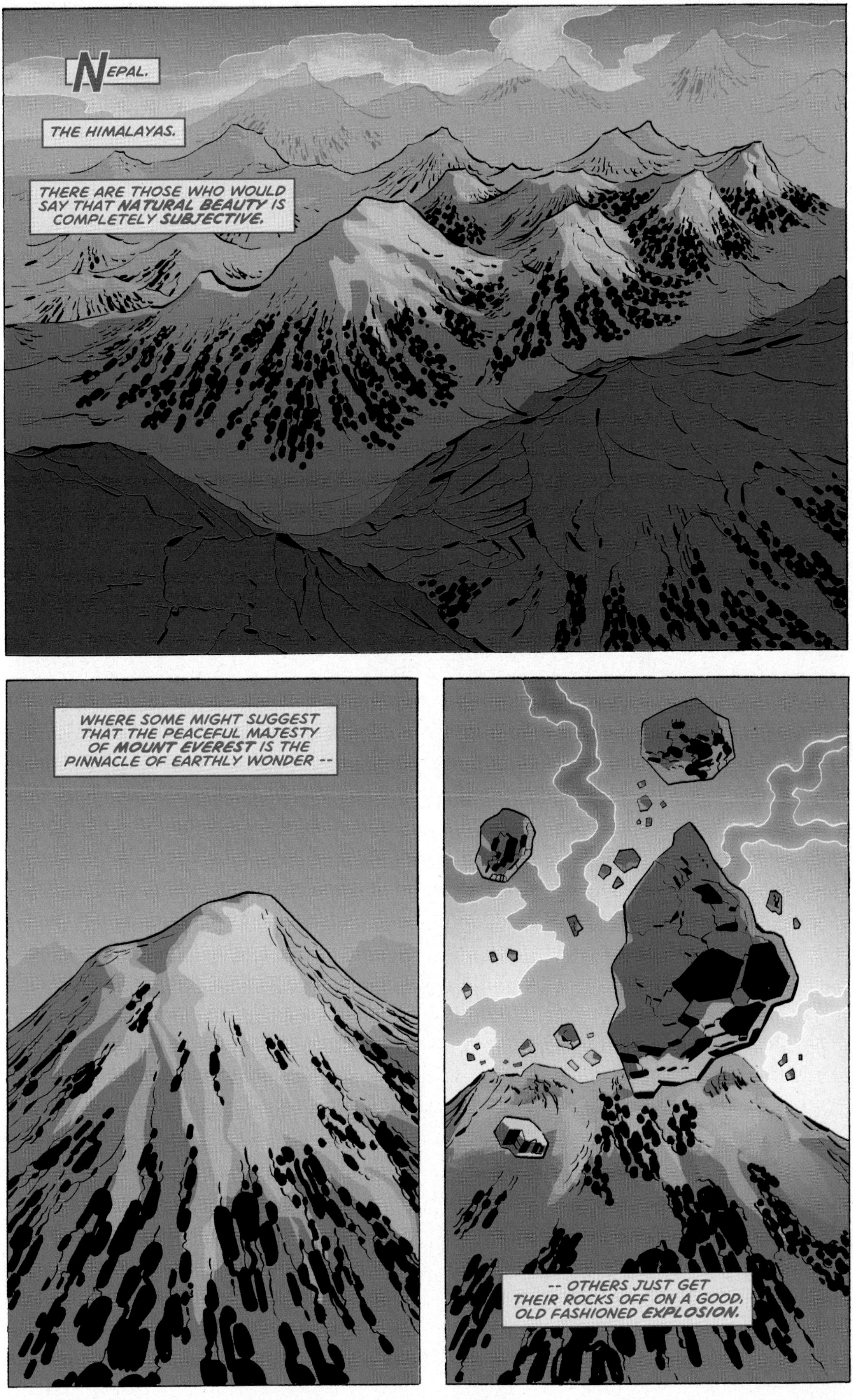
NEPAL.
THE HIMALAYAS.
THERE ARE THOSE WHO WOULD SAY THAT NATURAL BEAUTY IS COMPLETELY SUBJECTIVE.
WHERE SOME MIGHT SUGGEST THAT THE PEACEFUL MAJESTY OF MOUNT EVEREST IS THE PINNACLE OF EARTHLY WONDER --
-- OTHERS JUST GET THEIR ROCKS OFF ON A GOOD, OLD FASHIONED EXPLOSION.

AND AS THE HIGHEST PEAK ON THE PLANET DISINTEGRATES INTO *DUST*...

... *ANOTHER* PHENOMENON IS REVEALED. BEAUTIFUL IN ITS *OWN* WAY.

ALTHOUGH ANY "NATURAL" ASPECTS MIGHT BE SUBJECT TO DEBATE.

AND FROM DEEP WITHIN THIS ONCE PROUD EMBODIMENT OF MANKIND'S ASPIRATIONS TO CLIMB EVER HIGHER --

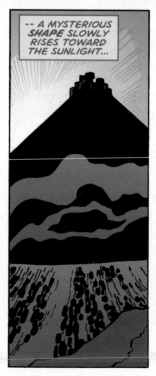

-- A MYSTERIOUS *SHAPE* SLOWLY RISES TOWARD THE SUNLIGHT...

... AND BEGINS ITS LONG, PREPROGRAMMED JOURNEY.

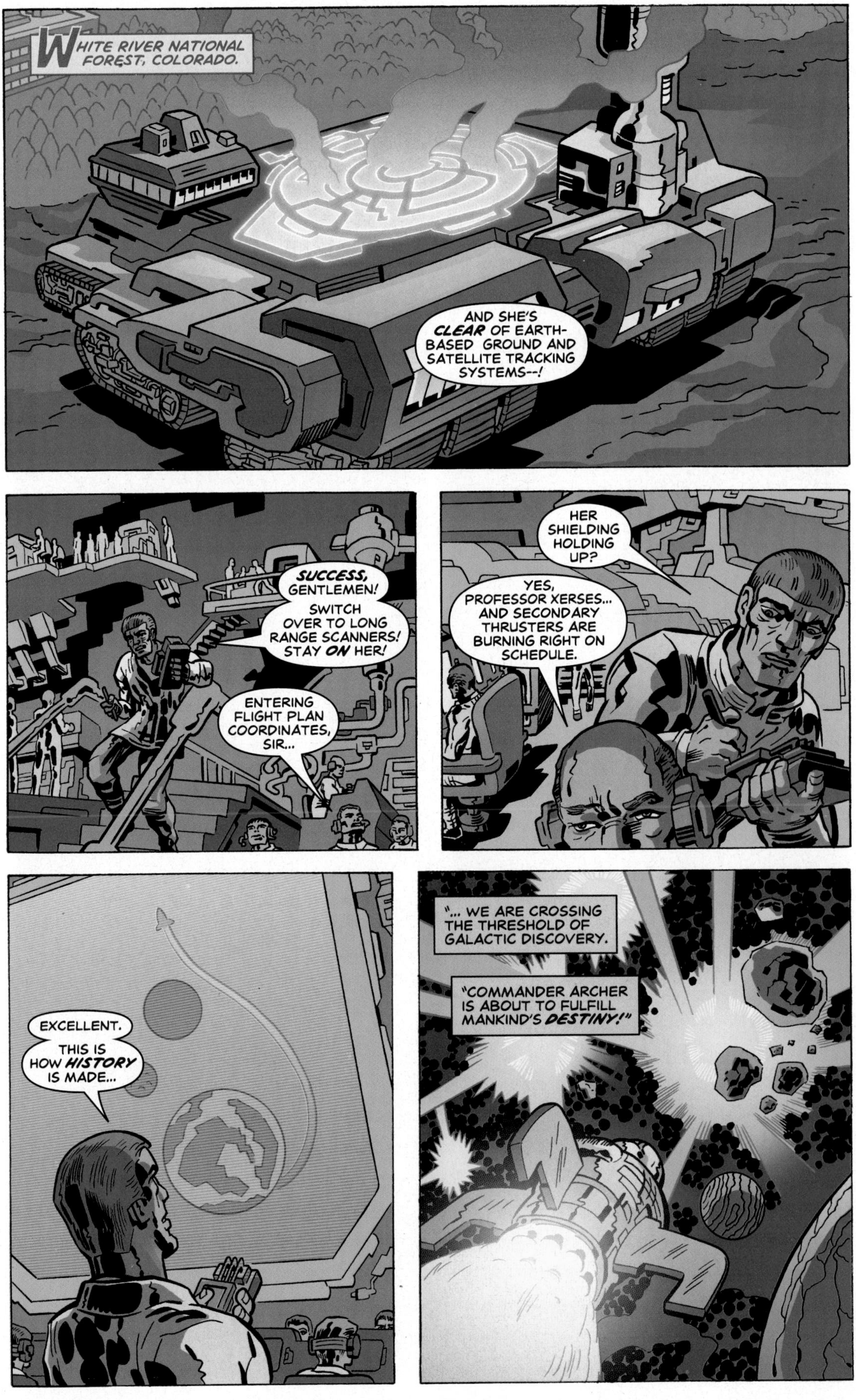
WHITE RIVER NATIONAL FOREST, COLORADO.
AND SHE'S CLEAR OF EARTH-BASED GROUND AND SATELLITE TRACKING SYSTEMS--!
SUCCESS, GENTLEMEN!
SWITCH OVER TO LONG RANGE SCANNERS! STAY ON HER!
ENTERING FLIGHT PLAN COORDINATES, SIR...
HER SHIELDING HOLDING UP?
YES, PROFESSOR XERSES... AND SECONDARY THRUSTERS ARE BURNING RIGHT ON SCHEDULE.
EXCELLENT.
THIS IS HOW HISTORY IS MADE...
"... WE ARE CROSSING THE THRESHOLD OF GALACTIC DISCOVERY.
"COMMANDER ARCHER IS ABOUT TO FULFILL MANKIND'S DESTINY!"

NEW YORK CITY

THE BLACKOUT CONTINUES...

HAS ANYONE HEARD WHAT THE HELL IS *GOING ON* HERE...?

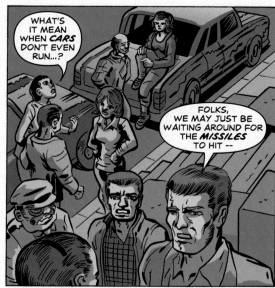

WHAT'S IT MEAN WHEN *CARS* DON'T EVEN RUN...?

FOLKS, WE MAY JUST BE WAITING AROUND FOR THE *MISSILES* TO HIT --

YOU'RE CRAZY! THIS ISN'T "*THE DAY AFTER*"...!

MAYBE IT'S GOT SOMETHING TO DO WITH THAT FREAKY *INFINITY* BUILDING --

AND INSIDE "THAT FREAKY INFINITY BUILDING"...

WELL, *THIS* IS EXCITING...!

MAXIM... STILL NOT PICKING UP ADAM...?

NOT ON *ANY* TELEPATHIC FREQUENCY. IT'S AS THOUGH I'M BEING *BLOCKED* SOMEHOW...

MAYBE CHANGE YOUR *DIET*, SPACE DOG --

ANGIE, *PLEASE.* NOT NOW.

WITHOUT POWER... WE CAN'T TRACK ADAM ELECTRONICALLY. AND I HAVE A FEELING WE *NEED* HIM...!

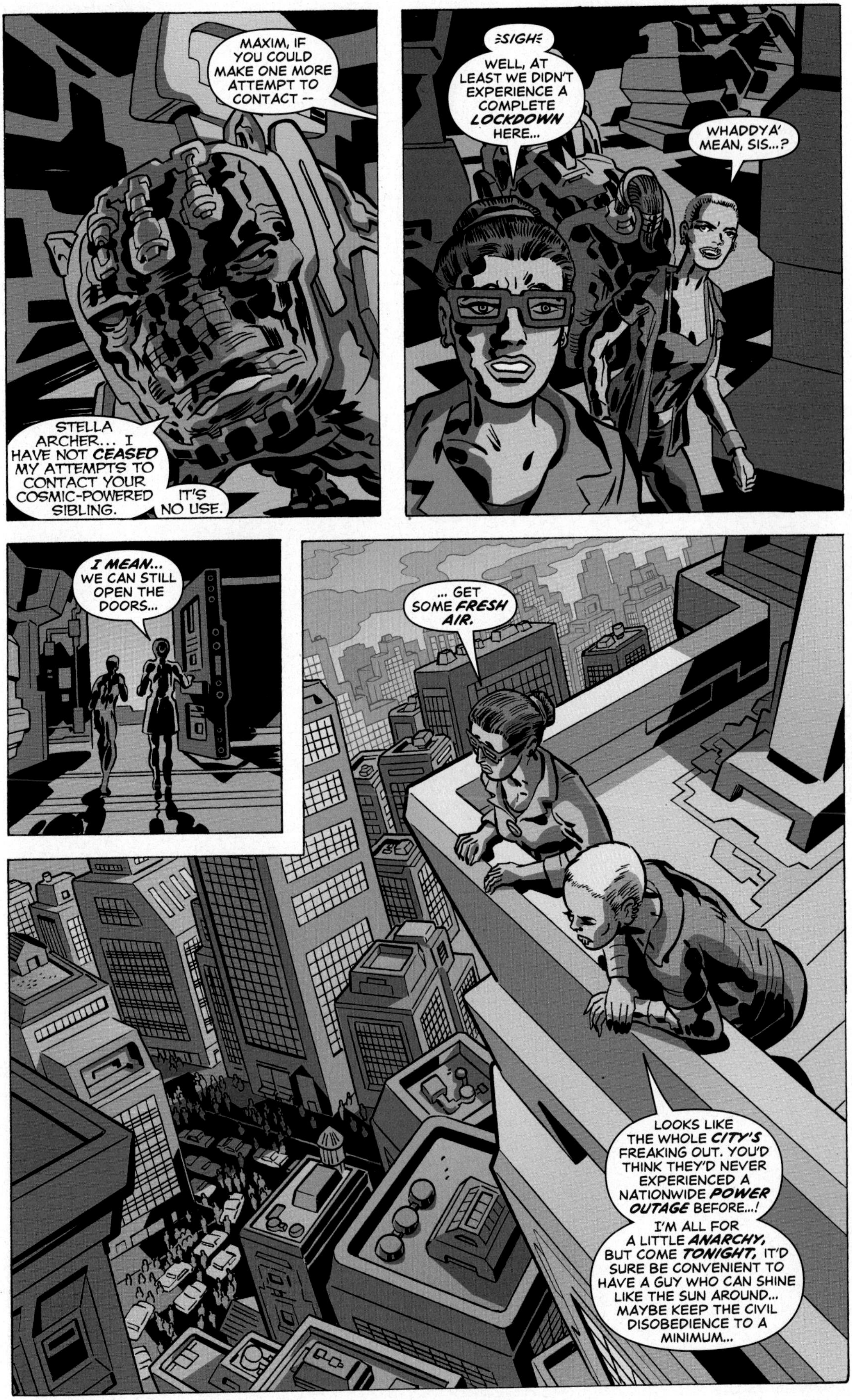
MAXIM, IF YOU COULD MAKE ONE MORE ATTEMPT TO CONTACT --
STELLA ARCHER... I HAVE NOT CEASED MY ATTEMPTS TO CONTACT YOUR COSMIC-POWERED SIBLING.
IT'S NO USE.
SIGH
WELL, AT LEAST WE DIDN'T EXPERIENCE A COMPLETE LOCKDOWN HERE...
WHADDYA' MEAN, SIS...?
I MEAN... WE CAN STILL OPEN THE DOORS...
... GET SOME FRESH AIR.
LOOKS LIKE THE WHOLE CITY'S FREAKING OUT. YOU'D THINK THEY'D NEVER EXPERIENCED A NATIONWIDE POWER OUTAGE BEFORE...!
I'M ALL FOR A LITTLE ANARCHY, BUT COME TONIGHT, IT'D SURE BE CONVENIENT TO HAVE A GUY WHO CAN SHINE LIKE THE SUN AROUND... MAYBE KEEP THE CIVIL DISOBEDIENCE TO A MINIMUM...

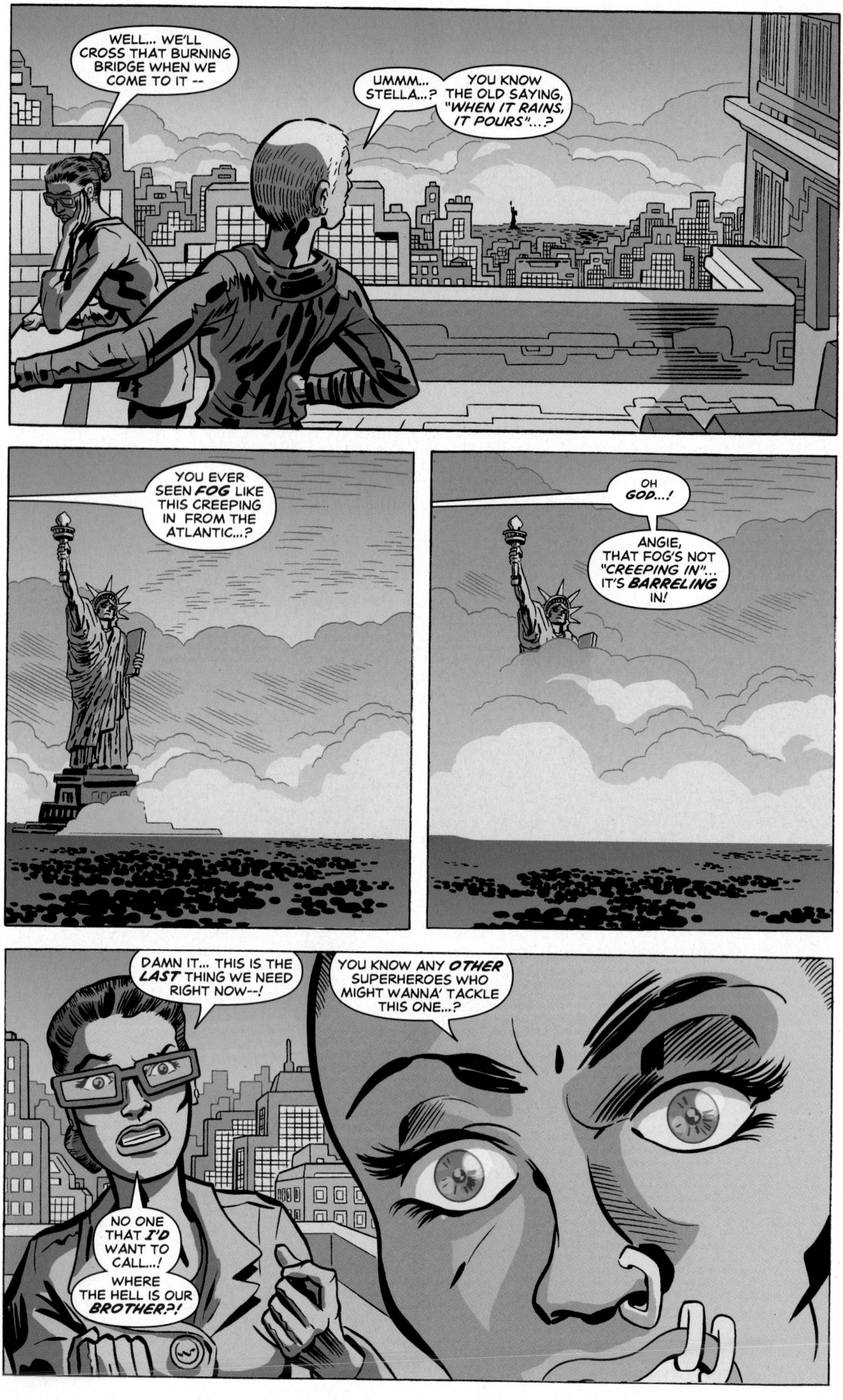
WELL... WE'LL CROSS THAT BURNING BRIDGE WHEN WE COME TO IT --
UMMM... STELLA...?
YOU KNOW THE OLD SAYING, "*WHEN IT RAINS, IT POURS*"...?
YOU EVER SEEN *FOG* LIKE THIS CREEPING IN FROM THE ATLANTIC...?
OH *GOD*...!
ANGIE, THAT FOG'S NOT "*CREEPING IN*"... IT'S *BARRELING* IN!
DAMN IT... THIS IS THE *LAST* THING WE NEED RIGHT NOW--!
YOU KNOW ANY *OTHER* SUPERHEROES WHO MIGHT WANNA' TACKLE THIS ONE...?
NO ONE THAT *I'D* WANT TO CALL...!
WHERE THE HELL IS OUR *BROTHER?!*

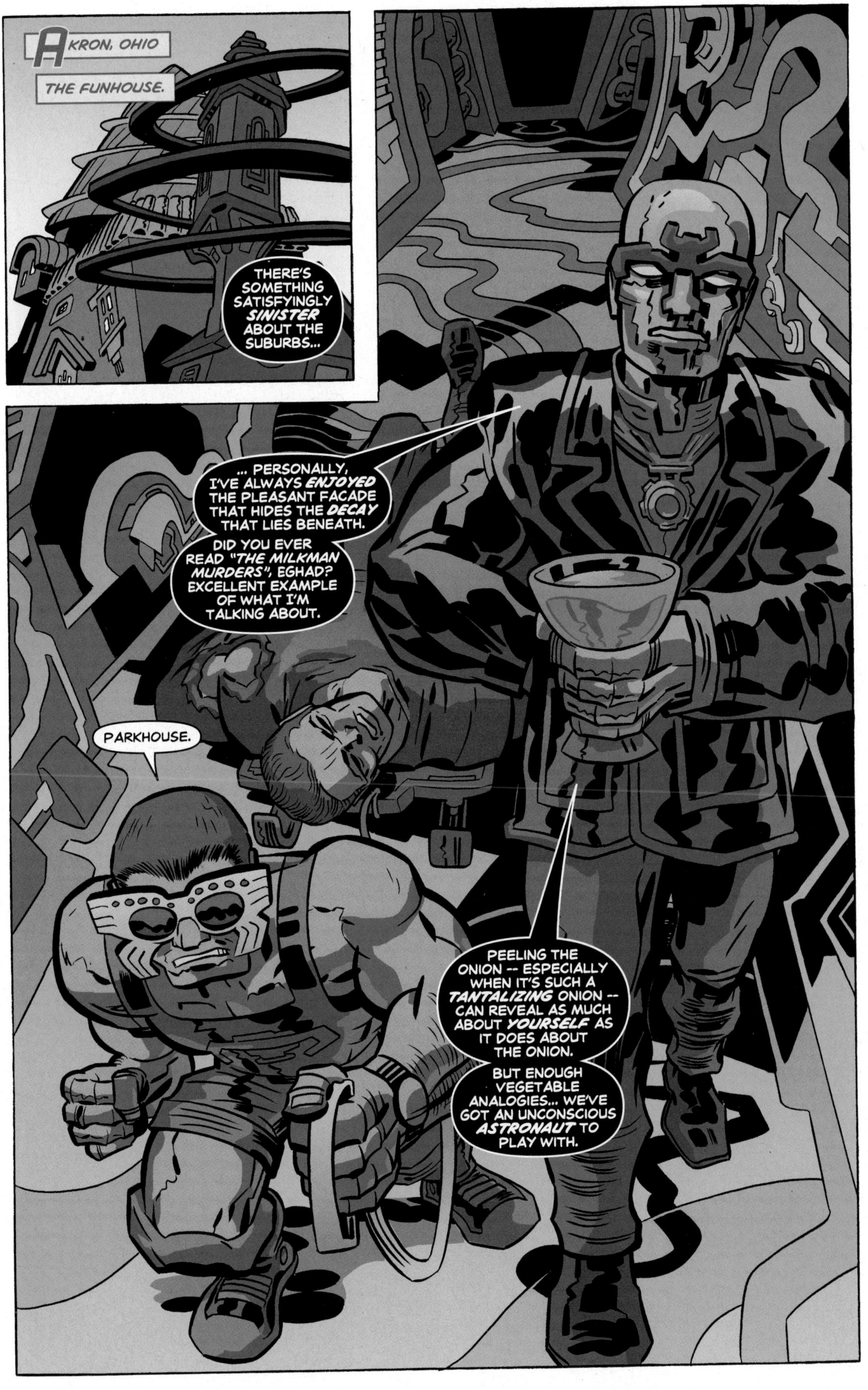
AKRON, OHIO
THE FUNHOUSE.
THERE'S SOMETHING SATISFYINGLY SINISTER ABOUT THE SUBURBS...
... PERSONALLY, I'VE ALWAYS ENJOYED THE PLEASANT FACADE THAT HIDES THE DECAY THAT LIES BENEATH.
DID YOU EVER READ "THE MILKMAN MURDERS", EGHAD? EXCELLENT EXAMPLE OF WHAT I'M TALKING ABOUT.
PARKHOUSE.
PEELING THE ONION -- ESPECIALLY WHEN IT'S SUCH A TANTALIZING ONION -- CAN REVEAL AS MUCH ABOUT YOURSELF AS IT DOES ABOUT THE ONION.
BUT ENOUGH VEGETABLE ANALOGIES... WE'VE GOT AN UNCONSCIOUS ASTRONAUT TO PLAY WITH.

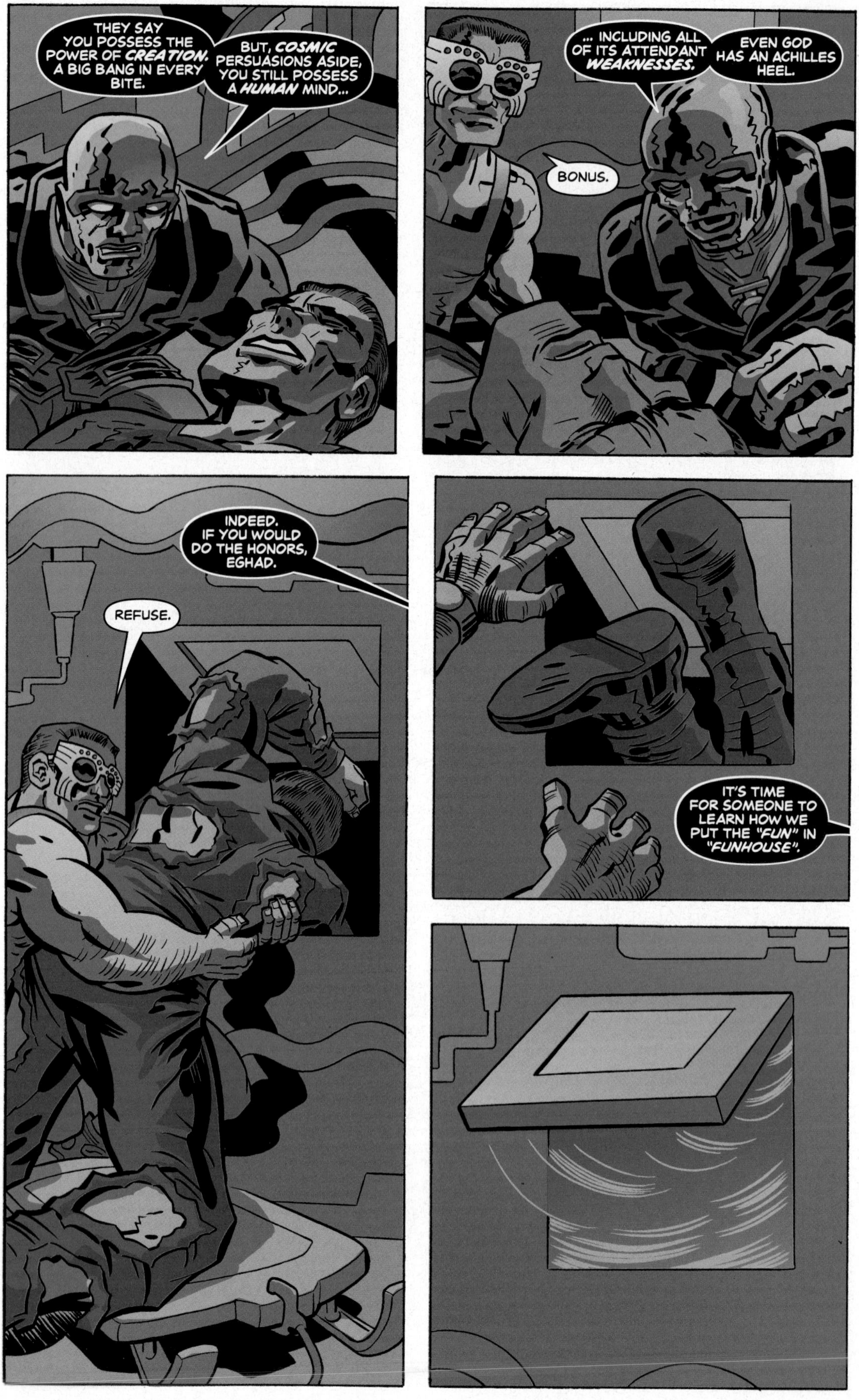
THEY SAY YOU POSSESS THE POWER OF CREATION. A BIG BANG IN EVERY BITE.
BUT, COSMIC PERSUASIONS ASIDE, YOU STILL POSSESS A HUMAN MIND...
... INCLUDING ALL OF ITS ATTENDANT WEAKNESSES.
EVEN GOD HAS AN ACHILLES HEEL.
BONUS.
INDEED. IF YOU WOULD DO THE HONORS, EGHAD.
REFUSE.
IT'S TIME FOR SOMEONE TO LEARN HOW WE PUT THE "FUN" IN "FUNHOUSE".

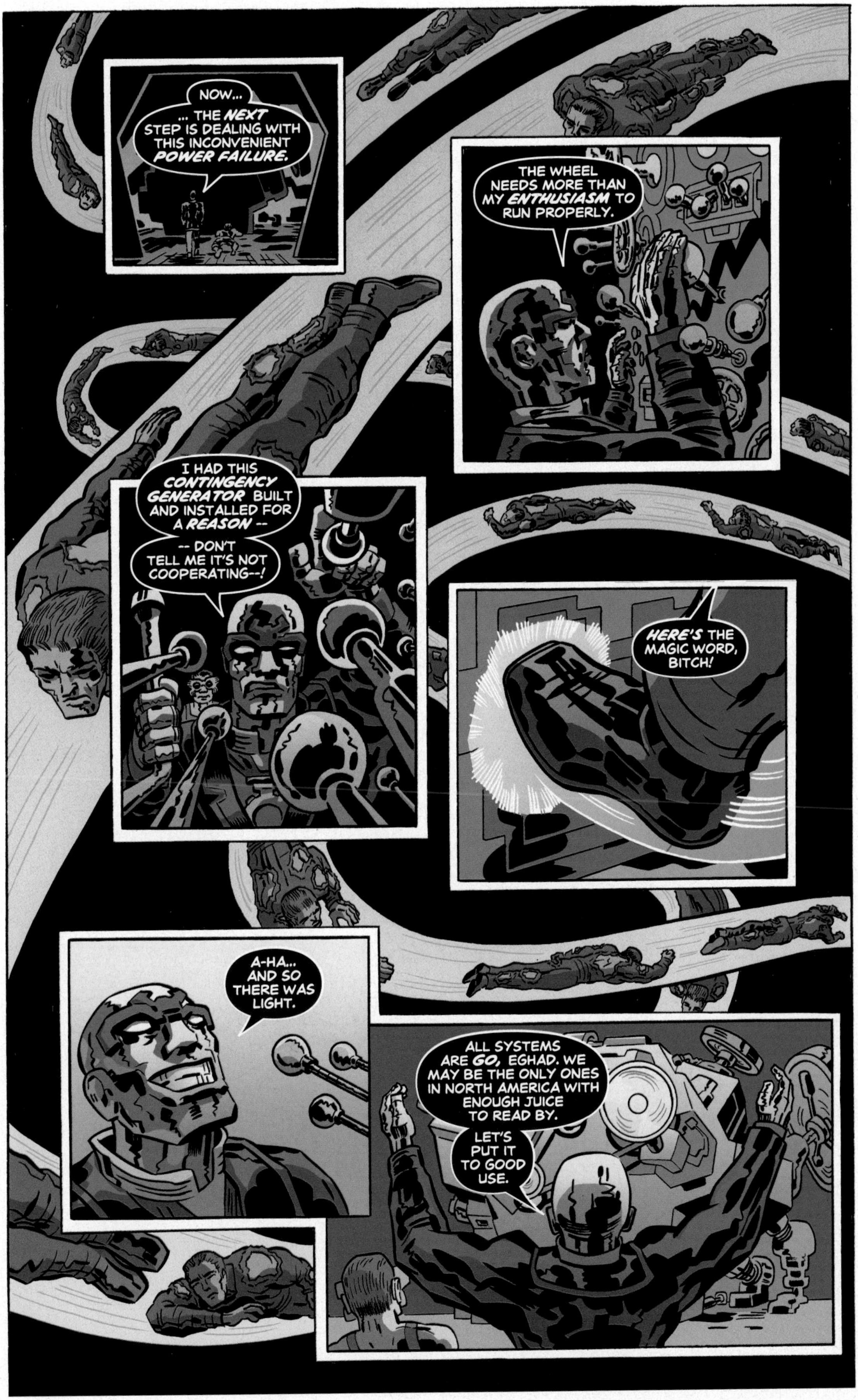
NOW...
... THE NEXT STEP IS DEALING WITH THIS INCONVENIENT POWER FAILURE.
THE WHEEL NEEDS MORE THAN MY ENTHUSIASM TO RUN PROPERLY.
I HAD THIS CONTINGENCY GENERATOR BUILT AND INSTALLED FOR A REASON --
-- DON'T TELL ME IT'S NOT COOPERATING--!
HERE'S THE MAGIC WORD, BITCH!
A-HA... AND SO THERE WAS LIGHT.
ALL SYSTEMS ARE GO, EGHAD. WE MAY BE THE ONLY ONES IN NORTH AMERICA WITH ENOUGH JUICE TO READ BY.
LET'S PUT IT TO GOOD USE.

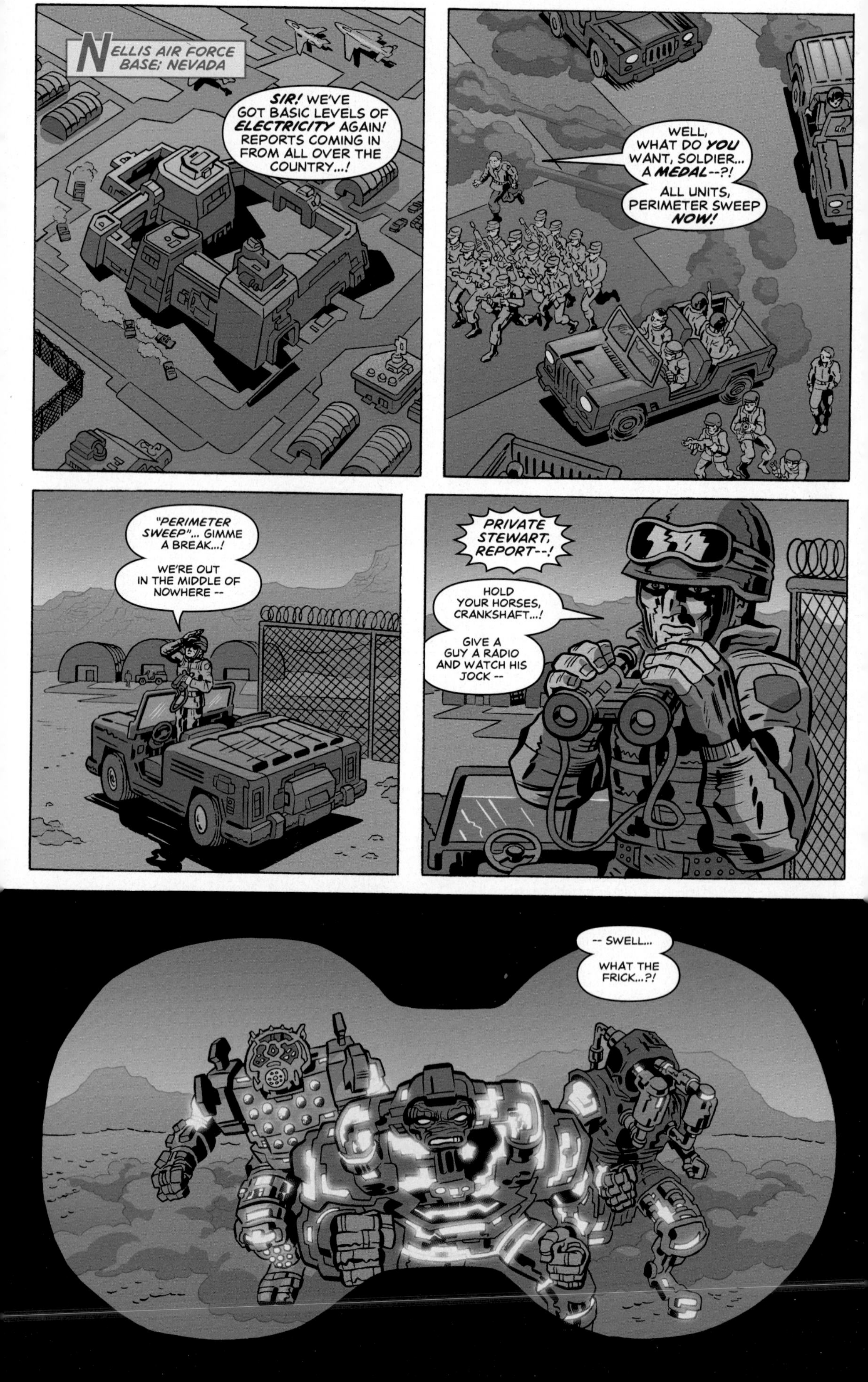
NELLIS AIR FORCE BASE; NEVADA
SIR! WE'VE GOT BASIC LEVELS OF ELECTRICITY AGAIN! REPORTS COMING IN FROM ALL OVER THE COUNTRY...!
WELL, WHAT DO YOU WANT, SOLDIER... A MEDAL--?!
ALL UNITS, PERIMETER SWEEP NOW!
"PERIMETER SWEEP"... GIMME A BREAK...!
WE'RE OUT IN THE MIDDLE OF NOWHERE --
PRIVATE STEWART, REPORT--!
HOLD YOUR HORSES, CRANKSHAFT...!
GIVE A GUY A RADIO AND WATCH HIS JOCK --
-- SWELL...
WHAT THE FRICK...?!

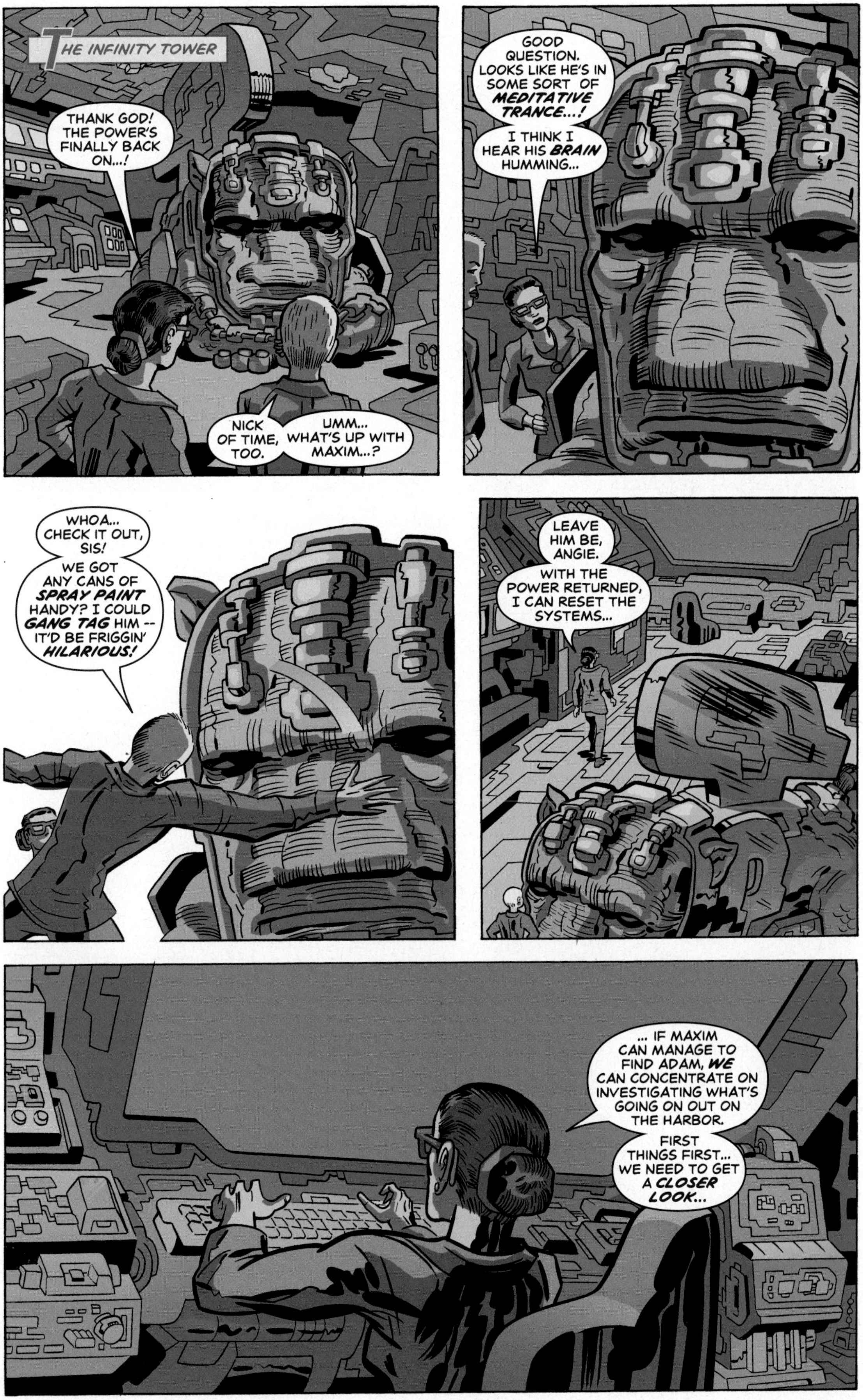
THE INFINITY TOWER
THANK GOD! THE POWER'S FINALLY BACK ON...!
NICK OF TIME, TOO.
UMM... WHAT'S UP WITH MAXIM...?
GOOD QUESTION. LOOKS LIKE HE'S IN SOME SORT OF MEDITATIVE TRANCE...!
I THINK I HEAR HIS BRAIN HUMMING...
WHOA... CHECK IT OUT, SIS!
WE GOT ANY CANS OF SPRAY PAINT HANDY? I COULD GANG TAG HIM -- IT'D BE FRIGGIN' HILARIOUS!
LEAVE HIM BE, ANGIE.
WITH THE POWER RETURNED, I CAN RESET THE SYSTEMS...
... IF MAXIM CAN MANAGE TO FIND ADAM, WE CAN CONCENTRATE ON INVESTIGATING WHAT'S GOING ON OUT ON THE HARBOR.
FIRST THINGS FIRST... WE NEED TO GET A CLOSER LOOK...

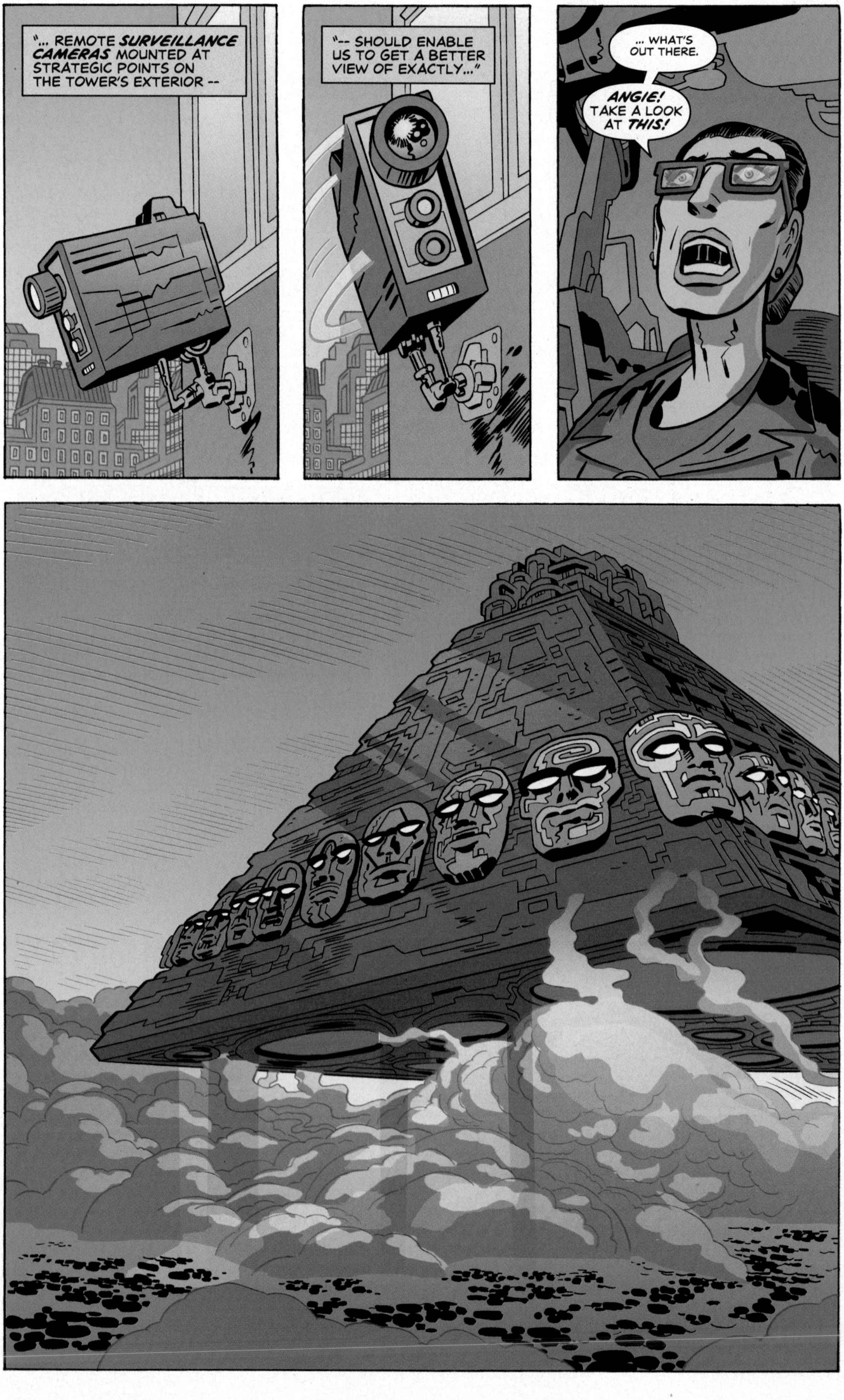
"... REMOTE SURVEILLANCE CAMERAS MOUNTED AT STRATEGIC POINTS ON THE TOWER'S EXTERIOR --
"-- SHOULD ENABLE US TO GET A BETTER VIEW OF EXACTLY..."
... WHAT'S OUT THERE.
ANGIE! TAKE A LOOK AT THIS!

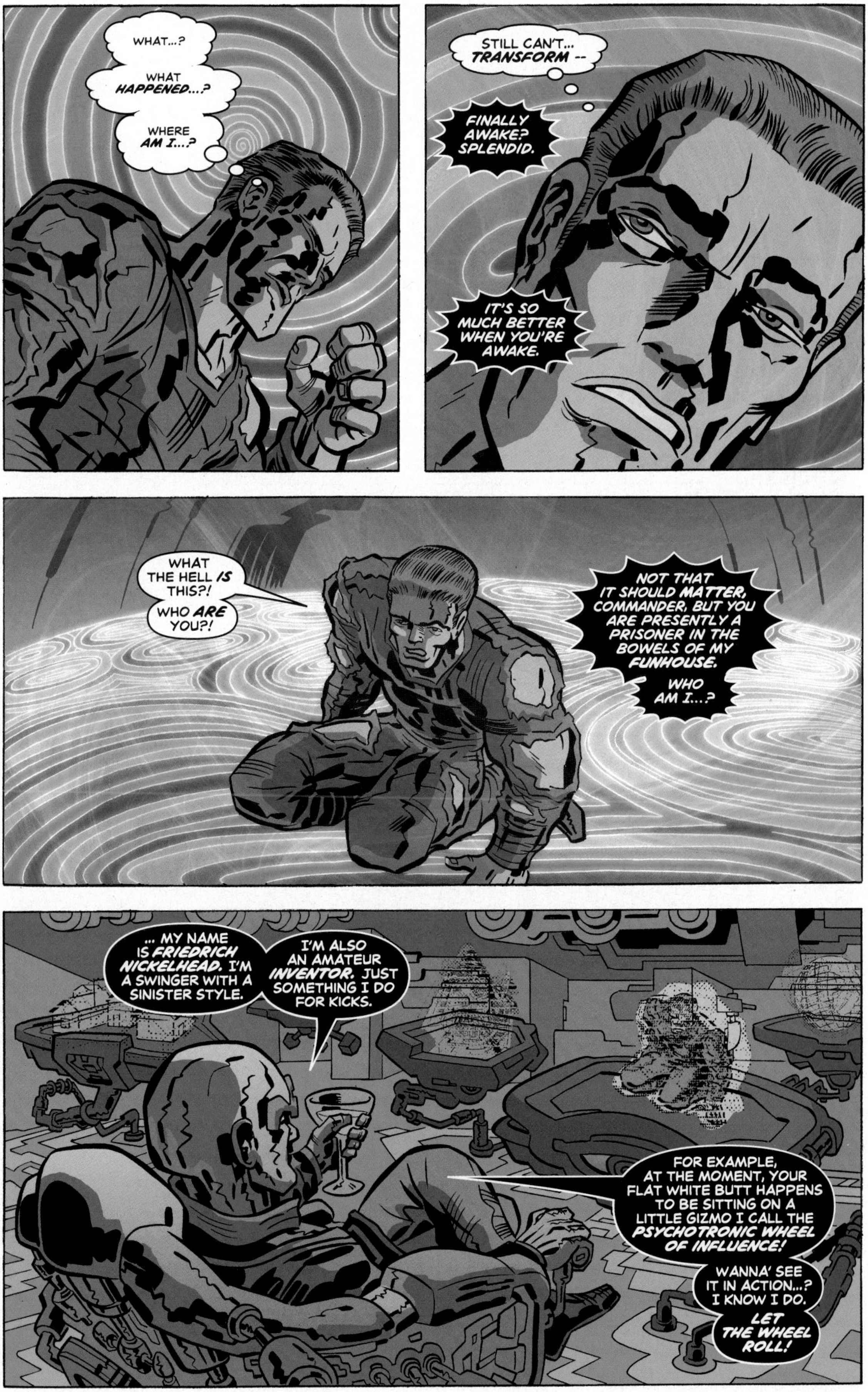
WHAT...?
WHAT HAPPENED...?
WHERE AM I...?
STILL CAN'T... TRANSFORM --
FINALLY AWAKE? SPLENDID.
IT'S SO MUCH BETTER WHEN YOU'RE AWAKE.
WHAT THE HELL IS THIS?!
WHO ARE YOU?!
NOT THAT IT SHOULD MATTER, COMMANDER, BUT YOU ARE PRESENTLY A PRISONER IN THE BOWELS OF MY FUNHOUSE.
WHO AM I...?
... MY NAME IS FRIEDRICH NICKELHEAD. I'M A SWINGER WITH A SINISTER STYLE.
I'M ALSO AN AMATEUR INVENTOR. JUST SOMETHING I DO FOR KICKS.
FOR EXAMPLE, AT THE MOMENT, YOUR FLAT WHITE BUTT HAPPENS TO BE SITTING ON A LITTLE GIZMO I CALL THE PSYCHOTRONIC WHEEL OF INFLUENCE!
WANNA' SEE IT IN ACTION...? I KNOW I DO.
LET THE WHEEL ROLL!

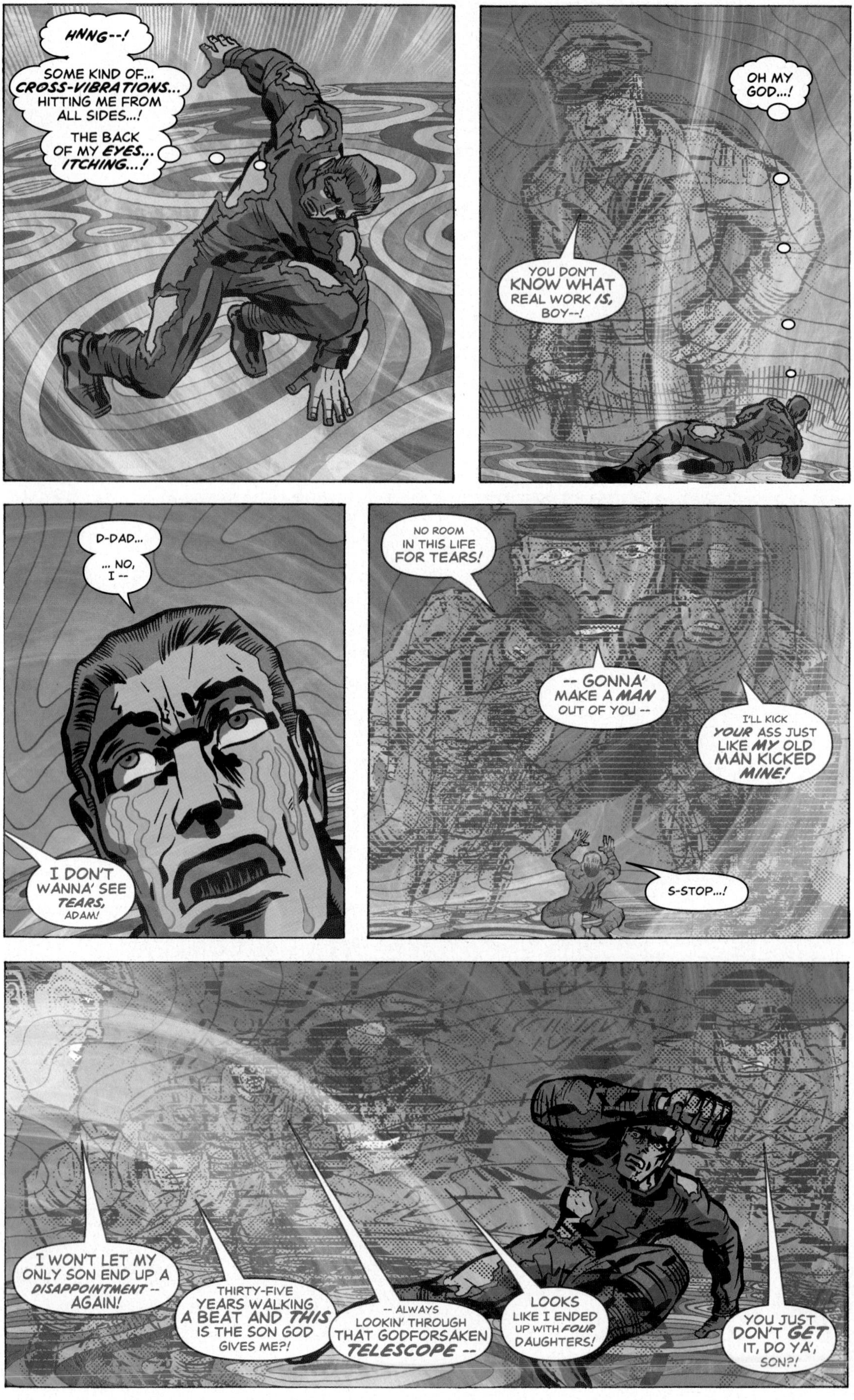
HNNG--!
SOME KIND OF... CROSS-VIBRATIONS... HITTING ME FROM ALL SIDES...!
THE BACK OF MY EYES... ITCHING...!
OH MY GOD...!
YOU DON'T KNOW WHAT REAL WORK IS, BOY--!
D-DAD...
... NO, I --
I DON'T WANNA' SEE TEARS, ADAM!
NO ROOM IN THIS LIFE FOR TEARS!
-- GONNA' MAKE A MAN OUT OF YOU --
I'LL KICK YOUR ASS JUST LIKE MY OLD MAN KICKED MINE!
S-STOP...!
I WON'T LET MY ONLY SON END UP A DISAPPOINTMENT -- AGAIN!
THIRTY-FIVE YEARS WALKING A BEAT AND THIS IS THE SON GOD GIVES ME?!
-- ALWAYS LOOKIN' THROUGH THAT GODFORSAKEN TELESCOPE --
LOOKS LIKE I ENDED UP WITH FOUR DAUGHTERS!
YOU JUST DON'T GET IT, DO YA', SON?!

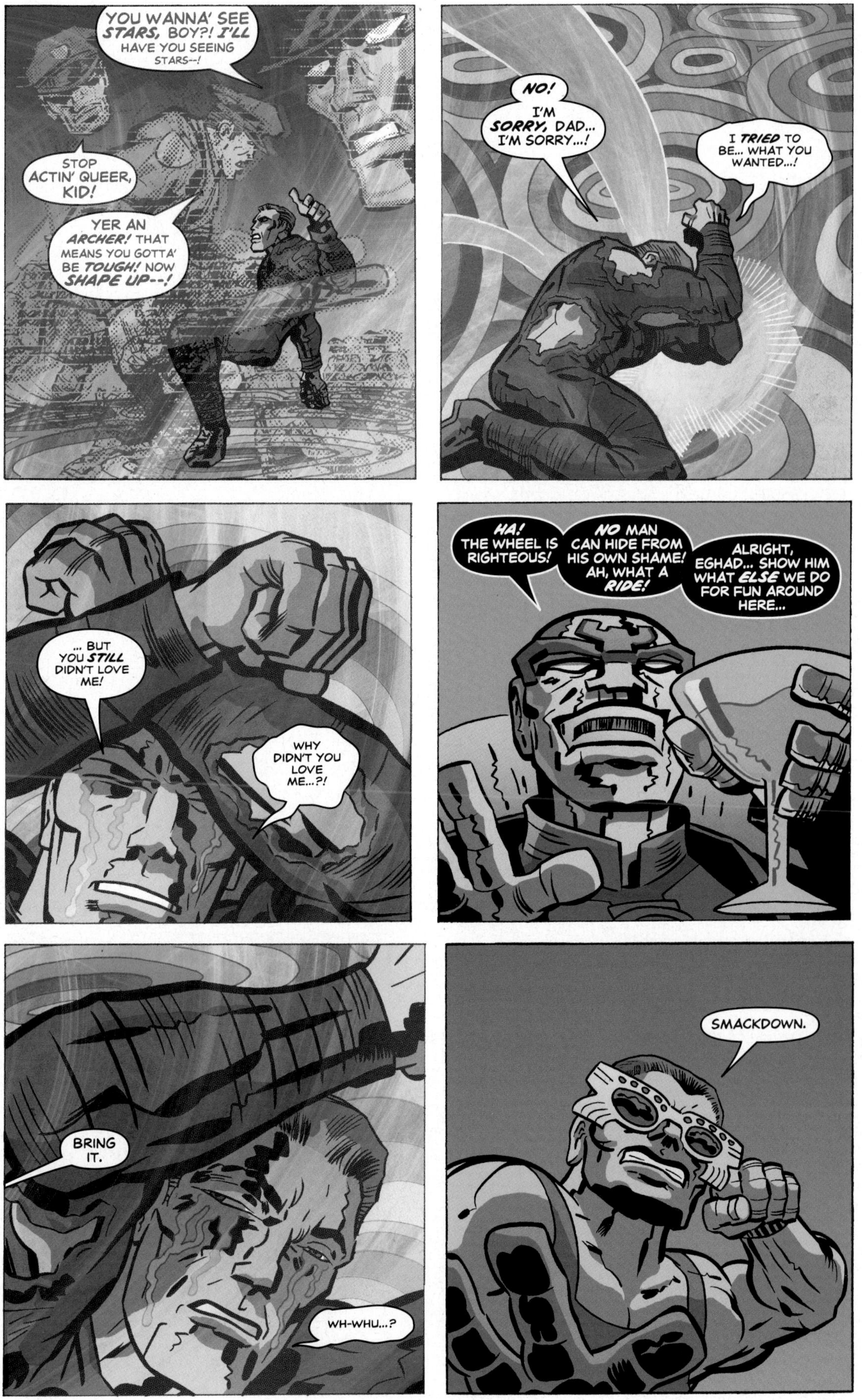
YOU WANNA' SEE STARS, BOY?! I'LL HAVE YOU SEEING STARS--!
STOP ACTIN' QUEER, KID!
YER AN ARCHER! THAT MEANS YOU GOTTA' BE TOUGH! NOW SHAPE UP--!
NO!
I'M SORRY, DAD... I'M SORRY...!
I TRIED TO BE... WHAT YOU WANTED...!
... BUT YOU STILL DIDN'T LOVE ME!
WHY DIDN'T YOU LOVE ME...?!
HA! THE WHEEL IS RIGHTEOUS!
NO MAN CAN HIDE FROM HIS OWN SHAME! AH, WHAT A RIDE!
ALRIGHT, EGHAD... SHOW HIM WHAT ELSE WE DO FOR FUN AROUND HERE...
BRING IT.
WH-WHU...?
SMACKDOWN.

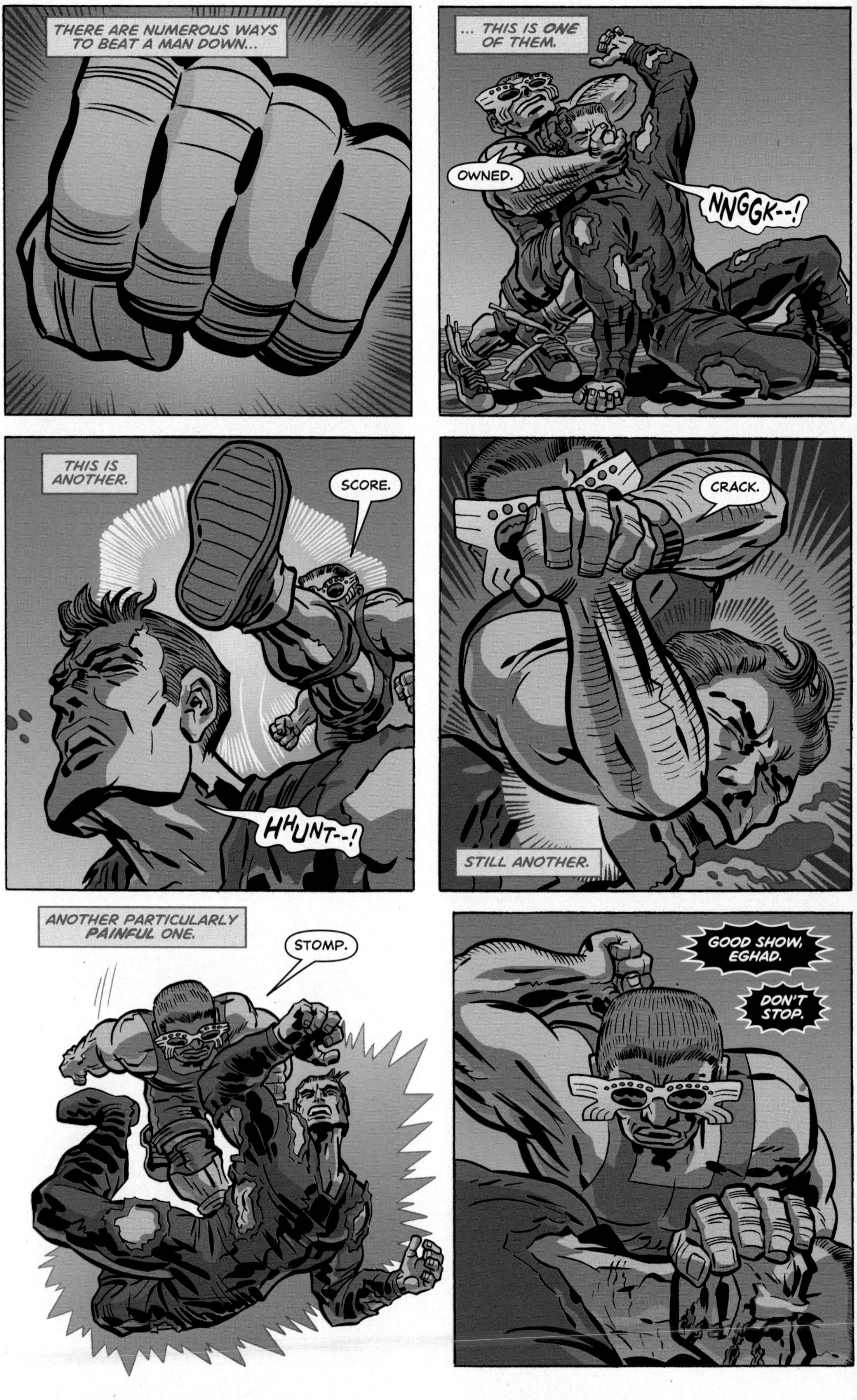
THERE ARE NUMEROUS WAYS TO BEAT A MAN DOWN...
... THIS IS ONE OF THEM.
OWNED.
NNGGK--!
THIS IS ANOTHER.
SCORE.
HHUNT--!
CRACK.
STILL ANOTHER.
ANOTHER PARTICULARLY PAINFUL ONE.
STOMP.
GOOD SHOW, EGHAD.
DON'T STOP.

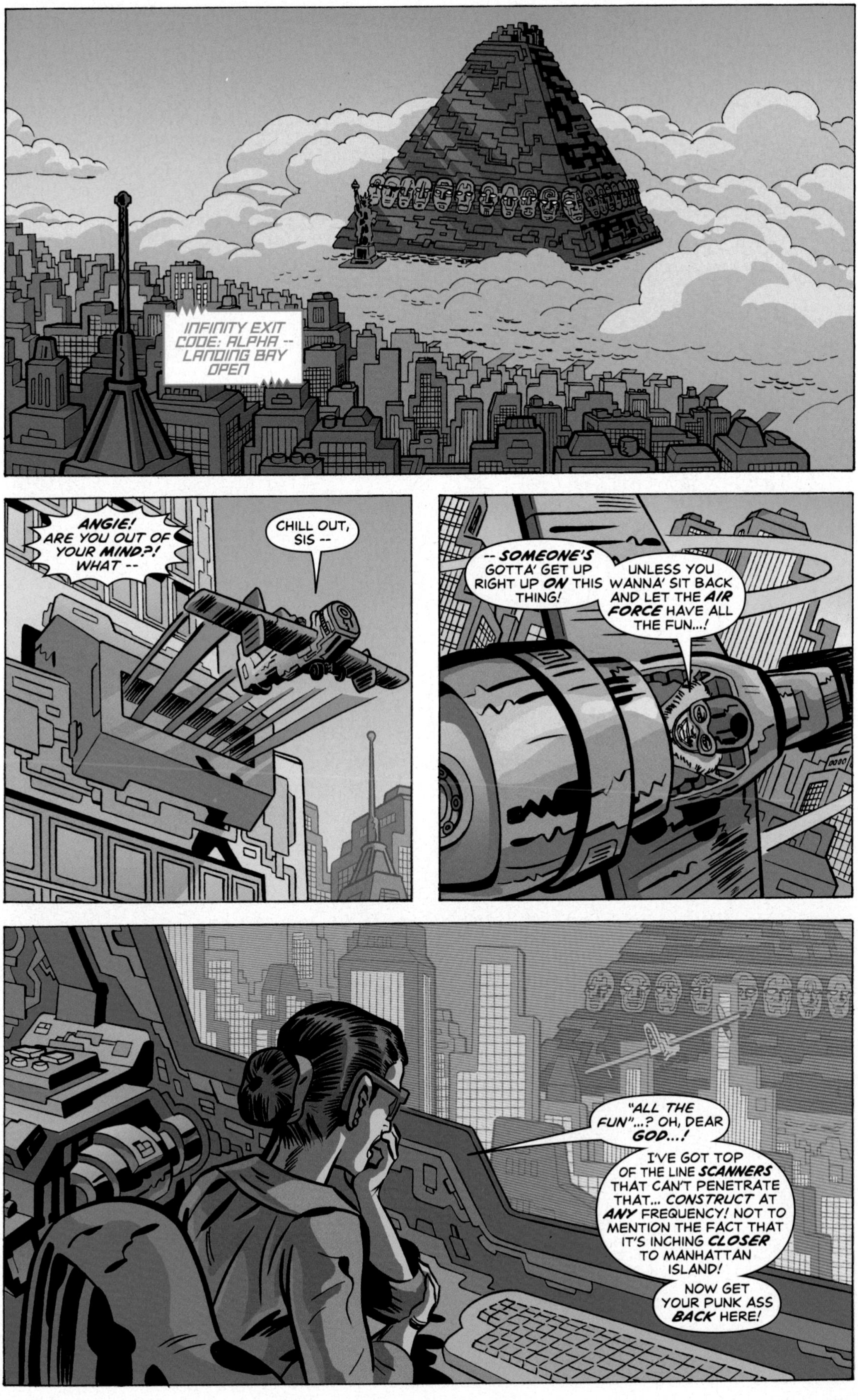
INFINITY EXIT CODE: ALPHA -- LANDING BAY OPEN
ANGIE! ARE YOU OUT OF YOUR MIND?! WHAT --
CHILL OUT, SIS --
-- SOMEONE'S GOTTA' GET UP RIGHT UP ON THIS THING!
UNLESS YOU WANNA' SIT BACK AND LET THE AIR FORCE HAVE ALL THE FUN...!
"ALL THE FUN"...? OH, DEAR GOD...!
I'VE GOT TOP OF THE LINE SCANNERS THAT CAN'T PENETRATE THAT... CONSTRUCT AT ANY FREQUENCY! NOT TO MENTION THE FACT THAT IT'S INCHING CLOSER TO MANHATTAN ISLAND!
NOW GET YOUR PUNK ASS BACK HERE!

NO CAN DO, "MOM"!

IF ADAM WERE HERE, *HE'D* BE DOING THIS EXACT THING! BUT HE'S *NOT*... SO IT'S UP TO *US*!

WATCH THIS ROLL!

YOU AND ADAM AREN'T EXACTLY *INTERCHANGEABLE,* ANGIE...!

SAYS *YOU*! THIS IS *MY* CITY --

-- TOO...?

OH, *DAMN*...!

NO!!

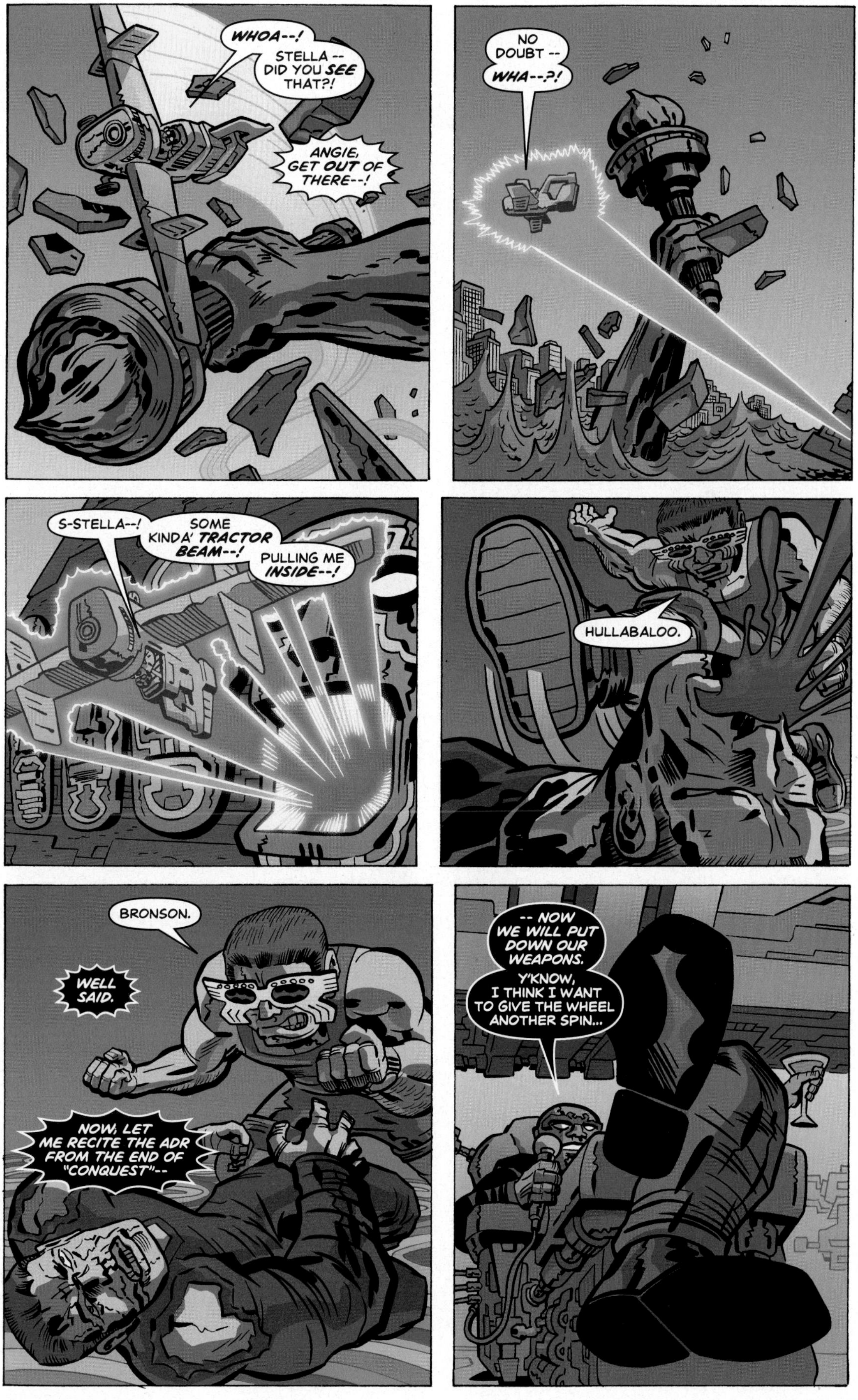
WHOA--! STELLA -- DID YOU SEE THAT?!
ANGIE, GET OUT OF THERE--!
NO DOUBT -- WHA--?!
S-STELLA--!
SOME KINDA' TRACTOR BEAM--!
PULLING ME INSIDE--!
HULLABALOO.
BRONSON.
WELL SAID.
NOW, LET ME RECITE THE ADR FROM THE END OF "CONQUEST"--
-- NOW WE WILL PUT DOWN OUR WEAPONS.
Y'KNOW, I THINK I WANT TO GIVE THE WHEEL ANOTHER SPIN...

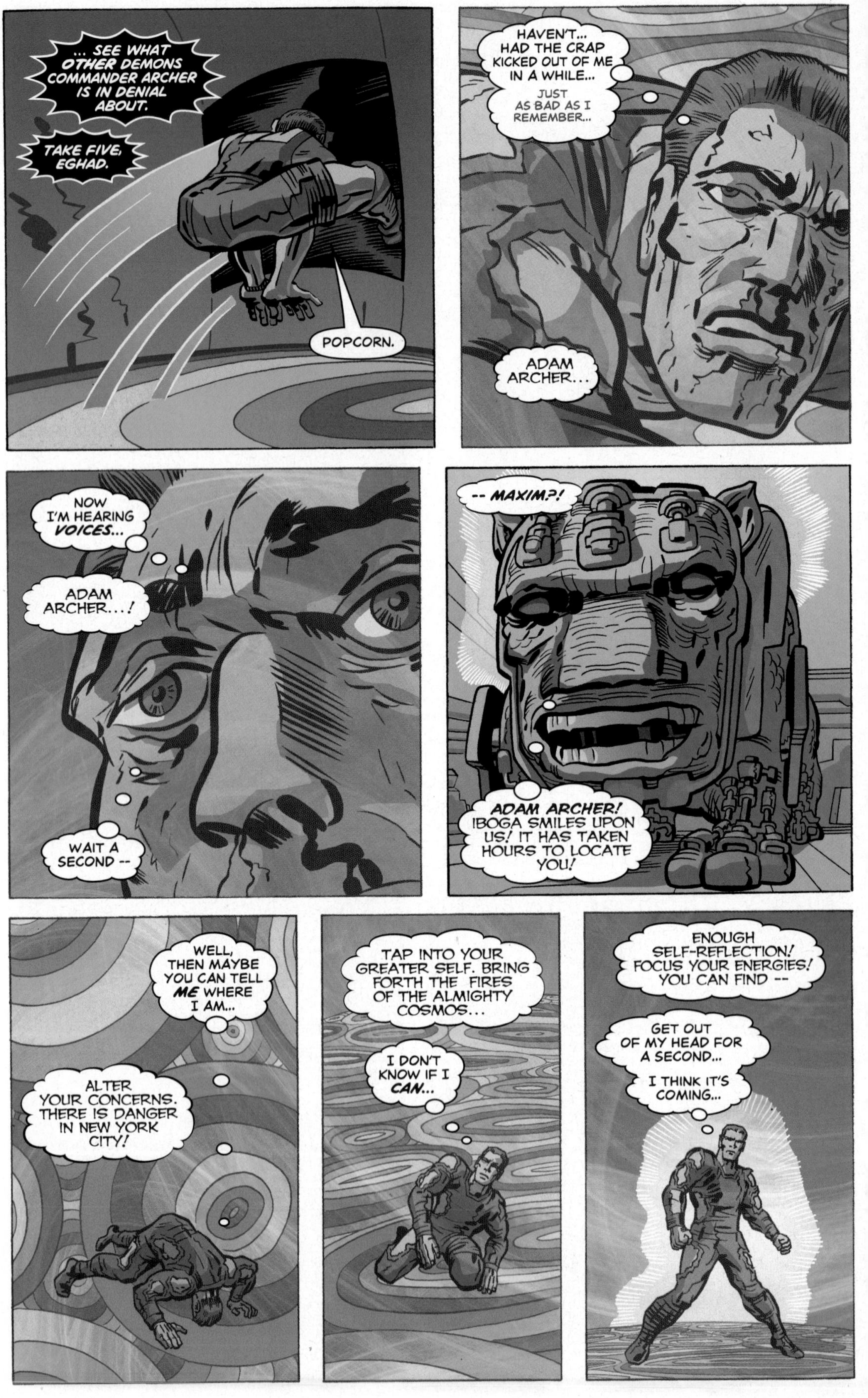
... SEE WHAT OTHER DEMONS COMMANDER ARCHER IS IN DENIAL ABOUT.
TAKE FIVE, EGHAD.
POPCORN.
HAVEN'T... HAD THE CRAP KICKED OUT OF ME IN A WHILE...
JUST AS BAD AS I REMEMBER...
ADAM ARCHER...
NOW I'M HEARING VOICES...
ADAM ARCHER...!
WAIT A SECOND --
-- MAXIM?!
ADAM ARCHER! IBOGA SMILES UPON US! IT HAS TAKEN HOURS TO LOCATE YOU!
WELL, THEN MAYBE YOU CAN TELL ME WHERE I AM...
ALTER YOUR CONCERNS. THERE IS DANGER IN NEW YORK CITY!
TAP INTO YOUR GREATER SELF. BRING FORTH THE FIRES OF THE ALMIGHTY COSMOS...
I DON'T KNOW IF I CAN...
ENOUGH SELF-REFLECTION! FOCUS YOUR ENERGIES! YOU CAN FIND --
GET OUT OF MY HEAD FOR A SECOND...
I THINK IT'S COMING...

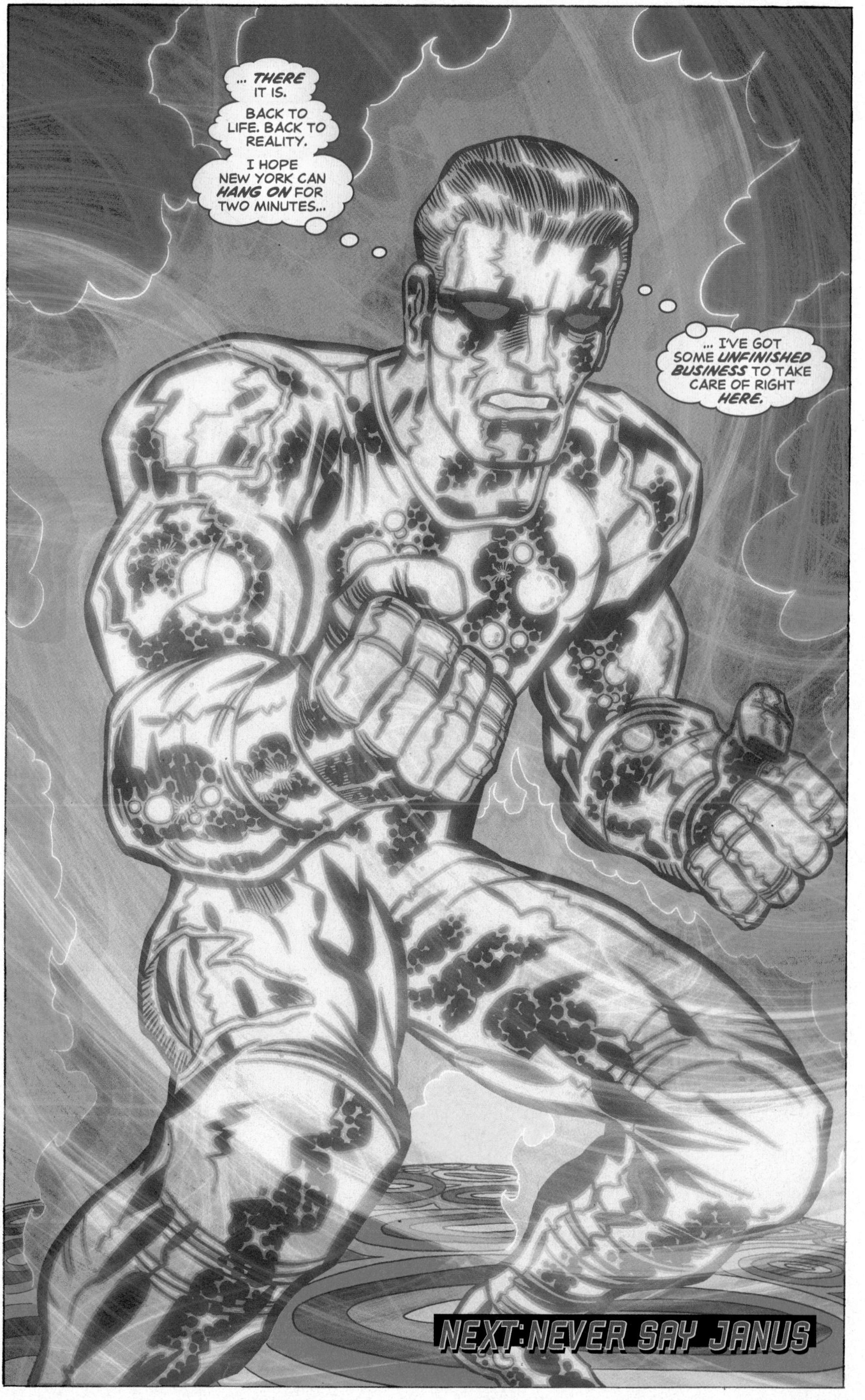
... THERE IT IS.
BACK TO LIFE. BACK TO REALITY.
I HOPE NEW YORK CAN HANG ON FOR TWO MINUTES...
... I'VE GOT SOME UNFINISHED BUSINESS TO TAKE CARE OF RIGHT HERE.
NEXT: NEVER SAY JANUS

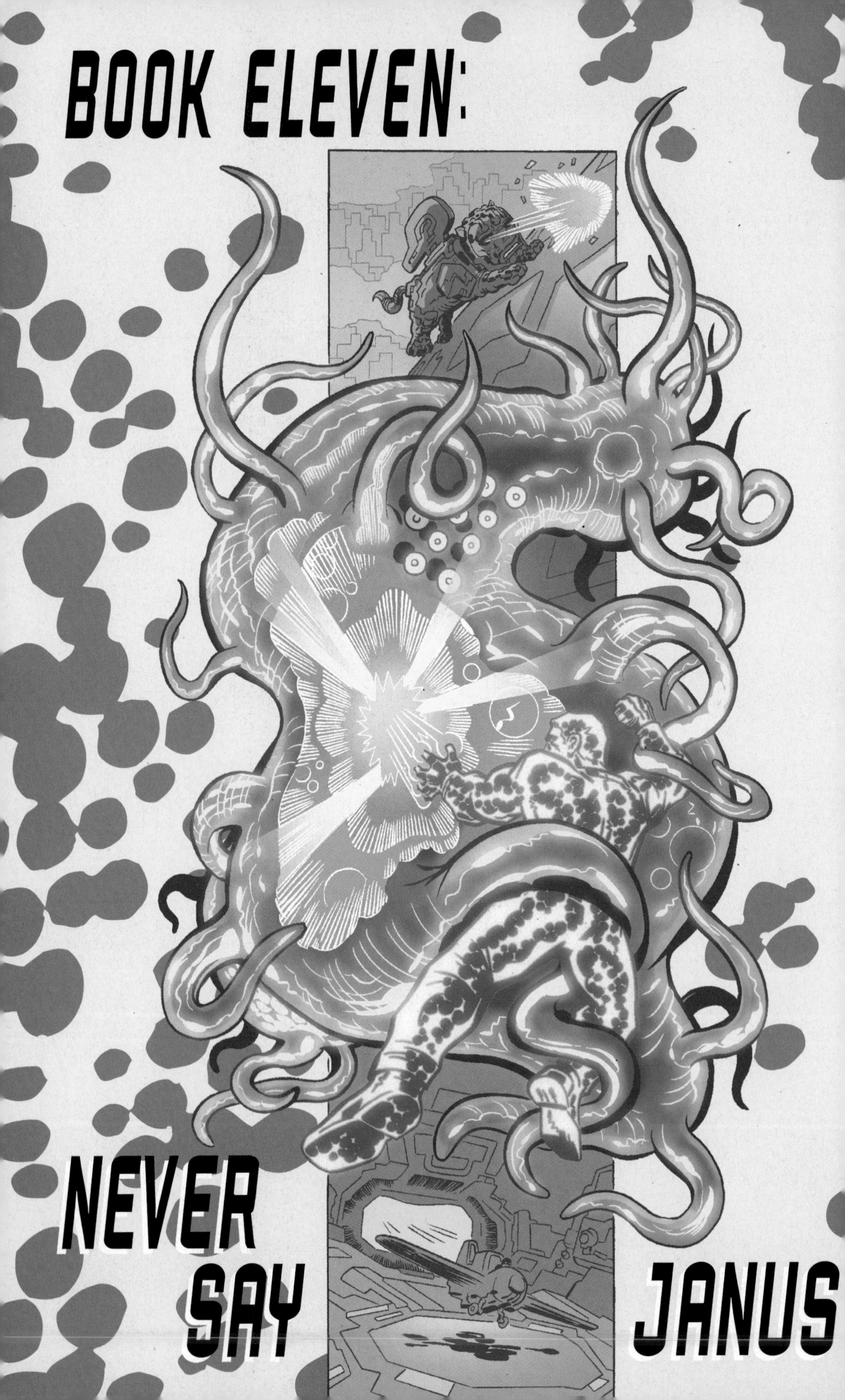
BOOK ELEVEN:
NEVER
SAY
JANUS

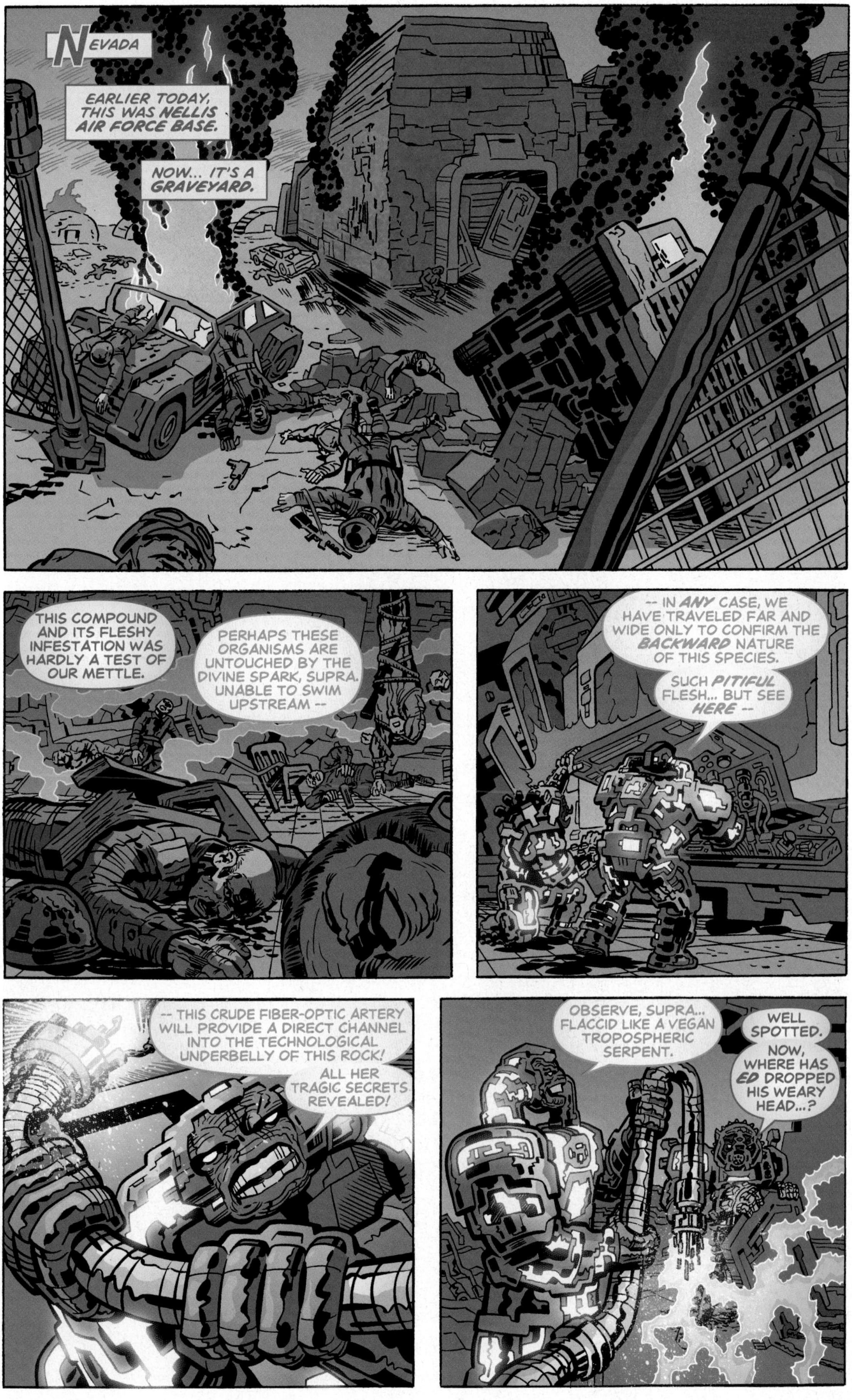
NEVADA
EARLIER TODAY, THIS WAS NELLIS AIR FORCE BASE.
NOW... IT'S A GRAVEYARD.
THIS COMPOUND AND ITS FLESHY INFESTATION WAS HARDLY A TEST OF OUR METTLE.
PERHAPS THESE ORGANISMS ARE UNTOUCHED BY THE DIVINE SPARK, SUPRA. UNABLE TO SWIM UPSTREAM --
-- IN ANY CASE, WE HAVE TRAVELED FAR AND WIDE ONLY TO CONFIRM THE BACKWARD NATURE OF THIS SPECIES.
SUCH PITIFUL FLESH... BUT SEE HERE --
-- THIS CRUDE FIBER-OPTIC ARTERY WILL PROVIDE A DIRECT CHANNEL INTO THE TECHNOLOGICAL UNDERBELLY OF THIS ROCK!
ALL HER TRAGIC SECRETS REVEALED!
OBSERVE, SUPRA... FLACCID LIKE A VEGAN TROPOSPHERIC SERPENT.
WELL SPOTTED.
NOW, WHERE HAS ED DROPPED HIS WEARY HEAD...?

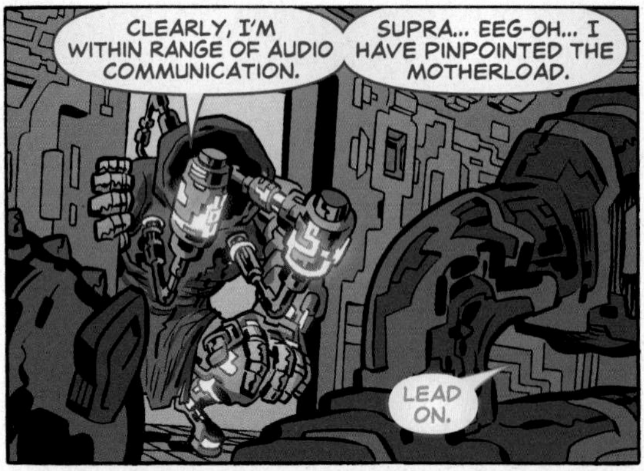
CLEARLY, I'M WITHIN RANGE OF AUDIO COMMUNICATION.
SUPRA... EEG-OH... I HAVE PINPOINTED THE MOTHERLOAD.
LEAD ON.

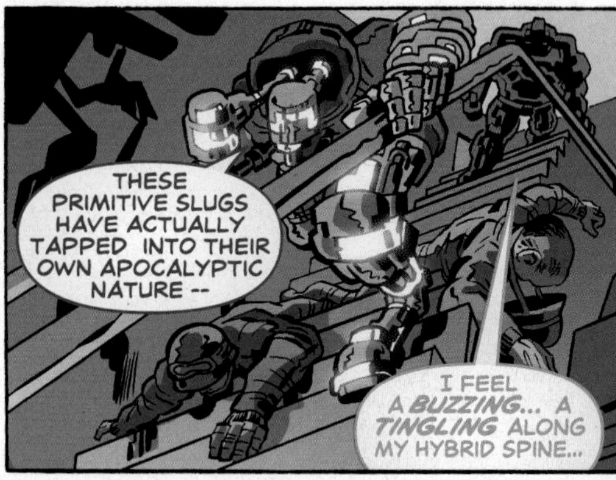
THESE PRIMITIVE SLUGS HAVE ACTUALLY TAPPED INTO THEIR OWN APOCALYPTIC NATURE --
I FEEL A BUZZING... A TINGLING ALONG MY HYBRID SPINE...

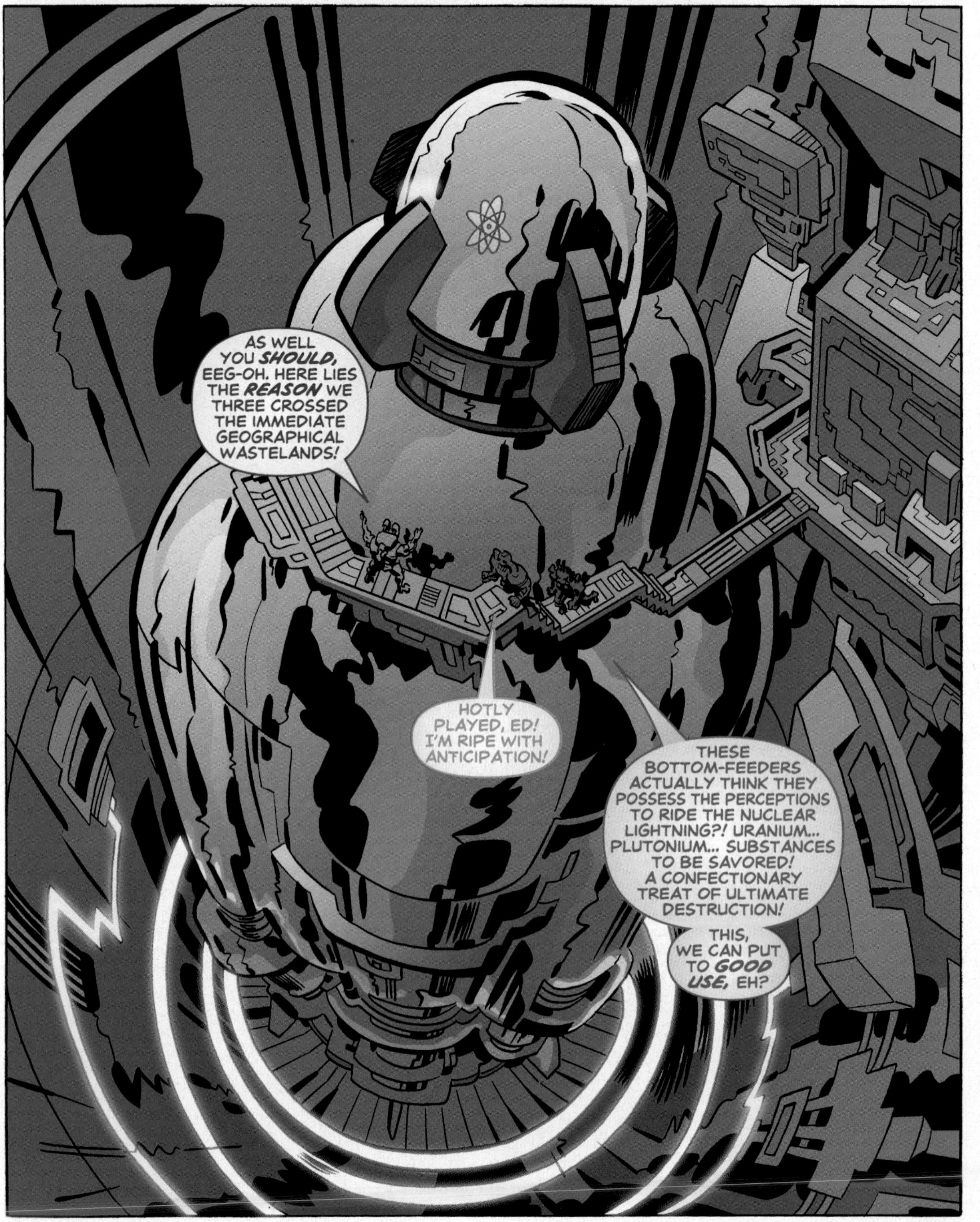
AS WELL YOU SHOULD, EEG-OH. HERE LIES THE REASON WE THREE CROSSED THE IMMEDIATE GEOGRAPHICAL WASTELANDS!
HOTLY PLAYED, ED! I'M RIPE WITH ANTICIPATION!
THESE BOTTOM-FEEDERS ACTUALLY THINK THEY POSSESS THE PERCEPTIONS TO RIDE THE NUCLEAR LIGHTNING?! URANIUM... PLUTONIUM... SUBSTANCES TO BE SAVORED! A CONFECTIONARY TREAT OF ULTIMATE DESTRUCTION!
THIS, WE CAN PUT TO GOOD USE, EH?

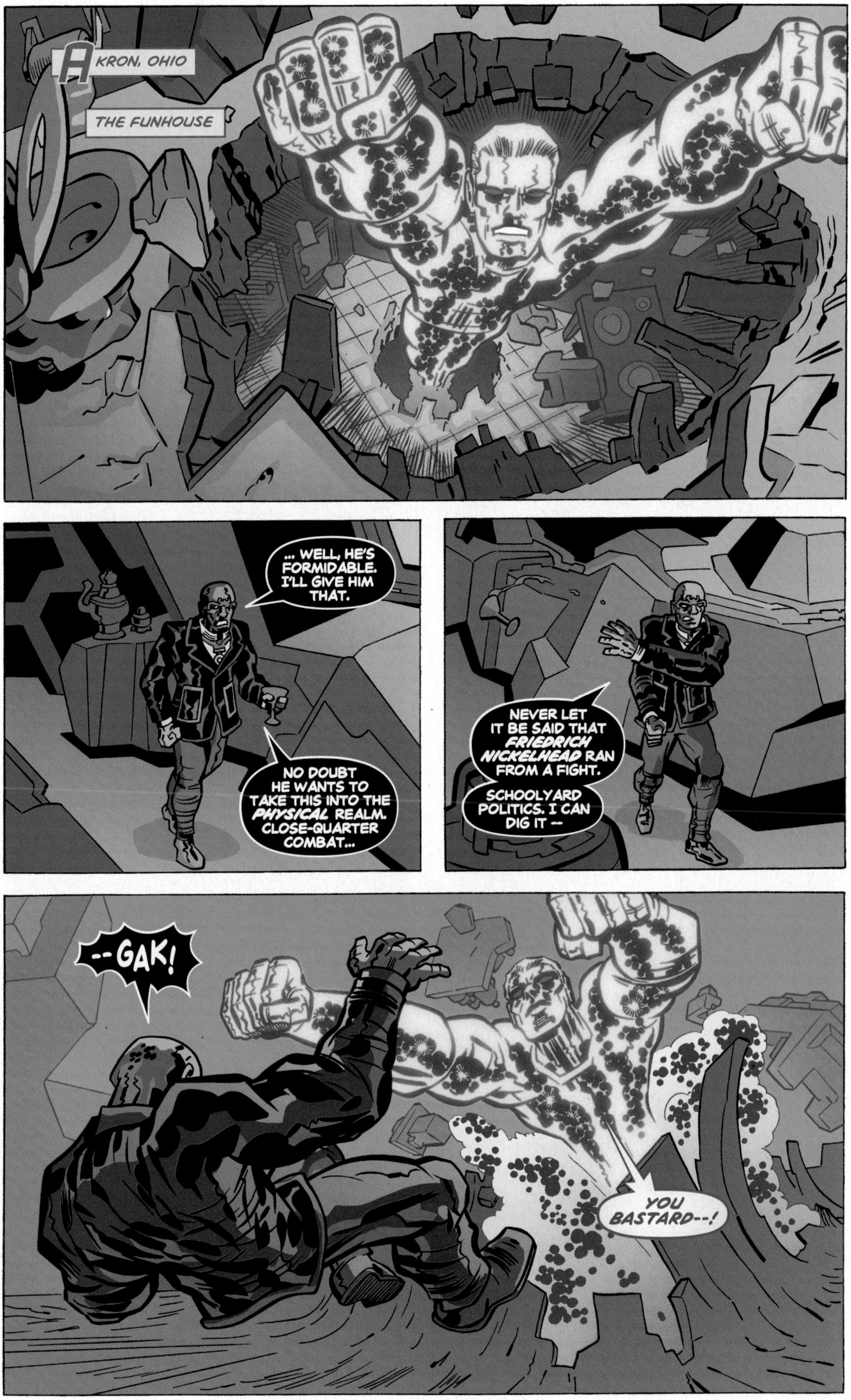
AKRON, OHIO
THE FUNHOUSE
... WELL, HE'S FORMIDABLE. I'LL GIVE HIM THAT.
NO DOUBT HE WANTS TO TAKE THIS INTO THE PHYSICAL REALM. CLOSE-QUARTER COMBAT...
NEVER LET IT BE SAID THAT FRIEDRICH NICKELHEAD RAN FROM A FIGHT.
SCHOOLYARD POLITICS. I CAN DIG IT --
--GAK!
YOU BASTARD--!

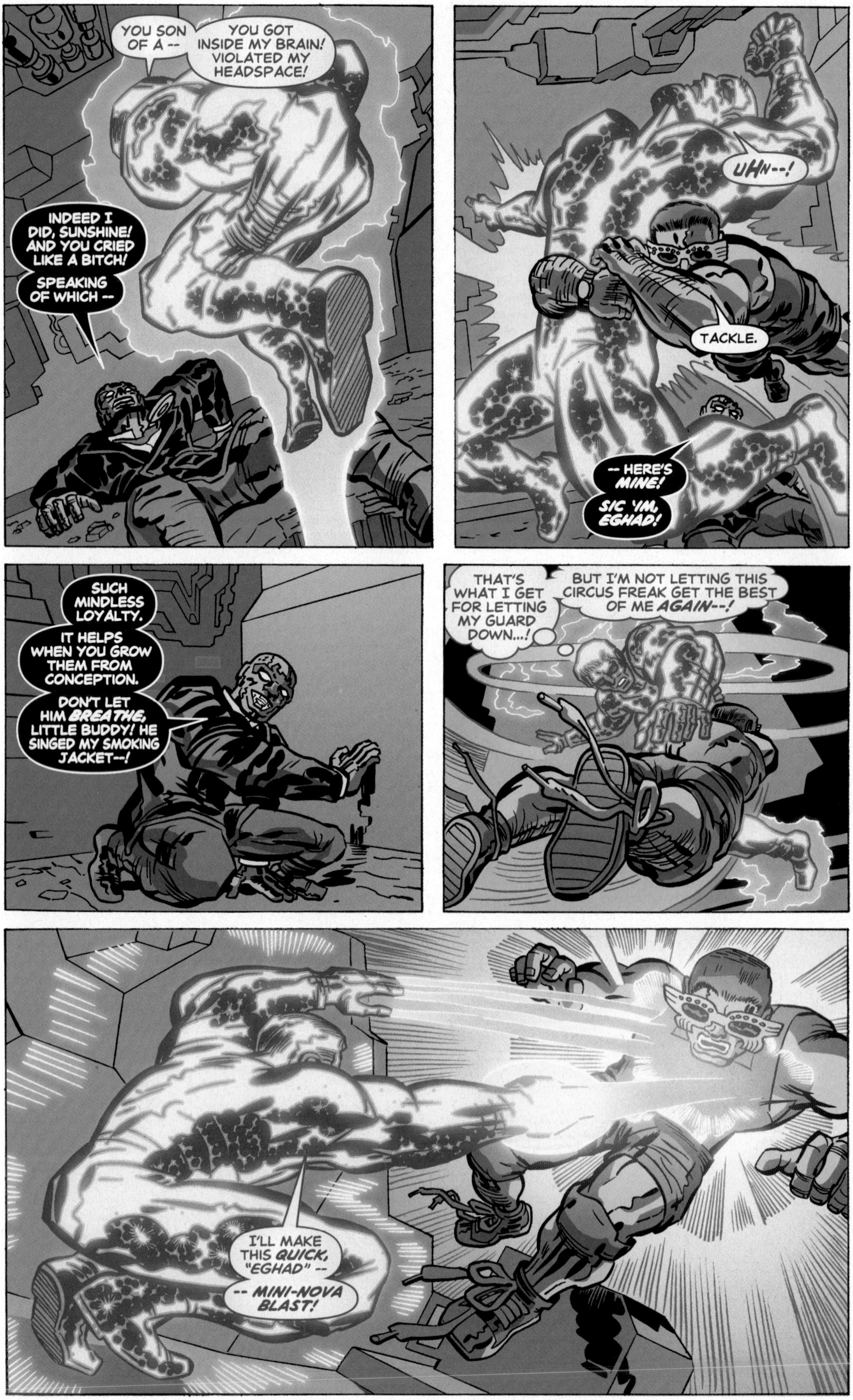
YOU SON OF A --
YOU GOT INSIDE MY BRAIN! VIOLATED MY HEADSPACE!
INDEED I DID, SUNSHINE! AND YOU CRIED LIKE A BITCH!
SPEAKING OF WHICH --
UHN--!
TACKLE.
-- HERE'S MINE!
SIC 'IM, EGHAD!
SUCH MINDLESS LOYALTY.
IT HELPS WHEN YOU GROW THEM FROM CONCEPTION.
DON'T LET HIM BREATHE, LITTLE BUDDY! HE SINGED MY SMOKING JACKET--!
THAT'S WHAT I GET FOR LETTING MY GUARD DOWN...!
BUT I'M NOT LETTING THIS CIRCUS FREAK GET THE BEST OF ME AGAIN--!
I'LL MAKE THIS QUICK, "EGHAD" --
-- MINI-NOVA BLAST!

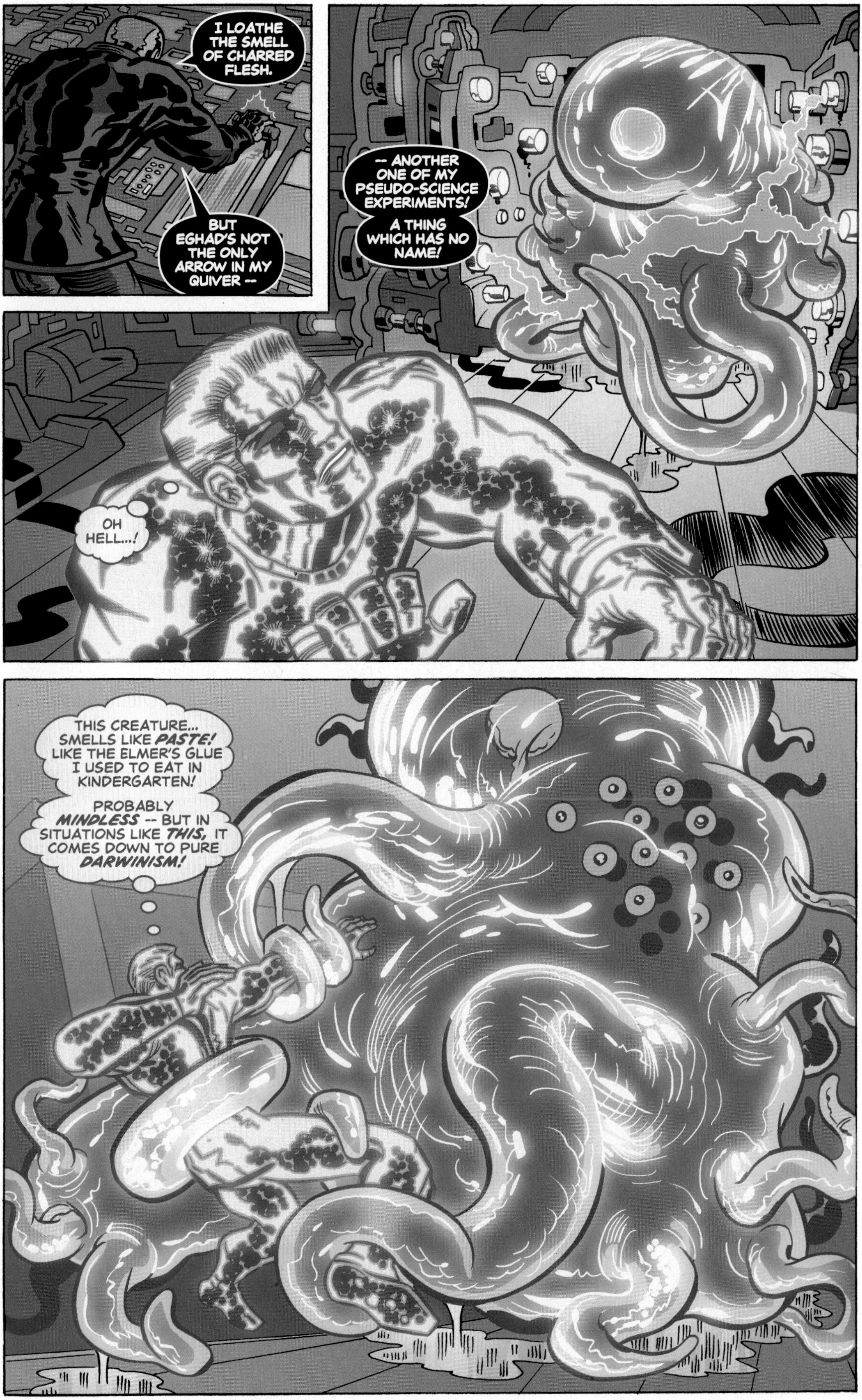
I LOATHE THE SMELL OF CHARRED FLESH.
BUT EGHAD'S NOT THE ONLY ARROW IN MY QUIVER --
-- ANOTHER ONE OF MY PSEUDO-SCIENCE EXPERIMENTS!
A THING WHICH HAS NO NAME!
OH HELL...!
THIS CREATURE... SMELLS LIKE PASTE! LIKE THE ELMER'S GLUE I USED TO EAT IN KINDERGARTEN!
PROBABLY MINDLESS -- BUT IN SITUATIONS LIKE THIS, IT COMES DOWN TO PURE DARWINISM!

BUT... MAYBE JUST A LITTLE *LOVE BLAST* WILL BE ENOUGH TO BACK IT OFF...!

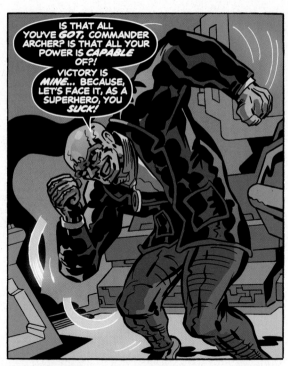

IS THAT ALL YOU'VE *GOT,* COMMANDER ARCHER? IS THAT ALL YOUR POWER IS *CAPABLE* OF?!

VICTORY IS *MINE...* BECAUSE, LET'S FACE IT, AS A SUPERHERO, YOU *SUCK!*

DON'T KNOW IF I CAN ARGUE THAT! AM I STILL FREAKED OUT FROM THE ATTEMPT TO FRY MY MIND?!

GOT TO... GET IT TOGETHER --

-- NOW!

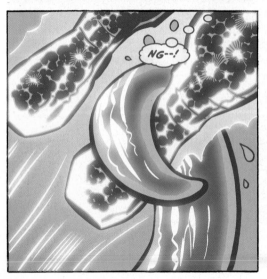

NG--!

OKAY... SO MUCH FOR *THAT* PLAN...!

DAMN THING'S... GROWING EXPONENTIALLY!

IT'S... GOT ITS OWN GRAVITATIONAL PULL...

... SUCKING ME IN--!

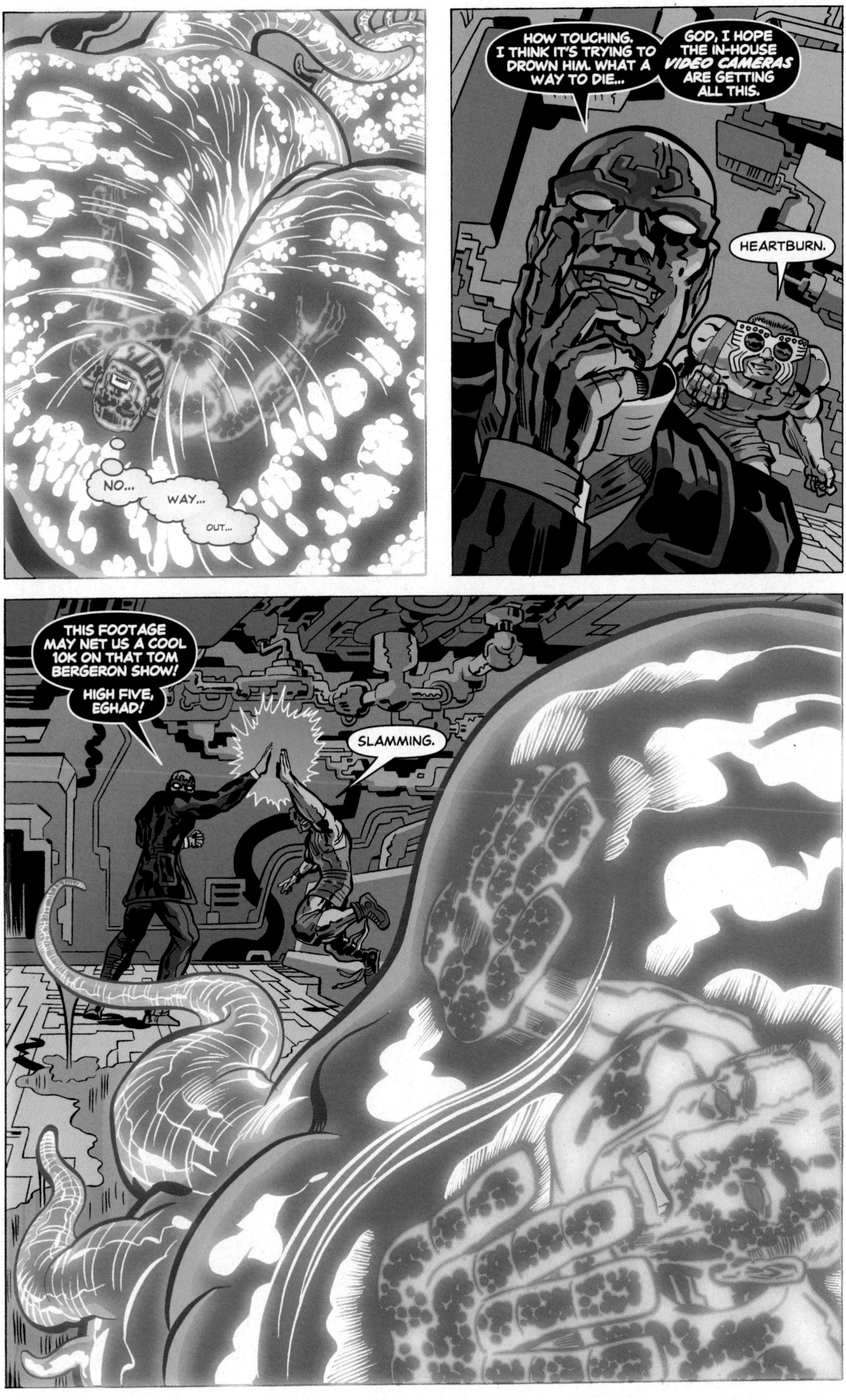
NO... WAY... OUT...
HOW TOUCHING. I THINK IT'S TRYING TO DROWN HIM. WHAT A WAY TO DIE...
GOD, I HOPE THE IN-HOUSE VIDEO CAMERAS ARE GETTING ALL THIS.
HEARTBURN.
THIS FOOTAGE MAY NET US A COOL 10K ON THAT TOM BERGERON SHOW!
HIGH FIVE, EGHAD!
SLAMMING.

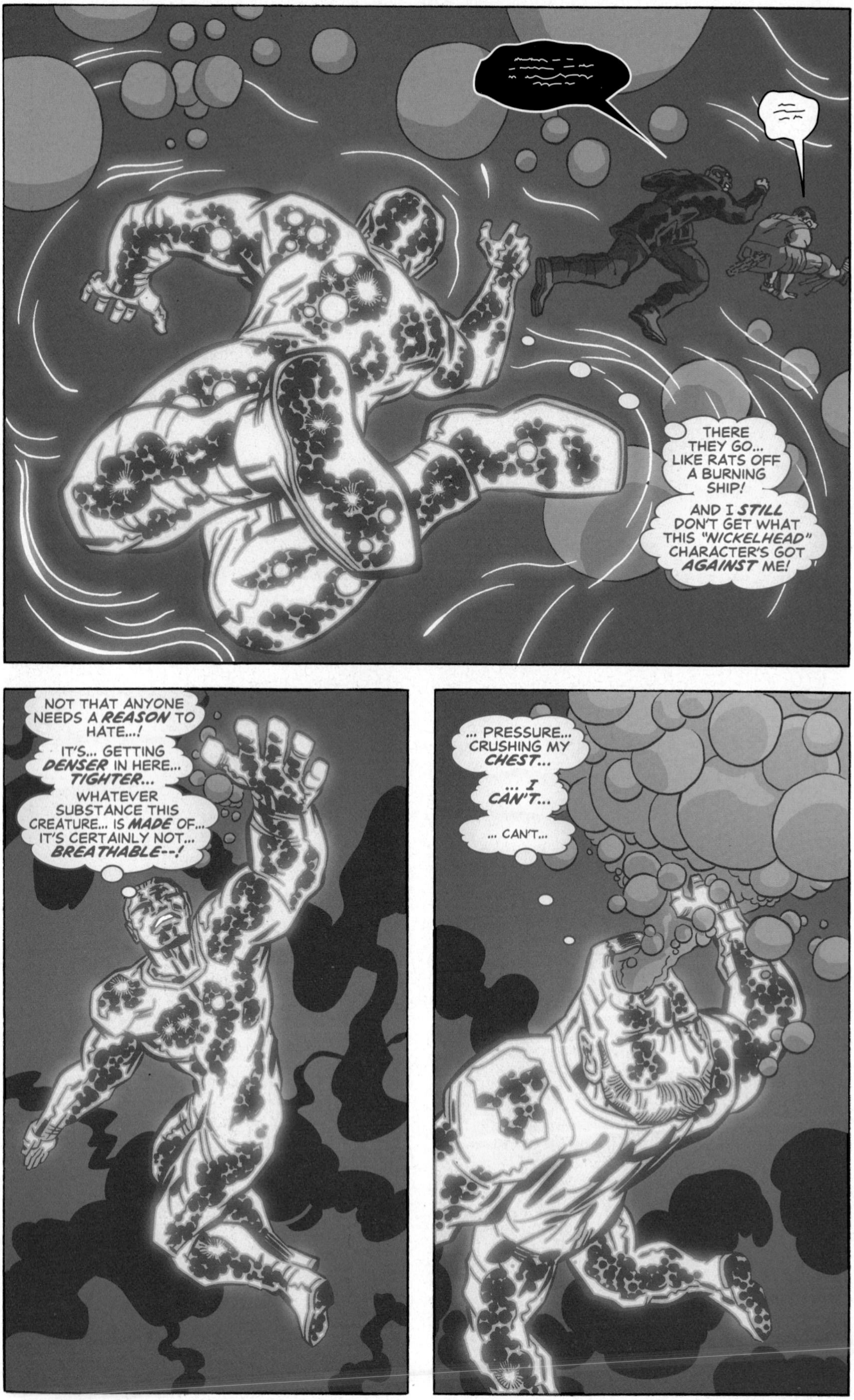

THERE THEY GO... LIKE RATS OFF A BURNING SHIP!
AND I STILL DON'T GET WHAT THIS "NICKELHEAD" CHARACTER'S GOT AGAINST ME!
NOT THAT ANYONE NEEDS A REASON TO HATE...!
IT'S... GETTING DENSER IN HERE... TIGHTER... WHATEVER SUBSTANCE THIS CREATURE... IS MADE OF... IT'S CERTAINLY NOT... BREATHABLE--!
... PRESSURE... CRUSHING MY CHEST...
... I CAN'T...
... CAN'T...

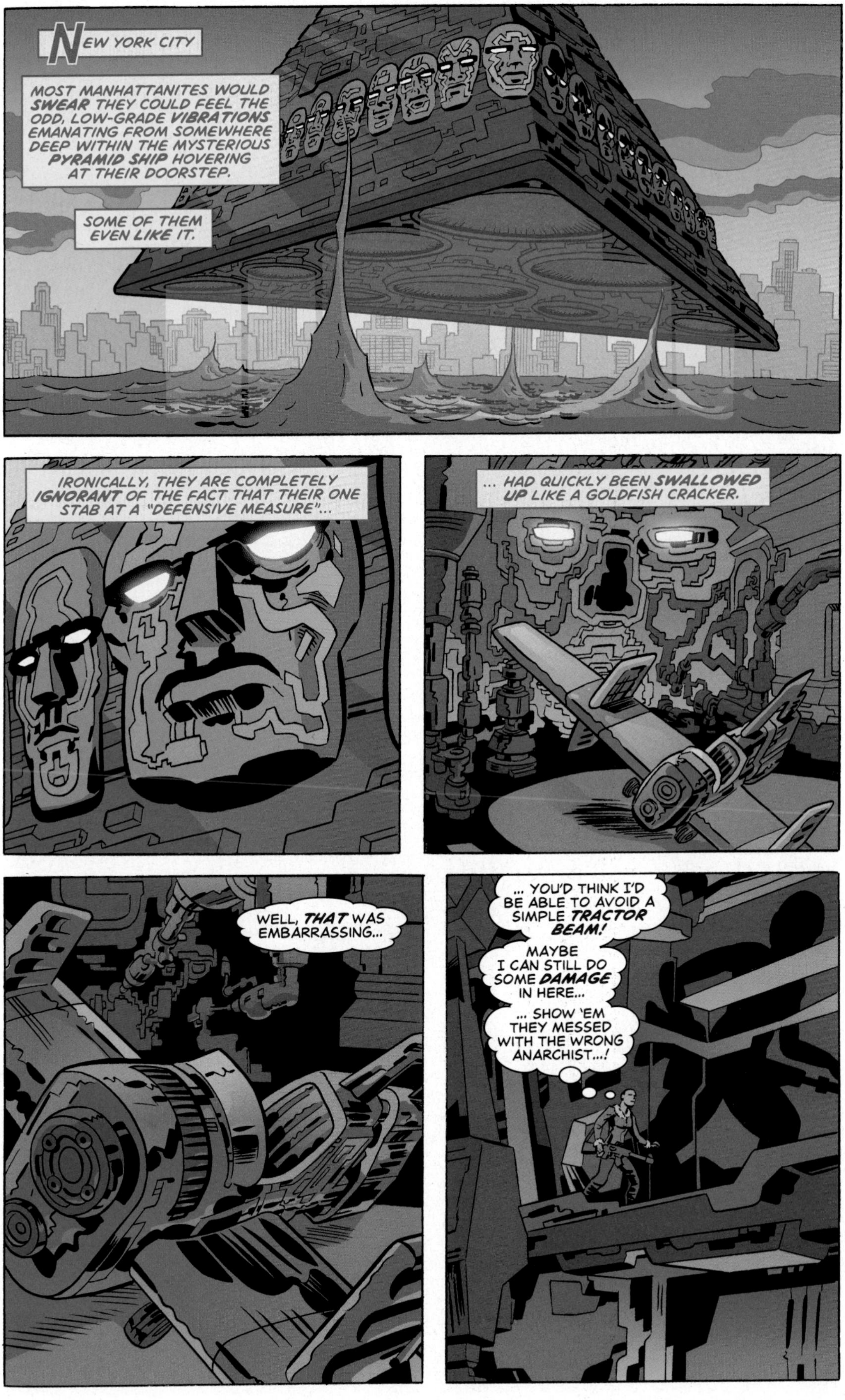
NEW YORK CITY
MOST MANHATTANITES WOULD SWEAR THEY COULD FEEL THE ODD, LOW-GRADE VIBRATIONS EMANATING FROM SOMEWHERE DEEP WITHIN THE MYSTERIOUS PYRAMID SHIP HOVERING AT THEIR DOORSTEP.
SOME OF THEM EVEN LIKE IT.
IRONICALLY, THEY ARE COMPLETELY IGNORANT OF THE FACT THAT THEIR ONE STAB AT A "DEFENSIVE MEASURE"...
... HAD QUICKLY BEEN SWALLOWED UP LIKE A GOLDFISH CRACKER.
WELL, THAT WAS EMBARRASSING...
... YOU'D THINK I'D BE ABLE TO AVOID A SIMPLE TRACTOR BEAM!
MAYBE I CAN STILL DO SOME DAMAGE IN HERE...
... SHOW 'EM THEY MESSED WITH THE WRONG ANARCHIST...!

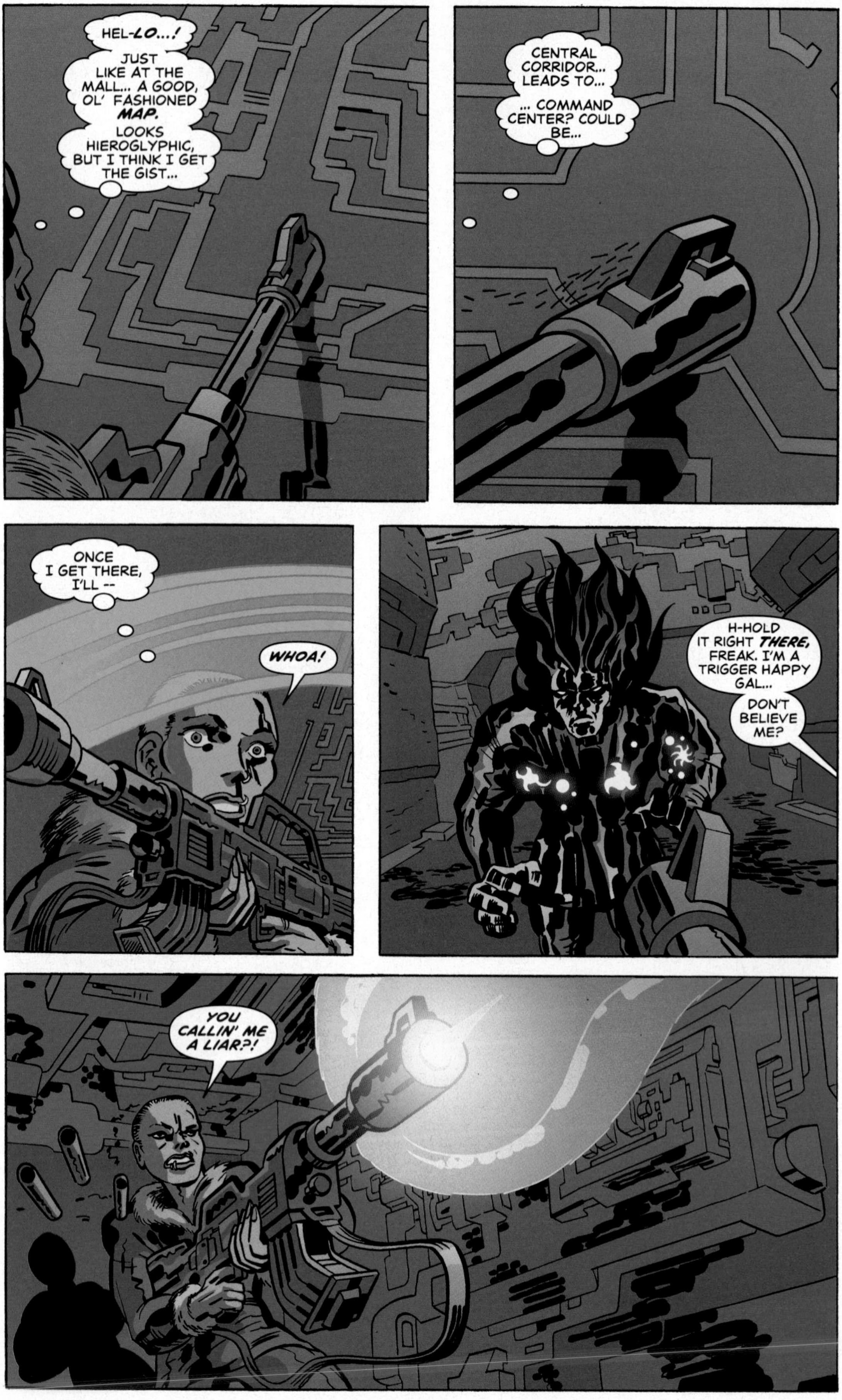

HEL-*LO*...!
JUST LIKE AT THE MALL... A GOOD, OL' FASHIONED ***MAP.***
LOOKS HIEROGLYPHIC, BUT I THINK I GET THE GIST...
CENTRAL CORRIDOR... LEADS TO...
... COMMAND CENTER? COULD BE...
ONCE I GET THERE, I'LL --
WHOA!
H-HOLD IT RIGHT ***THERE,*** FREAK. I'M A TRIGGER HAPPY GAL...
DON'T BELIEVE ME?
YOU CALLIN' ME A LIAR?!

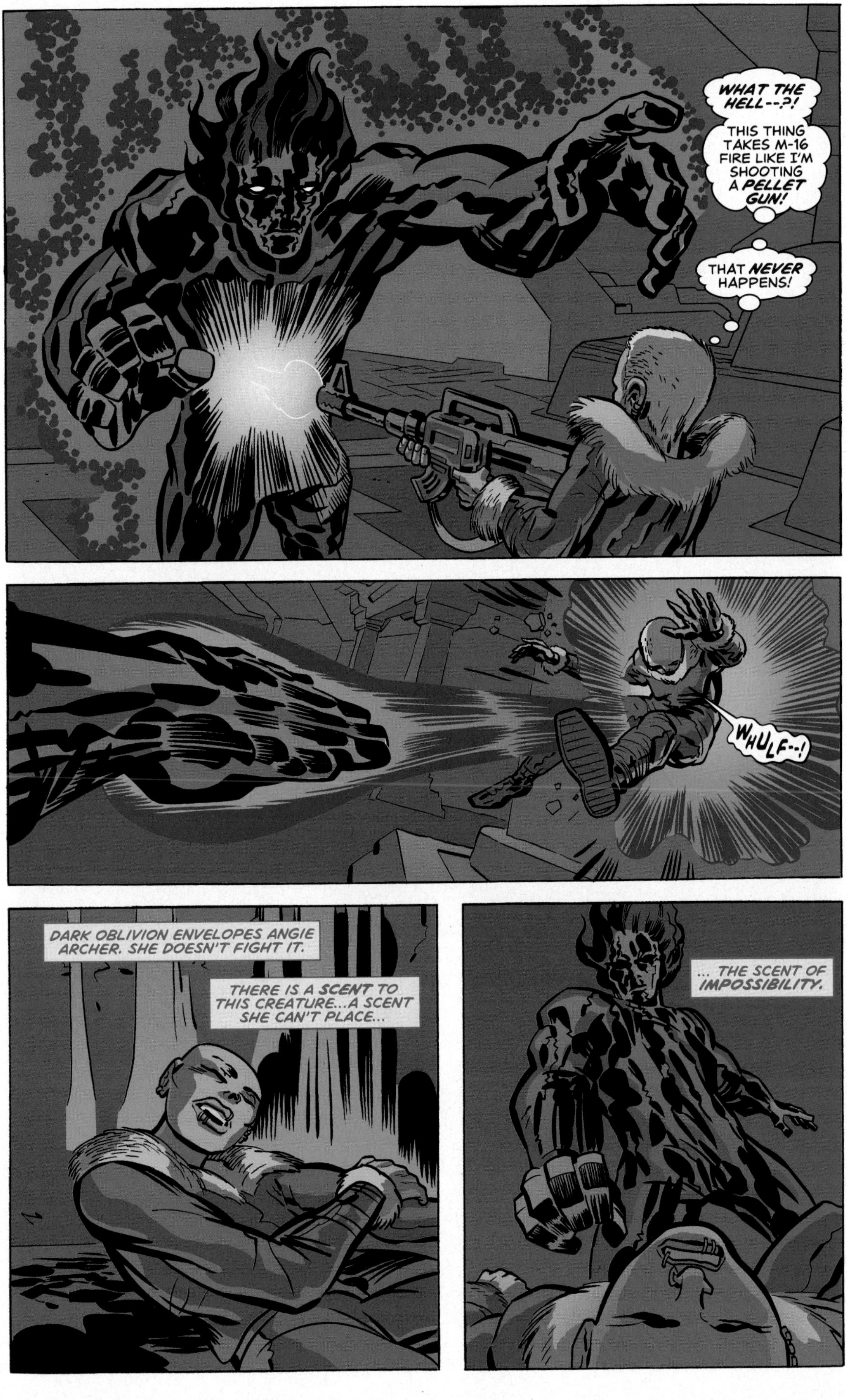
WHAT THE HELL--?!
THIS THING TAKES M-16 FIRE LIKE I'M SHOOTING A PELLET GUN!
THAT NEVER HAPPENS!
WHULF--!
DARK OBLIVION ENVELOPES ANGIE ARCHER. SHE DOESN'T FIGHT IT.
THERE IS A SCENT TO THIS CREATURE...A SCENT SHE CAN'T PLACE...
... THE SCENT OF IMPOSSIBILITY.

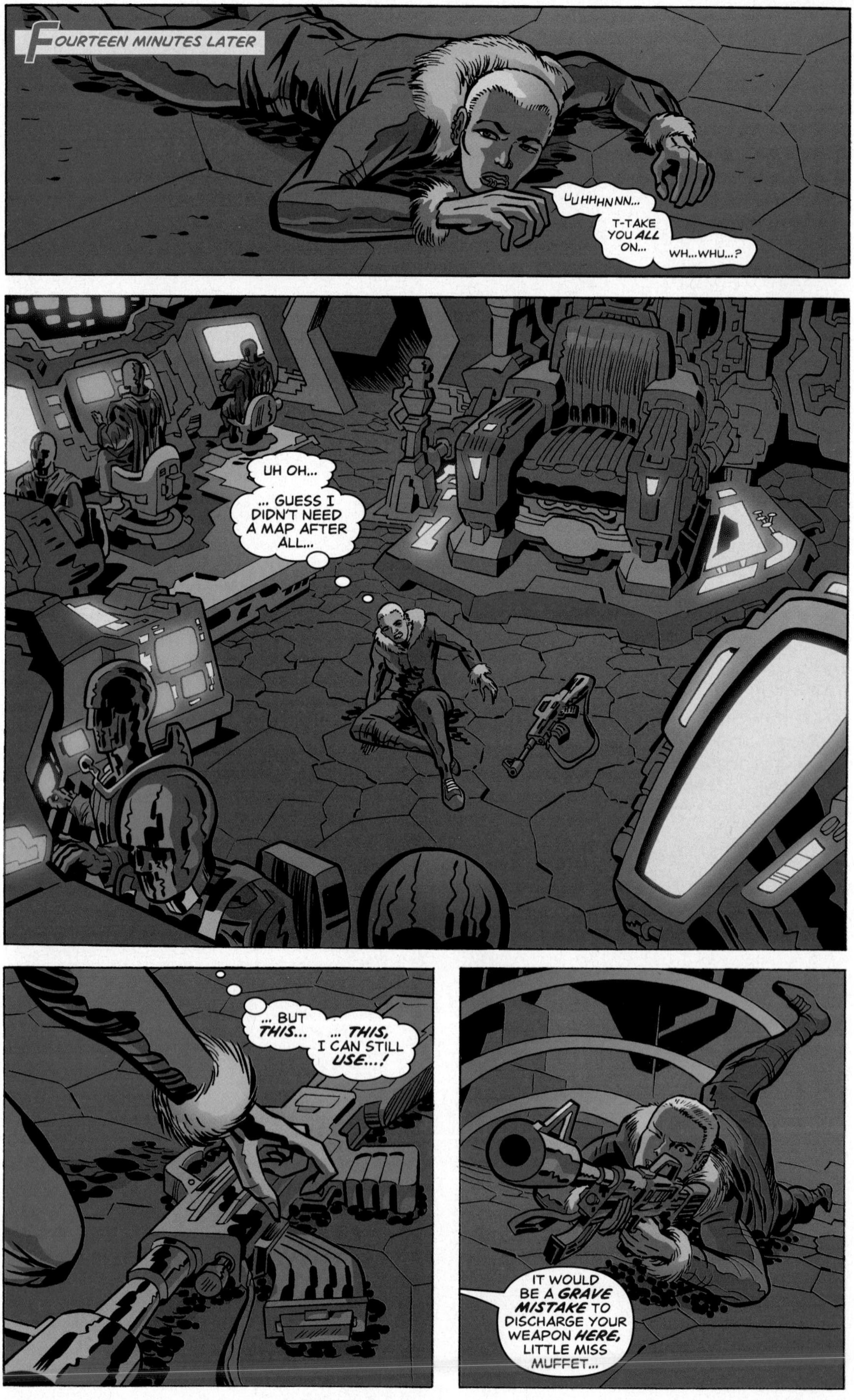
FOURTEEN MINUTES LATER
UUHHHNNN...
T-TAKE YOU ALL ON...
WH...WHU...?
UH OH...
... GUESS I DIDN'T NEED A MAP AFTER ALL...
... BUT THIS...
... THIS, I CAN STILL USE...!
IT WOULD BE A GRAVE MISTAKE TO DISCHARGE YOUR WEAPON HERE, LITTLE MISS MUFFET...

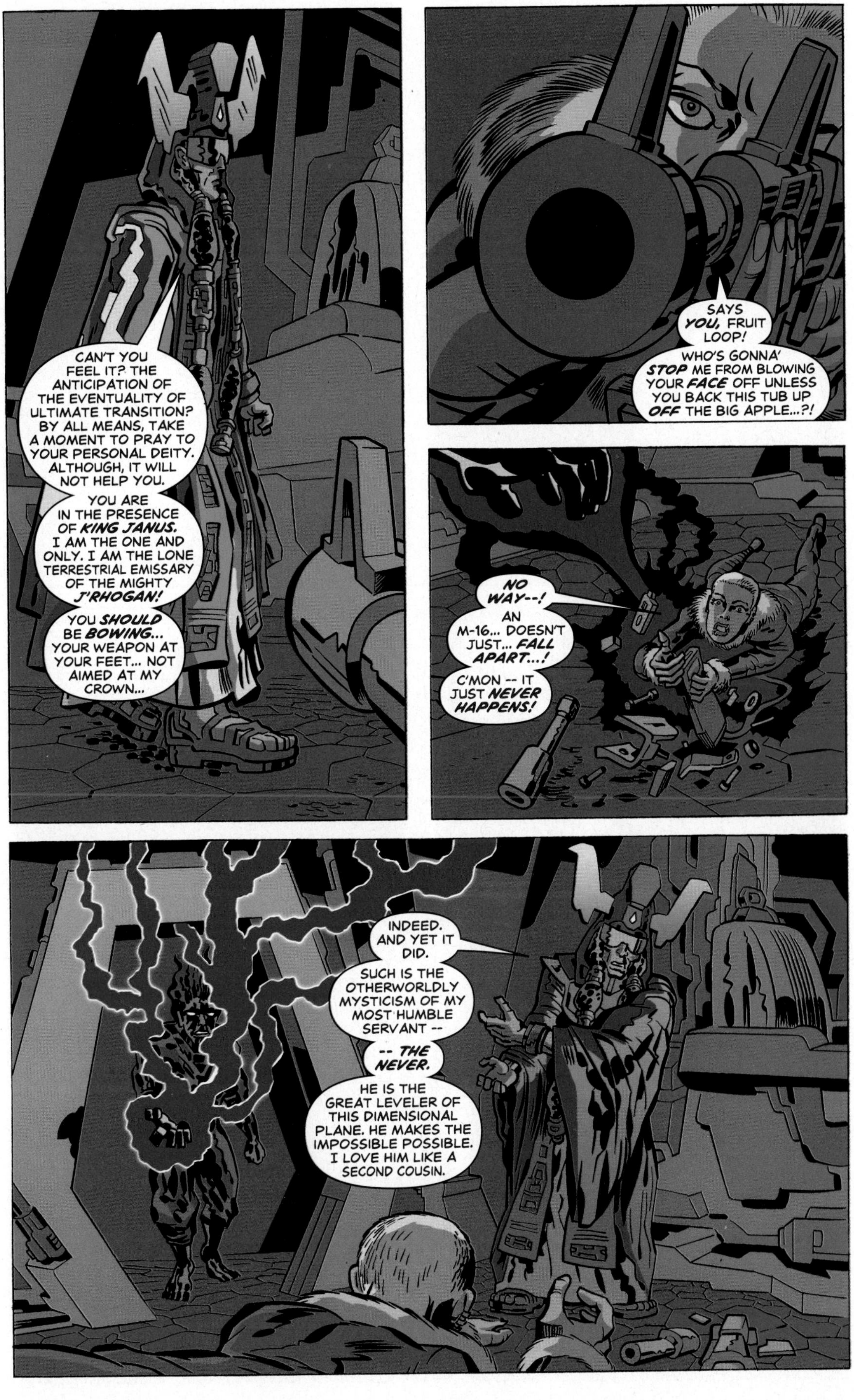
CAN'T YOU FEEL IT? THE ANTICIPATION OF THE EVENTUALITY OF ULTIMATE TRANSITION? BY ALL MEANS, TAKE A MOMENT TO PRAY TO YOUR PERSONAL DEITY. ALTHOUGH, IT WILL NOT HELP YOU.
YOU ARE IN THE PRESENCE OF KING JANUS. I AM THE ONE AND ONLY. I AM THE LONE TERRESTRIAL EMISSARY OF THE MIGHTY J'RHOGAN!
YOU SHOULD BE BOWING... YOUR WEAPON AT YOUR FEET... NOT AIMED AT MY CROWN...
SAYS YOU, FRUIT LOOP!
WHO'S GONNA' STOP ME FROM BLOWING YOUR FACE OFF UNLESS YOU BACK THIS TUB UP OFF THE BIG APPLE...?!
NO WAY--!
AN M-16... DOESN'T JUST... FALL APART...!
C'MON -- IT JUST NEVER HAPPENS!
INDEED. AND YET IT DID.
SUCH IS THE OTHERWORLDLY MYSTICISM OF MY MOST HUMBLE SERVANT --
-- THE NEVER.
HE IS THE GREAT LEVELER OF THIS DIMENSIONAL PLANE. HE MAKES THE IMPOSSIBLE POSSIBLE. I LOVE HIM LIKE A SECOND COUSIN.

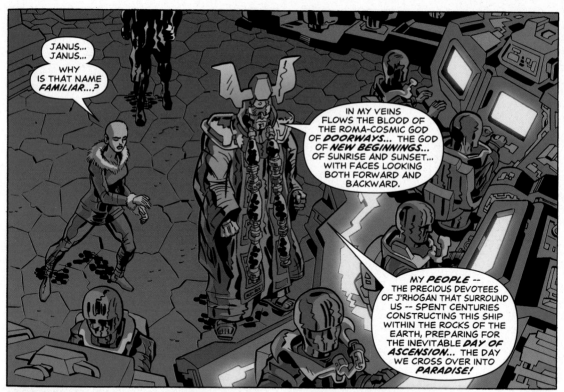

JANUS... JANUS... WHY IS THAT NAME *FAMILIAR...?*

IN MY VEINS FLOWS THE BLOOD OF THE ROMA-COSMIC GOD OF *DOORWAYS*... THE GOD OF *NEW BEGINNINGS*... OF SUNRISE AND SUNSET... WITH FACES LOOKING BOTH FORWARD AND BACKWARD.

MY *PEOPLE* -- THE PRECIOUS DEVOTEES OF J'RHOGAN THAT SURROUND US -- SPENT CENTURIES CONSTRUCTING THIS SHIP WITHIN THE ROCKS OF THE EARTH, PREPARING FOR THE INEVITABLE *DAY OF ASCENSION*... THE DAY WE CROSS OVER INTO *PARADISE!*

PARADISE, HUH? I'M GUESSING YOU DON'T MEAN CENTRAL PARK...

THIS TEEMING METROPOLIS SERVES A *PURPOSE,* BALD ONE. SUCH IS THE LAW OF *CAUSE* AND *EFFECT.*

DUE TO THE MYSTICAL *ENERGIES* RELEASED DURING THE ORGY OF CARNAGE, A MOMENTARY *PORTAL* WILL OPEN... ONE THAT WILL DELIVER OUR PEOPLE TO THE PROMISED LAND!

CAN I GET AN AFFIRMATION?

"ORGY OF CARNAGE"...? WHAT THE HELL ARE YOU *TALKIN'* ABOUT?!

LANGUAGE, CHILD. THE ROMA-COSMIC CALENDAR IDENTIFIES THE *FIFTEENTH OF MAY* OF THIS YEAR AS A SPIRITUALLY POTENT DATE... THE DAY OF RECKONING FOR MY PEOPLE --

-- THAT DAY HAS ARRIVED. *TODAY.* TO PROVIDE THE NECESSARY EVENT WHICH WILL *OPEN* THE DOORWAY TO BLESSED J'RHOGAN'S DIMENSION...

... WE SHALL *DESTROY* THE ISLAND YOU CALL "MANHATTAN".

OH, CRAP...

... *THIS* IS WHY I *HATE* ORGANIZED RELIGION...!

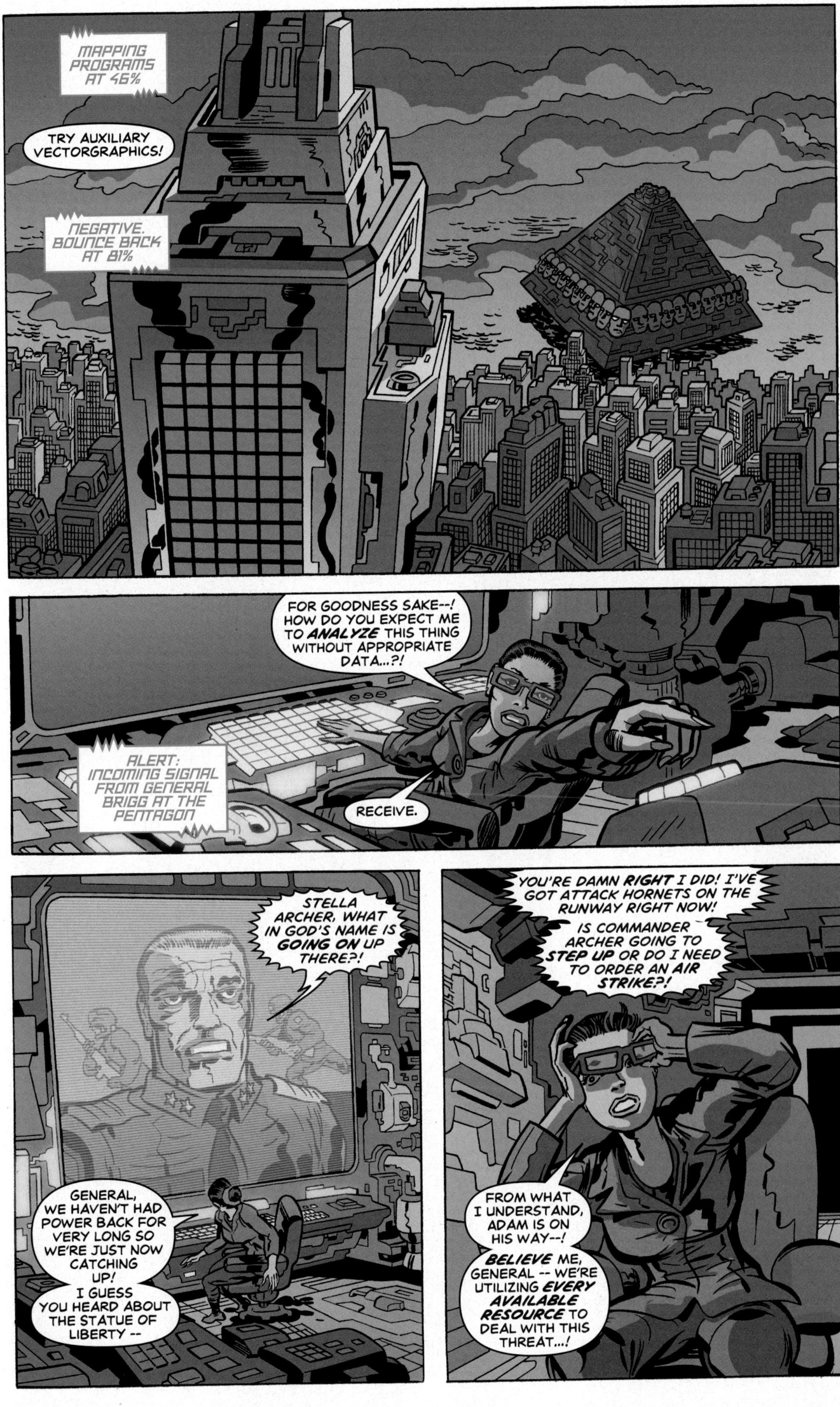
MAPPING PROGRAMS AT 46%
TRY AUXILIARY VECTORGRAPHICS!
NEGATIVE. BOUNCE BACK AT 81%
FOR GOODNESS SAKE--! HOW DO YOU EXPECT ME TO ANALYZE THIS THING WITHOUT APPROPRIATE DATA...?!
ALERT: INCOMING SIGNAL FROM GENERAL BRIGG AT THE PENTAGON
RECEIVE.
STELLA ARCHER, WHAT IN GOD'S NAME IS GOING ON UP THERE?!
GENERAL, WE HAVEN'T HAD POWER BACK FOR VERY LONG SO WE'RE JUST NOW CATCHING UP!
I GUESS YOU HEARD ABOUT THE STATUE OF LIBERTY --
YOU'RE DAMN RIGHT I DID! I'VE GOT ATTACK HORNETS ON THE RUNWAY RIGHT NOW!
IS COMMANDER ARCHER GOING TO STEP UP OR DO I NEED TO ORDER AN AIR STRIKE?!
FROM WHAT I UNDERSTAND, ADAM IS ON HIS WAY--!
BELIEVE ME, GENERAL -- WE'RE UTILIZING EVERY AVAILABLE RESOURCE TO DEAL WITH THIS THREAT...!

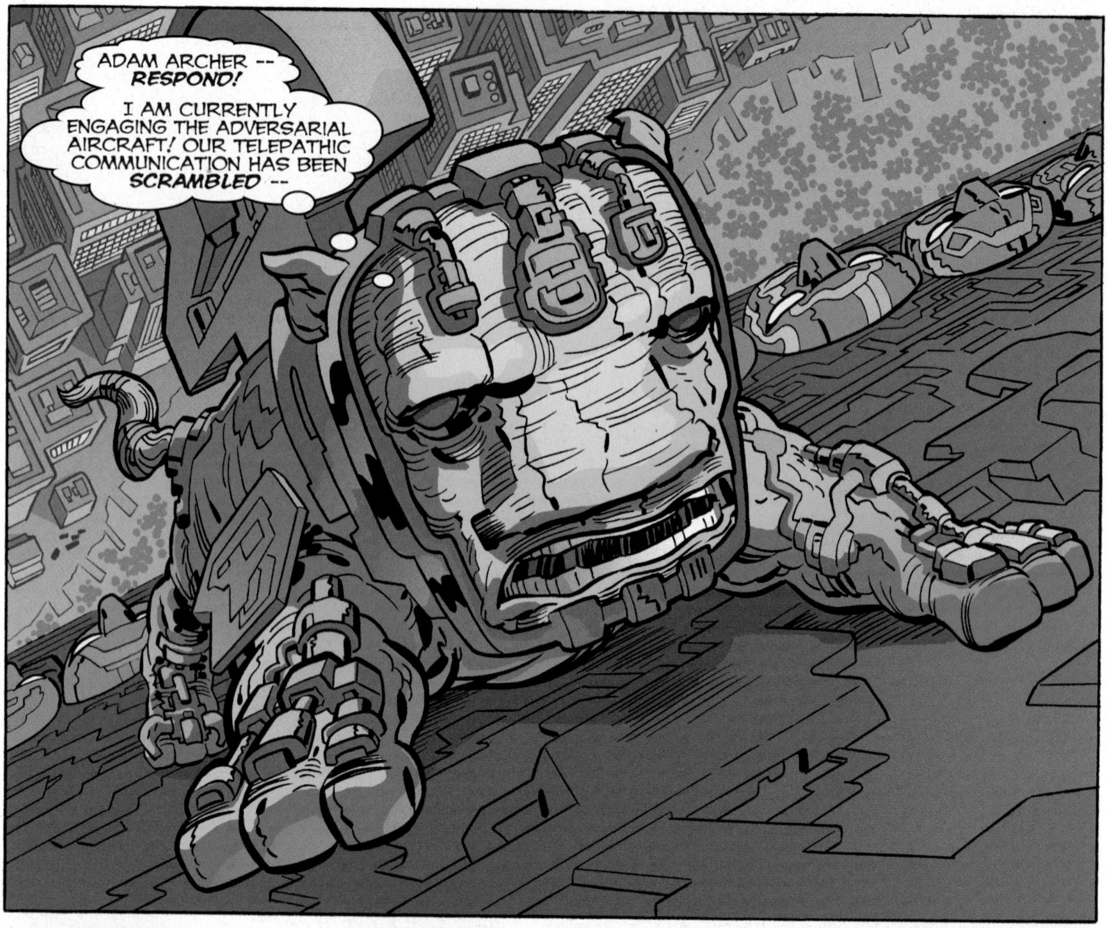
ADAM ARCHER -- RESPOND!
I AM CURRENTLY ENGAGING THE ADVERSARIAL AIRCRAFT! OUR TELEPATHIC COMMUNICATION HAS BEEN SCRAMBLED --

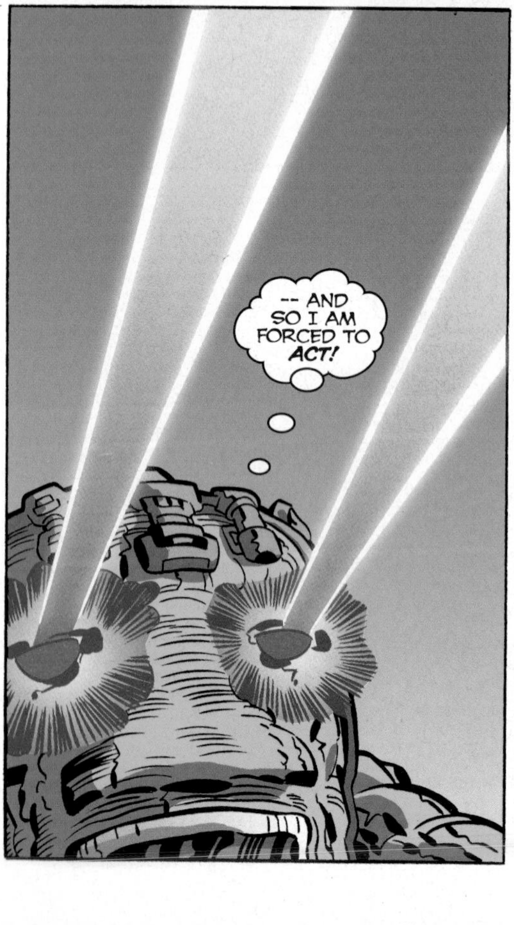
-- AND SO I AM FORCED TO ACT!

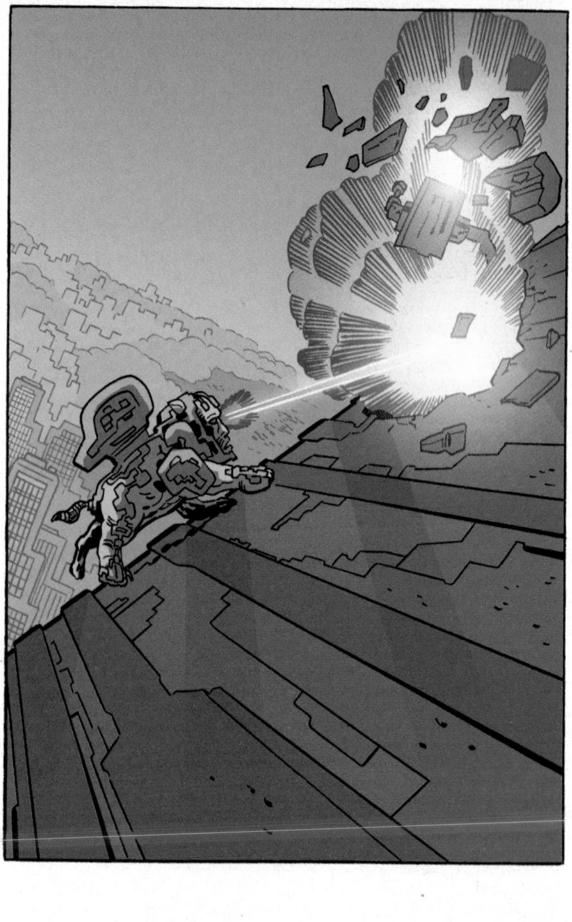

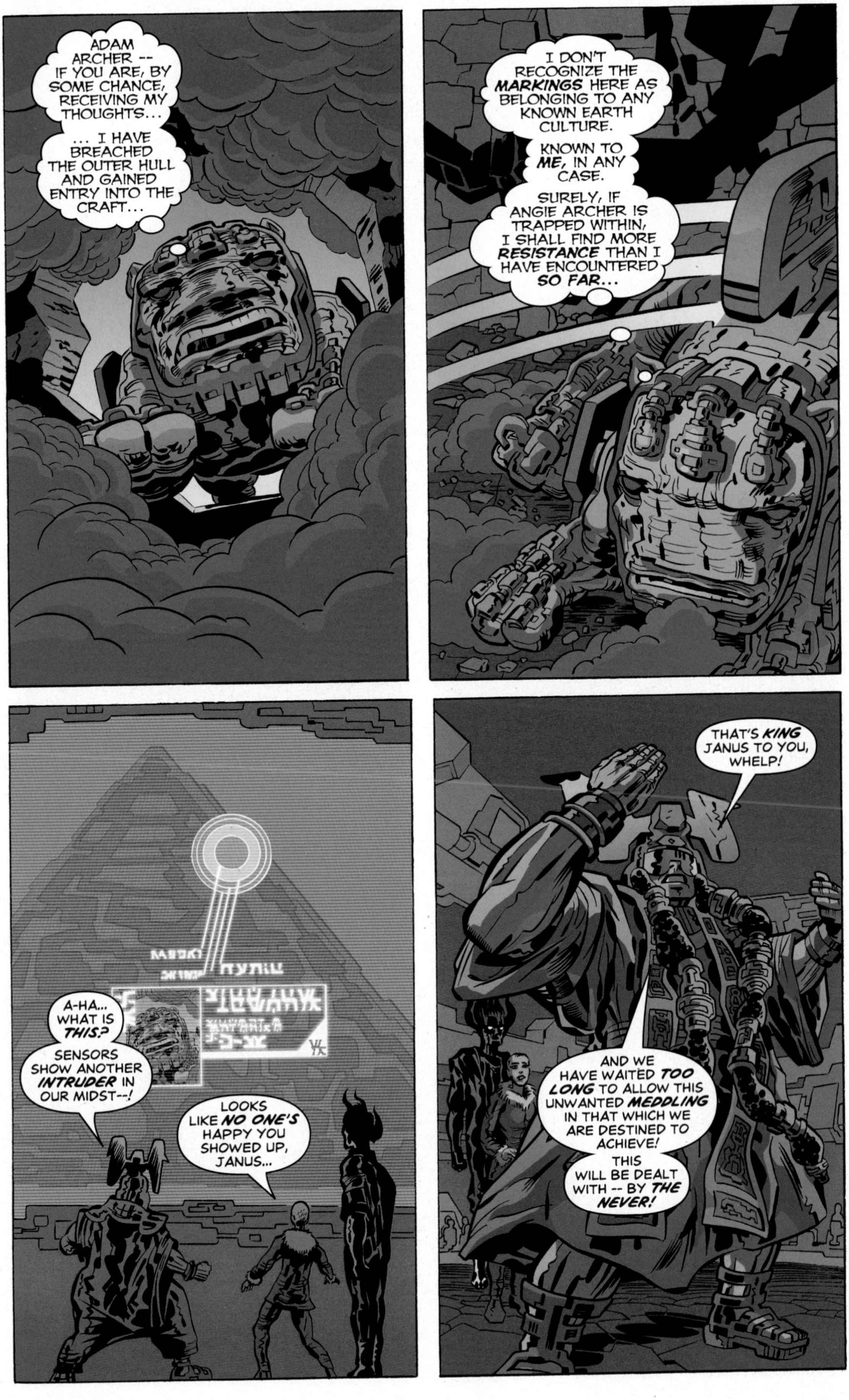
ADAM ARCHER -- IF YOU ARE, BY SOME CHANCE, RECEIVING MY THOUGHTS...
... I HAVE BREACHED THE OUTER HULL AND GAINED ENTRY INTO THE CRAFT...
I DON'T RECOGNIZE THE MARKINGS HERE AS BELONGING TO ANY KNOWN EARTH CULTURE.
KNOWN TO ME, IN ANY CASE.
SURELY, IF ANGIE ARCHER IS TRAPPED WITHIN, I SHALL FIND MORE RESISTANCE THAN I HAVE ENCOUNTERED SO FAR...
A-HA... WHAT IS THIS?
SENSORS SHOW ANOTHER INTRUDER IN OUR MIDST--!
LOOKS LIKE NO ONE'S HAPPY YOU SHOWED UP, JANUS...
THAT'S KING JANUS TO YOU, WHELP!
AND WE HAVE WAITED TOO LONG TO ALLOW THIS UNWANTED MEDDLING IN THAT WHICH WE ARE DESTINED TO ACHIEVE!
THIS WILL BE DEALT WITH -- BY THE NEVER!

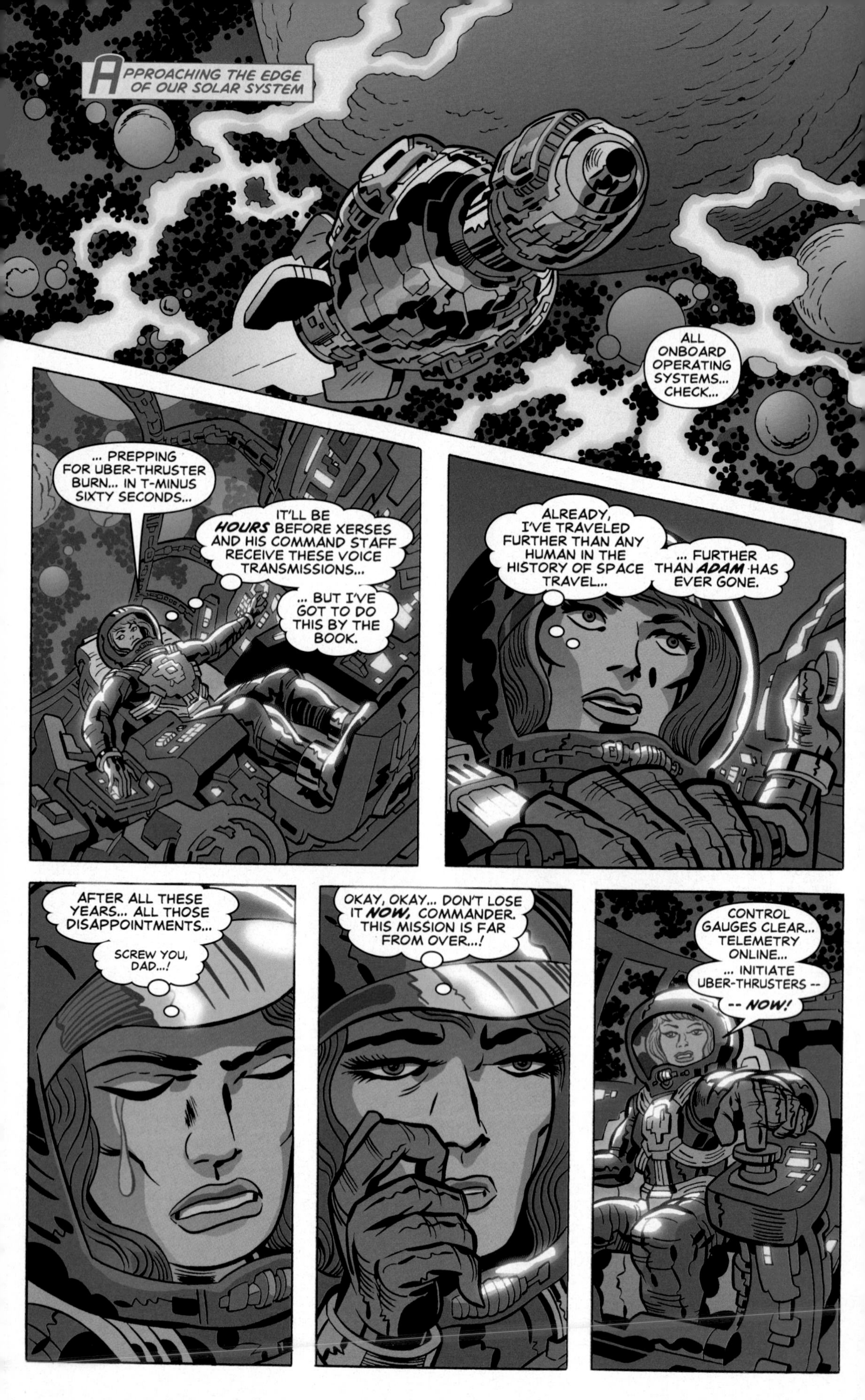
APPROACHING THE EDGE OF OUR SOLAR SYSTEM
ALL ONBOARD OPERATING SYSTEMS... CHECK...
... PREPPING FOR UBER-THRUSTER BURN... IN T-MINUS SIXTY SECONDS...
IT'LL BE HOURS BEFORE XERSES AND HIS COMMAND STAFF RECEIVE THESE VOICE TRANSMISSIONS...
... BUT I'VE GOT TO DO THIS BY THE BOOK.
ALREADY, I'VE TRAVELED FURTHER THAN ANY HUMAN IN THE HISTORY OF SPACE TRAVEL...
... FURTHER THAN ADAM HAS EVER GONE.
AFTER ALL THESE YEARS... ALL THOSE DISAPPOINTMENTS...
SCREW YOU, DAD...!
OKAY, OKAY... DON'T LOSE IT NOW, COMMANDER. THIS MISSION IS FAR FROM OVER...!
CONTROL GAUGES CLEAR... TELEMETRY ONLINE...
... INITIATE UBER-THRUSTERS --
-- NOW!

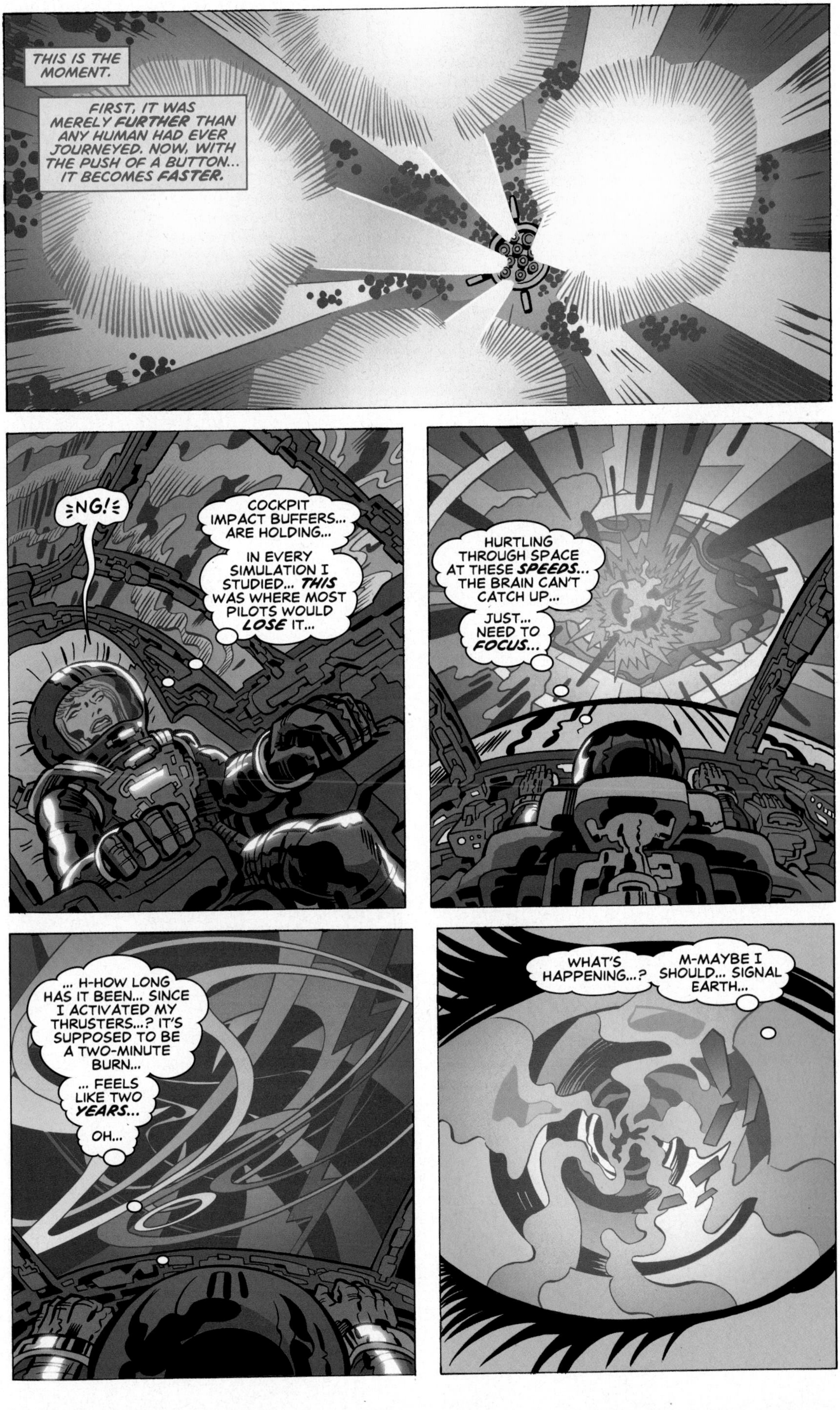
THIS IS THE MOMENT.
FIRST, IT WAS MERELY FURTHER THAN ANY HUMAN HAD EVER JOURNEYED. NOW, WITH THE PUSH OF A BUTTON... IT BECOMES FASTER.
NG!
COCKPIT IMPACT BUFFERS... ARE HOLDING...
IN EVERY SIMULATION I STUDIED... THIS WAS WHERE MOST PILOTS WOULD LOSE IT...
HURTLING THROUGH SPACE AT THESE SPEEDS... THE BRAIN CAN'T CATCH UP...
JUST... NEED TO FOCUS...
... H-HOW LONG HAS IT BEEN... SINCE I ACTIVATED MY THRUSTERS...? IT'S SUPPOSED TO BE A TWO-MINUTE BURN...
... FEELS LIKE TWO YEARS...
OH...
WHAT'S HAPPENING...?
M-MAYBE I SHOULD... SIGNAL EARTH...

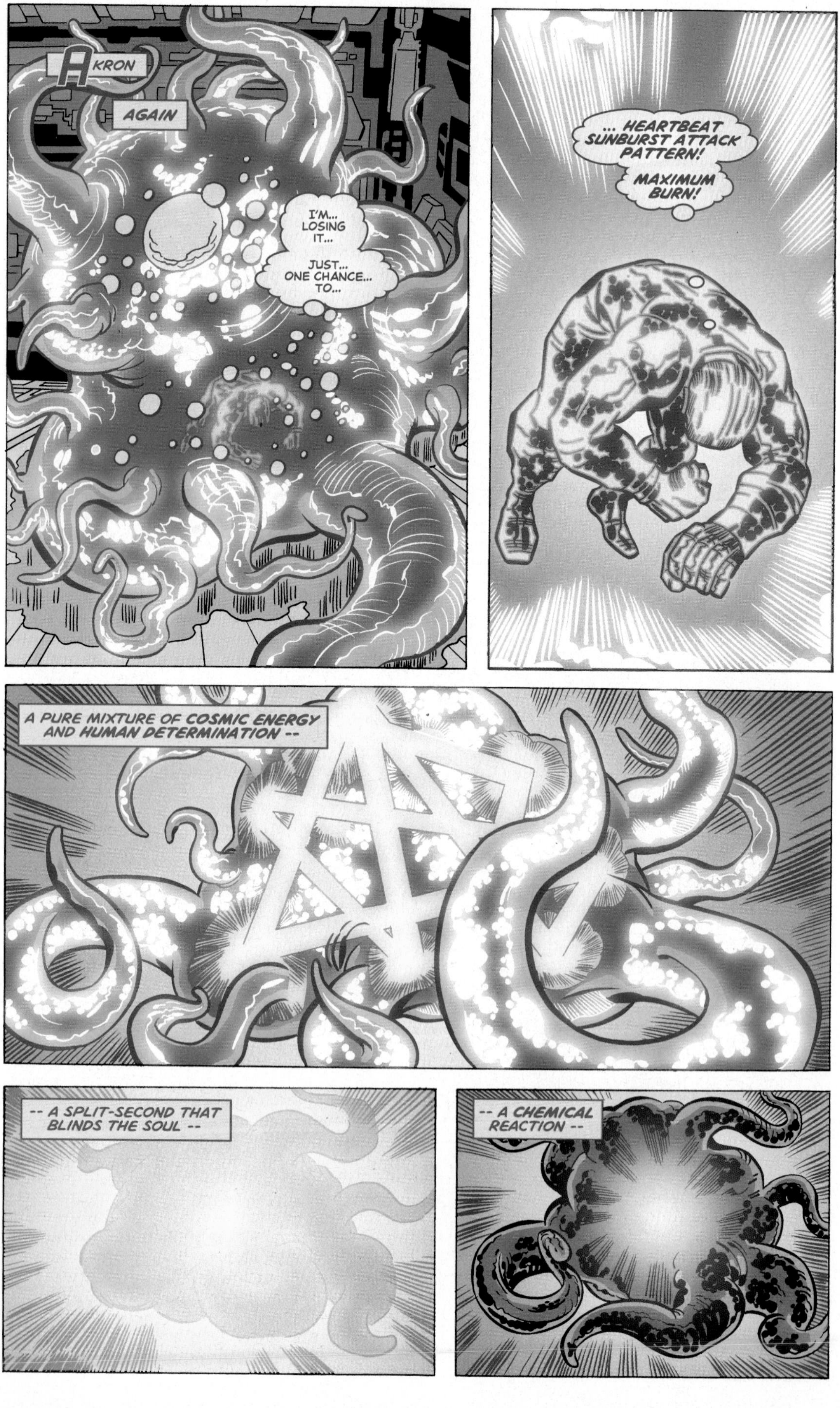
AKRON
AGAIN
I'M... LOSING IT...
JUST... ONE CHANCE... TO...
... HEARTBEAT SUNBURST ATTACK PATTERN!
MAXIMUM BURN!
A PURE MIXTURE OF COSMIC ENERGY AND HUMAN DETERMINATION --
-- A SPLIT-SECOND THAT BLINDS THE SOUL --
-- A CHEMICAL REACTION --

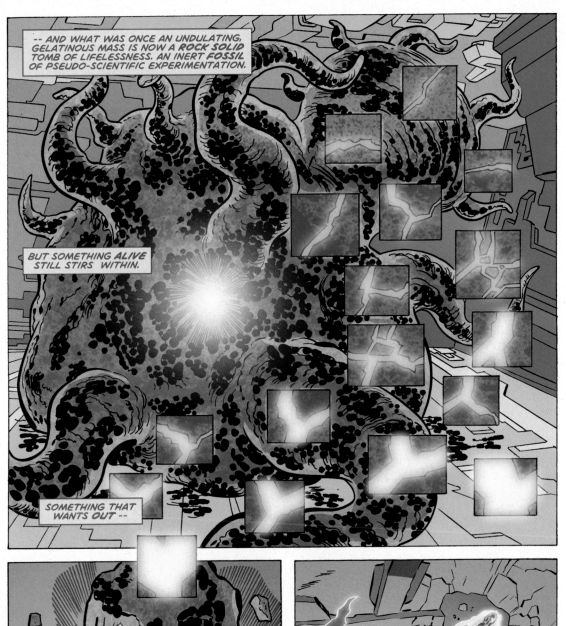

-- AND WHAT WAS ONCE AN UNDULATING, GELATINOUS MASS IS NOW A *ROCK SOLID* TOMB OF LIFELESSNESS. AN INERT FOSSIL OF PSEUDO-SCIENTIFIC EXPERIMENTATION.

BUT SOMETHING *ALIVE* STILL STIRS WITHIN.

SOMETHING THAT WANTS *OUT* --

HUHN--!

NICKELHEAD'S *ESCAPED*... ANOTHER VICTORY I *CAN'T* CLAIM...

... AND I'VE WASTED TOO MUCH TIME HERE ALREADY...!

DAMMIT.

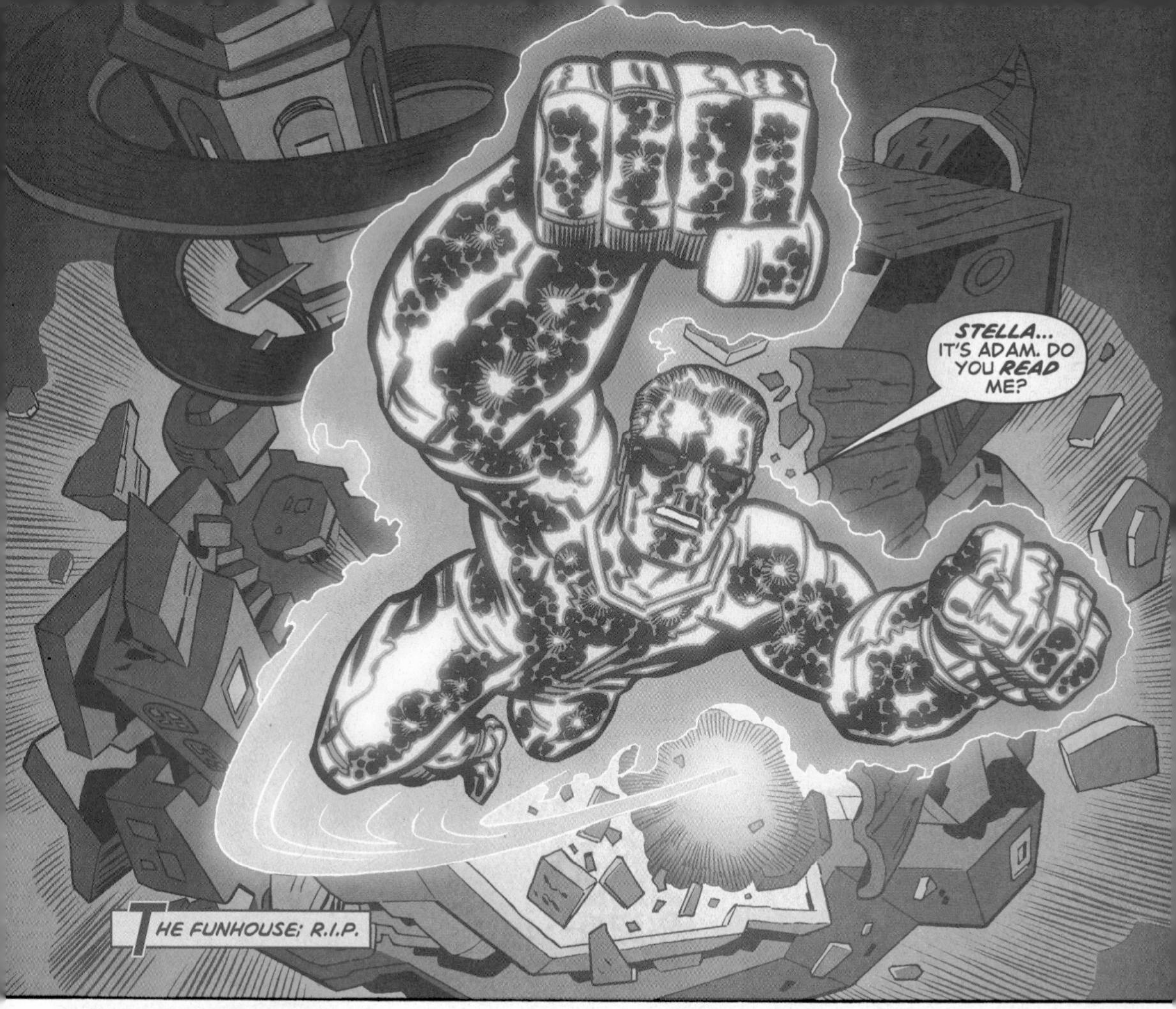
STELLA... IT'S ADAM. DO YOU READ ME?
THE FUNHOUSE: R.I.P.

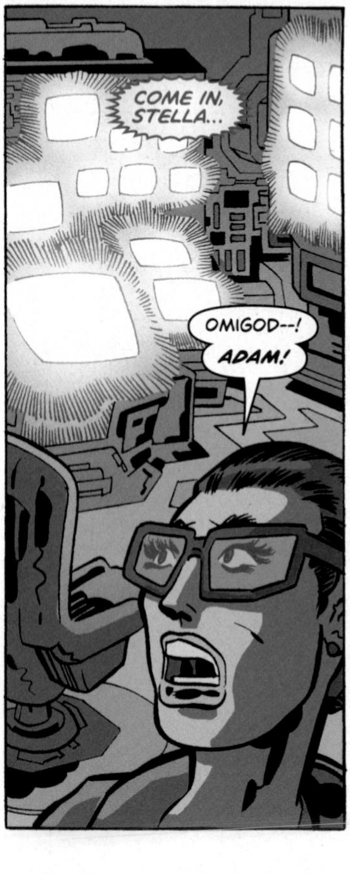
COME IN, STELLA...
OMIGOD--! ADAM!

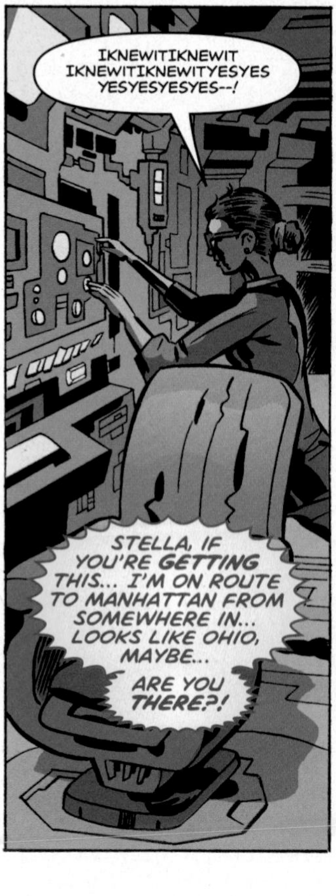
IKNEWITIKNEWIT IKNEWITIKNEWITYESYES YESYESYESYES--!
STELLA, IF YOU'RE GETTING THIS... I'M ON ROUTE TO MANHATTAN FROM SOMEWHERE IN... LOOKS LIKE OHIO, MAYBE...
ARE YOU THERE?!

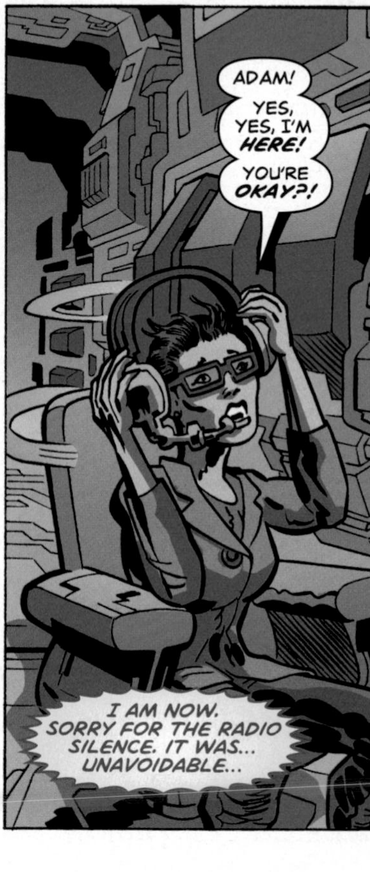
ADAM!
YES, YES, I'M HERE!
YOU'RE OKAY?!
I AM NOW. SORRY FOR THE RADIO SILENCE. IT WAS... UNAVOIDABLE...

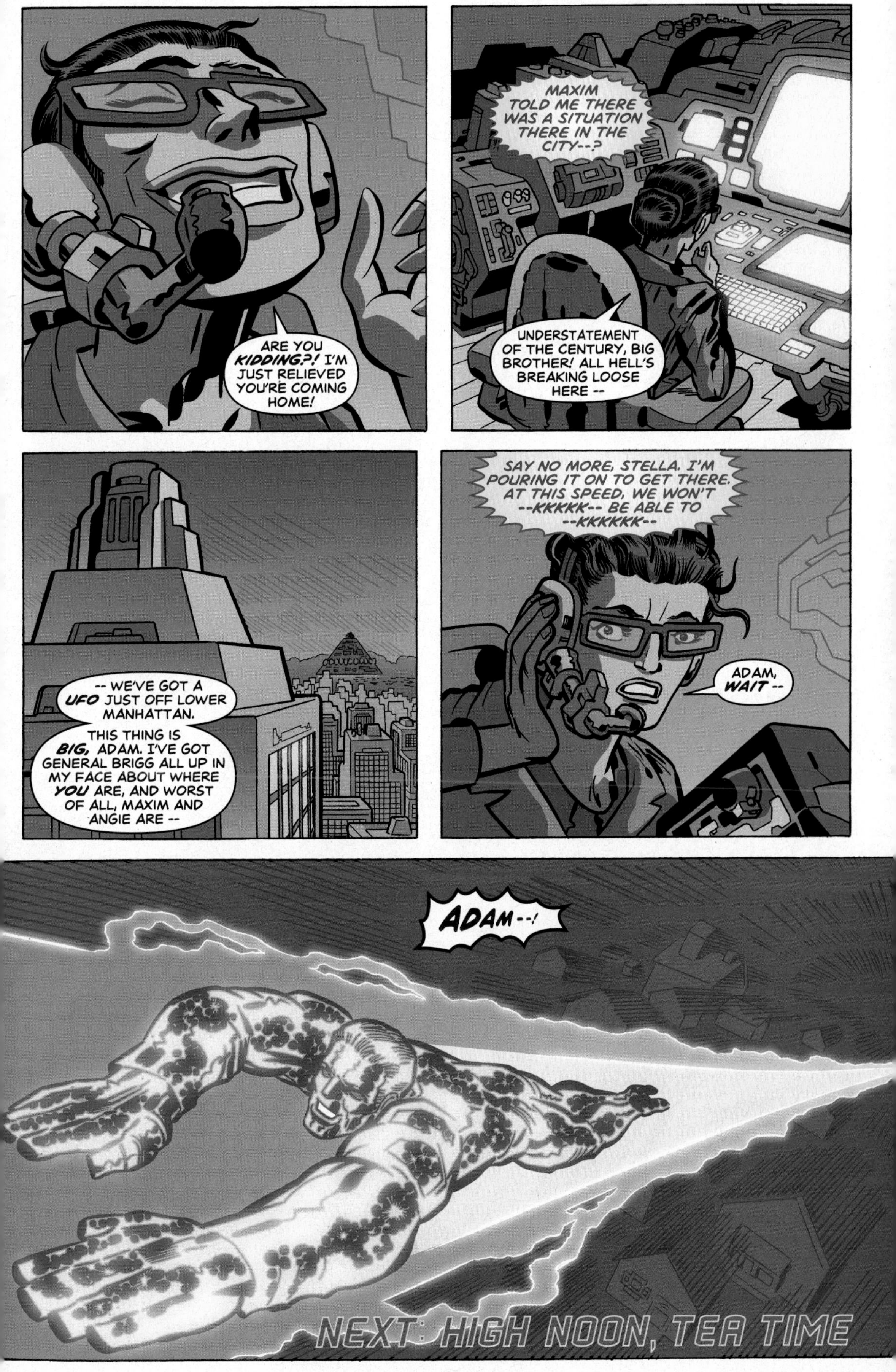
MAXIM TOLD ME THERE WAS A SITUATION THERE IN THE CITY--?
ARE YOU KIDDING?! I'M JUST RELIEVED YOU'RE COMING HOME!
UNDERSTATEMENT OF THE CENTURY, BIG BROTHER! ALL HELL'S BREAKING LOOSE HERE --
-- WE'VE GOT A UFO JUST OFF LOWER MANHATTAN.
THIS THING IS BIG, ADAM. I'VE GOT GENERAL BRIGG ALL UP IN MY FACE ABOUT WHERE YOU ARE, AND WORST OF ALL, MAXIM AND ANGIE ARE --
SAY NO MORE, STELLA. I'M POURING IT ON TO GET THERE. AT THIS SPEED, WE WON'T --KKKKK-- BE ABLE TO --KKKKKK--
ADAM, WAIT --
ADAM--!
NEXT: HIGH NOON, TEA TIME

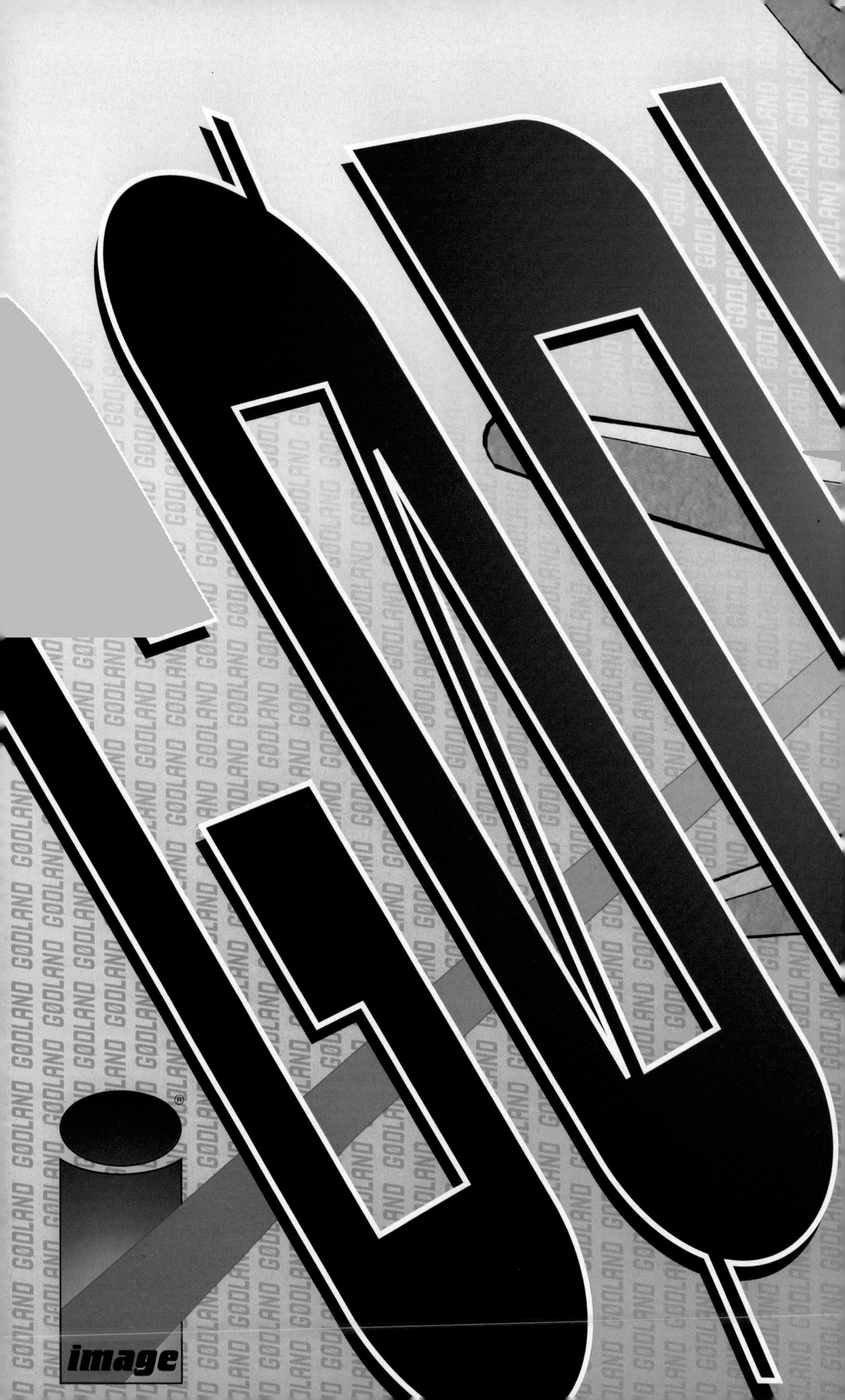
GODLAND
image

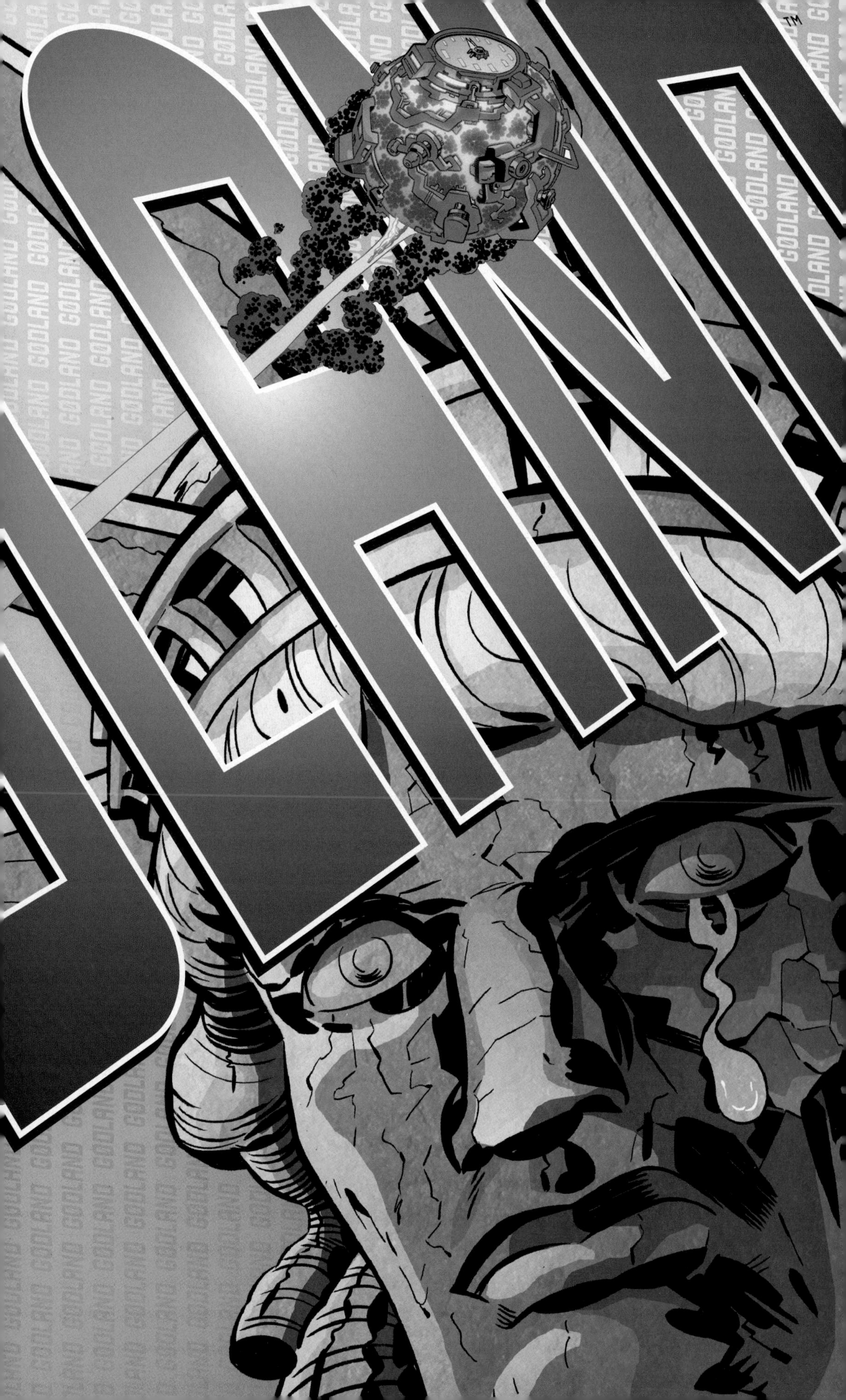
GODLAND
™

BOOK TWELVE:

HIGH NOON, TEA TIME

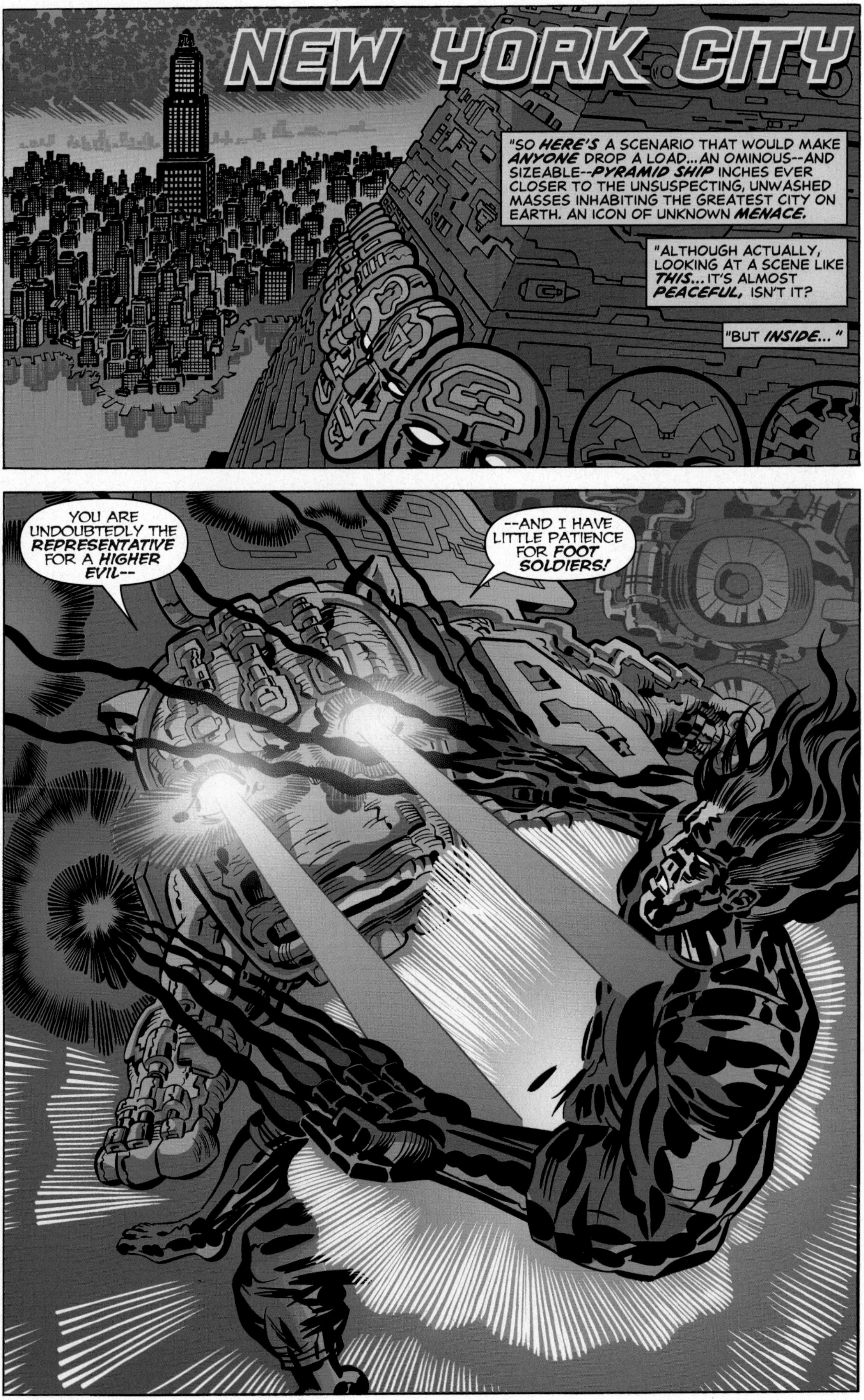
NEW YORK CITY
"SO HERE'S A SCENARIO THAT WOULD MAKE ANYONE DROP A LOAD...AN OMINOUS--AND SIZEABLE--PYRAMID SHIP INCHES EVER CLOSER TO THE UNSUSPECTING, UNWASHED MASSES INHABITING THE GREATEST CITY ON EARTH. AN ICON OF UNKNOWN MENACE.
"ALTHOUGH ACTUALLY, LOOKING AT A SCENE LIKE THIS... IT'S ALMOST PEACEFUL, ISN'T IT?
"BUT INSIDE..."
YOU ARE UNDOUBTEDLY THE REPRESENTATIVE FOR A HIGHER EVIL--
--AND I HAVE LITTLE PATIENCE FOR FOOT SOLDIERS!

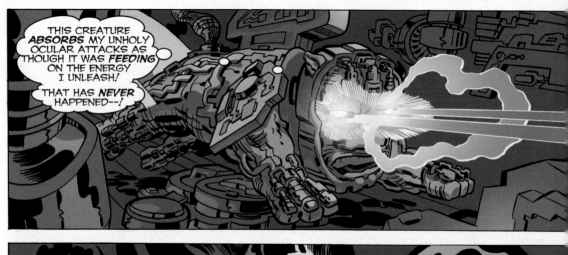

THIS CREATURE *ABSORBS* MY UNHOLY OCULAR ATTACKS AS THOUGH IT WAS *FEEDING* ON THE ENERGY I UNLEASH!

THAT HAS *NEVER* HAPPENED--!

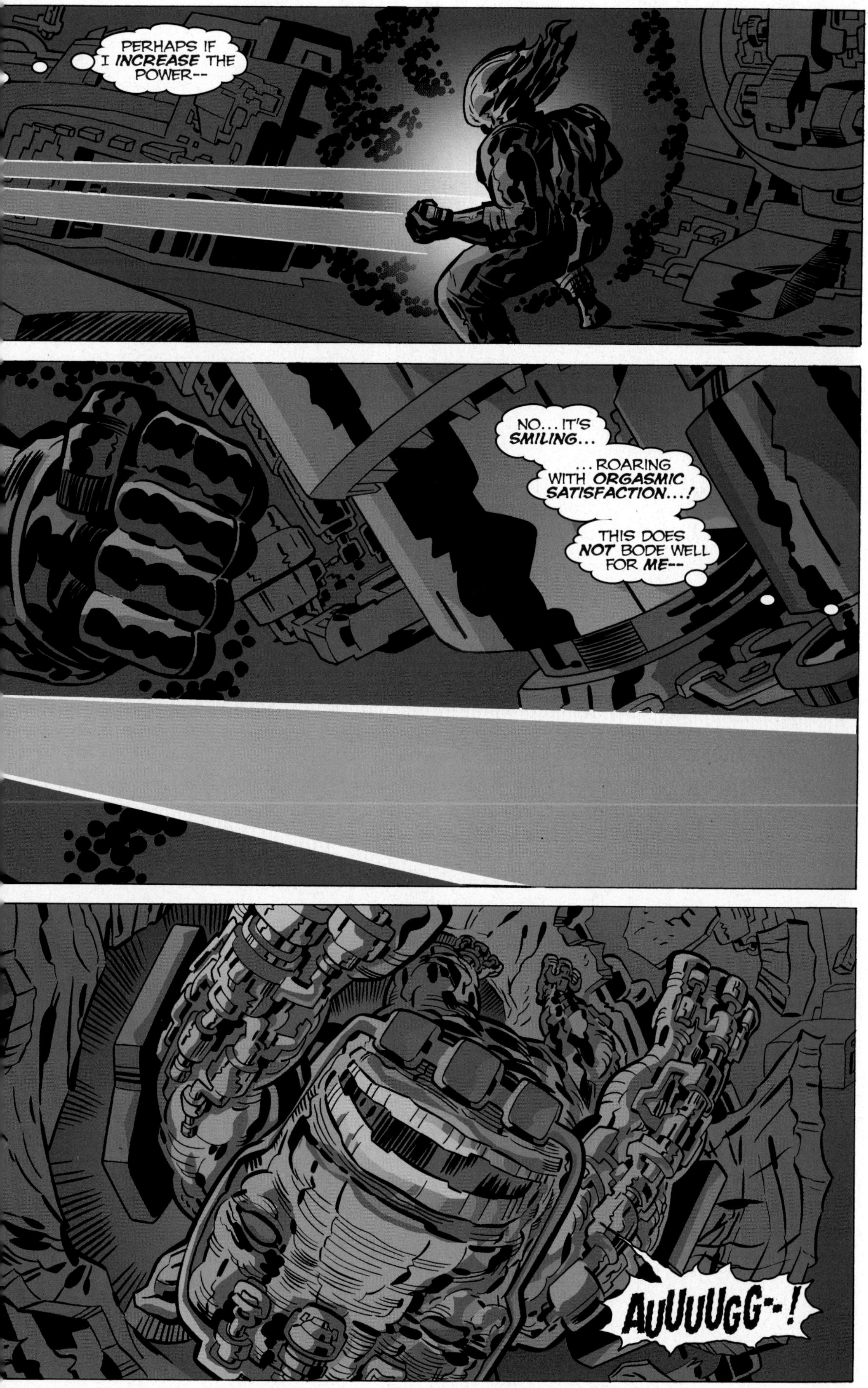
PERHAPS IF I INCREASE THE POWER--
NO... IT'S SMILING...
...ROARING WITH ORGASMIC SATISFACTION...!
THIS DOES NOT BODE WELL FOR ME--
AUUUUGG--!

BY NOW, THE NEVER WILL HAVE EFFECTIVELY *ELIMINATED* OUR UNWANTED GUEST. IT'S WHAT HE DOES BEST.

KNEEL BEFORE THE GLORY THAT IS *KING JANUS,* SCRUB.

NNNGG... YOU GOT... NO *IDEA* WHAT YOU'RE *UP* AGAINST, LIBERACE...

G-GET *OFFA* ME...!

DO I LOOK WORRIED? THE ALMIGHTY *J'RHOGAN* HAS INFUSED ME WITH GRAND PURPOSE. NO EARTHLY OPPOSITION WILL CAUSE *ME* TO BLINK!

WELL, *GUESS WHAT,* ANTENNA-HEAD-- "EARTHLY OPPOSITION" DOESN'T COME *CLOSE* TO DESCRIBING WHAT *YOU'RE* UP AGAINST--!

MY *BROTHER'S* GONNA' SHOVE THAT SILK ROBE STRAIGHT UP YOUR--

NONSENSE. I'M GOING TO *SHOW* YOU SOMETHING... SOMETHING NO OTHER MODERN MORTAL WILL EVER BE BLESSED TO *SEE...*

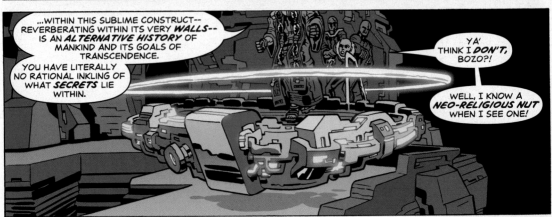

...WITHIN THIS SUBLIME CONSTRUCT-- REVERBERATING WITHIN ITS VERY *WALLS*-- IS AN *ALTERNATIVE HISTORY* OF MANKIND AND ITS GOALS OF TRANSCENDENCE.

YOU HAVE LITERALLY NO RATIONAL INKLING OF WHAT *SECRETS* LIE WITHIN.

YA' THINK I *DON'T,* BOZO?!

WELL, I KNOW A *NEO-RELIGIOUS NUT* WHEN I SEE ONE!

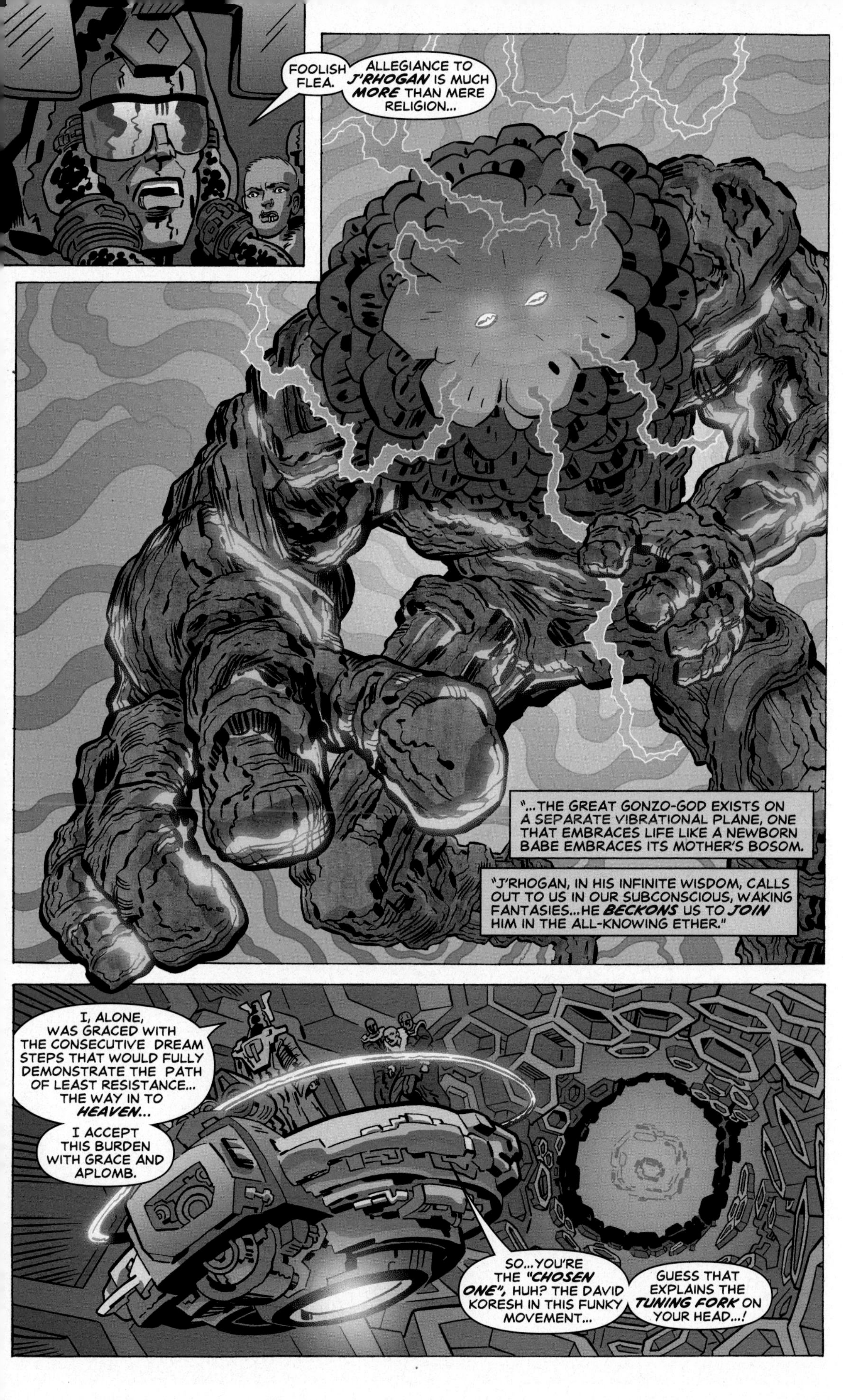
FOOLISH FLEA.
ALLEGIANCE TO J'RHOGAN IS MUCH MORE THAN MERE RELIGION...
"...THE GREAT GONZO-GOD EXISTS ON A SEPARATE VIBRATIONAL PLANE, ONE THAT EMBRACES LIFE LIKE A NEWBORN BABE EMBRACES ITS MOTHER'S BOSOM.
"J'RHOGAN, IN HIS INFINITE WISDOM, CALLS OUT TO US IN OUR SUBCONSCIOUS, WAKING FANTASIES...HE BECKONS US TO JOIN HIM IN THE ALL-KNOWING ETHER."
I, ALONE, WAS GRACED WITH THE CONSECUTIVE DREAM STEPS THAT WOULD FULLY DEMONSTRATE THE PATH OF LEAST RESISTANCE... THE WAY IN TO HEAVEN...
I ACCEPT THIS BURDEN WITH GRACE AND APLOMB.
SO...YOU'RE THE "CHOSEN ONE", HUH? THE DAVID KORESH IN THIS FUNKY MOVEMENT...
GUESS THAT EXPLAINS THE TUNING FORK ON YOUR HEAD...!

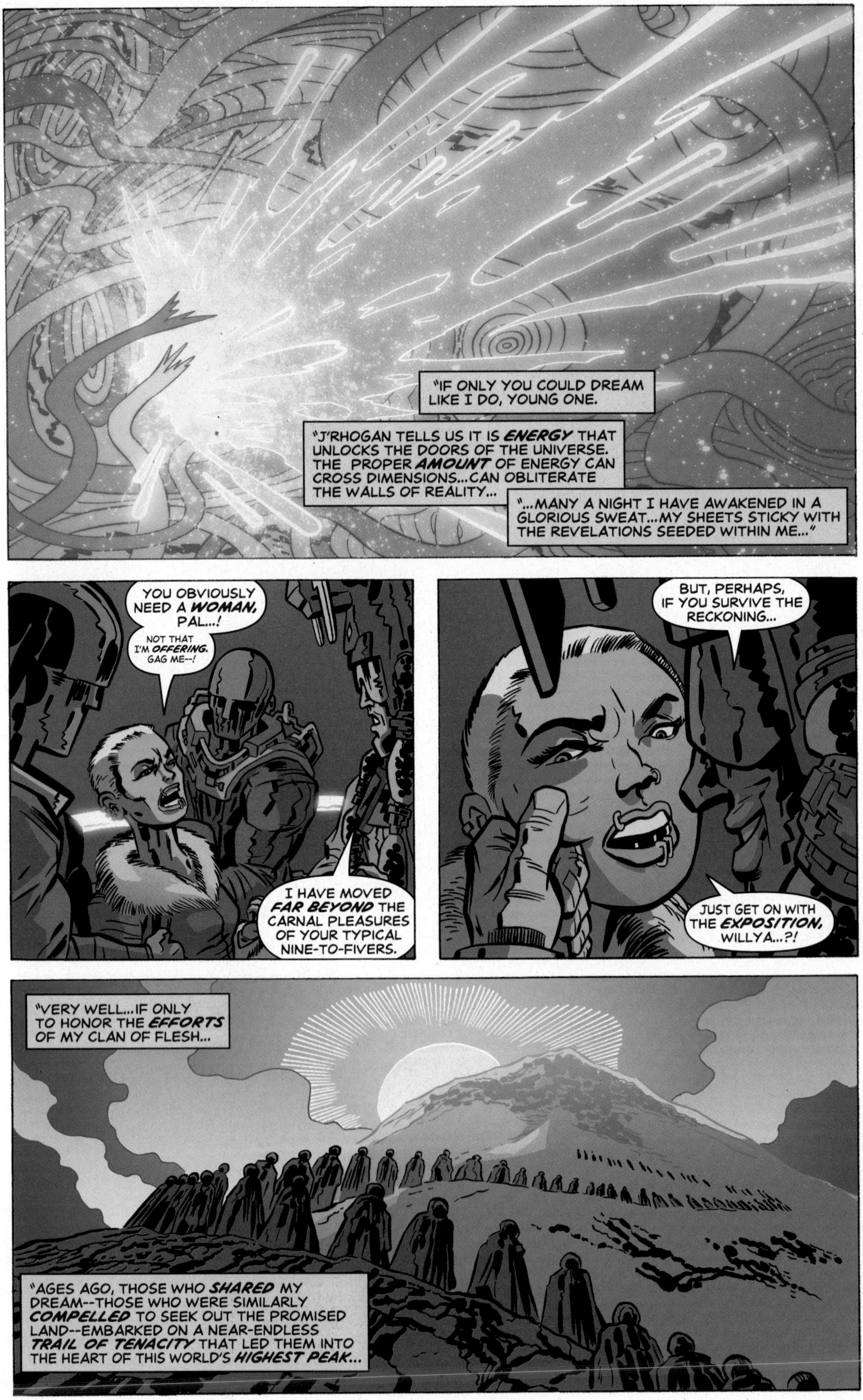
"IF ONLY YOU COULD DREAM LIKE I DO, YOUNG ONE.
"J'RHOGAN TELLS US IT IS ENERGY THAT UNLOCKS THE DOORS OF THE UNIVERSE. THE PROPER AMOUNT OF ENERGY CAN CROSS DIMENSIONS...CAN OBLITERATE THE WALLS OF REALITY...
"...MANY A NIGHT I HAVE AWAKENED IN A GLORIOUS SWEAT...MY SHEETS STICKY WITH THE REVELATIONS SEEDED WITHIN ME..."
YOU OBVIOUSLY NEED A WOMAN, PAL...!
NOT THAT I'M OFFERING. GAG ME--!
I HAVE MOVED FAR BEYOND THE CARNAL PLEASURES OF YOUR TYPICAL NINE-TO-FIVERS.
BUT, PERHAPS, IF YOU SURVIVE THE RECKONING...
JUST GET ON WITH THE EXPOSITION, WILLYA...?!
"VERY WELL...IF ONLY TO HONOR THE EFFORTS OF MY CLAN OF FLESH...
"AGES AGO, THOSE WHO SHARED MY DREAM--THOSE WHO WERE SIMILARLY COMPELLED TO SEEK OUT THE PROMISED LAND--EMBARKED ON A NEAR-ENDLESS TRAIL OF TENACITY THAT LED THEM INTO THE HEART OF THIS WORLD'S HIGHEST PEAK...

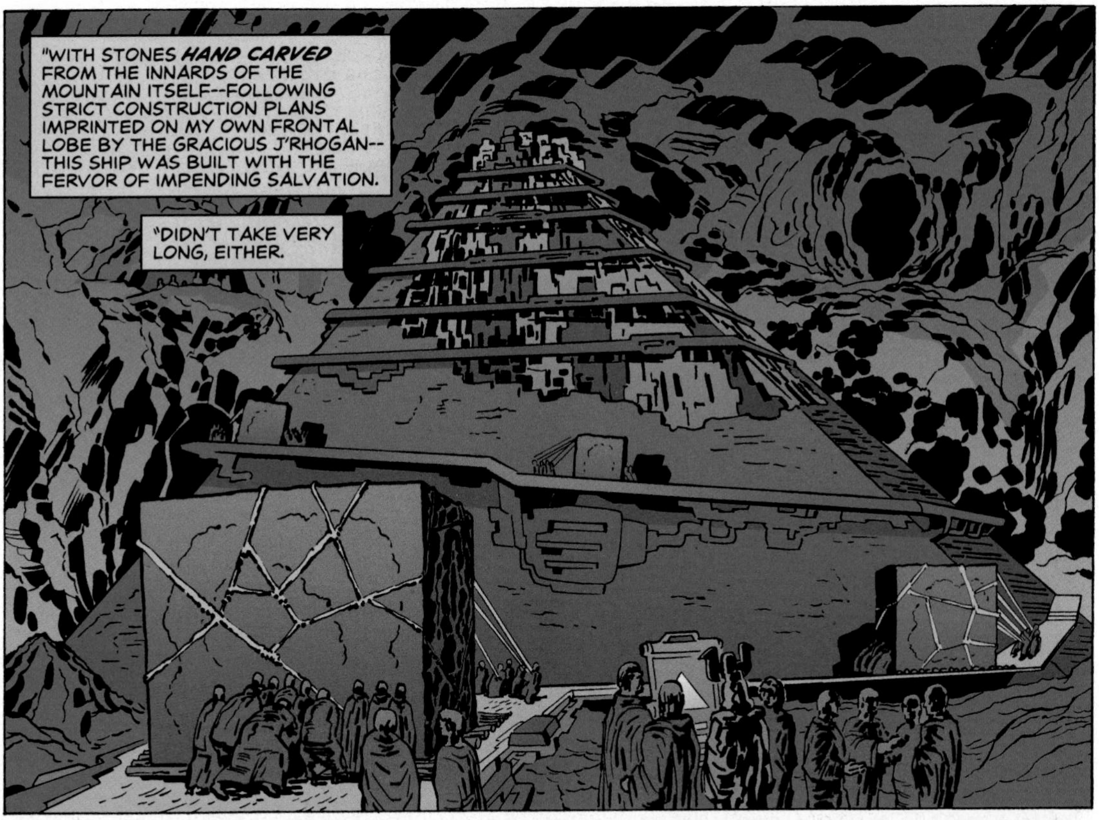
"WITH STONES HAND CARVED FROM THE INNARDS OF THE MOUNTAIN ITSELF--FOLLOWING STRICT CONSTRUCTION PLANS IMPRINTED ON MY OWN FRONTAL LOBE BY THE GRACIOUS J'RHOGAN--THIS SHIP WAS BUILT WITH THE FERVOR OF IMPENDING SALVATION.
"DIDN'T TAKE VERY LONG, EITHER.

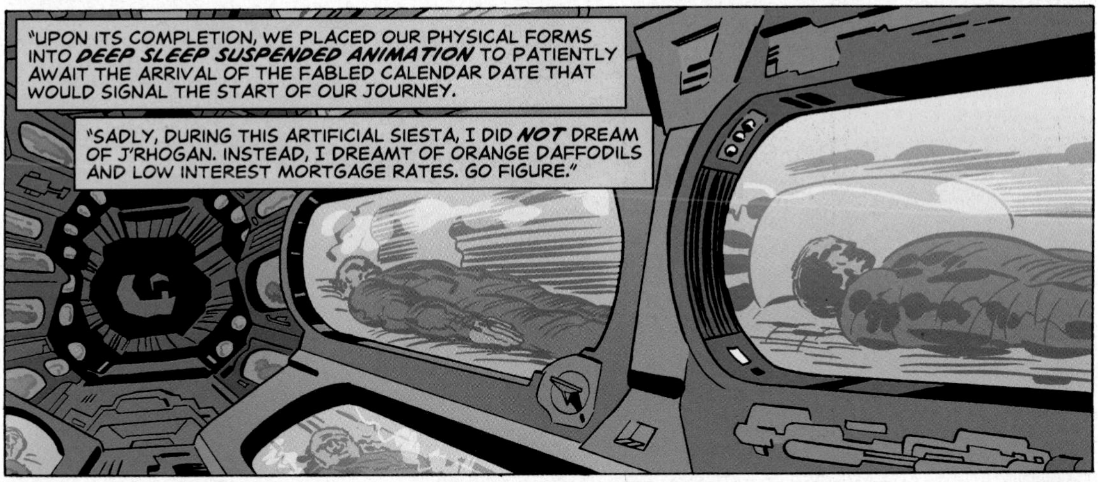
"UPON ITS COMPLETION, WE PLACED OUR PHYSICAL FORMS INTO DEEP SLEEP SUSPENDED ANIMATION TO PATIENTLY AWAIT THE ARRIVAL OF THE FABLED CALENDAR DATE THAT WOULD SIGNAL THE START OF OUR JOURNEY.
"SADLY, DURING THIS ARTIFICIAL SIESTA, I DID NOT DREAM OF J'RHOGAN. INSTEAD, I DREAMT OF ORANGE DAFFODILS AND LOW INTEREST MORTGAGE RATES. GO FIGURE."

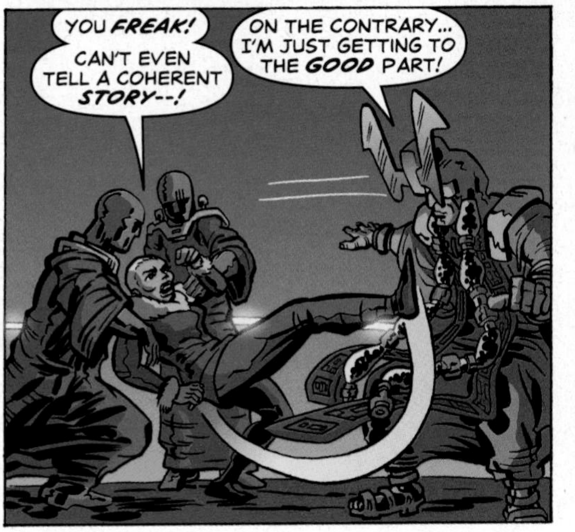
YOU FREAK! CAN'T EVEN TELL A COHERENT STORY--!
ON THE CONTRARY... I'M JUST GETTING TO THE GOOD PART!

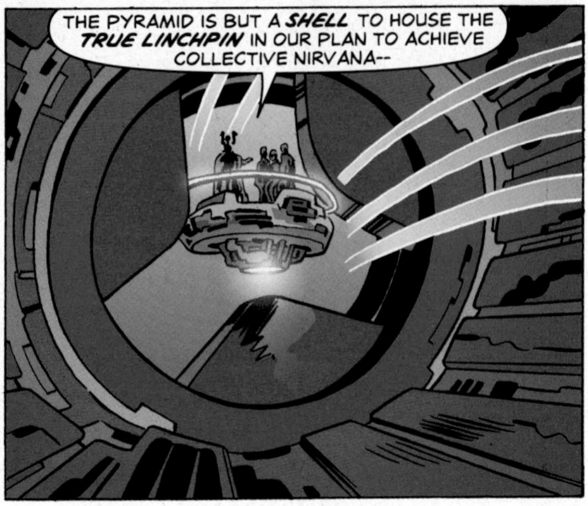
THE PYRAMID IS BUT A SHELL TO HOUSE THE TRUE LINCHPIN IN OUR PLAN TO ACHIEVE COLLECTIVE NIRVANA--

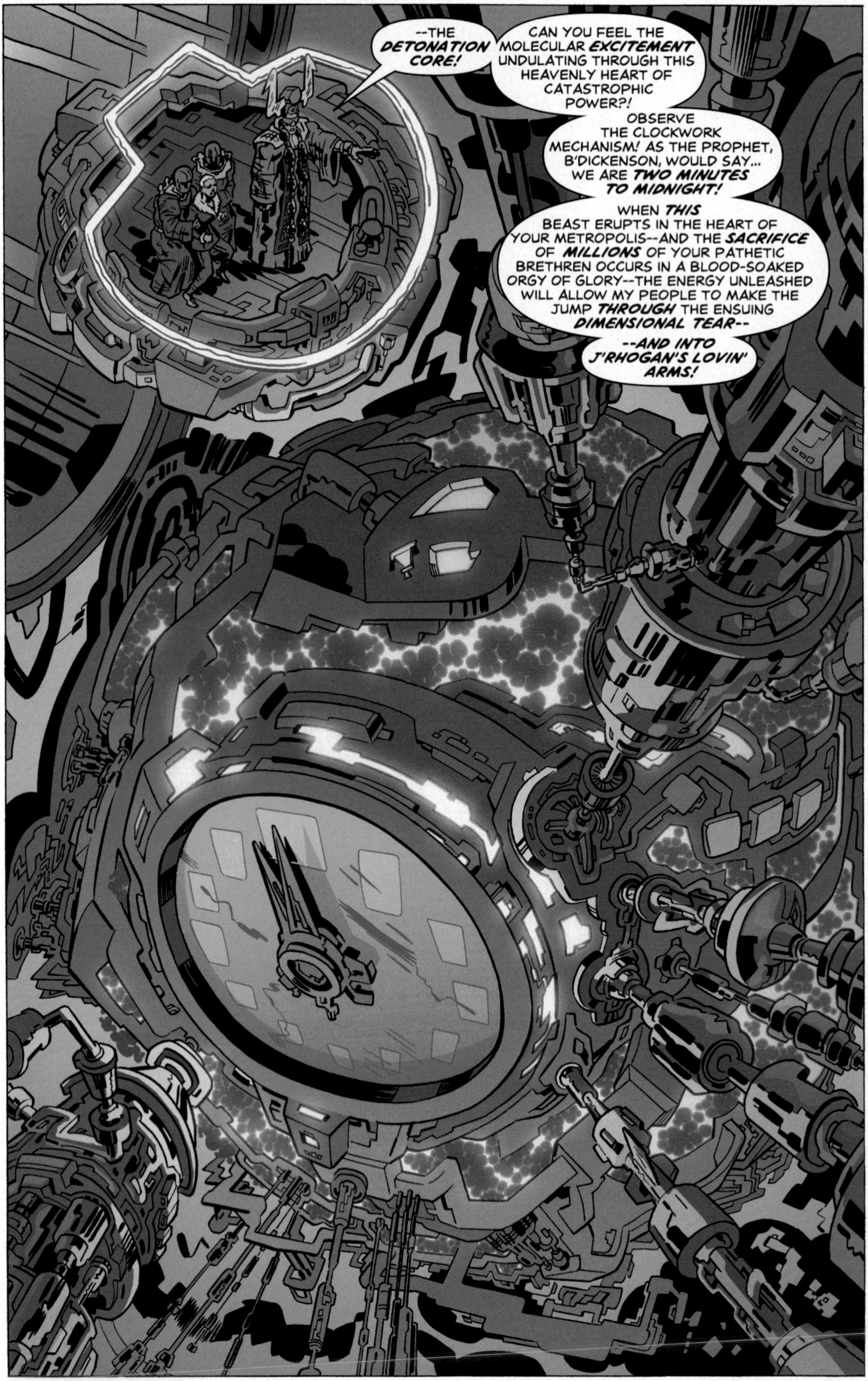
--THE DETONATION CORE!
CAN YOU FEEL THE MOLECULAR EXCITEMENT UNDULATING THROUGH THIS HEAVENLY HEART OF CATASTROPHIC POWER?!
OBSERVE THE CLOCKWORK MECHANISM! AS THE PROPHET, B'DICKENSON, WOULD SAY... WE ARE TWO MINUTES TO MIDNIGHT!
WHEN THIS BEAST ERUPTS IN THE HEART OF YOUR METROPOLIS--AND THE SACRIFICE OF MILLIONS OF YOUR PATHETIC BRETHREN OCCURS IN A BLOOD-SOAKED ORGY OF GLORY--THE ENERGY UNLEASHED WILL ALLOW MY PEOPLE TO MAKE THE JUMP THROUGH THE ENSUING DIMENSIONAL TEAR--
--AND INTO J'RHOGAN'S LOVIN' ARMS!

ALERT: INCOMING SIGNAL FROM GENERAL BRIGG--

THAT'S *ONE* CALL I'M *NOT* ANSWERING RIGHT NOW--!

WHAT ON EARTH WOULD I TELL HIM ANYWAY?!

"SORRY, GENERAL...BUT MY *LITTLE SISTER* AND AN *ALIEN DOG CREATURE* ARE *INSIDE* THAT THING... TRYING TO STOP IT FROM DOING TO *MANHATTAN* WHAT IT DID TO THE *STATUE OF LIBERTY*...

...FIGHTING THE GOOD FIGHT UNTIL MY *BROTHER* ARRIVES!" WONDER IF *THAT* EXPLANATION WOULD FLY WITH THE MILITARY...?

ADAM!

ADAM, DO YOU *READ* ME?!

IT'S NO USE. HE'S MOVING *TOO FAST.* GOD HELP US IF HE OVERSHOOTS NEW YORK--!

WAIT-- THERE HE *IS*...

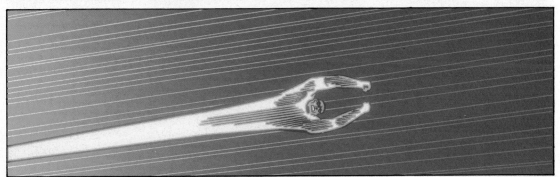

"...MOMENT OF TRUTH, BIG BROTHER. THIS IS A CHANCE TO BE A BONA FIDE *SUPERHERO.*

"DON'T BLOW IT."

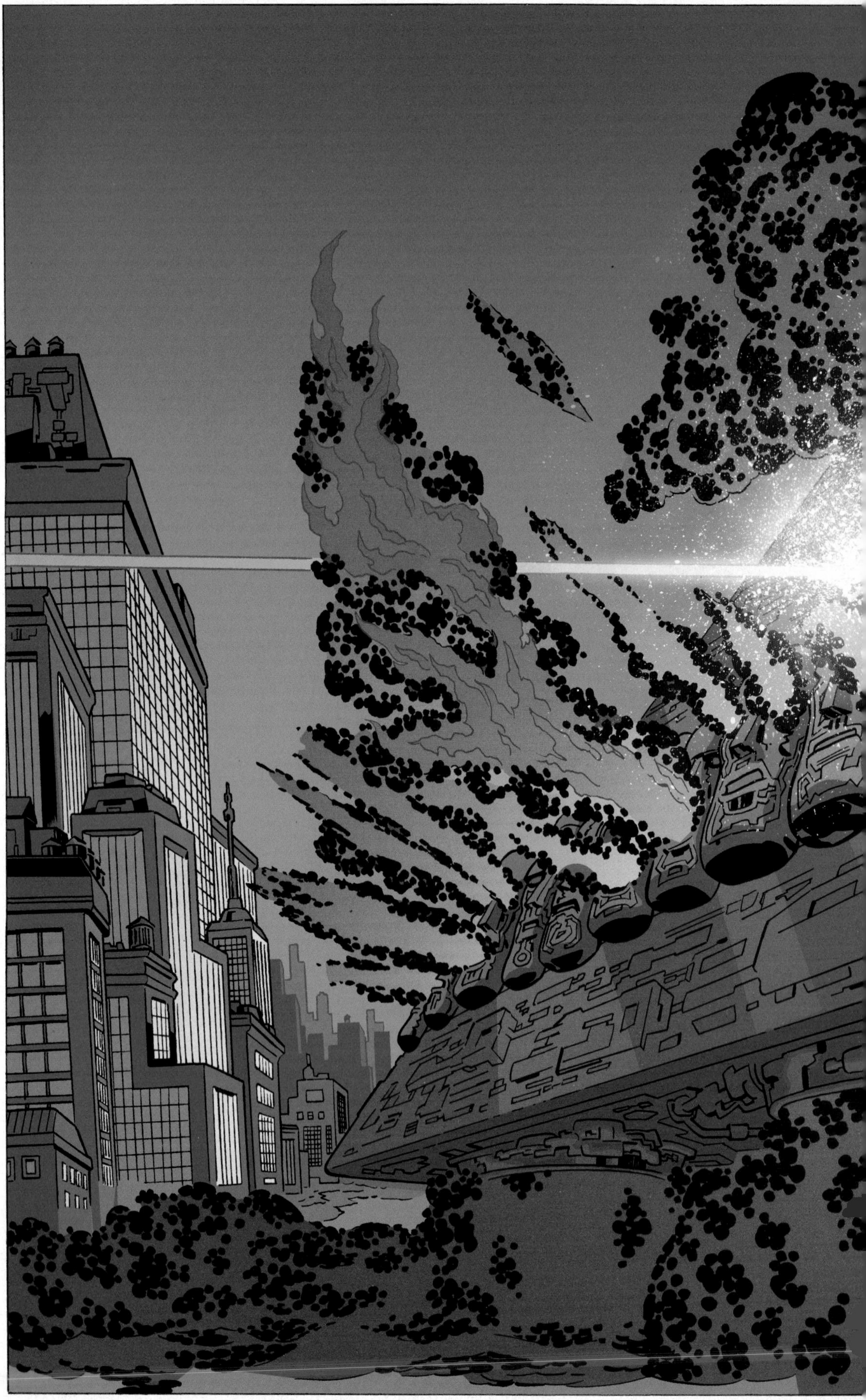

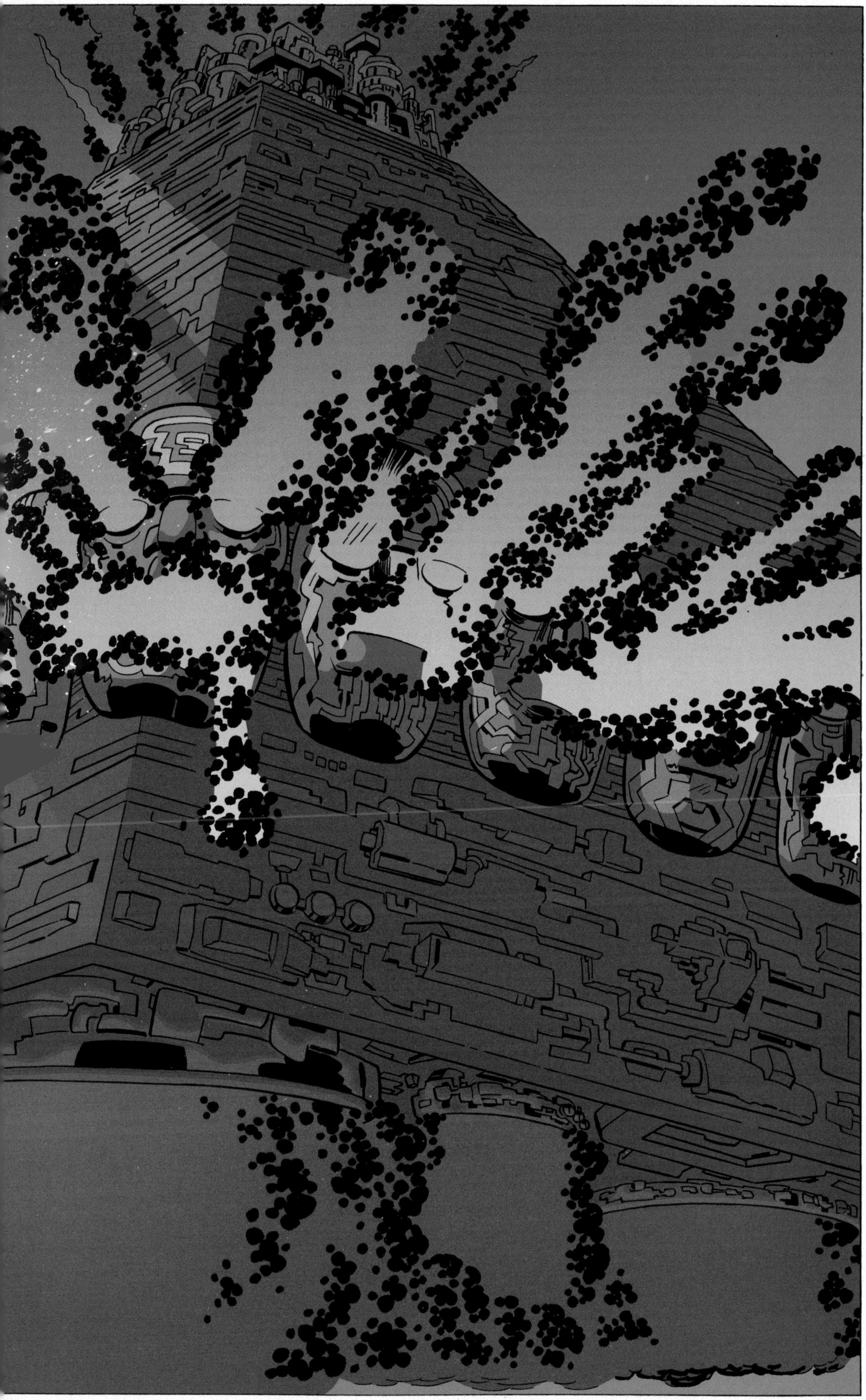

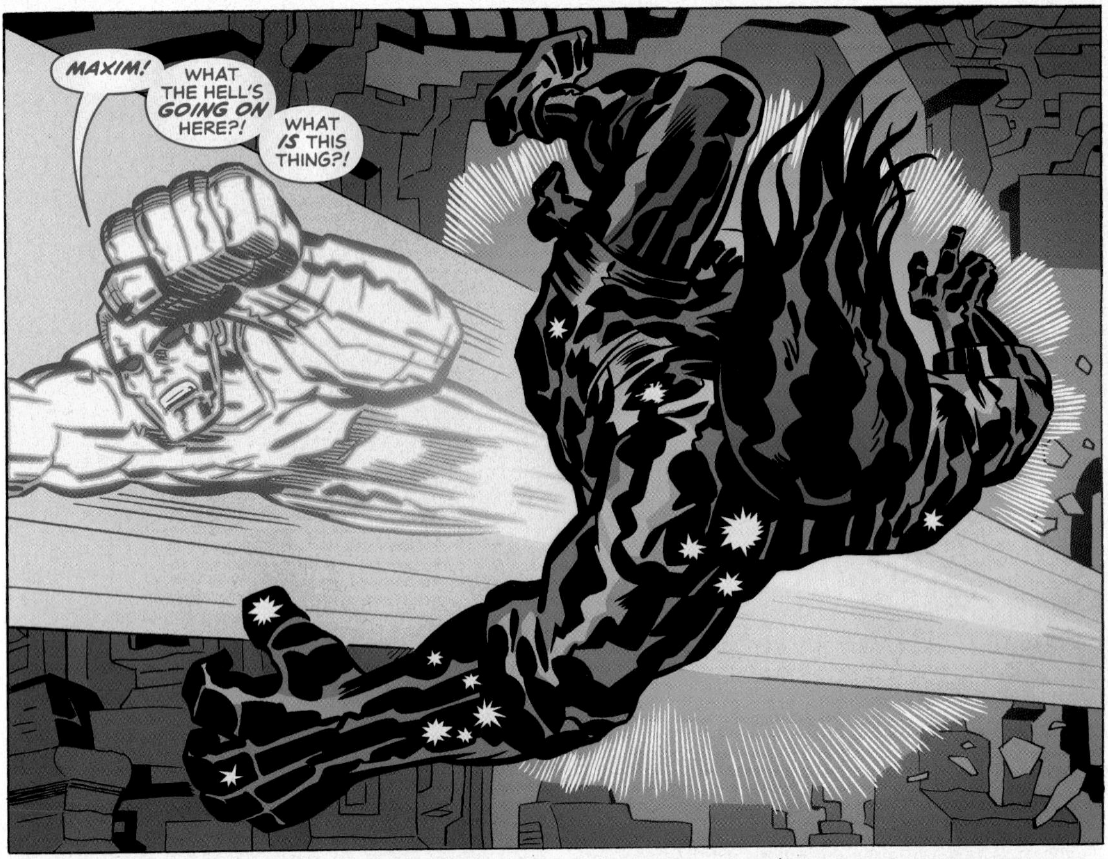
MAXIM!
WHAT THE HELL'S GOING ON HERE?!
WHAT IS THIS THING?!

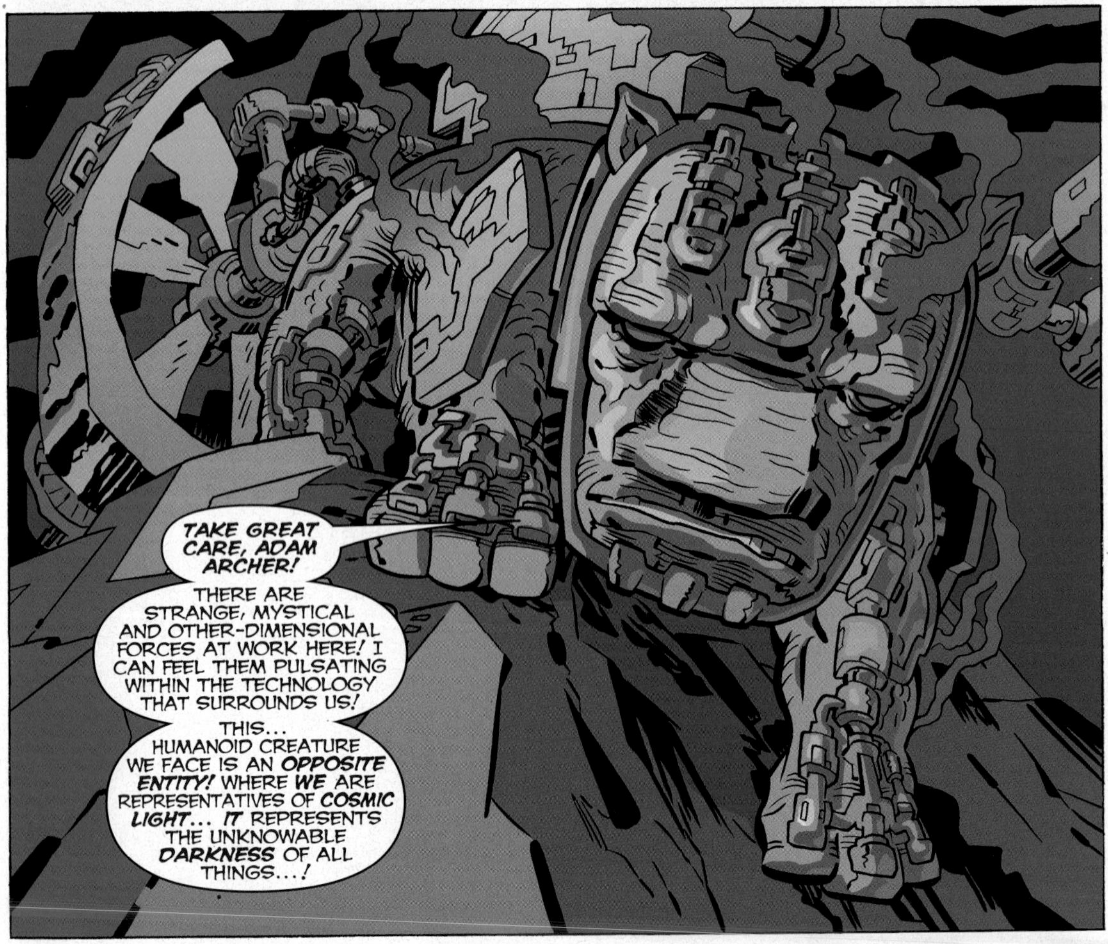
TAKE GREAT CARE, ADAM ARCHER!
THERE ARE STRANGE, MYSTICAL AND OTHER-DIMENSIONAL FORCES AT WORK HERE! I CAN FEEL THEM PULSATING WITHIN THE TECHNOLOGY THAT SURROUNDS US!
THIS... HUMANOID CREATURE WE FACE IS AN OPPOSITE ENTITY! WHERE WE ARE REPRESENTATIVES OF COSMIC LIGHT... IT REPRESENTS THE UNKNOWABLE DARKNESS OF ALL THINGS...!

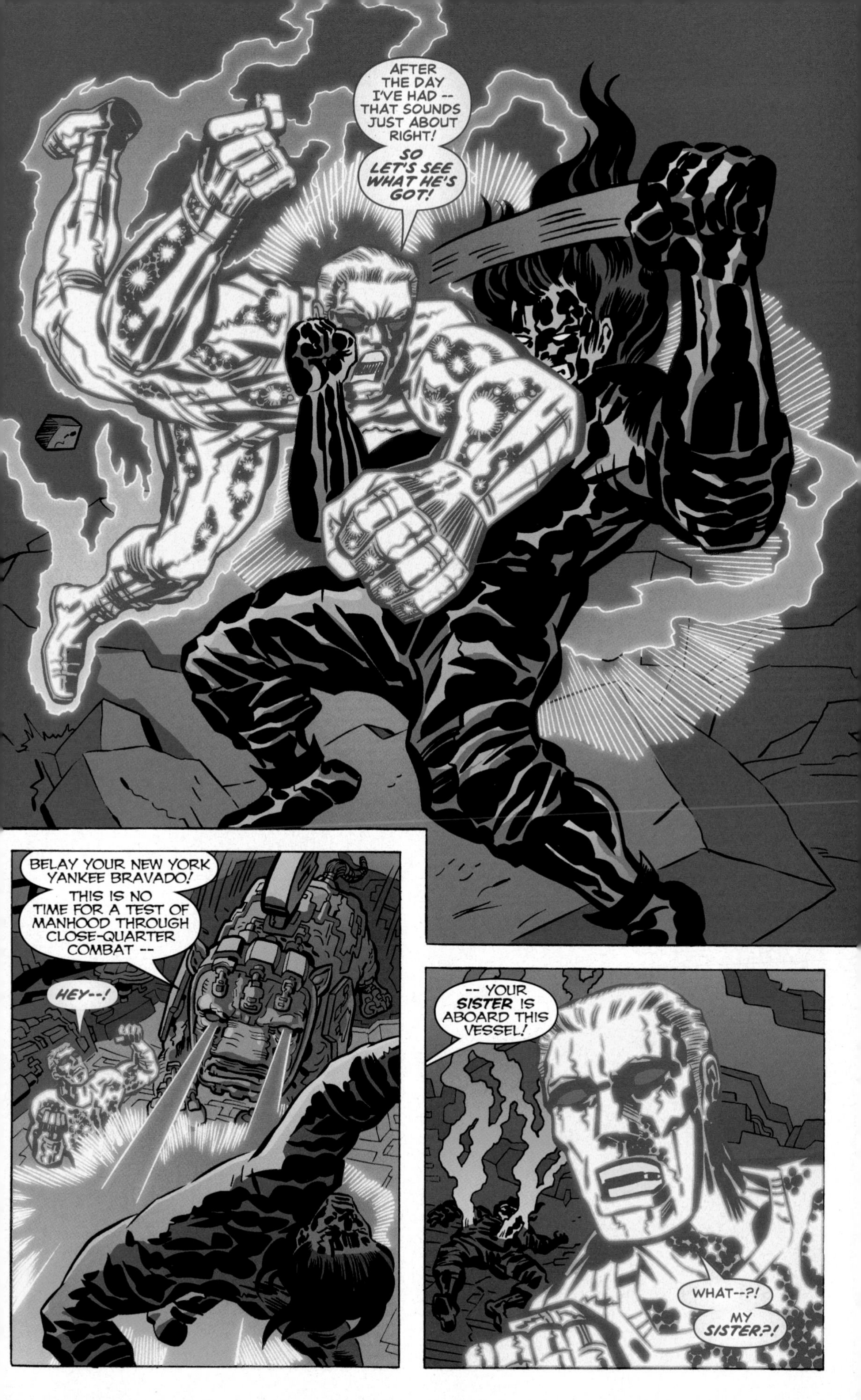
AFTER THE DAY I'VE HAD -- THAT SOUNDS JUST ABOUT RIGHT!
SO LET'S SEE WHAT HE'S GOT!
BELAY YOUR NEW YORK YANKEE BRAVADO! THIS IS NO TIME FOR A TEST OF MANHOOD THROUGH CLOSE-QUARTER COMBAT --
HEY--!
-- YOUR SISTER IS ABOARD THIS VESSEL!
WHAT--?!
MY SISTER?!

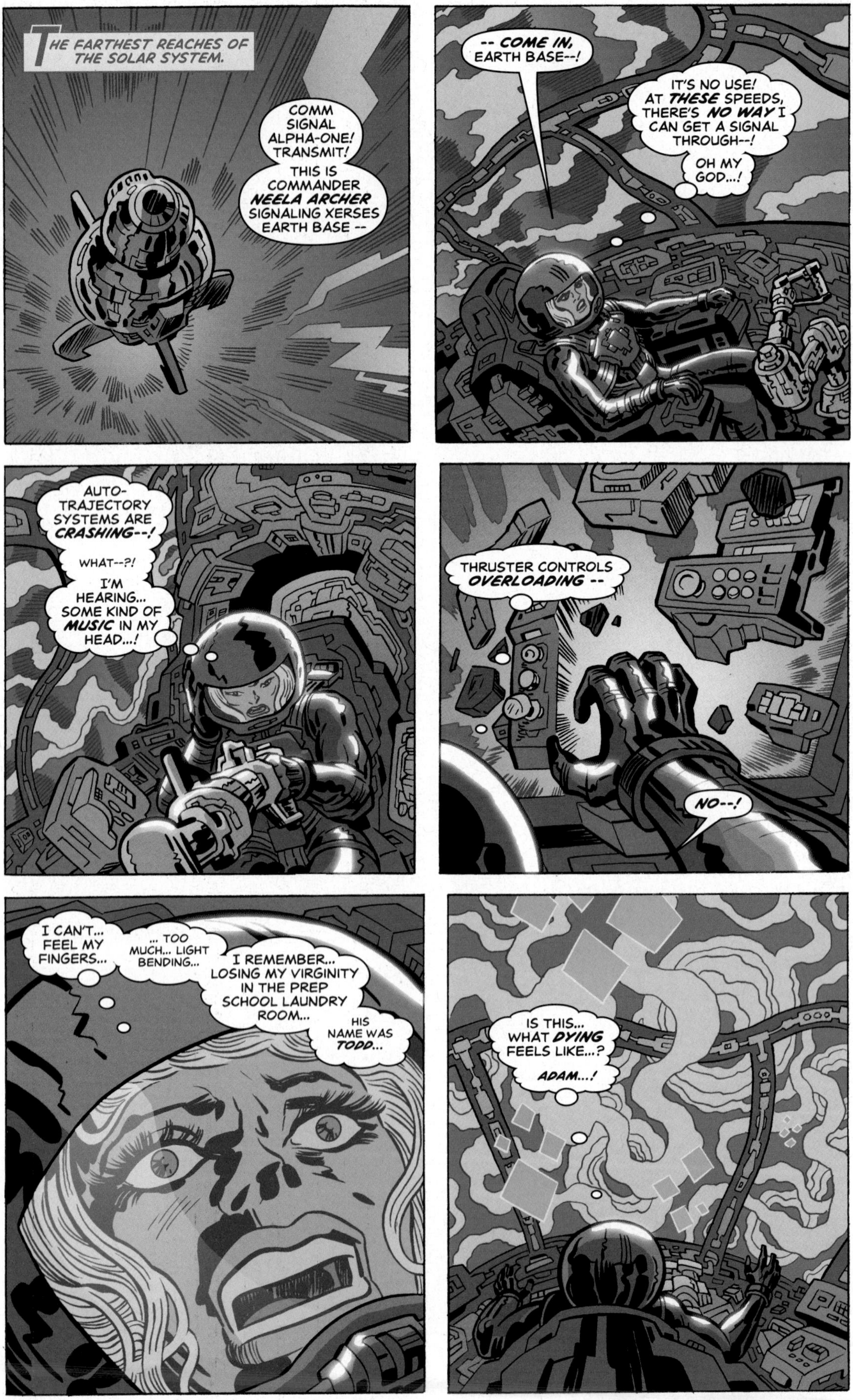
THE FARTHEST REACHES OF THE SOLAR SYSTEM.
COMM SIGNAL ALPHA-ONE! TRANSMIT!
THIS IS COMMANDER NEELA ARCHER SIGNALING XERSES EARTH BASE --
-- COME IN, EARTH BASE--!
IT'S NO USE! AT THESE SPEEDS, THERE'S NO WAY I CAN GET A SIGNAL THROUGH--!
OH MY GOD...!
AUTO-TRAJECTORY SYSTEMS ARE CRASHING--!
WHAT--?!
I'M HEARING... SOME KIND OF MUSIC IN MY HEAD...!
THRUSTER CONTROLS OVERLOADING --
NO--!
I CAN'T... FEEL MY FINGERS...
... TOO MUCH... LIGHT BENDING...
I REMEMBER... LOSING MY VIRGINITY IN THE PREP SCHOOL LAUNDRY ROOM...
HIS NAME WAS TODD...
IS THIS... WHAT DYING FEELS LIKE...?
ADAM...!

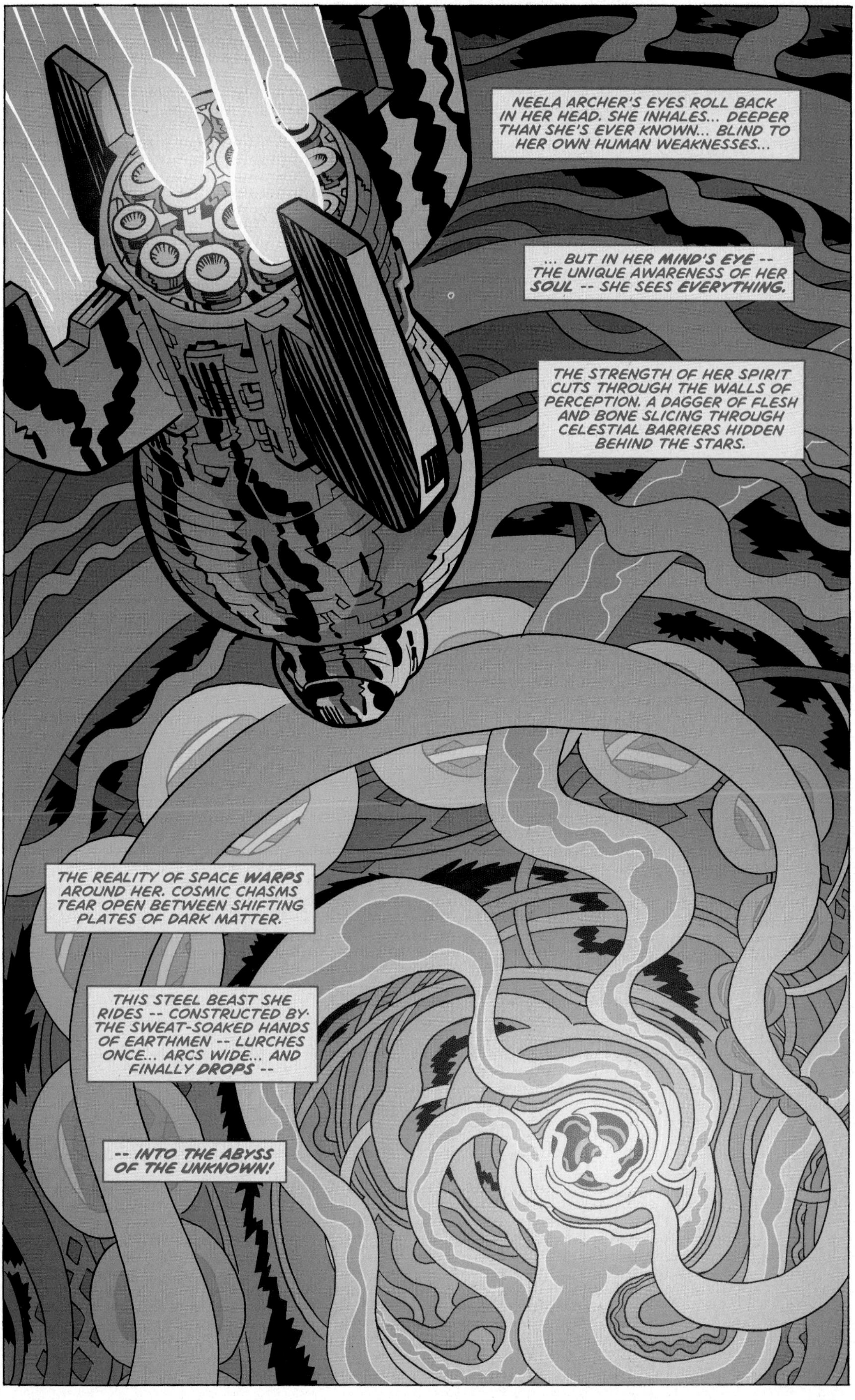
NEELA ARCHER'S EYES ROLL BACK IN HER HEAD. SHE INHALES... DEEPER THAN SHE'S EVER KNOWN... BLIND TO HER OWN HUMAN WEAKNESSES...
... BUT IN HER MIND'S EYE -- THE UNIQUE AWARENESS OF HER SOUL -- SHE SEES EVERYTHING.
THE STRENGTH OF HER SPIRIT CUTS THROUGH THE WALLS OF PERCEPTION. A DAGGER OF FLESH AND BONE SLICING THROUGH CELESTIAL BARRIERS HIDDEN BEHIND THE STARS.
THE REALITY OF SPACE WARPS AROUND HER. COSMIC CHASMS TEAR OPEN BETWEEN SHIFTING PLATES OF DARK MATTER.
THIS STEEL BEAST SHE RIDES -- CONSTRUCTED BY THE SWEAT-SOAKED HANDS OF EARTHMEN -- LURCHES ONCE... ARCS WIDE... AND FINALLY DROPS --
-- INTO THE ABYSS OF THE UNKNOWN!

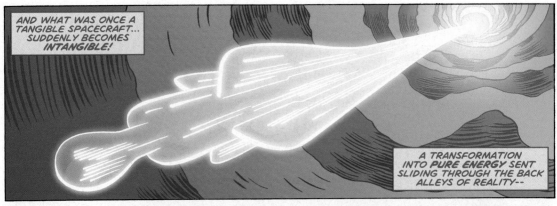

AND WHAT WAS ONCE A TANGIBLE SPACECRAFT... SUDDENLY BECOMES INTANGIBLE!

A TRANSFORMATION INTO *PURE ENERGY* SENT SLIDING THROUGH THE BACK ALLEYS OF REALITY--

--AND, IN THE BLINK OF A HUMAN EYE, VIOLENTLY RECONSTITUTING ITSELF...

...SOMEWHERE ELSE.

COMM-SIGNAL! ALERT ONE! ALERT ONE!

LOCATOR TECH IS *COMPLETELY OFF-LINE!* NO *CLUE* WHERE I AM--

MY NAME IS NEELA ARCHER. MY NAME IS NEELA ARCHER. MY NAME IS NEELA ARCHER.

I'M AN ASTRONAUT. I'M AN ASTRONAUT. I'M AN ASTRONAUT. I'M AN--

--ASTRONAUT...

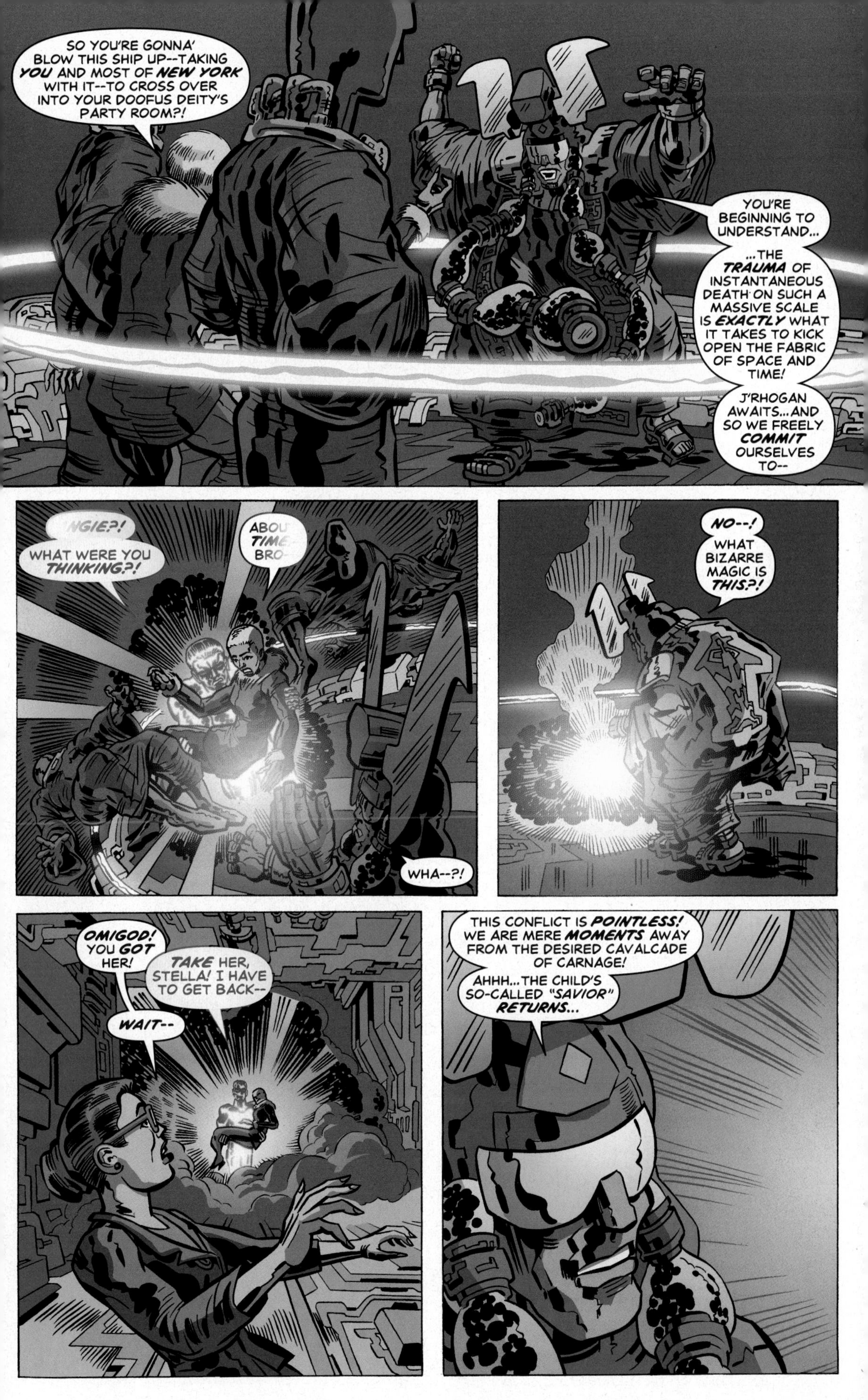
SO YOU'RE GONNA' BLOW THIS SHIP UP--TAKING *YOU* AND MOST OF *NEW YORK* WITH IT--TO CROSS OVER INTO YOUR DOOFUS DEITY'S PARTY ROOM?!
YOU'RE BEGINNING TO UNDERSTAND...
...THE *TRAUMA* OF INSTANTANEOUS DEATH ON SUCH A MASSIVE SCALE IS *EXACTLY* WHAT IT TAKES TO KICK OPEN THE FABRIC OF SPACE AND TIME!
J'RHOGAN AWAITS...AND SO WE FREELY *COMMIT* OURSELVES TO--
NGIE?!
WHAT WERE YOU *THINKING?!*
ABOU *TIME*-- BRO--
WHA--?!
NO--!
WHAT BIZARRE MAGIC IS *THIS?!*
OMIGOD! YOU *GOT* HER!
TAKE HER, STELLA! I HAVE TO GET BACK--
WAIT--
THIS CONFLICT IS *POINTLESS!* WE ARE MERE *MOMENTS* AWAY FROM THE DESIRED CAVALCADE OF CARNAGE!
AHHH...THE CHILD'S SO-CALLED *"SAVIOR" RETURNS...*

I *MIGHT'VE* GIVEN YOU A CHANCE TO *EXPLAIN* YOURSELF--

--BUT THAT WAS BEFORE YOU MADE MY *SISTER* YOUR *PRISONER!*

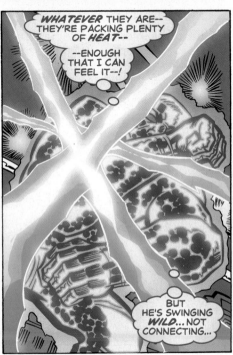

WHATEVER THEY ARE-- THEY'RE PACKING PLENTY OF *HEAT*--

--ENOUGH THAT I CAN *FEEL* IT--!

BUT HE'S SWINGING *WILD*...NOT CONNECTING...

NOT EXACTLY AN *EXPERT* WITH THOSE THINGS, *ARE* YOU?!

NK!

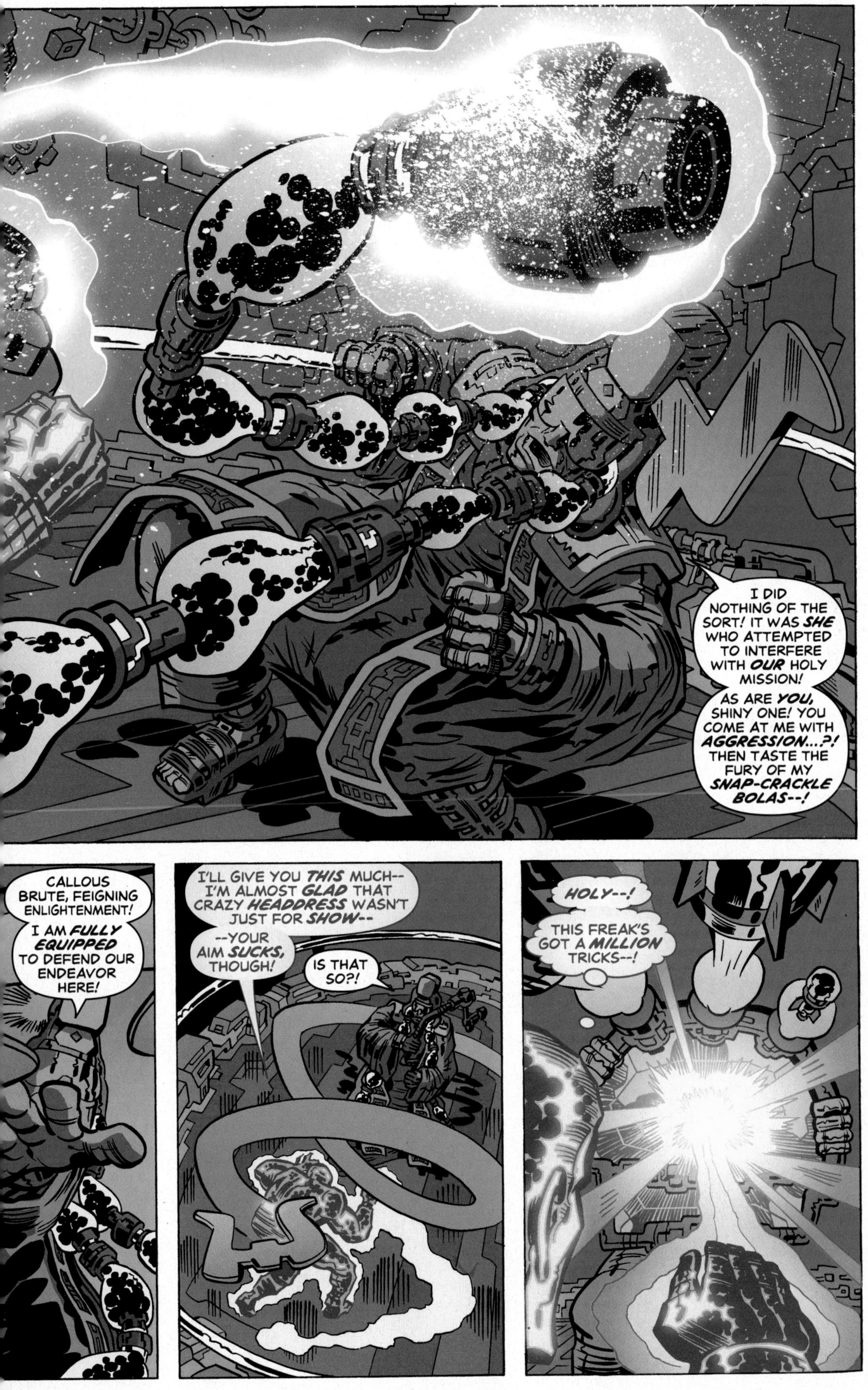
I DID NOTHING OF THE SORT! IT WAS SHE WHO ATTEMPTED TO INTERFERE WITH OUR HOLY MISSION!
AS ARE YOU, SHINY ONE! YOU COME AT ME WITH AGGRESSION...?! THEN TASTE THE FURY OF MY SNAP-CRACKLE BOLAS--!
CALLOUS BRUTE, FEIGNING ENLIGHTENMENT!
I AM FULLY EQUIPPED TO DEFEND OUR ENDEAVOR HERE!
I'LL GIVE YOU THIS MUCH-- I'M ALMOST GLAD THAT CRAZY HEADDRESS WASN'T JUST FOR SHOW--
--YOUR AIM SUCKS, THOUGH!
IS THAT SO?!
HOLY--!
THIS FREAK'S GOT A MILLION TRICKS--!

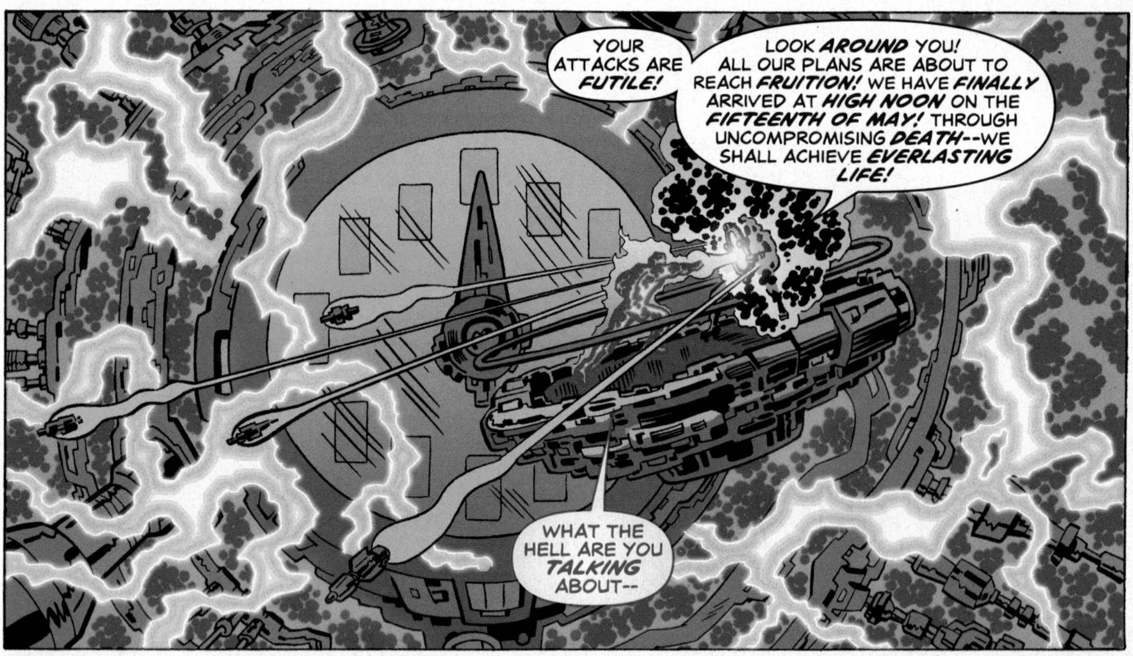
YOUR ATTACKS ARE *FUTILE!*
LOOK *AROUND* YOU! ALL OUR PLANS ARE ABOUT TO REACH *FRUITION!* WE HAVE *FINALLY* ARRIVED AT *HIGH NOON* ON THE *FIFTEENTH OF MAY!* THROUGH UNCOMPROMISING *DEATH*--WE SHALL ACHIEVE *EVERLASTING LIFE!*
WHAT THE HELL ARE YOU *TALKING* ABOUT--

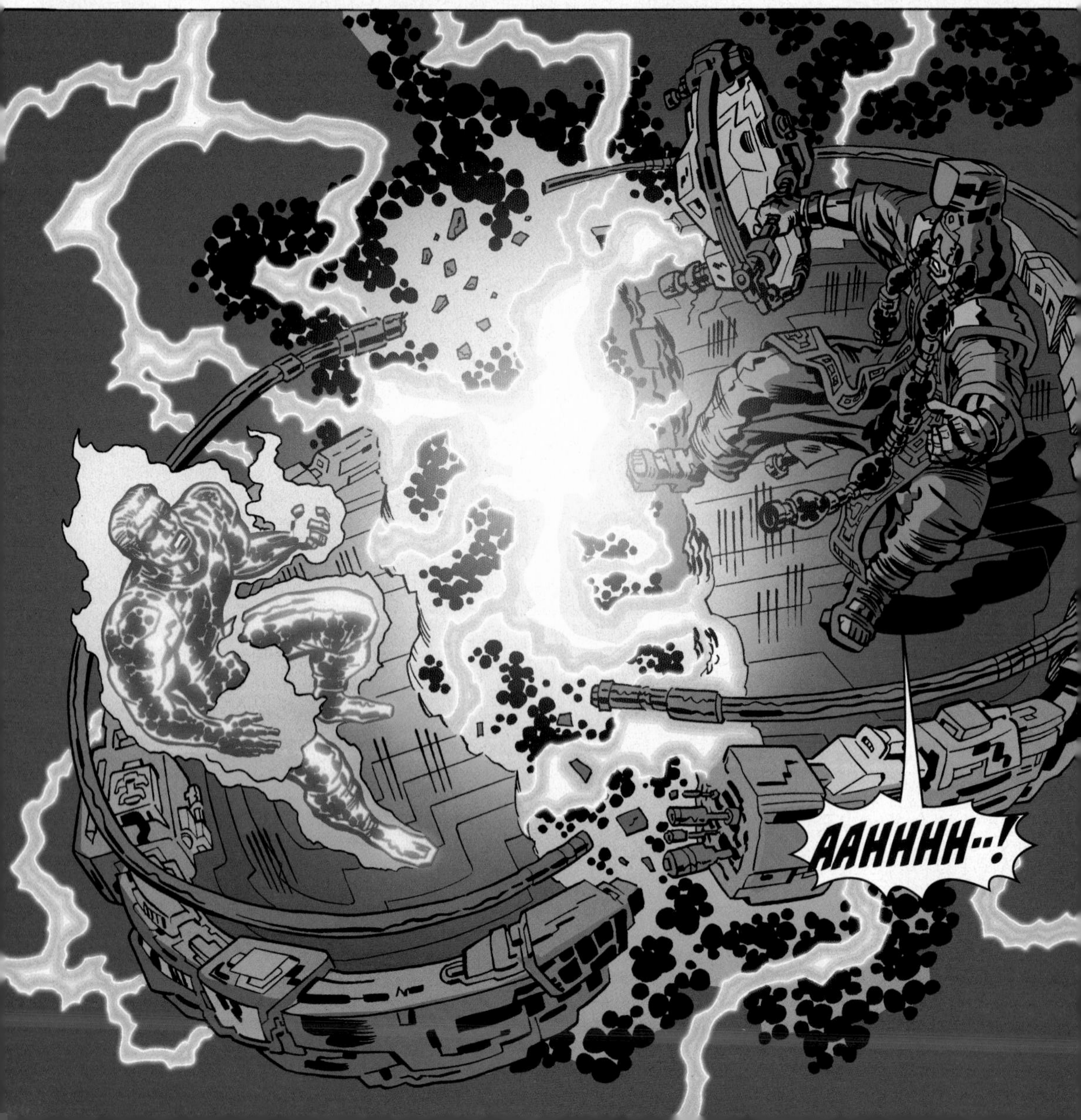
AAHHHH--!

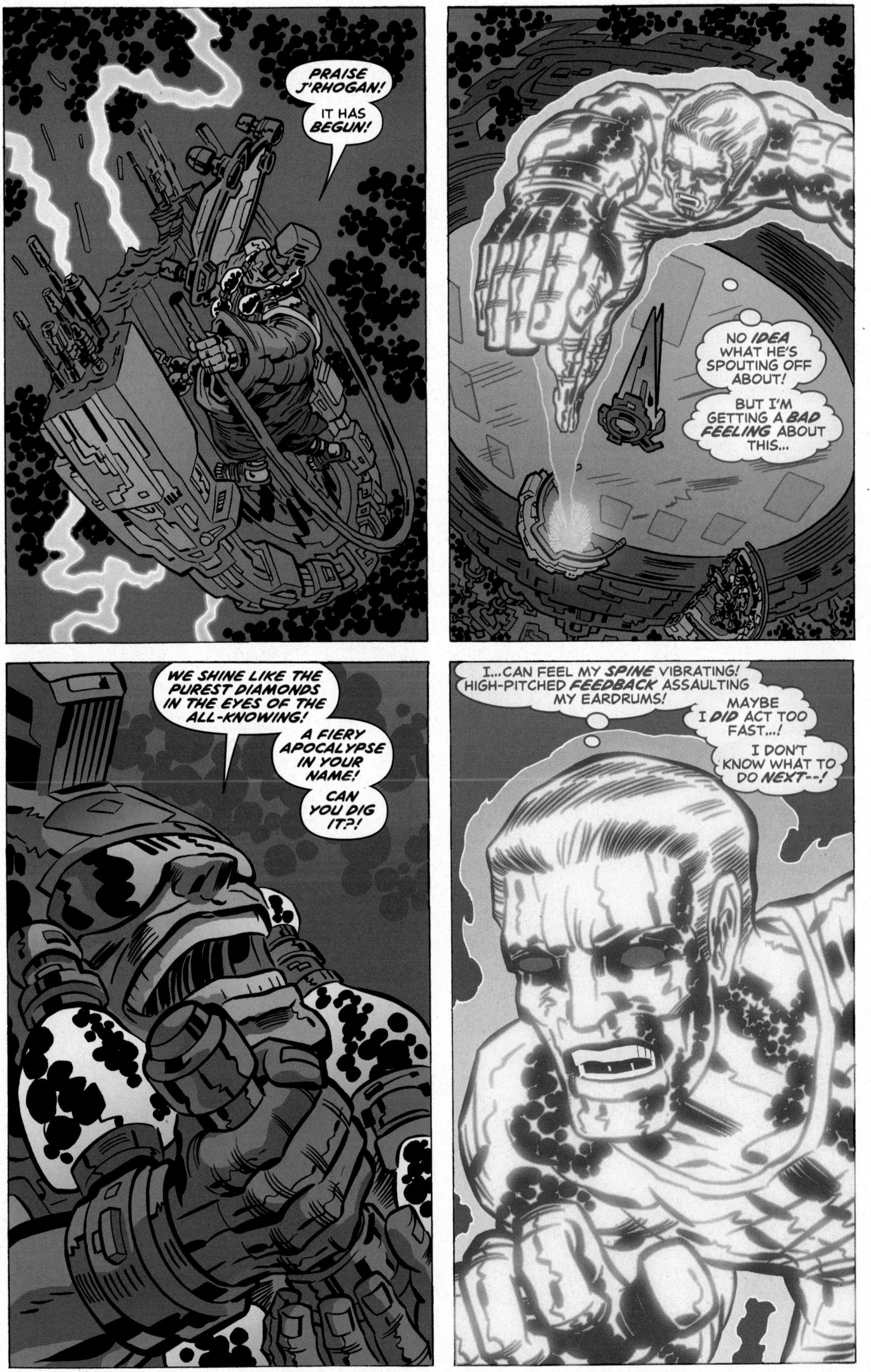
PRAISE J'RHOGAN!
IT HAS BEGUN!
NO IDEA WHAT HE'S SPOUTING OFF ABOUT!
BUT I'M GETTING A BAD FEELING ABOUT THIS...
WE SHINE LIKE THE PUREST DIAMONDS IN THE EYES OF THE ALL-KNOWING!
A FIERY APOCALYPSE IN YOUR NAME!
CAN YOU DIG IT?!
I...CAN FEEL MY SPINE VIBRATING! HIGH-PITCHED FEEDBACK ASSAULTING MY EARDRUMS!
MAYBE I DID ACT TOO FAST...!
I DON'T KNOW WHAT TO DO NEXT--!

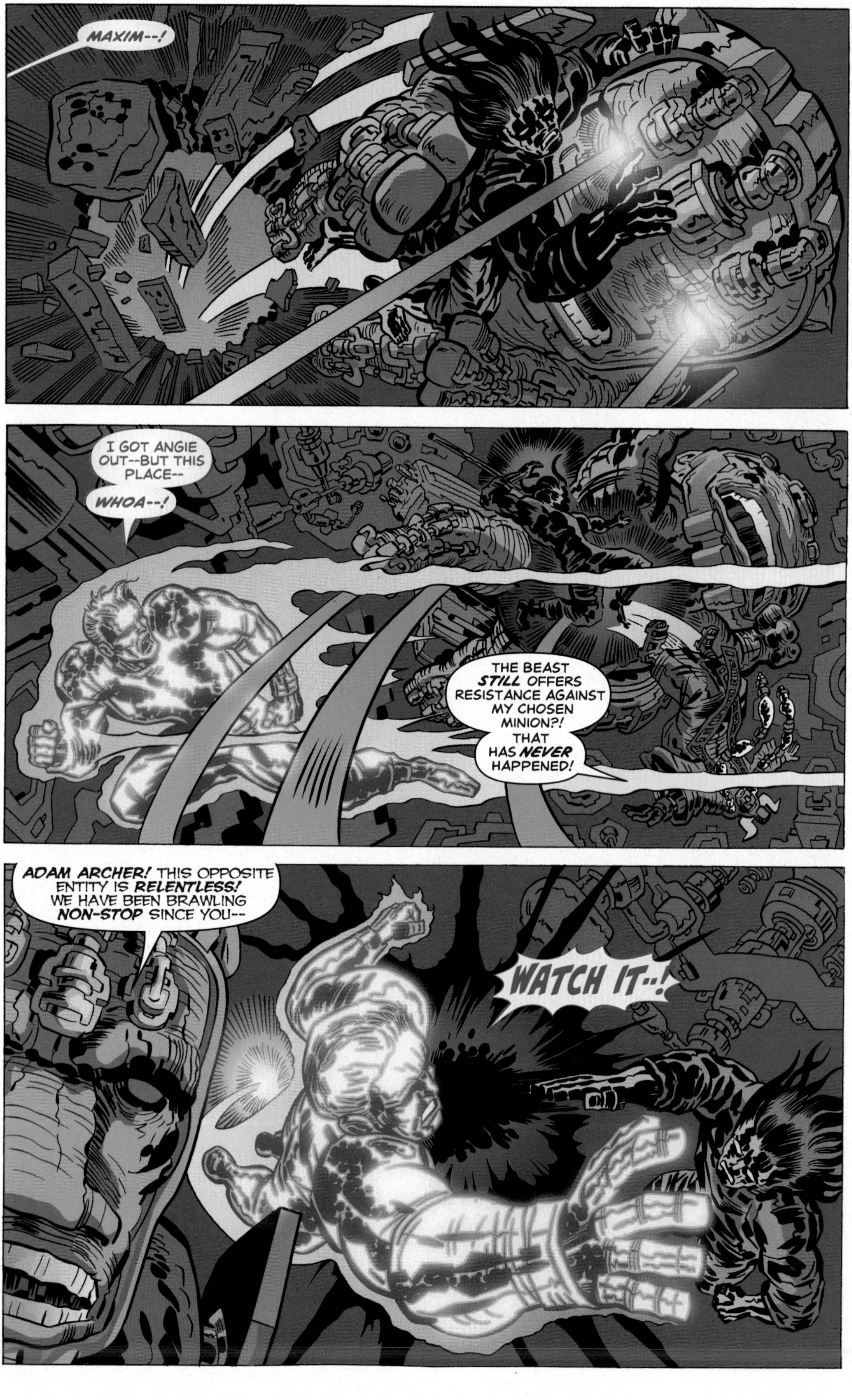
MAXIM--!
I GOT ANGIE OUT--BUT THIS PLACE--
WHOA--!
THE BEAST STILL OFFERS RESISTANCE AGAINST MY CHOSEN MINION?! THAT HAS NEVER HAPPENED!
ADAM ARCHER! THIS OPPOSITE ENTITY IS RELENTLESS! WE HAVE BEEN BRAWLING NON-STOP SINCE YOU--
WATCH IT--!

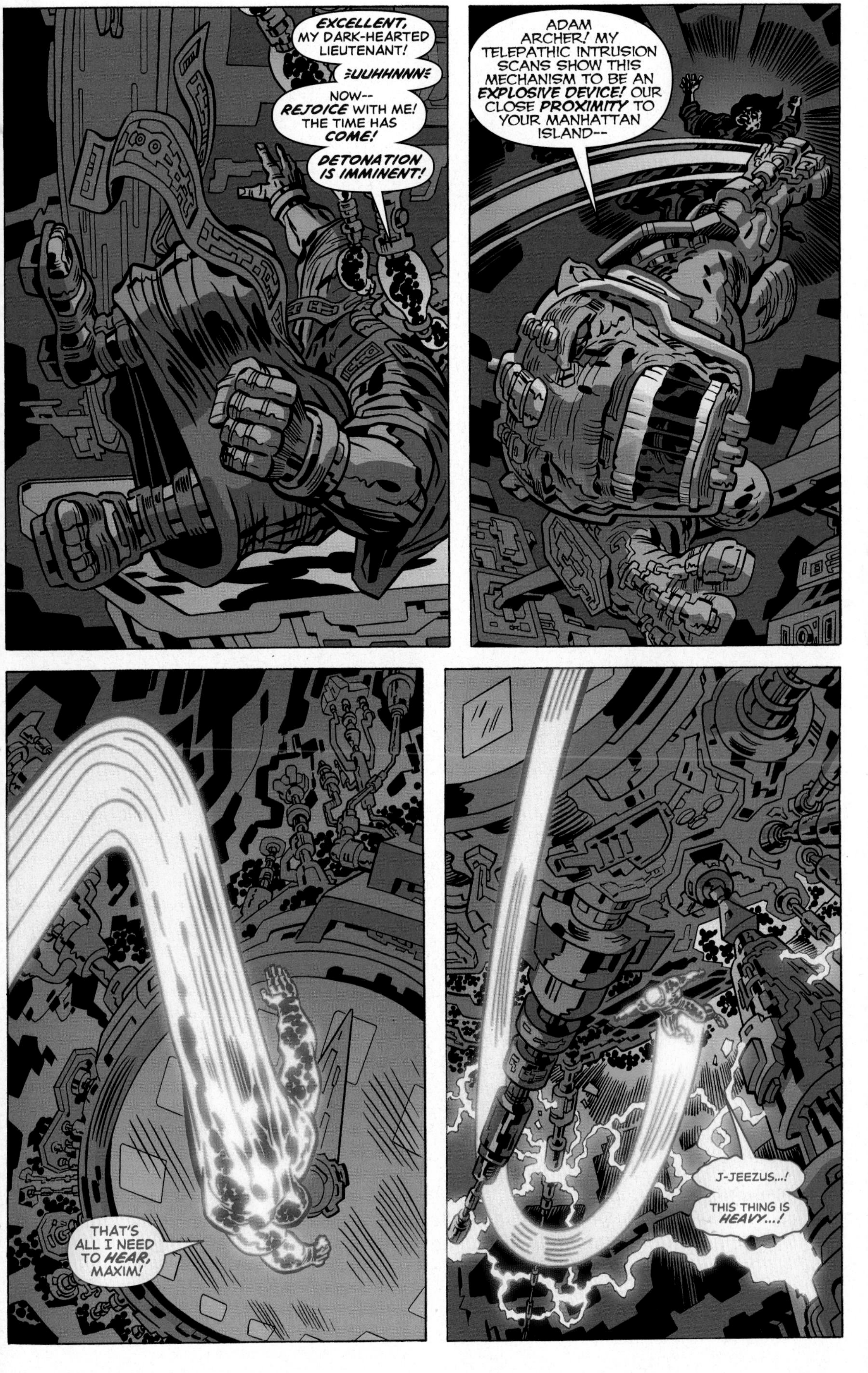
EXCELLENT, MY DARK-HEARTED LIEUTENANT!
UUHHNNN
NOW-- REJOICE WITH ME! THE TIME HAS COME!
DETONATION IS IMMINENT!
ADAM ARCHER! MY TELEPATHIC INTRUSION SCANS SHOW THIS MECHANISM TO BE AN EXPLOSIVE DEVICE! OUR CLOSE PROXIMITY TO YOUR MANHATTAN ISLAND--
THAT'S ALL I NEED TO HEAR, MAXIM!
J-JEEZUS...!
THIS THING IS HEAVY...!

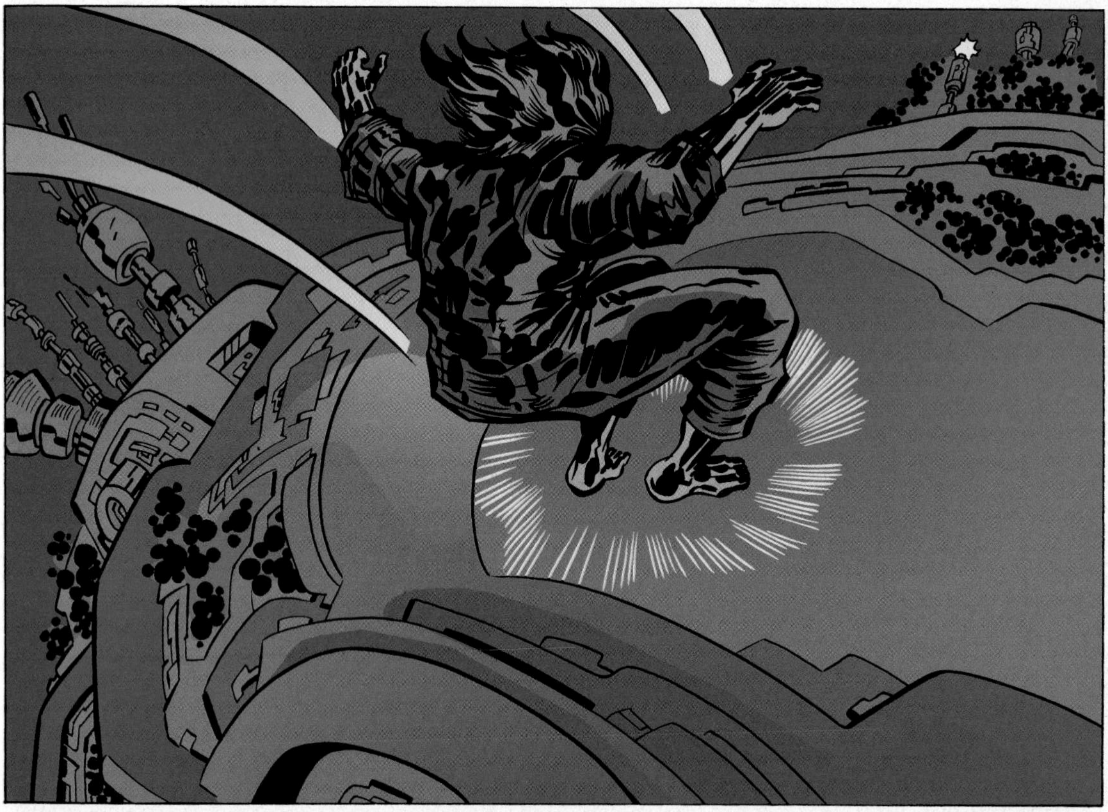

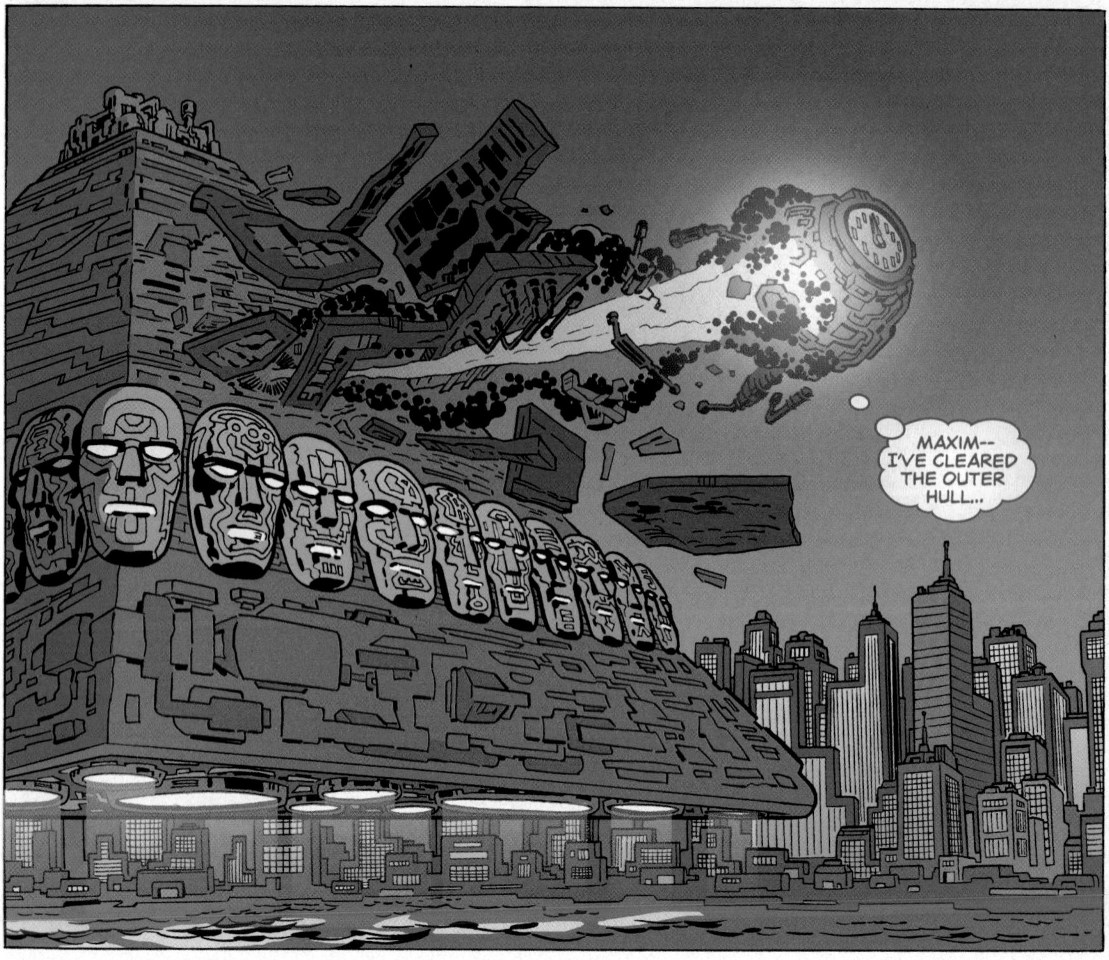
MAXIM--
I'VE CLEARED
THE OUTER
HULL...

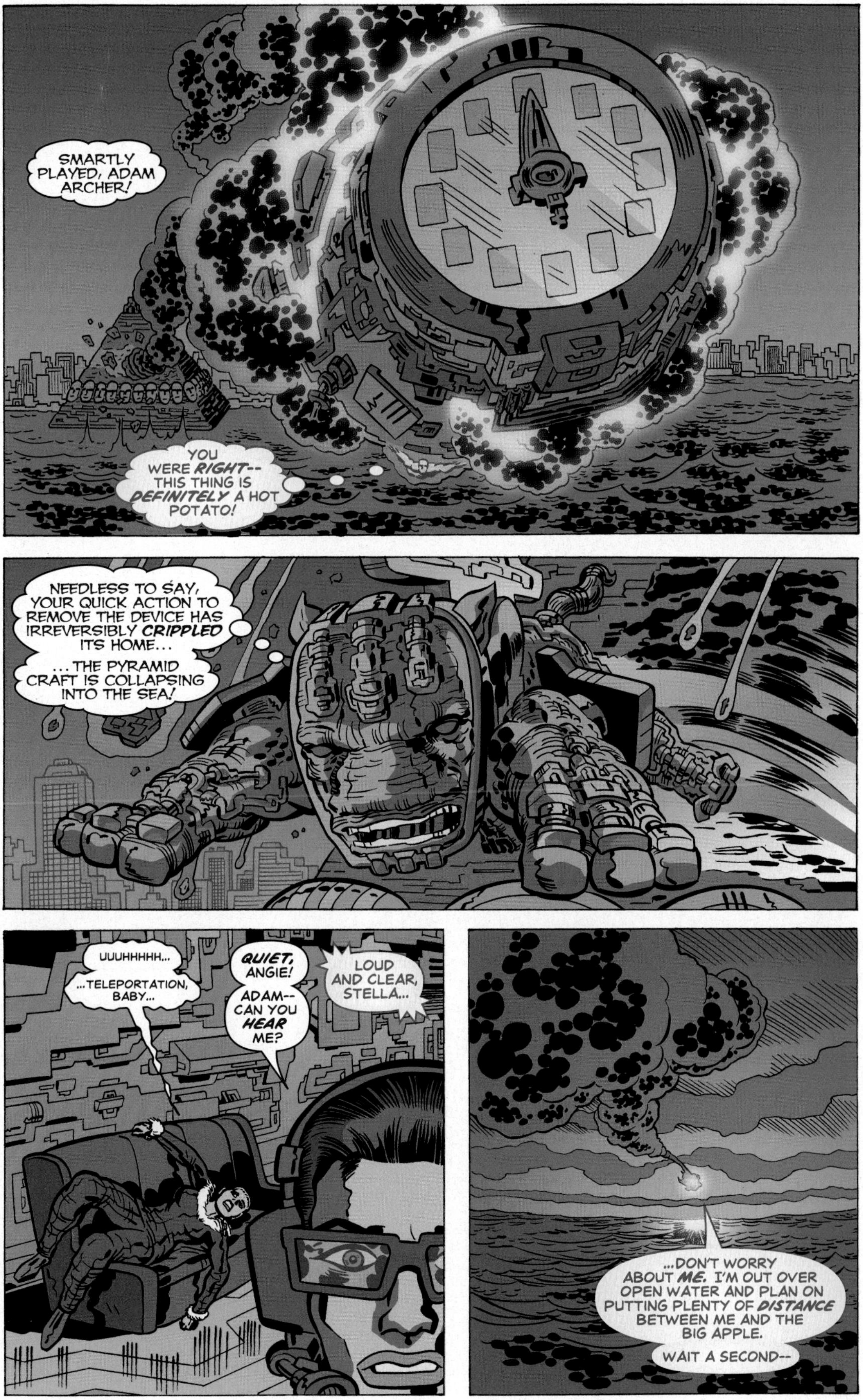

SMARTLY PLAYED, ADAM ARCHER!
YOU WERE RIGHT-- THIS THING IS DEFINITELY A HOT POTATO!
NEEDLESS TO SAY, YOUR QUICK ACTION TO REMOVE THE DEVICE HAS IRREVERSIBLY CRIPPLED ITS HOME...
...THE PYRAMID CRAFT IS COLLAPSING INTO THE SEA!
UUUHHHHH...
...TELEPORTATION, BABY...
QUIET, ANGIE!
ADAM-- CAN YOU HEAR ME?
LOUD AND CLEAR, STELLA...
...DON'T WORRY ABOUT ME. I'M OUT OVER OPEN WATER AND PLAN ON PUTTING PLENTY OF DISTANCE BETWEEN ME AND THE BIG APPLE.
WAIT A SECOND--

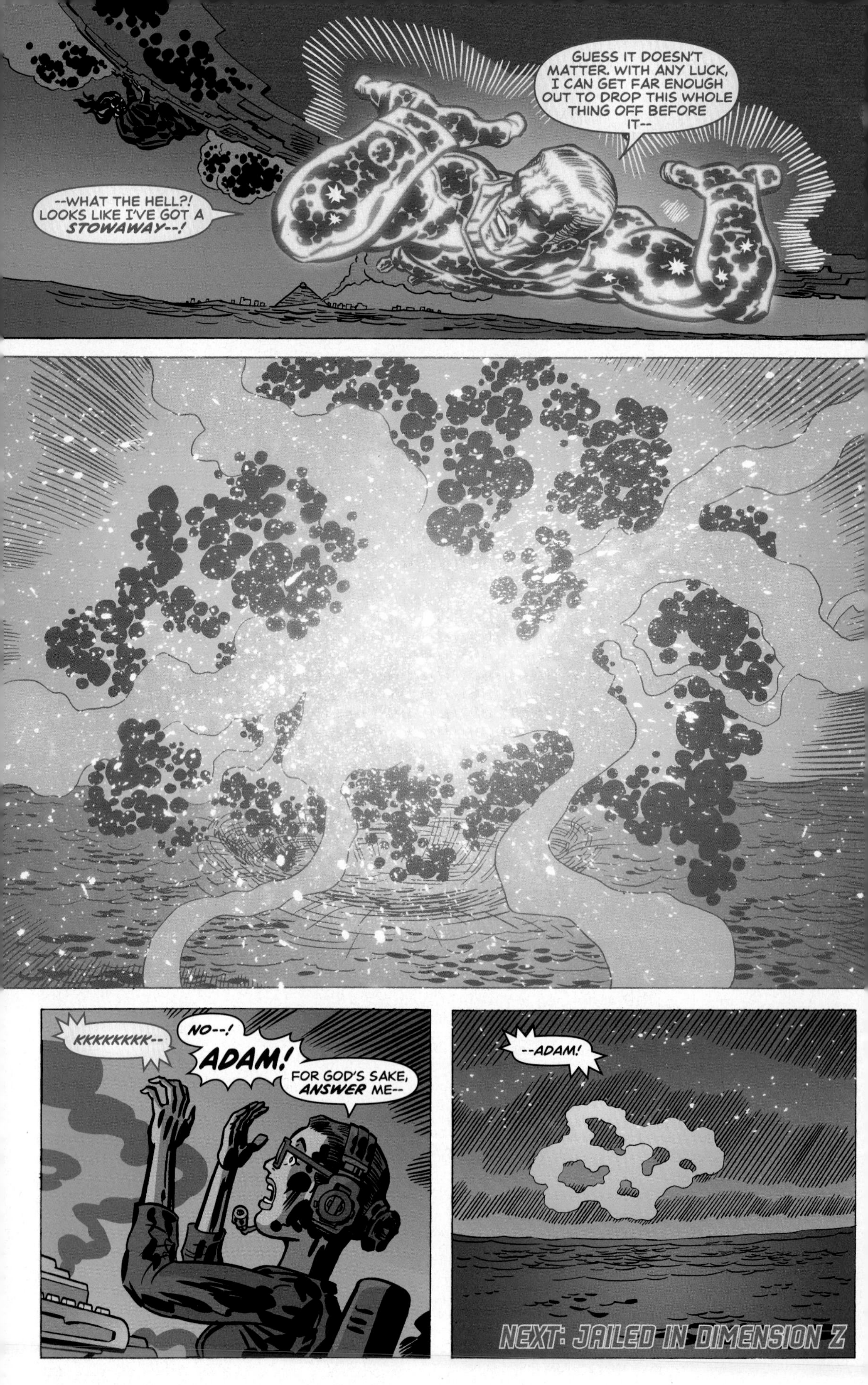

GUESS IT DOESN'T MATTER. WITH ANY LUCK, I CAN GET FAR ENOUGH OUT TO DROP THIS WHOLE THING OFF BEFORE IT--
--WHAT THE HELL?! LOOKS LIKE I'VE GOT A STOWAWAY--!
KKKKKKKK--
NO--! ADAM!
FOR GOD'S SAKE, ANSWER ME--
--ADAM!
NEXT: JAILED IN DIMENSION Z

HOLIDAY SPECIAL:
BASIL'S EARLY EARLY CHRISTMAS

Image Merrily Presents:

GODLAND

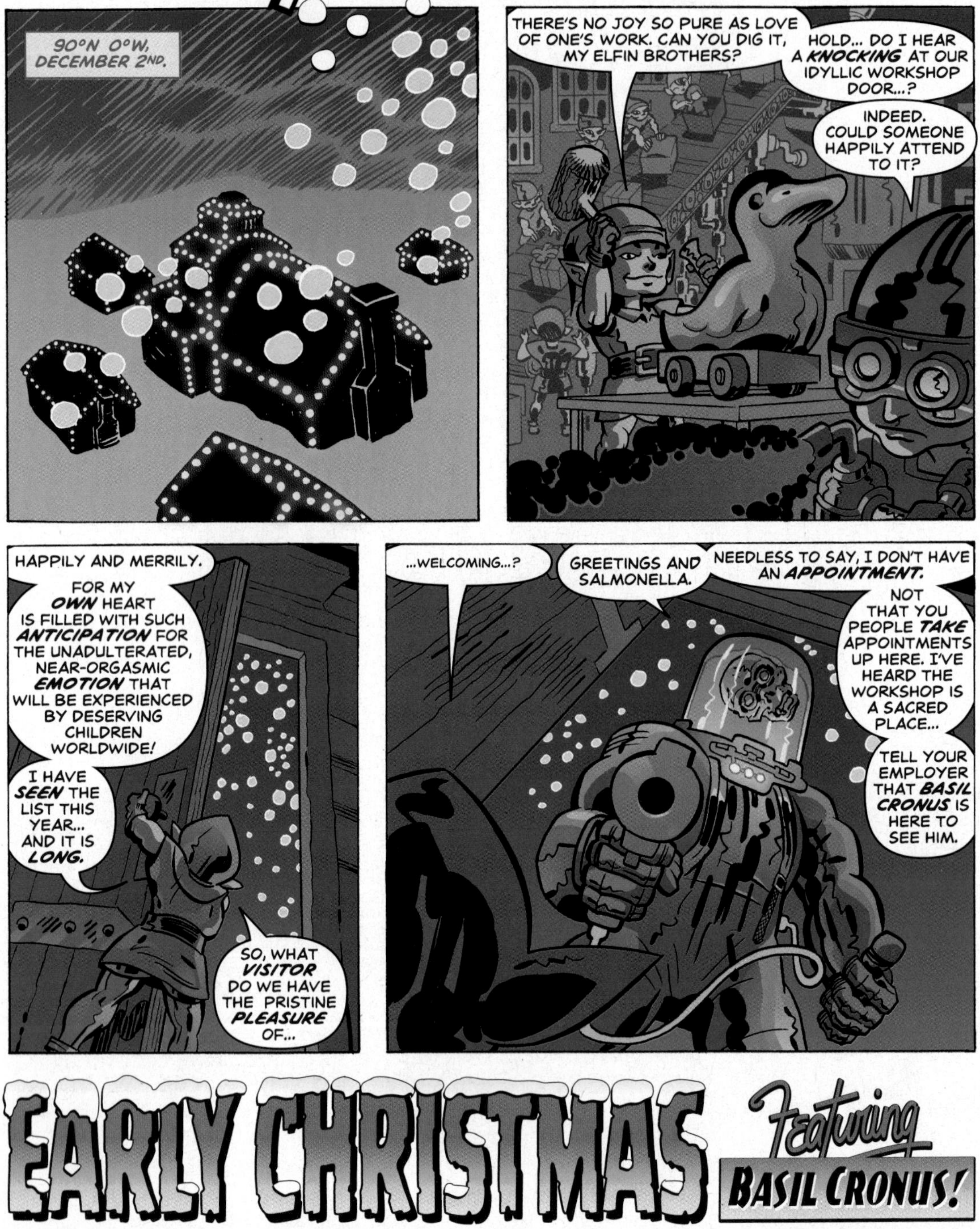
90°N 0°W, DECEMBER 2ND.
THERE'S NO JOY SO PURE AS LOVE OF ONE'S WORK. CAN YOU DIG IT, MY ELFIN BROTHERS?
HOLD... DO I HEAR A KNOCKING AT OUR IDYLLIC WORKSHOP DOOR...?
INDEED. COULD SOMEONE HAPPILY ATTEND TO IT?
HAPPILY AND MERRILY.
FOR MY OWN HEART IS FILLED WITH SUCH ANTICIPATION FOR THE UNADULTERATED, NEAR-ORGASMIC EMOTION THAT WILL BE EXPERIENCED BY DESERVING CHILDREN WORLDWIDE!
I HAVE SEEN THE LIST THIS YEAR... AND IT IS LONG.
SO, WHAT VISITOR DO WE HAVE THE PRISTINE PLEASURE OF...
...WELCOMING...?
GREETINGS AND SALMONELLA.
NEEDLESS TO SAY, I DON'T HAVE AN APPOINTMENT.
NOT THAT YOU PEOPLE TAKE APPOINTMENTS UP HERE. I'VE HEARD THE WORKSHOP IS A SACRED PLACE...
TELL YOUR EMPLOYER THAT BASIL CRONUS IS HERE TO SEE HIM.

EARLY CHRISTMAS Featuring BASIL CRONUS!

Unwrapped for you by Joe Casey & Tom Scioli

Smokin' Colors by Nick Filardi, Comicraft's Rich & Jimmy did Snow on the logo

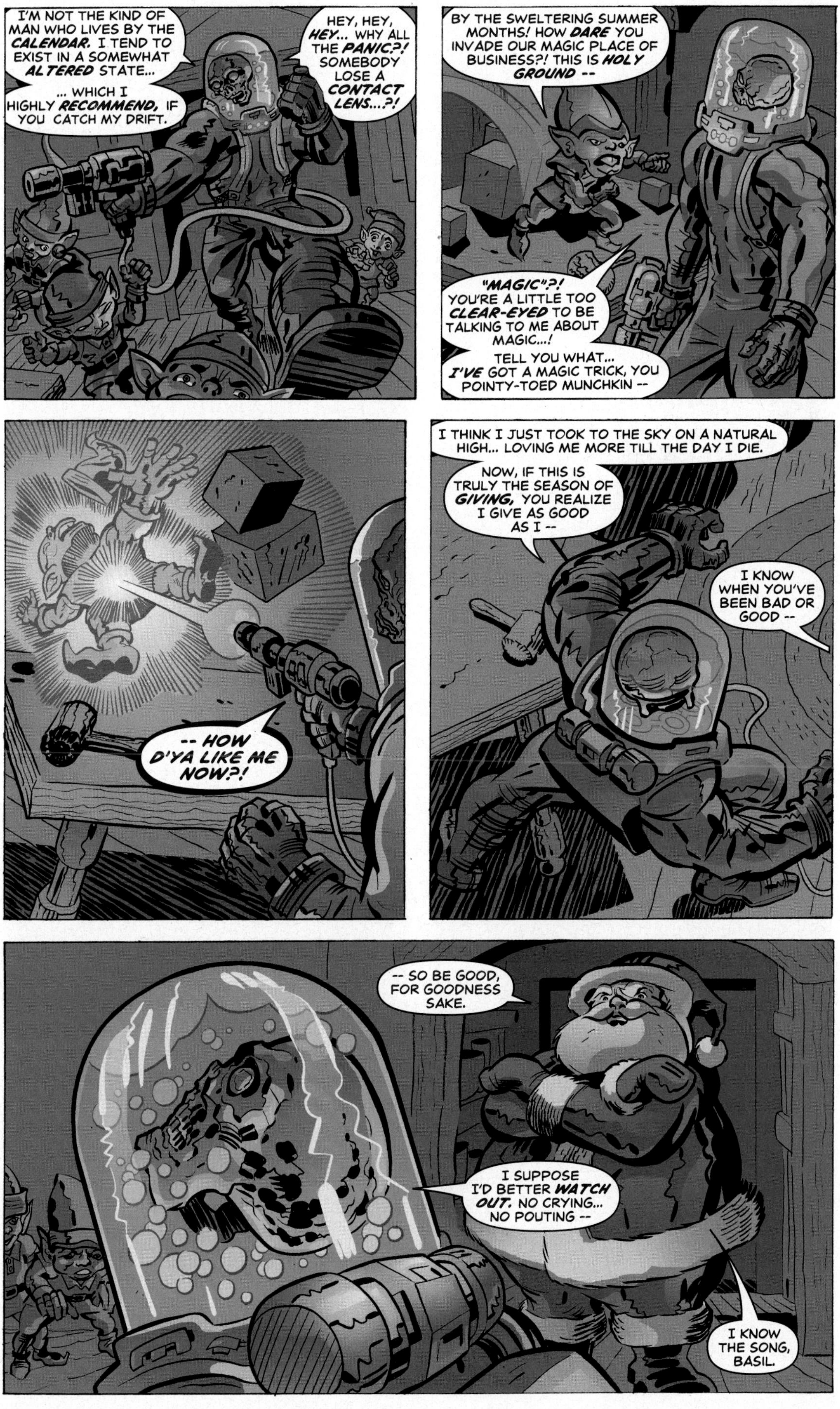
I'M NOT THE KIND OF MAN WHO LIVES BY THE CALENDAR. I TEND TO EXIST IN A SOMEWHAT ALTERED STATE...
... WHICH I HIGHLY RECOMMEND, IF YOU CATCH MY DRIFT.
HEY, HEY, HEY... WHY ALL THE PANIC?! SOMEBODY LOSE A CONTACT LENS...?!
BY THE SWELTERING SUMMER MONTHS! HOW DARE YOU INVADE OUR MAGIC PLACE OF BUSINESS?! THIS IS HOLY GROUND --
"MAGIC"?! YOU'RE A LITTLE TOO CLEAR-EYED TO BE TALKING TO ME ABOUT MAGIC...!
TELL YOU WHAT... I'VE GOT A MAGIC TRICK, YOU POINTY-TOED MUNCHKIN --
-- HOW D'YA LIKE ME NOW?!
I THINK I JUST TOOK TO THE SKY ON A NATURAL HIGH... LOVING ME MORE TILL THE DAY I DIE.
NOW, IF THIS IS TRULY THE SEASON OF GIVING, YOU REALIZE I GIVE AS GOOD AS I --
I KNOW WHEN YOU'VE BEEN BAD OR GOOD --
-- SO BE GOOD, FOR GOODNESS SAKE.
I SUPPOSE I'D BETTER WATCH OUT. NO CRYING... NO POUTING --
I KNOW THE SONG, BASIL.

SAVE THE CUTE HOLIDAY CHEER FOR THE MERCHANDISING, FAT MAN!

HO, HO, *HOLD* IT...

...NO NEED TO BRANDISH A FIREARM. YOU'RE IN A PACIFIST ENVIRONMENT.

YOU'RE NO ABBIE HOFFMAN. WE *BOTH* KNOW THAT. THIS IS MATERIALISM AT ITS FINEST. NOW *HOP TO IT!* I'M HERE FOR --

SWARM, BROTHER BUILDERS!

GOTCHA--!

HNNGG--!

MUST BE... A *TEAMSTER* THING--!

NONE OF THOSE HI-JINKS IN HERE, SOLDIER...!

NOW, NOW... LET'S ALL TAKE A DEEP BREATH... ELF AND JUNKIE ALIKE. NO MORE VIOLENCE! FROM *ANYONE!*

REMEMBER... WHAT DREAMS MAY COME FROM UNEXPECTED GUESTS...

SOMEBODY CALL HALLMARK...! LOOK, I DIDN'T COME *EMPTY-HANDED*, PAPA KRINGLE! I KNOW IT'S *EARLY*... BUT I'VE GOT A *THING* ON THE TWENTY-FIFTH!

AND SO... YOU HAVE TRAVELED *HERE.*

WHY...?

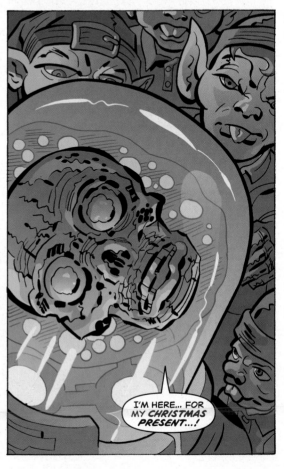

I'M HERE... FOR MY *CHRISTMAS PRESENT...!*

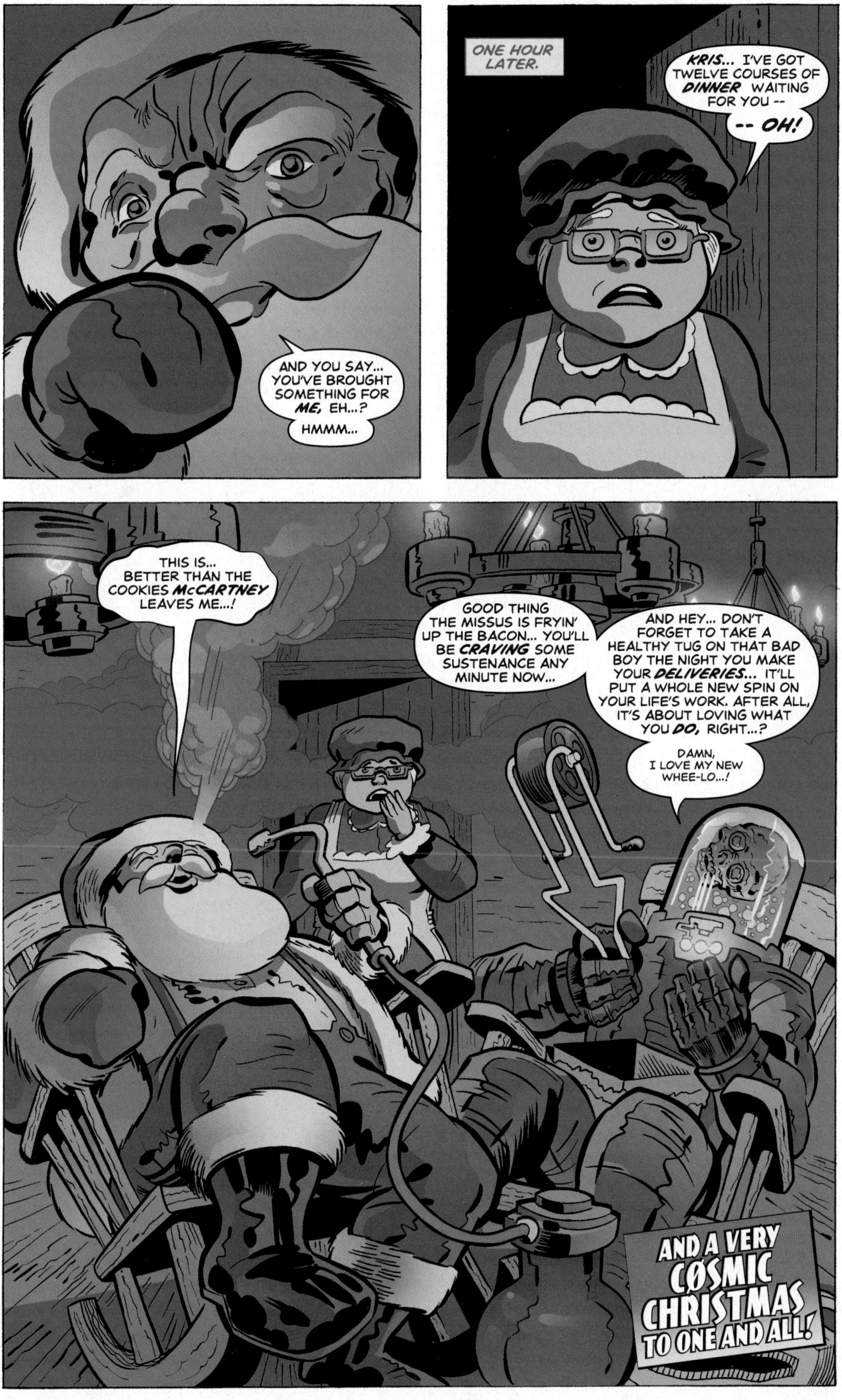
AND YOU SAY... YOU'VE BROUGHT SOMETHING FOR ME, EH...?
HMMM...
ONE HOUR LATER.
KRIS... I'VE GOT TWELVE COURSES OF DINNER WAITING FOR YOU --
-- OH!
THIS IS... BETTER THAN THE COOKIES McCARTNEY LEAVES ME...!
GOOD THING THE MISSUS IS FRYIN' UP THE BACON... YOU'LL BE CRAVING SOME SUSTENANCE ANY MINUTE NOW...
AND HEY... DON'T FORGET TO TAKE A HEALTHY TUG ON THAT BAD BOY THE NIGHT YOU MAKE YOUR DELIVERIES... IT'LL PUT A WHOLE NEW SPIN ON YOUR LIFE'S WORK. AFTER ALL, IT'S ABOUT LOVING WHAT YOU DO, RIGHT...?
DAMN, I LOVE MY NEW WHEE-LO...!
AND A VERY CØSMIC CHRISTMAS TO ONE AND ALL!

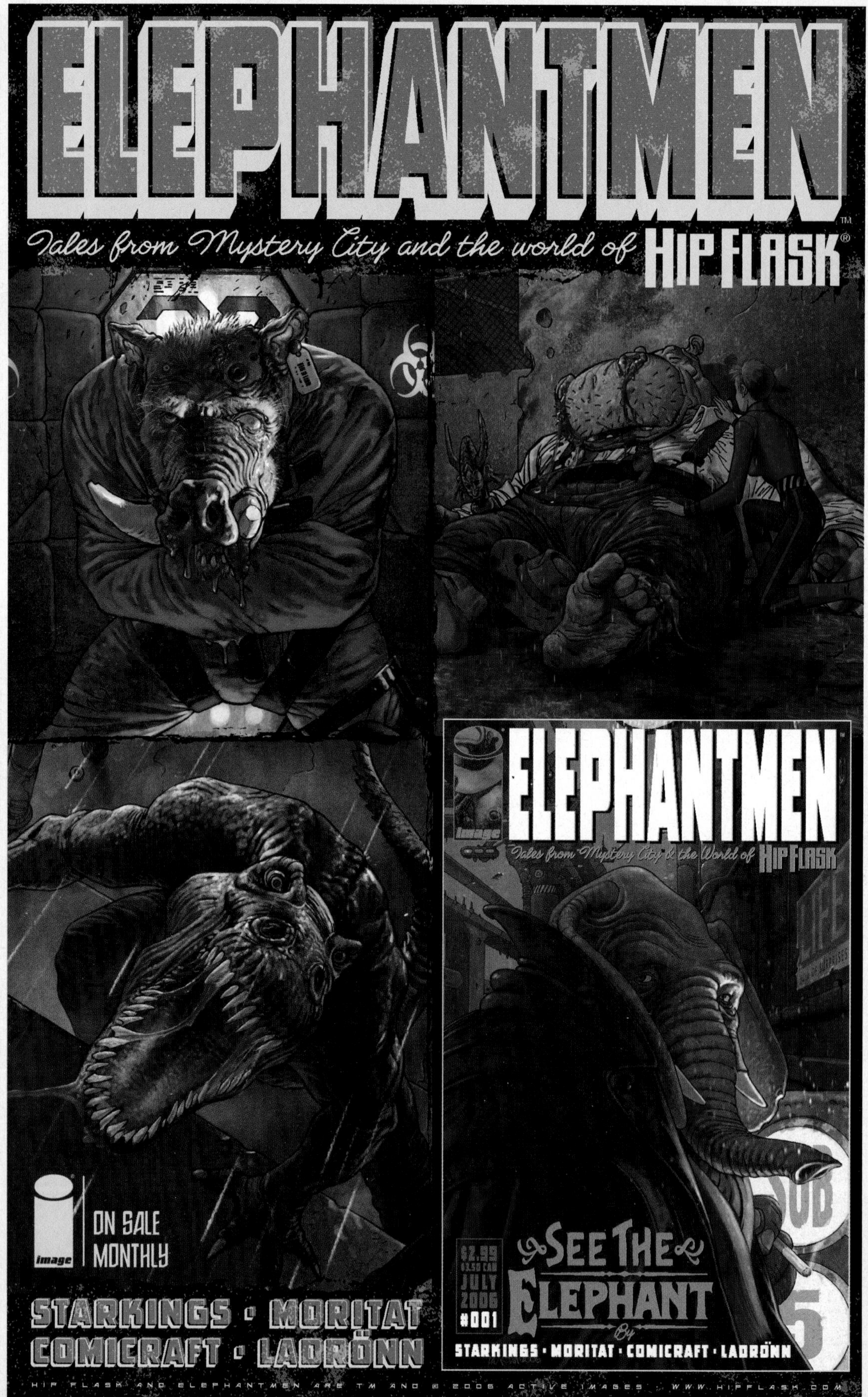
ELEPHANTMEN™
Tales from Mystery City and the world of HIP FLASK®
ELEPHANTMEN
Tales from Mystery City & the World of HIP FLASK
$2.99
$3.50 CAN
JULY
2006
#001
SEE THE ELEPHANT
By
STARKINGS · MORITAT · COMICRAFT · LADRÖNN
ON SALE
MONTHLY
STARKINGS · MORITAT
COMICRAFT · LADRÖNN
HIP FLASK AND ELEPHANTMEN ARE TM AND © 2006 ACTIVE IMAGES · WWW.HIPFLASK.COM